ADVENTURES IN ENGLISH LITERATURE

VOLUME
4

The Modern Age

J. B. PRIESTLEY

JOSEPHINE SPEAR

O. B. DAVIS

Series Editor: MARY RIVES BOWMAN

Harcourt Brace Jovanovich

New York   Chicago   San Francisco
Atlanta   Dallas   and   London

J. B. PRIESTLEY, literary critic and historian as well as one of England's most renowned playwrights, essayists, and novelists, is a frequent visitor to these shores. Among the versatile Mr. Priestley's best-known works are the critical history *Literature and Western Man,* the essay collection *Midnight on the Desert,* the novel *The Good Companions,* and the recent *Charles Dickens: A Pictorial Biography.* He is also co-editor of two twelfth-grade books in the ADVENTURES IN GOOD BOOKS series: *Four English Novels* and *Four English Biographies.*

JOSEPHINE SPEAR, who is co-editor of the Olympic Edition of *Adventures in English Literature,* has been Chairman of the English Department at the University School of Indiana University since 1954. Dr. Spear received her A.B. degree in English from DePauw University. She did her graduate work in education (M.S., Ed.D.) at Indiana University and is a former president of the Indiana Council of Teachers of English.

O. B. DAVIS, who edited the text of *Typhoon* and wrote the accompanying study material, holds degrees in English from Princeton University (A.B.) and Johns Hopkins University (M.A.). His teaching career began in 1949 when he became a Master of English at Kent School, Kent, Connecticut; since 1954 he has been Chairman of the English Department at Kent. Mr. Davis is co-editor of three volumes in the ADVENTURES IN GOOD BOOKS SERIES: *Four English Novels, Four American Novels,* and *Four English Biographies.*

The Series Editor, **MARY RIVES BOWMAN**, holds degrees in English from the University of Texas (B.A.) and the University of Chicago (M.A.) and has also done graduate work in English at the University of Colorado and at East Texas State College. She has been active in various professional organizations and has devoted much of her time to the training and supervision of high school English teachers. She is co-editor of three earlier editions of *Adventures in American Literature* and of two editions of *Adventures for Readers,* Books 1 and 2.

Copyright © 1963, 1958, copyright 1952, 1949, 1946, 1941, 1938, 1931
by Harcourt Brace Jovanovich, Inc.

PRINTED IN THE UNITED STATES OF AMERICA

ISBN 0-15-335810-6

CONTENTS

Modern Biography

Modern Essays

Modern Drama

The Modern Novel

NOTE: The initials J. B. P. are used throughout as the signature of Mr. Priestley.

THE TWENTIETH CENTURY

1900–

THIS AGE of ours represents the triumph of science, invention, technology, and social welfare. Man travels faster and faster, further and further. He is able to invent machines that do more and more work for him. By means of public health services and the use of antibiotics he has been able to save countless millions of lives that would have been lost in any former age. The mass of people in Western Europe and North America are better fed, housed, clothed, and educated than ever before in history. On all this—and much more—we can congratulate ourselves.

SOME MODERN PROBLEMS

But there is another side to the picture, and unless we take a look at it we cannot understand our age and the literature it has produced. This century has known already the two most destructive and terrible wars in all history, and it is not yet out of danger of a third world war that would destroy our whole civilization. Science can save lives but, with two-thirds of the world's inhabitants threatened with starvation, does not yet know any quick way of producing food for the steadily increasing populations of the earth. It may be important to reach the moon and travel through space, but it is even more important to make sure that all the people on this planet are adequately fed, housed, and clothed, and that they have at least a chance of good health.

THE MODERN TEMPER

In spite of our wonderful scientific and technological advances, we in this century are curiously lacking in big new ideas. It is a fact that almost all the ideas that have shaped both our thought and our history in the twentieth century actually belong to the nineteenth century. This is true of Communism, Socialism, Fascism, Anarchism, in politics. The theory of evolution, which has had immense influence on modern thought, also originated in the nineteenth century. No great new religious idea has been developed in our own age. Even Freud, the father of psychoanalysis and depth psychology, is more a nineteenth- than a twentieth-century figure. In all the ideas that relate men to one another or to some spiritual principle in the universe, this age has owed almost everything to the past.

What is most startlingly new and belongs essentially to this time of ours is what men are discovering not on the human scale but in the immensely large and the unimaginably tiny realms of galaxies and stars, atoms, electrons and protons. The mathematicians and astronomers and their theory of relativity, and the nuclear physicists, who may either destroy us with their H-bombs or save us by offering us new sources of energy, are in the forefront of our picture of contemporary life. Both sets of scientists deal with highly abstract and difficult ideas so far removed from any human scale that it is difficult to relate them to our own lives. This situation, in which man no longer seems at home in his world but merely poised perilously between gigantic stars and whirling atoms, is not easily accepted even by imaginative men and women and has been partly responsible for introducing into literature more than a suggestion of bewilderment, doubt, and despair. We wonder who and what we are.

TWENTIETH-CENTURY BRITAIN

In this age three important things have happened to Britain. She has lost the dominant position she had during the nineteenth century and now must accept third place, behind the United States and Russia. Secondly, she has had to face two ruinous wars which have cost her lives (chiefly of young healthy men) she could ill spare, the destruction and loss of much property, especially during World War II (1939–45), and the continued loss of investments abroad that had once made London the financial capital of the world. Thirdly—a gain now instead of a loss —first through the Liberal Party, then through the Labor Party, she has raised the standard of life of the working people and has finally created a welfare state, which makes itself responsible for the health, employment, housing, education, and pensions of the great mass of the population. Everybody makes some kind of contribution to finance this welfare program. Much of it would be impossible without exceptionally heavy taxation—directly through income and surtaxes and indirectly through high duties on tobacco, liquor, imported luxuries, and what are really sales taxes (much heavier than any in America) on a variety of goods.

FROM EMPIRE TO COMMONWEALTH

During the first half of the century what had been the British Empire became the British Commonwealth. This is not merely a change of name. Ireland, except for Ulster, declared itself an independent republic in 1921. In 1947 so did India and Pakistan, though nominally remaining within the Commonwealth. In the early years of the century, Canada, Australia, and New Zealand became dominions—self-governing and independent nations—within the Commonwealth. And now the people in West Africa and elsewhere are, with British help, creating states of their own, like Ghana and Nigeria. People who have a prejudice against Britain often sneer at her for "losing her Empire," but this is to misjudge the more liberal British attitude toward her former possessions. The more liberal and progressive idea was always that Britain had been holding these territories in trust for their inhabitants, who when they were ready to govern themselves should be encouraged to do so. Many brutal and stupid things have been done in the name of British imperialism—and such things have always been denounced by the more enlightened British themselves—but the idea behind the British Commonwealth of gradually bringing new states and nations into existence is one of the noblest and most creative political ideas that history can show us, fit companion to the idea that inspired the American Constitution.

No doubt in earlier years Britain's colonial possessions were exploited for commercial purposes and were financially beneficial to Britain. Today the heavily-taxed Briton finds himself helping to run these areas at a financial loss. Not only· is he still responsible for their protection (adding to the size and cost of Army, Navy, and Air Force), but he must also subsidize their development into independent and economically strong nations. Moreover, the large dominions have no financial responsibility to Britain herself. Canada, the wealthiest of them, is not even within "the sterling area" (that is, the area using the British pound sterling) but has her own dollar currency. The ties between Britain and the dominions are in fact more sentimental than economic. Nevertheless, in each of the two world wars, the dominions hastened to support Britain with men and materials as well as with financial assistance.

INFLUENCE OF THE WARS ON LITERATURE

The influence of the two great wars, even upon English literature, has been so great that something must be said about them. This is all the more important because Americans cannot help regarding these wars as being much shorter and less crippling than they seemed, and actually were, to the British.

For Britain, World War I began in August 1914, and ended in November 1918. During that time almost a million young Britons were killed outright. The slaughter was terrible, especially during the Battle of the Somme, which began in July 1916. (In that month, more than half the young men I had known as boys were killed.) Since many battalions had been recruited largely from single cities, after which they were named, these cities were plunged at once into mourning when their battalions were mowed down by machine guns. The effect of these ghastly casualties was powerful and lasting, both on surviving soldiers themselves—poets like Siegfried Sassoon (1886–   ) and Robert Graves (1895–   )—and on the civilians at home. A certain optimism, the nineteenth-century conviction that progress must forever continue, which can also be found in twentieth-century figures such as Shaw (1856–1950) and Wells (1866–1946) and Arnold Bennett (1867–1931) vanished from Britain.

The younger creative writers and critics from 1919 onward turned in disgust from public affairs (from which the war developed, and, much influenced by writers abroad, turned from man in society to man in the inner world of his mind. Whatever was associated with the world before the war was condemned or ignored because it was that world which had produced the war. Even rebels like Shaw and Wells never recovered the popularity among "advanced" young writers and critics that they had had before 1914.

THE NEW WRITING

Literature had now a much narrower base. It was regarded as something that could appeal only to a very small minority, the cultured few. The old idea that good literature could be enjoyed by almost everybody did not survive into the 1920's, which was very much a period of new writing that might be called "highbrow" and "precious." The work of these writers—T. S. Eliot (1888–   ), James Joyce (1882–1941), Virginia Woolf (1882–1941), for example—was often difficult and deliberately obscure. If ordinary people could not understand such writing, then so much the worse for ordinary people, who, anyhow, had plenty of rubbish to amuse them. This was the more extreme literary attitude during the 1920's.

One reason for this defiant and rather "snooty" attitude was the enormous development throughout the 1920's and 30's (and, indeed, down to this day) of what are generally referred to as "mass media." These are the popular press, including both newspapers and magazines with large circulations; films; radio; and, of course more recently, television. All these were held to be the enemies of real literature. Young creative writers felt themselves in danger of being overwhelmed by these mass media. So they had to keep a long way off and do something very different. If so much was being made easily acceptable to the ordinary public, then real literature, not meant for such people, could afford to be difficult, could even glory in its difficulty.

(A personal note: It was impossible, during the 1920's and 30's, for a youngish writer in England to have both a large and enthusiastic public and a good literary reputation at the same time. So when I published *The Good Companions,* which sold about a million copies, I immediately lost any literary reputation I had had and did not get it back for years. I mention this to show that here, in this introduction, I am writing about what I know from personal experience.)

WORLD WAR II

For Britain World War II lasted from 1939 to 1945. During most of 1940 and most of 1941 Britain was alone facing Hitler, who first threatened invasion and then launched bombing attacks on London and many other English cities. The destruction in this war was staggering (in a single night millions and millions of books were destroyed by fire, the result of incendiary bombs in the city of London), but the loss of life among the armed forces was less than that in the previous war, though the *civilian* casualties, those killed or severely wounded, numbered about 250,000. There was nothing like the growing disillusionment and bitterness of the first war, if only because few illusions remained when the second war began. Indeed many of us feel that the spirit of the English was higher during World War II than it had been before or has been since. Among other things, there was a tremendous demand for good reading and theater, for music and the visual arts. It was during the war that what is now called the British Arts Council was born. By dispensing government grants to worthy nonprofit cultural projects which otherwise would be unable to exist, this organization has done much to encourage the arts in Britain.

THE POLITICAL SCENE

As a result of the Parliamentary reform bills passed during the later years of Victoria's reign and the growth of stronger local self-government and increasingly widened suffrage, control of the government, both in Britain and in her colonies, passed more and more from royalty and the aristocracy to the middle and lower classes. Accompanying the more popular form of government was more extensive social legislation which continued throughout the following years, characterizing the period both before and after World War I, and indeed before and after World War II, during which Winston Churchill as prime minister did so much to marshal the country's forces for survival and final victory.

Many Americans are surprised that in the General Election of 1945

Winston Churchill was defeated. But the point is that Churchill (whose personal popularity was as high as ever) was the head of the Conservative Party, and it was Clement Attlee and the opposing Labor Party that answered the mood of the time, especially for the younger people. The result was the welfare state, which the Conservatives kept intact when Churchill led them back to power again in 1951. Churchill served as prime minister until 1955 when, at the age of 81, he retired from public life. Government leadership and the leadership of the Conservative Party was then placed in the hands of Anthony Eden, who in 1957 was in turn succeeded by Harold Macmillan.

Despite the fact that the original welfare state represented for Britain a completely new approach to economic and social affairs, certain hopes of some of the younger people, who wanted a more radical social democracy, were never realized. This defeat, together with an increasingly materialistic outlook among people in general, explains the basic dissatisfaction, the cynicism, of many of the younger English writers such as Kingsley Amis (1922–   ), John Wain (1925–   ), John Osborne (1929–   ), and John Braine (1922–   ). They dislike the complacent, materialistic, selfish mood and atmosphere of their time, so obviously lacking in ideals and public spirit. They, too, would like to fight for something, but they cannot find a cause to adopt.

THE ARTS IN CONTEMPORARY BRITAIN

Although there is a reasonably high level of accomplishment in most literary forms—poetry, fiction, drama—in postwar Britain, there is still a disappointing lack of really outstanding figures, figures ready to belong to world literature. The giants are very slow to arrive. But this may have something to do with the state of the public mind, for, as we have already seen, it is when some form of literature (like the drama in the Elizabethan Age, the novel in the Victorian) is important and exciting to people in general that great work is achieved in those forms. A public that is more concerned about "television personalities" than it is about authors is in no condition to nourish great literature.

Certain modern developments should be noted. The wide popularity of paperbacks, beginning with the *Penguin* series that originally sold for about a dime, brought good reading to a very large public. These paperbacks, however, were of little or no financial help to young authors, and they killed the more literary magazines and the market for short stories. Also, as in America, with the costs of publishing rising all the time, it was more and more difficult for young poets to find publishers. (On the other hand, poets and playwrights have been not ungenerously assisted by the British Broadcasting Corporation, and, to a lesser extent, by the Arts Council.) As for the theater, it is always about to become much better but on the whole remains much the same. Just as it began to recover from the triumphant competition of the films, it had to meet the challenge of television. It is true that London probably has more plays running at any time than any other city in the world. Nevertheless, too high a proportion of these plays have no literary nor even dramatic value.

At this time of writing—for the situation can easily change—contemporary English literature and the production of good new work suffer from certain handicaps. One is that the former middle class, which liked to buy books and literary reviews and seats for good plays, is dwindling and is comparatively hard up, whereas the very large working class, which at last has leisure and some money to spend, has not yet discovered an interest in books and authors. Perhaps a more serious handicap, though it might disappear any time, is that the contemporary atmosphere, tone, mood, flavor, of Britain as a society possesses a certain staleness and want of imagination and inspiration. This does not encourage the creation of fine literature on any scale. England, like the rest of the world, is now sadly short of great and illuminating ideas. But when they come, they will be reflected, as they have so often been before, in English literature.

J. B. P.

MODERN SHORT STORIES

Although Dickens at the height of his popularity wrote some short stories, the modern English short story makes its appearance some years after his death, beginning in the 1880's. The interest in this form was strongest probably from 1885–1930. The names associated with the short story would include Stevenson, Hardy, Kipling, H. G. Wells, Conrad, Somerset Maugham, Lawrence, O'Connor, Katherine Mansfield, and A. E. Coppard.

Clearly there has been no lack of work in the short story in Britain. Yet literary and critical interest in the short story has never been as great in Britain as it has been in the United States, France, and possibly Germany. Although writers like Stevenson, Kipling, and Wells still enjoy large sales for their short stories, it is a fact, which many British publishers have been reluctantly compelled to acknowledge, that it is very difficult to sell volumes of short stories by new writers to the British reading public, which has never really taken the short story to its heart. (Coppard, an excellent writer and widely praised by critics, had comparatively small sales in Britain, in spite of his fine reputation.) This public indifference to the short story is probably due to the fact that English readers enjoy a leisurely display and development of character, something which is impossible in the short story form.

We must make a distinction, however, between the true short story, which really is short, and much longer tales—long short stories—that come somewhere between the true short story and the novel. (There is no proper term for this kind of fiction in English, but, borrowing from the Italian, *novella* might do.) Both Conrad and Maugham, for example, have done some of their best work in these longer tales, which are particularly suitable for stories with exotic backgrounds, if only because they are not too short for some elaborate descriptive passages and the creation of a special atmosphere. Quite often, three or four of these tales together are sufficient to make up a fair-sized volume.

Both Kipling and Wells made admirable use of the shorter short story form. The stories of neither of these writers, however, are usually very short, both men needing a certain length in order to develop an action. The short story in their hands tends to be a fully realized tale in miniature, complete with characters, action, atmosphere, and background. In the stories they write, something definitely happens. [A minor master of this form of tale, which he always most cunningly plotted, was the humorist W. W. Jacobs (1846–1943), who could also on occasion write a convincing tale of horror. And so, with even more force and subtlety, could the poet Walter de la Mare.] There can be no doubt that it is this type of short story, which keeps us in suspense, that the British reading public prefers to any other.

A later and generally shorter kind of story, which has little or no action, no plot in the old sense of the term, but depends instead on insight into character, the ability to suggest a mood or atmosphere, can be found in the work of Katherine Mansfield. She did not invent it, for stories of this kind were being written in the 1890's, but she gave it emotional intensity and poetic feeling. She and her contemporaries, all writing about the time of World War I, were very much under the influence of Anton Chekhov (1860–1904), the Russian master of the short story, whose work was first appearing at that time in English translations.

A friend and contemporary of Katherine Mansfield was D. H. Lawrence (1885–1930), many of whose short stories are more satisfying than all but two or three of his novels. Lawrence is able to combine something of the emotional intensity and poetic feeling of the Mansfield type of story with the plot development of the older short story writers. Many of his stories are based on real incidents and characters who were friends and acquaintances.

A. E. Coppard at his best has much in common with both Mansfield and Lawrence, though he tends to write more elaborately. But what distinguishes him from them is a kind of sly and almost rustic humor. A self-educated man, who in his time tried all manner of jobs, Coppard had a great knowledge of all the byways and out-of-the-way places of southern England, almost like that of a gypsy, and he put this knowledge to good use in his short stories. There is a rather similar rustic background in many of the early stories of the novelist H. E. Bates.

Some of the more distinguished women writers, like Rebecca West (1892–   ) and the Anglo-Irish Elizabeth Bowen (1899–   ), have turned occasionally, and with success, to the short story. But there are very few women writers since Katherine Mansfield who have specialized in this form. Irish writers, male and female, have produced fine short stories; it is a form that seems to suit the Irish.

Few things are easier to write than a mediocre short story, especially when nothing much happens in it. But good short stories, giving us so much in so little space, are very hard indeed to write. Their authors are more like poets than like novelists. There is, however, one trap that even good short story writers are rarely able to avoid. This might be called "false finality," which tries to persuade us that all is over forever with a character because he or she does, or fails to do, something or other. "As he closed the door, he knew that life could never be the same again"—that kind of thing, true enough at the moment but false in its finality. But at its best the short story offers us a wonderfully clear little window through which we can see something of the lights and shadows, the heights and depths, of life in this world.

J. B. P.

The Lagoon

JOSEPH CONRAD 1857–1924

Joseph Conrad was the pen name of a Polish youth who became one of the most remarkable figures in twentieth-century English literature. Until he was twenty-one, he could speak no English. He did not begin his writing career until he was thirty, and yet became one of England's great novelists.

From early youth, Conrad yearned for a life at sea and, when seventeen, left home to become a sailor. While on shipboard on a Congo river steamer, he began his first novel, *Almayer's Folly*. Later, retiring from the merchant marine, he began to write steadily. (A detailed sketch of his life and work appears on page 309, preceding his novel *Typhoon*.)

The sea is never far away in a Conrad story. Like Herman Melville in American literature, Conrad is the great storyteller of the sea in English fiction. In novels (*The Secret Sharer, Victory, Lord Jim,* and others), in long stories ("Youth," "The End of the Tether"), and in short stories like "The Lagoon," the sounds and moods of the sea run through his writing. But Conrad stories are not travelogues. Vigorously and with keen psychological insight, he is always probing into the hidden motives and problems of men. The grandeur of the sea and the mystery of tropic shores or shady riverbanks are typical Conrad settings for memorable character studies.

THE WHITE MAN, leaning with both arms over the roof of the little house in the stern of the boat, said to the steersman:

"We will pass the night in Arsat's clearing. It is late."

The Malay only grunted, and went on looking fixedly at the river. The white man rested his chin on his crossed arms and gazed at the wake of the boat. At the end of the straight avenue of forests cut by the intense glitter of the river, the sun appeared unclouded and dazzling, poised low over the water that shone smoothly like a band of metal. The forests, somber and dull, stood motionless and silent on each side of the broad stream. At the foot of big, towering trees, trunkless nipa palms rose from the mud of the bank, in bunches of leaves enormous and heavy, that hung unstirring over the brown swirl of eddies. In the stillness of the air every tree, every leaf, every bough, every tendril of creeper and every petal of minute blossoms seemed to have been bewitched into an immobility perfect and final. Nothing moved on the river but the eight paddles that rose flashing regularly, dipped together with a single splash, while the steersman swept right and left with a periodic and sudden flourish of his blade describing a glinting semicircle above his head. The churned-up water frothed alongside with a confused murmur. And the white man's canoe, advancing upstream in the short-lived disturbance of its own making, seemed to enter the portals of a land from which the very memory of motion had forever departed.

The white man, turning his back upon the setting sun, looked along the empty and broad expanse of the sea reach. For the last three miles of its course the wandering, hesitating river, as if enticed irresistibly by the freedom of an open horizon, flows straight into the sea, flows straight to the east—to the east that harbors both light and darkness. Astern of the boat the repeated call of some bird, a cry discordant and feeble, skipped along over the smooth water and lost itself, before it could reach the other shore, in the breathless silence of the world.

The steersman dug his paddle into the stream, and held hard with stiffened arms, his body thrown forward. The water gurgled aloud; and suddenly the long straight reach seemed to pivot on its center, the forests swung in a semicircle, and the slanting beams of sunset touched the broadside of the canoe with a fiery glow, throwing the slender and distorted shadows of its crew upon the streaked glitter of the river. The white man turned to look ahead. The course of the boat had been altered at right angles to the stream, and the carved dragonhead on its prow was pointing now at a gap in the fringing bushes of the bank. It glided through, brushing the overhanging twigs, and disappeared from the river like some slim and amphibious creature leaving the water for its lair in the forests.

The narrow creek was like a ditch: tortuous, fabulously deep; filled with gloom under the thin strip of pure and shining blue of the heaven.

Immense trees soared up, invisible behind the festooned draperies of creepers. Here and there, near the glistening blackness of the water, a twisted root of some tall tree showed among the tracery of small ferns, black and dull, writhing and motionless, like an arrested snake. The short words of the paddlers reverberated loudly between the thick and somber walls of vegetation. Darkness oozed out from between the trees, through the tangled maze of the creepers, from behind the great fantastic and unstirring leaves; the darkness, mysterious and invincible; the darkness scented and poisonous of impenetrable forests.

The men poled in the shoaling water. The creek broadened, opening out into a wide sweep of a stagnant lagoon. The forests receded from the marshy bank, leaving a level strip of bright green, reedy grass to frame the reflected blueness of the sky. A fleecy pink cloud drifted high above, trailing the delicate coloring of its image under the floating leaves and the silvery blossoms of the lotus. A little house, perched on high piles, appeared black in the distance. Near it, two tall nibong palms, that seemed to have come out of the forests in the background, leaned slightly over the ragged roof, with a suggestion of sad tenderness and care in the droop of their leafy and soaring heads.

The steersman, pointing with his paddle, said, "Arsat is there. I see his canoe fast between the piles."

The polers ran along the sides of the boat glancing over their shoulders at the end of the day's journey. They would have preferred to spend the night somewhere else than on this lagoon of weird aspect and ghostly reputation. Moreover, they disliked Arsat, first as a stranger, and also because he who repairs a ruined house, and dwells in it, proclaims that he is not afraid to live amongst the spirits that haunt the places abandoned by mankind. Such a man can disturb the course of fate by glances or words; while his familiar ghosts are not easy to propitiate by casual wayfarers upon whom they long to wreak the malice of their human master. White men care not for such things, being unbelievers and in league with the Father of Evil, who leads them unharmed through the invisible dangers of this world. To the warnings of the righteous they oppose an offensive pretense of disbelief. What is there to be done?

So they thought, throwing their weight on the end of their long poles. The big canoe glided on swiftly, noiselessly, and smoothly, toward Arsat's clearing, till, in a great rattling of poles thrown down, and the loud murmurs of "Allah be praised!" it came with a gentle knock against the crooked piles below the house.

The boatmen with uplifted faces shouted discordantly, "Arsat! O Arsat!" Nobody came. The white man began to climb the rude ladder giving access to the bamboo platform before the house. The juragan[1] of the boat said sulkily, "We will cook in the sampan,[2] and sleep on the water."

"Pass my blankets and the basket," said the white man, curtly.

He knelt on the edge of the platform to receive the bundle. Then the boat shoved off, and the white man, standing up, confronted Arsat, who had come out through the low door of his hut. He was a man young, powerful, with broad chest and muscular arms. He had nothing on but his sarong.[3] His head was bare. His big, soft eyes stared eagerly at the white man, but his voice and demeanor were composed as he asked, without any words of greeting:

"Have you medicine, Tuan?"[4]

"No," said the visitor in a startled tone. "No. Why? Is there sickness in the house?"

"Enter and see," replied Arsat, in the same calm manner, and turning short round, passed again through the small doorway. The white man, dropping his bundles, followed.

In the dim light of the dwelling he made out on a couch of bamboos a woman stretched on her back under a broad sheet of red cotton cloth. She lay still, as if dead; but her big eyes, wide open, glittered in the gloom, staring upward at the slender rafters, motionless and unseeing. She was in a high fever, and evidently unconscious. Her cheeks were sunk slightly, her lips were partly open, and on the young face there was the ominous and fixed expression—the absorbed, contemplating expression of the unconscious who are going to die. The two men stood looking down at her in silence.

"Has she been long ill?" asked the traveler.

"I have not slept for five nights," answered the Malay, in a deliberate tone. "At first she heard voices calling her from the water and struggled against me who held her. But since the sun of today rose she hears nothing—she hears not me. She sees nothing. She sees not me—me!"

He remained silent for a minute, then asked softly:

"Tuan, will she die?"

"I fear so," said the white man, sorrowfully. He had known Arsat

---

[1] *juragan:* native leader or captain.
[2] *sampan:* flat-bottomed boat, used in river and harbor traffic.
[3] *sarong:* skirt or kilt worn by both sexes in the Malay Peninsula.
[4] *Tuan:* term of respect, like Sir, used by natives to white men.

years ago, in a far country in times of trouble and danger, when no friendship is to be despised. And since his Malay friend had come unexpectedly to dwell in the hut on the lagoon with a strange woman, he had slept many times there, in his journeys up and down the river. He liked the man who knew how to keep faith in council and how to fight without fear by the side of his white friend. He liked him—not so much perhaps as a man likes his favorite dog—but still he liked him well enough to help and ask no questions, to think sometimes vaguely and hazily in the midst of his own pursuits, about the lonely man and the long-haired woman with audacious face and triumphant eyes, who lived together hidden by the forests—alone and feared.

The white man came out of the hut in time to see the enormous conflagration of sunset put out by the swift and stealthy shadows that, rising like a black and impalpable vapor above the treetops, spread over the heaven, extinguishing the crimson glow of floating clouds and the red brilliance of departing daylight. In a few moments all the stars came out above the intense blackness of the earth and the great lagoon gleaming suddenly with reflected lights resembled an oval patch of night sky flung down into the hopeless and abysmal night of the wilderness. The white man had some supper out of the basket, then collecting a few sticks that lay about the platform, made up a small fire, not for warmth, but for the sake of the smoke, which would keep off the mosquitoes. He wrapped himself in the blankets and sat with his back against the reed wall of the house, smoking thoughtfully.

Arsat came through the doorway with noiseless steps and squatted down by the fire. The white man moved his outstretched legs a little.

"She breathes," said Arsat in a low voice, anticipating the expected question. "She breathes and burns as if with a great fire. She speaks not; she hears not—and burns!"

He paused for a moment, then asked in a quiet, incurious tone:

"Tuan . . . will she die?"

The white man moved his shoulders uneasily and uttered in a hesitating manner:

"If such is her fate."

"No, Tuan," said Arsat, calmly. "If such is my fate. I hear, I see, I wait. I remember . . . Tuan, do you remember the old days? Do you remember my brother?"

"Yes," said the white man. The Malay rose suddenly and went in. The other, sitting still outside, could hear the voice in the hut. Arsat said: "Hear me! Speak!" His words were succeeded by a complete silence. "O Diamelen!" he cried, suddenly. After that cry there was a deep sigh. Arsat came out and sank down again in his old place.

They sat in silence before the fire. There was no sound within the house, there was no sound near them; but far away on the lagoon they could hear the voices of the boatmen ringing fitful and distinct on the calm water. The fire in the bow of the sampan shone faintly in the distance with a hazy red glow. Then it died out. The voices ceased. The land and the water slept invisible, unstirring, and mute. It was as though there had been nothing left in the world but the glitter of stars streaming, ceaseless and vain, through the black stillness of the night.

The white man gazed straight before him into the darkness with wide-open eyes. The fear and fascination, the inspiration and the wonder of death—of death near, unavoidable, and unseen, soothed the unrest of his race and stirred the most indistinct, the most intimate of his thoughts. The ever-ready suspicion of evil, the gnawing suspicion that lurks in our hearts, flowed out into the stillness round him—into the stillness profound and dumb, and made it appear untrustworthy and infamous, like the placid and impenetrable mask of an unjustifiable violence. In that fleeting and powerful disturbance of his being, the earth, enfolded in the starlight peace, became a shadowy country of inhuman strife, a battlefield of phantoms terrible and charming, august or ignoble, struggling ardently for the possession of our helpless hearts. An unquiet and mysterious country of inextinguishable desires and fears.

A plaintive murmur rose in the night; a murmur saddening and startling, as if the great solitudes of surrounding woods had tried to whisper into his ear the wisdom of their immense and lofty indifference. Sounds hesitating and vague floated in the air round him, shaped themselves slowly into words; and at last flowed on gently in a murmuring stream of soft and monotonous sentences. He stirred like a man waking up and changed his position slightly. Arsat, motionless and shadowy, sitting with bowed head under the stars, was speaking in a low and dreamy tone:

". . . for where can we lay down the heaviness of our trouble but in a friend's heart? A man must speak of war and of love. You, Tuan, know what war is, and you have seen me in time of danger seek death as other men seek life! A writing may be lost; a lie may be written; but what the eye has seen is truth and remains in the mind!"

"I remember," said the white man, quietly. Arsat went on with mournful composure:

"Therefore I shall speak to you of love. Speak in the night. Speak before both night and love are gone—and the eye of day looks upon my sorrow and my shame; upon my blackened face; upon my burnt-up heart."

A sigh, short and faint, marked an almost imperceptible pause, and then his words flowed on, without a stir, without a gesture.

"After the time of trouble and war was over and you went away from my country in the pursuit of your desires, which we, men of the islands, cannot understand, I and my brother became again, as we had been before, the swordbearers of the Ruler. You know we were men of family, belonging to a ruling race, and more fit than any to carry on our right shoulder the emblem of power. And in time of prosperity Si Dendring showed us favor, as we, in time of sorrow, had showed to him the faithfulness of our courage. It was a time of peace. A time of deer hunts and cockfights; of idle talks and foolish squabbles between men whose bellies are full and weapons are rusty. But the sower watched the young rice shoots grow up without fear, and the traders came and went, departed lean and returned fat into the river of peace. They brought news, too. Brought lies and truth mixed together, so that no man knew when to rejoice and when to be sorry. We heard from them about you also. They had seen you here and had seen you there. And I was glad to hear, for I remembered the stirring times, and I always remembered you, Tuan, till the time came when my eyes could see nothing in the past, because they had looked upon the one who is dying there—in the house."

He stopped to exclaim in an intense whisper, "O Mara bahia! O Calamity!" then went on speaking a little louder:

"There's no worse enemy and no better friend than a brother, Tuan, for one brother knows another, and in perfect knowledge is strength for good or evil. I loved my brother. I went to him and told him that I could see nothing but one face, hear nothing but one voice. He told me: 'Open your heart so that she can see what is in it—and wait. Patience is wisdom. Inchi Midah may die or our Ruler may throw off his fear of a woman!' . . . I waited— . . . You remember the lady with the veiled face, Tuan, and the fear of our Ruler before her cunning and temper. And if she wanted her servant, what could I do? But I fed the hunger of my heart on short glances and stealthy words. I loitered on the path to the bathhouses in the daytime, and when the sun had fallen behind the forest I crept along the jasmine hedges of the women's courtyard. Unseeing, we spoke to one another through the scent of flowers, through the veil of leaves, through the blades of long grass that stood still before our lips; so great was our prudence, so faint was the murmur of our great longing. The time passed swiftly . . . and there were whispers among women—and our enemies watched—my brother was gloomy, and I began to think of killing and of a fierce death. . . . We are of a people who take what they want—like you whites. There is a time when a man should forget loyalty and respect. Might and authority are given to rulers, but to all men is given love and strength and courage. My brother said, 'You shall take her from their midst. We are two who are like one.' And I answered, 'Let it be soon, for I find no warmth in sunlight that does not shine upon her.' Our time came when the Ruler and all the great people went to the mouth of the river to fish by torchlight. There were hundreds of boats, and on the white sand, between the water and the forests, dwellings of leaves were built for the households of the Rajahs. The smoke of cooking fires was like a blue mist of the evening, and many voices rang in it joyfully. While they were making the boats ready to beat up the fish, my brother came to me and said, 'Tonight!' I looked to my weapons, and when the time came our canoe took its place in the circle of boats carrying the torches. The lights blazed on the water, but behind the boats there was darkness. When the shouting began and the excitement made them like mad we dropped out. The water swallowed our fire, and we floated back to the shore that was dark with only here and there the glimmer of embers. We could hear the talk of slave girls among the sheds. Then we found a place deserted and silent. We waited there. She came. She came running along the shore, rapid and leaving no trace, like a leaf driven by the wind into the sea. My brother said gloomily, 'Go and take her; carry her into our boat.' I lifted her in my arms. She panted. Her heart was beating against my breast. I said, 'I take you from those people. You came to the cry of my heart, but my arms take you into my boat against the will of the great!' 'It is right,' said my brother. 'We are men who take what we want and can hold it against many. We should have taken her in daylight.' I said, 'Let us be off'; for since she was in my boat I began to think of our Ruler's many men. 'Yes. Let us be off,' said my brother. 'We are cast out and this boat is our country now— and the sea is our refuge.' He lingered with his foot on the shore, and I entreated him to hasten, for I remembered the strokes of her heart against my breast and thought that two men cannot withstand a hundred. We left, paddling downstream close to the bank; and as we passed by the creek where they were fishing, the great shouting had ceased, but the murmur of voices was loud like the humming of insects flying at noonday. The boats floated, clustered together, in the red light of torches, under a black roof of smoke; and men talked of their sport. Men that boasted, and praised, and jeered—men that would have been our friends in the morning, but on that night were already our enemies. We paddled swiftly past. We had no more friends in the country of our birth. She sat in the middle of the canoe with covered face; silent as she is now; unseeing as she is now—and I had no regret at what I was leaving because I could hear her breathing close to me—as I can hear her now."

He paused, listened with his ear turned to the doorway, then shook his head and went on:

"My brother wanted to shout the cry of challenge—one cry only—to let the people know we were freeborn robbers who trusted our arms and the great sea. And again I begged him in the name of our love to be silent. Could I not hear her breathing close to me? I knew the pursuit would come quick enough. My brother loved me. He dipped his paddle without a splash. He only said, 'There is a half a man in you now—the other half is in that woman. I can wait. When you are a whole man again, you will come back with me here to shout defiance. We are sons of the same mother.' I made no answer. All my strength and all my spirit were in my hands that held the paddle—for I longed to be with her in a safe place beyond the reach of men's anger and of women's spite. My love was so great, that I thought it could guide me to a country where death was unknown, if I could only escape from Inchi Midah's fury and from our Ruler's sword. We paddled with haste, breathing through our teeth. The blades bit deep into the smooth water. We passed out of the river; we flew in clear channels among the shallows. We skirted the black coast; we skirted the sand beaches where the sea speaks in whispers to the land; and the gleam of white sand flashed back past our boat, so swiftly she ran upon the water. We spoke not. Only once I said, 'Sleep, Diamelen, for soon you may want all your strength.' I heard the sweetness of her voice, but I never turned my head. The sun rose and still we went on. Water fell from my face like rain from a cloud. We flew in the light and heat. I never looked back, but I knew that my brother's eyes, behind me, were looking steadily ahead, for the boat went as straight as a bushman's dart, when it leaves the end of the sumpitan.[1] There was no better paddler, no better steersman than my brother. Many times, together, we had won races in that canoe. But we

[1] *sumpitan:* a kind of blowgun for discharging a dart, used by natives of Borneo and adjacent islands.

never had put out our strength as we did then—then, when for the last time we paddled together! There was no braver or stronger man in our country than my brother. I could not spare the strength to turn my head and look at him, but every moment I heard the hiss of his breath getting louder behind me. Still he did not speak. The sun was high. The heat clung to my back like a flame of fire. My ribs were ready to burst, but I could no longer get enough air into my chest. And then I felt I must cry out with my last breath, 'Let us rest!' . . . 'Good!' he answered; and his voice was firm. He was strong. He was brave. He knew not fear and no fatigue. . . . My brother!"

A murmur powerful and gentle, a murmur vast and faint; the murmur of trembling leaves, of stirring boughs, ran through the tangled depths of the forests, ran over the starry smoothness of the lagoon, and the water between the piles lapped the slimy timber once with a sudden splash. A breath of warm air touched the two men's faces and passed on with a mournful sound—a breath loud and short like an uneasy sigh of the dreaming earth.

Arsat went on in an even, low voice.

"We ran our canoe on the white beach of a little bay close to a long tongue of land that seemed to bar our road; a long wooded cape going far into the sea. My brother knew that place. Beyond the cape a river has its entrance, and through the jungle of that land there is a narrow path. We made a fire and cooked rice. Then we lay down to sleep on the soft sand in the shade of our canoe, while she watched. No sooner had I closed my eyes than I heard her cry of alarm. We leaped up. The sun was halfway down the sky already, and coming in sight in the opening of the bay we saw a prau[1] manned by many paddlers. We knew it at once; it was one of our Rajah's praus. They were watching the shore, and saw us. They beat the gong, and turned the head of the prau into the bay. I felt my heart become weak within my breast. Diamelen sat on the sand and covered her face. There was no escape by sea. My brother laughed. He had the gun you had given him, Tuan, before you went away, but there was only a handful of powder. He spoke to me quickly: 'Run with her along the path. I shall keep them back, for they have no firearms, and landing in the face of a man with a gun is certain death for some. Run with her. On the other side of that wood there is a fisherman's house—and a canoe. When I have fired all the shots I will

---

[1] prau: swift Malayan vessel with sharp prow and stern, which can sail equally well prow or stern first.

follow. I am a great runner, and before they can come up we shall be gone. I will hold out as long as I can, for she is but a woman—that can neither run nor fight, but she has your heart in her weak hands.' He dropped behind the canoe. The prau was coming. She and I ran, and as we rushed along the path I heard shots. My brother fired—once—twice —and the booming of the gong ceased. There was silence behind us. That neck of land is narrow. Before I heard my brother fire the third shot I saw the shelving shore, and I saw the water again; the mouth of a broad river. We crossed a grassy glade. We ran down to the water. I saw a low hut above the black mud, and a small canoe hauled up. I heard another shot behind me. I thought, 'That is his last charge.' We rushed down to the canoe; a man came running from the hut, but I leaped on him, and we rolled together in the mud. Then I got up, and he lay still at my feet. I don't know whether I had killed him or not. I and Diamelen pushed the canoe afloat. I heard yells behind me, and I saw my brother run across the glade. Many men were bounding after him. I took her in my arms and threw her into the boat, then leaped in myself. When I looked back I saw that my brother had fallen. He fell and was up again, but the men were closing round him. He shouted, 'I am coming!' The men were close to him. I looked. Many men. Then I looked at her. Tuan, I pushed the canoe! I pushed it into deep water. She was kneeling forward looking at me, and I said, 'Take your paddle,' while I struck the water with mine. Tuan, I heard him cry. I heard him cry my name twice; and I heard voices shouting, 'Kill! Strike!' I never turned back. I heard him calling my name again with a great shriek, as when life is going out together with the voice—and I never turned my head. My own name! . . . My brother! Three times he called—but I was not afraid of life. Was she not there in that canoe? And could I not with her find a country where death is forgotten— where death is unknown!"

The white man sat up. Arsat rose and stood, an indistinct and silent figure above the dying embers of the fire. Over the lagoon a mist drifting and low had crept, erasing slowly the glittering images of the stars. And now a great expanse of white vapor covered the land: it flowed cold and gray in the darkness, eddied in noiseless whirls round the tree trunks and about the platform of the house, which seemed to float upon a restless and impalpable illusion of a sea. Only far away the tops of the trees stood outlined on the twinkle of heaven, like a somber and forbidding shore—a coast deceptive, pitiless and black.

Arsat's voice vibrated loudly in the profound peace.

"I had her there! I had her! To get her I would have faced all mankind. But I had her—and—"

His words went out ringing into the empty distances. He paused, and seemed to listen to them dying away very far—beyond help and beyond recall. Then he said quietly:

"Tuan, I loved my brother."

A breath of wind made him shiver. High above his head, high above the silent sea of mist the drooping leaves of the palms rattled together with a mournful and expiring sound. The white man stretched his legs. His chin rested on his chest, and he murmured sadly without lifting his head:

"We all love our brothers."

Arsat burst out with an intense whispering violence—

"What did I care who died? I wanted peace in my own heart."

He seemed to hear a stir in the house—listened—then stepped in noiselessly. The white man stood up. A breeze was coming in fitful puffs. The stars shone paler as if they had retreated into the frozen depths of immense space. After a chill gust of wind there were a few seconds of perfect calm and absolute silence. Then from behind the black and wavy line of the forests a column of golden light shot up into the heavens and spread over the semicircle of the eastern horizon. The sun had risen. The mist lifted, broke into drifting patches, vanished into thin flying wreaths; and the unveiled lagoon lay, polished and black, in the heavy shadows at the foot of the wall of trees. A white eagle rose over it with a slanting and ponderous flight, reached the clear sunshine and appeared dazzlingly brilliant for a moment, then soaring higher, became a dark and motionless speck before it vanished into the blue as if it had left the earth forever. The white man, standing gazing upward before the doorway, heard in the hut a confused and broken murmur of distracted words ending with a loud groan. Suddenly Arsat stumbled out with outstretched hands, shivered, and stood still for some time with fixed eyes. Then he said:

"She burns no more."

Before his face the sun showed its edge above the treetops rising steadily. The breeze freshened; a great brilliance burst upon the lagoon, sparkled on the rippling water. The forests came out of the clear shadows of the morning, became distinct, as if they had rushed nearer—to stop short in a great stir of leaves, of nodding boughs, of swaying branches. In the merciless sunshine the whisper of unconscious life grew louder, speaking in an incomprehensible voice round the dumb darkness of that human sorrow. Arsat's eyes wandered slowly, then stared at the rising sun.

"I can see nothing," he said half aloud to himself.

"There is nothing," said the white man, moving to the edge of the platform and waving his hand to his boat. A shout came faintly over the lagoon and the sampan began to glide toward the abode of the friend of ghosts.

"If you want to come with me, I will wait all the morning," said the white man, looking away upon the water.

"No, Tuan," said Arsat, softly. "I shall not eat or sleep in this house, but I must first see my road. Now I can see nothing—see nothing! There is no light and no peace in the world; but there is death—death for many. We are sons of the same mother—and I left him in the midst of enemies; but I am going back now."

He drew a long breath and went on in a dreamy tone:

"In a little while I shall see clear enough to strike—to strike. But she has died, and . . . now . . . darkness."

He flung his arms wide open, let them fall along his body, then stood still with unmoved face and stony eyes, staring at the sun. The white man got down into his canoe. The polers ran smartly along the sides of the boat, looking over their shoulders at the beginning of a weary journey. High in the stern, his head muffled up in white rags, the juragan sat moody, letting his paddle trail in the water. The white man, leaning with both arms over the grass roof of the little cabin, looked at the shining ripple of the boat's wake. Before the sampan passed out of the lagoon into the creek he lifted his eyes. Arsat had not moved. He stood lonely in the searching sunshine; and he looked beyond the great light of a cloudless day into the darkness of a world of illusions.

READING THE SHORT STORY

Short stories are often read for enjoyment only. Although enjoyment is always important, reading short stories becomes an even more satisfying experience if we examine this literary type from the point of view of form and technique. For many readers the answers to two questions are often enlightening: *Why* was this short story written? *How* does it achieve its effects? You will find that these questions can be used in evaluating any short story you read. Try to answer them by examining Joseph Conrad's "The Lagoon."

THE PURPOSE OF THE STORY

Conrad's story is the death of Arsat's wife and the events leading up to it. But what is the idea behind the story? What are Arsat's values and standards of behavior? What conflict does he face in the situation he describes? Why has Arsat failed to find that peace which he said he wanted in his own heart? Is the story a tragedy because of the failure of a faithful, courageous man to act courageously and faithfully in a moment of crisis? To answer such questions we must go beyond the plot of the story and look at its structure, its characters, its atmosphere.

STRUCTURE

This story is unusual in its development. Try dividing it into the following sections: (1) *introduction,* the arrival of the white trader to spend the night with Arsat; (2) *transition,* illness of Diamelen; (3) *big scene,* Arsat's story of the winning of Diamelen and his brother's death; (4) *transition,* death of Diamelen; (5) *final scene,* Arsat's poignant grief.

If you were planning a television production of this story, how much time out of a total of thirty minutes would you give to each part of it? What method would you use to convey a single impression of the first scene? While telling of their last hours together, Conrad uses the "flashback" technique to explain why Arsat and Diamelen are living on the isolated lagoon. At what point in the story is the flashback completed? How does Arsat react to his wife's death? Is Diamelen's death the real tragedy of Arsat's life? What attitude toward Arsat does Conrad seem to have? How do the answers to these questions help you to see why Conrad constructed the story as he did?

CHARACTERS

Arsat's love for Diamelen and the intensity of his grief at her death can be traced throughout the story. His first words to the visitor are, "Have you medicine, Tuan?" Later he asks, "Tuan, will she die?" About to lose what he holds most dear, Arsat is in the depths of despair. His character has also been revealed in a crisis he himself describes. He must be judged both by his actions toward his brother and toward Diamelen. What evidence is there that Arsat is essentially a courageous man?

A complex individual, Arsat's character is revealed through *conversation, action, direct description,* and *interaction with other characters.* Notice how he speaks to the white trader, how he refers to his brother. Where does Conrad indicate what is going on in Arsat's mind by describing what he is doing? Point out short passages that describe Arsat to the reader.

What do you learn about the character of Arsat's brother? How is his character important to the story?

Although Diamelen is a somewhat ephemeral character, her relationship with Arsat should be considered. She never speaks, only cries out during the escape. However, the fact remains that she loved Arsat enough to risk her life for him.

ATMOSPHERE

Conrad's poetic descriptions of remote waters and forests create a sense of mystery. They not only furnish clear pictures for the reader but also establish a mood. Conrad takes care to create the actual physical setting of his story and to suggest its influence on the characters. In the first few paragraphs he conveys a sense of awe by his descriptions of the deep silence and the beauty of the scene. It is by choosing significant details that the author sets the tone and creates the atmosphere. Reread the second paragraph of the story, beginning "The Malay . . . ," and note Conrad's method of conveying a single impression of a scene—in this case, its stillness.

Go over the story again pointing out how Conrad uses specific details to convey a single impression.

The Old Venerable

A. E. COPPARD 1878–1957

Alfred Edgar Coppard, a recognized master of the short story, was born in Folkestone, Kent, of a tailor and a housemaid. At the age of nine he left school and was apprenticed to a London tailor. Later, as an errand boy, he began reading poetry. While he was employed in Oxford as an accountant for an engineering firm, he became the friend of Aldous Huxley and other student writers at the University there.

This group of eager writers gave him the inspiration and encouragement he needed to become a writer himself. Giving up his job, Coppard moved to a hut in the Chiltern Hills, northwest of London, and for two years devoted all his time to writing. He endured extreme poverty, but was justified when *Adam and Eve and Pinch Me,* his first volume of short stories, appeared. This book, published by the Golden Cockerel Press, is already a collector's item. Other collections which followed are *Fishmonger's Fiddle, The Field of Mustard,* and *Tapster's Tapestry.* At the time of his death,

Coppard was working on an autobiography, which has been published posthumously under the title *It's Me, O Lord.*

For many years, A. E. Coppard was neglected by the reading public, but today he is praised for both his poetry and short stories. He has been influenced considerably by folk literature. Because he began writing seriously after World War I, he is often included among the postwar writers. He really is not one of them, however, for he has no psychological answers to give, no sociological theories to advance, simply a story to tell. In "The Old Venerable," Coppard demonstrates that he is at his best in realistic, robust tales of rural life.

Down in the village the women called him "the dirty old man," the children did not seem to notice him, and their fathers called him "the Owd Venrable," or old Dick, with a sigh as of vague envy. There was little cause for that, he living in a wood in a little old tent shanty built of boughs and string and tarpaulin, with a heap of straw to sleep on. Outside the tent was his fire, and he had dwelt there so long that the mound of wood ash had grown almost as big as his house. Seventy years old he was, an old venerable ragged crippled man using two sticks, with a cheery voice and a truculent spirit, but honest as spring water, sharing his last drop with the last man or the first—he invariably shared theirs. When he was drunk he sang, when he was not drunk he talked for evermore about nothing, to nobody, for his tent was in a wood, a little clearing in a great wood, and the wood was away, a long way, from anywhere, so that he lived, as you might say, on air and affability and primed his starved heart with hope. A man like that could hope for anything, and a mere anything—twopence—would bring him bliss, but his undeviating aspiration, an ambition as passionate as it was supine, was to possess a donkey. He had pestered many sympathetic people who had the means; often he had sent out that dove of his fancy from the ark of his need, but it had never returned, at least not with a donkey; and never an ass fell like a bolt from heaven. If it had done, it would surely have taken no hurt, such a grand wood it was, miles of it, growing up and down the hills and hills, and so thickly bosomed that if you had fallen from a balloon into the top of that wood it would have been at the last like sinking into a feather bed. And full of birds and game. And gamekeepers. The keepers did not like him to be there, it was unnatural to them, but keepers come and go, the shooting was let to a syndicate, and he had been there so long that new keepers found him where the old ones had left him. They even made use of him; he swept the rides and alley-ways for the shooters, marked down the nests of pheasants, and kept observation on rabbits and weasels and the flocks of pigeons which anybody was welcome to shoot. Sometimes he earned a few shillings by plashing[1] hedgerows or hoeing a field of roots, but mostly he was a "kindler," he gathered firewood and peddled it on a hand truck around the villages. That was why he dreamed of donkey and nothing but donkey; a creature whose four feet together were not so big as one of its ears, would carry double and treble the load of kindling and make him a rich man.

One day he tramped right over to the head keeper's house to deliver a message, and there Tom Hussey had shown him a litter of retriever puppies he was tending. They had a pedigree, Tom Hussey said, as long as the shafts of a cart; the mother herself was valued at fifty golden guineas,[2] but the sire belonged to Lord Camover and bank notes wouldn't buy that dog, nor love nor money—not even the crown of England. There they were, six puppies just weaned and scrambling about, beautiful bouncing creatures, all except one that seemed quiet and backward.

"That one?" Tom Hussey said; "I be going to kill her. Sha's got a sort of rupture in her navel."

"Don't do that," said old Dick, for he knew a lot about dogs as well as birds and lambs and donkeys. "Give it to I." And Tom Hussey gave him the pup then and there, and he took it home to his tent and bandaged it artfully with a yard strip of canvas, and called it Sossy because it was so pert.

Every day the old man attended to that bandage round Sossy's stomach —he knew a whole lot about dogs—and the dog throve and grew, and every night nuzzled in the straw beside him; and Dick rejoiced. They lived heartily, for Dick was a nimble hand with a wire, and rabbits were plentiful, and he was always begging for bones and suchlike for his Sossy. Everywhere in that wood he took Sossy with him and he trained her so in the arts of obedience that she knew what he wanted even if he only winked one eye. After about six months of this he took off her bandage for the last time and threw it away. There she was, cured and fit and perfect, a fine sweet flourishing thing. What a glossy coat! What a bushy tail! And her eyes—they made you dream of things!

Awhile after that Tom Hussey came into the wood to shoot some pigeons. There was always a great flock of them somewhere in the

[1] *plashing:* cutting and intertwining branches to make a hedge.
[2] *guineas:* at the time of the story a guinea was worth 21 shillings, or about $5.

wood, and when they rose up from the trees the whirr of their thousand wings was like the roar of a great wave. Well, Tom Hussey came, and as he passed near the tent he called out the good of the morning to old Dick.

"Come here," cried Dick, and Tom Hussey went, and when he saw that dog you could have split him with a lath of wood he was so astonished. Sossy danced round him in a rare flurry, nuzzling at his pockets.

"She's hungry," he said.

"No, she ain't. Get down, you great devil! No, she ain't hungry, she's just had a saucepan full o' shackles—get down!—that saucepan there what I washes myself in."

When Tom Hussey shot a pigeon she stood to the gun and brought the bird back like an angel.

"Dick, you can swap that dog for a donkey whenever you've a mind to," Tom Hussey said.

"Ain't she got a mouth? I tell you," Dick cried joyfully.

"Like silk," was the rejoinder.

"It's a gift."

"Born," chanted Tom Hussey.

"It's a gift, I tell you."

"Born. She's worth twenty pounds. You sell that bitch and get you a donkey, quick."

"No," deliberated the veteran, "I shan't do that."

"Twenty pound she's worth, of good money."

"I shan't have 'ee, I tell you."

"You sell that bitch and get you a donkey. That's my last word to you," Tom Hussey said as he stalked away.

But that "Owd Venrable" was a far-seeing sagacious creature, a very artful old man he was, and when the time came for it he and Tom Hussey conjured up a deal between themselves. It would have been risky for Tom Hussey, but as he was changing to another estate he chanced it and he connived and Sossy was mated on the sly to one of his master's finest retrievers, as good as ever stepped into a covert, and by all accounts the equal of Lord Camover's dog that had begot Sossy. So when Tom Hussey departed, there was old Dick with his valuable dog, looking forward to the few weeks hence when Sossy would have the finest bred puppies of their kind in the land. He scarcely dared to compute their value, but it would surely be enough to relegate the idea of a donkey to the limbo of outworn and mean conceits. No, if all went well he would have a change of life altogether. He would give up the old tent; it was rotting, he was tired of it. If things came wonderful well he would buy a nag and a little cart and a few cokernuts and he would travel the round of the fairs and see something of the world again. Nothink like cokernuts for a profitable trade.

This roseate[1] dream so tinted every moment of his thoughts that he lived, as you might say, like a poet, cherishing the dog, the source and promise of these ideals, with fondness and joy. The only cloud on the horizon of bliss was the new gamekeeper, a sprag young fellow, who had taken a deep dislike to him. Old Dick soon became aware of this animosity, for the new keeper kept a strict watch upon his neighborhood and walked about kicking over Dick's snares, impounding his wires, and complaining of his dirty habits and his poaching. And it was true, he *was* dirty, he had lost his pride, and he *did* poach, just a little, for he had a belly that hungered like any other man's, and he had a dog.

Early one morning as Dick was tending his fire the new keeper strolled up. He was a wry-mouthed, slow-speaking young chap, and he lounged there with his gun under his arm and his hands in his pockets. Neither spoke for a while, but at last the keeper said:

"It burns well."

"Huh, and so would you burn well," grinned the old man, "if I cut you atop of it."

For fully two minutes the young keeper made no retort, he was a rather enraging young keeper. Then he said: "Ah, and what do you think you may be doing round here?"

The old man flung a few pinches of tea into a can of boiling water.

"You get on with your job, young feller, and I'll get on with mine."

"What *is* your job?"

The "Owd Venrable" eyed him angrily.

"My job? I'll tell you—it's to mind my own business. You'll learn that for yourself later on, I 'spects, when you get the milk outer your mouth—you ought to, however. Wait till yer be as old as I."

"Ah," drawled the keeper, "I don't mind waiting."

"I met chaps like you before," the old man began to thunder. "Thousands on 'em. D'you know what happened to the last one?"

"Died of fleabites, I shouldn't wonder," was the placid rejoinder.

"I had him on the hop. When he warn't thinking," the old man, ruminating, grinned, "I wuz! I give him a kick o' the stomach as fetched him

---

[1] *roseate:* tinged with the color rose; used figuratively to mean optimistic.

atween wind and water, and down he went, clean as a smelt. D'you know what I did then?"

"Picked his pocket, I shouldn't wonder."

"Yah! Never stole nothing from no man, 'cept it was my own. Clean as a smelt, I tell you."

"Well," the new keeper slowly said, shifting his gun from the left arm to the right, "I can take a hiding from any man. . . ."

"Ah, and from any old woman, too, I should say."

". . . from any man," continued the imperturbable one, "as can give it me—if you know of one." He began to pick his teeth with a matchstick. "Did you get my message?" he more briskly added.

"What message?"

"I sent you a message."

"Then you sent it by a wet hen. I ain't had no message."

"I know you had it, but I'll tell you again. I've got orders to clear you out of this wood, you and your dog. You can take your time, don't want to be hard on you, but out you goes, and soon, you and your dog."

"Well, we can go, my cunning feller, we can go."

"That's right, then."

"We can go—when we've a mind to. But who's a-going to look arter my job?"

"What job's that?"

"Huh, what job!" the old man disgustedly groaned. "Why, who's a-going to keep an eye on things, and they poachers, thousands on 'em, just waiting for to catch I asleep! But they can't do it."

"Naw, I shouldn't think anyone *could* sleep in a hole like that!"

"Yah, I could sleep, I could sleep a sack o' taters rotten! And who's a-going to clear up when the storms been shamracking about the place? I cleans up the paths, I cleans 'em for one and all, and I cleans 'em for you. Some I does it right for and some I does it wrong. If I did it right for all, I'd be out of this world, seemly."

"Who asked you to? Nobody asked you to, we can do without it, and we can do without you. So now I've told you." With that the young keeper sauntered airily away.

"Yah!" the Old Venerable called after him. "Clean as a smelt, I tell you, clean as a smelt"; and as long as his adversary remained in view he continued to remind him of that excellent conclusion.

But despite his contempt the old man was perturbed; he knew the game was up, he would have to seek a lodging elsewhere. By the grace of fortune the blow had come just when it could least concern him; all he wanted was time for Sossy to rear her pups, and then he would go; then he would gaily, driving his horse and cart like a man of property all over that Berkshire and that Oxfordshire.

A week later Sossy was safely delivered of nine puppies. Miracles are possible—they must be—but it is not possible to anticipate a miracle: a litter of nine! They were born in the tent beside the man, and they all —Dick, Sossy, and the nine morsels—slept together, and in a few days, although Sossy, despite heroic feeding, began to grow lean, the pups were fat as slugs.

When they were seven days old the man got up one morning to go to a job of hedging. It was a bright, draughty[1] March morn, and he noted the look of the early pink clouds. A fine day promised, though some of the clouds had a queer shape like a goose with its head turned back-wards. That boded something! The blackies and thrushers sang beautiful. After Sossy had fed somewhat daintily from the same pot of "shackles" as himself, old Dick hung the sack over the tent opening and left her mothering the pups. He limped off to work. The hedge he was laying was on an upland farm that overlooked his wood. At midday when he lunched he could sit and stare over the vast stern brownness that was so soon to unbend in unbelievable trellises of leaves. Already the clearings and banks were freckled with primroses, the nut thickets hung with showers of yellow pods, and the pilewort's cresset in the hedge was a beam to wandering bees. In all that vastitude there was one tiny hole into which he had crept like a snail for years and years, but it was too small to hide him for ever and ever. So now they would go, he and Sossy.

Just beside him was a pond and the barns of the farm. Two white horses were nuzzling each other in the croft, and a magpie watched them from the cone of a stack. A red ox at the pond snuffled in the water, and as it lifted its head to stare at the old man, streams of water pattered back from its hairy lips. Deftly the ox licked with its tongue first one nostril, then the other, but water still dribbled from its mouth in one long glutinous[2] stripe. A large cloud hung above the scene, brood-ing, white and silent as a swan. Old Dick rose and stretched himself; the wind had died. When the afternoon had worn on he ceased work and turned home. Half-way through the woods he came to a clearing full of primroses, and on a bank, with her muzzle in a rich clump of the blooms, lay his dog, shot through the breast. The old man knelt down

---

[1] *draughty:* drafty.
[2] *glutinous* (gloo'tĭ·nŭs): gluey in nature.

beside his dog, but there was nothing he could do, she had been dead a long time. He recalled hearing the shot of a gun, hours ago, not a sharp report, but sullen. Perhaps she had gone out for a scamper and had been chasing a rabbit, or perhaps she had left her litter in order to come to him. The keeper had shot her, shot a poor man's dog, shot her dead. There was nothing he could do, the doom had come crushing even time in its swiftness.

"Fizzled and mizzled I am now," he said forlornly, "and that's a fact."

He left there and, conversing angrily, pottered home to his tent. Two of the pups were already dead. The others were helpless, and he was helpless; there was nothing he could do for them, they were too young to feed by hand, and he had nothing to feed them with. He crawled out of the tent to suck a long drink from the bucket of water that stood outside, and then he knelt there gazing without vision at the smoldering fire.

"I know, yes, I know what I can do," he mumbled, picking up his long, heavy billhook.[1] "Just a smack o' that behind his earhole and he won't take no more hidings from e'er a man or a woman neither. Tipet, I says, and he'd be done, he'd be done in a couple o' minutes, ah, quicker, quicker'n you could say smoke." He dashed the billhook to the earth and groaned. "Oh I be fair fizzled and mizzled now, I be, ah." He sat up and pulled the bucket between his legs. Picking up one of the pups he plopped it into the bucket. "There's your donkey," he gurgled, "huh, huh, huh! And there"—as he plopped the others in one by one—"goes your cob and your cart and your cokernuts. And there"—as he dashed the last one violently in.

After a while the old man rose and emptied the drowned bodies into a heap of bushes; the clash of the bucket as he flung it back only fretted[2] the silence of the wood for a few moments.

[1] *billhoo'* : a cutting or pruning instrument with a hooked point.
[2] *fretted:* disturbed.

A REALISTIC TALE

1. First, check the exact meaning of the word *venerable*. Who used this word in reference to the old man? Explain how they used it. Does the word really describe him? Why do you think the author chose this word? What did the other members of the village think of the old man?

2. Why was the old man allowed to stay in the wood? Explain how he

lived "on air and affability and primed his starved heart with hope." What became of his "roseate dream"?

3. Give reasons for the antagonism which develops between the old man and the new gamekeeper. Where in the story do you first become aware of the gamekeeper's plan of revenge?

4. Describe the old man's feelings when he first finds his dog. How do these feelings change from this point to the end of the story? Has the old man been treated unjustly?

ANALYZING CONFLICT

The conflict in a short story is often what most easily captures the interest of the reader. Consider the conflict in "The Lagoon"—the problem Arsat faces in the situation he describes to the white man. Can you describe his struggle? This conflict becomes important to you, the reader. Whether or not you agree with the decision he makes is determined by your own analysis of the conflict.

What is conflict? Conflict can be discord between personalities, ideas, interests, and even cultures. Man can be in conflict with nature. There can be conflict between characters—in a clash of worldly wisdom with unworldly innocence, for example. Because of the many different kinds of conflict to be found—as many kinds as there are in life itself—it is important for you to learn to recognize the conflict in the particular story that you are reading.

In "The Old Venerable" there is a conflict that for the old man moves toward tragedy. Where is the conflict first set in motion? Find the paragraph in which the first warning of tragedy appears. Describe the conflict at this point in the story. Now consider how the old man's antagonism toward the gamekeeper is developed. Does the conflict become just a clash of the personalities of the gamekeeper and the Old Venerable, or is it more than this? Note the Old Venerable's lack of struggle at the end, his complete defeat, the end of the conflict. Try to state briefly in your own words what you believe to be the major conflict in this story.

The Japanese Quince

JOHN GALSWORTHY 1867–1933

The year before his death John Galsworthy was awarded the Nobel Prize for Literature. It was a well-deserved honor, for Galsworthy had been writing distinguished fiction and drama for a third of a century.

In his person, Galsworthy represented the best tradition of England—descent from a cultivated family of Surrey, education at Harrow and Oxford, and training in the law. Though he did not practice his profession, his legal turn of mind emerges in his writings. Concerned with the problems his characters must face, he is always the unbiased judge, not the prosecuting attorney. No other modern writer gives quite the same impression of sane and balanced judgment of his characters. He shows so clearly why people act as they do that the reader can scarcely condemn even the most unpleasant of them. His great social dramas suggest the nature of their conflicts by their titles: *Justice*—the irony of how the process of law wrecks the life of a weak character; *Strife*—the devastating results of capital-labor troubles; *Escape*—the emotional experiences of an escaped convict; *Loyalties*—the cross-purposes of allegiances when a crime is involved.

As a writer of novels, Galsworthy created the Forsyte family and followed their fortunes through several generations, beginning with the Victorians. Three of his novels were combined into *The Forsyte Saga*, one of the best-loved works of this century. A later volume, *A Modern Comedy*, brings the younger Forsytes through World War I.

Galsworthy was always keenly aware of the tastes of his time. He was one of the first playwrights to use natural, colloquial speech in his plays rather than the stilted speech prevalent in earlier drama.

Although you are given only a brief glimpse of Mr. Nilson in "The Japanese Quince," Galsworthy provides considerable illumination of his character's life. There are passages which give you clues to an understanding of what Mr. Nilson's life is like and of the social class to which he belongs. Watch for these as you read.

As MR. NILSON, well known in the City,[1] opened the window of his dressing room on Campden Hill, he experienced a peculiar sweetish sensation in the back of his throat, and a feeling of emptiness just under his fifth rib. Hooking the window back, he noticed that a little tree in the Square Gardens had come out in blossom, and that the thermometer stood at sixty. "Perfect morning," he thought; "spring at last!"

Resuming some meditations on the price of Tintos,[2] he took up an ivory-backed handglass and scrutinized his face. His firm, round, well-opened, clear gray eyes wore a reassuring appearance of good health. Putting on his black frock coat, he went downstairs.

In the dining room his morning paper was laid out on the sideboard. Mr. Nilson had scarcely taken it in his hand when he again became aware

---

[1] *City:* the financial and commercial section of London.
[2] *Tintos:* red Madeira wines.

of that queer feeling. Somewhat concerned, he went to the French window and descended the scrolled iron steps into the fresh air. A cuckoo clock struck eight.

"Half an hour to breakfast," he thought; "I'll take a turn in the Gardens."

He had them to himself, and proceeded to pace the circular path with his morning paper clasped behind him. He had scarcely made two revolutions, however, when it was borne in on him that, instead of going away in the fresh air, the feeling had increased. He drew several deep breaths, having heard deep breathing recommended by his wife's doctor; but they augmented rather than diminished the sensation—as of some sweetish liquor in course within him, together with a faint aching just above his heart. Running over what he had eaten the night before, he could recollect no unusual dish, and it occurred to him that it might possibly be some smell affecting him. But he could detect nothing except a faint sweet lemony scent, rather agreeable than otherwise, which evidently emanated from the bushes budding in the sunshine. He was on the point of resuming his promenade, when a blackbird close by burst into song, and, looking up, Mr. Nilson saw at a distance of perhaps five yards a little tree, in the heart of whose branches the bird was perched. He stood staring curiously at this tree, recognizing it for that which he had noticed from his window. It was covered with young blossoms, pink and white, and little bright green leaves both round and spiky; and on all this blossom and these leaves the sunlight glistened. Mr. Nilson smiled; the little tree was so alive and pretty! And instead of passing on, he stayed there smiling at the tree.

"Morning like this!" he thought; "and here I am the only person in the Square who has the—to come out and—!" But he had no sooner conceived this thought than he saw quite near him a man with his hands behind him, who was also staring up and smiling at the little tree. Rather taken aback, Mr. Nilson ceased to smile, and looked furtively at the stranger. It was his next-door neighbor, Mr. Tandram, well known in the City, who had occupied the adjoining house for some five years. Mr. Nilson perceived at once the awkwardness of his position, for, being married, they had not yet had occasion to speak to one another. Doubtful as to his proper conduct, he decided at last to murmur: "Fine morning!" and was passing on, when Mr. Tandram answered: "Beautiful, for the time of year!" Detecting a slight nervousness in his neighbor's voice, Mr. Nilson was embolded to regard him openly. He was of about Mr. Nilson's own height, with firm, well-colored cheeks, neat brown moustaches, and round, well-opened, clear gray eyes; and he was wearing a black frock coat. Mr. Nilson noticed that he had his morning paper clasped behind him as he looked up at the little tree. And, visited somehow by the feeling that he had been caught out, he said abruptly:

"Er—can you give me the name of that tree?"

Mr. Tandram answered:

"I was about to ask you that," and stepped toward it. Mr. Nilson also approached the tree.

"Sure to have its name on, I should think," he said.

Mr. Tandram was the first to see the little label, close to where the blackbird had been sitting. He read it out.

"Japanese quince!"

"Ah!" said Mr. Nilson, "thought so. Early flowerers."

"Very," assented Mr. Tandram, and added: "Quite a feelin' in the air today."

Mr. Nilson nodded.

"It was a blackbird singin'," he said.

"Blackbirds," answered Mr. Tandram. "I prefer them to thrushes myself; more body in the note." And he looked at Mr. Nilson in an almost friendly way.

"Quite," murmured Mr. Nilson. "These exotics, they don't bear fruit. Pretty blossom!" and he again glanced up at the blossom, thinking: "Nice fellow, this, I rather like him."

Mr. Tandram also gazed at the blossom. And the little tree, as if appreciating their attention, quivered and glowed. From a distance the blackbird gave a loud, clear call. Mr. Nilson dropped his eyes. It struck him suddenly that Mr. Tandram looked a little foolish; and, as if he had seen himself, he said: "I must be going in. Good morning!"

A shade passed over Mr. Tandram's face, as if he, too, had suddenly noticed something about Mr. Nilson.

"Good morning," he replied, and clasping their journals to their backs they separated.

Mr. Nilson retraced his steps toward his garden window, walking slowly so as to avoid arriving at the same time as his neighbor. Having seen Mr. Tandram mount his scrolled iron steps, he ascended his own in turn. On the top step he paused.

With the slanting spring sunlight darting and quivering into it, the Japanese quince seemed more living than a tree. The blackbird had returned to it, and was chanting out his heart.

Mr. Nilson sighed; again he felt that queer sensation, that choky feeling in his throat.

The sound of a cough or sigh attracted his attention. There, in the shadow of his French window, stood Mr. Tandram, also looking forth across the Gardens at the little quince tree.

Unaccountably upset, Mr. Nilson turned abruptly into the house, and opened his morning paper.

A GLIMPSE OF LIFE

1. Find the clues which suggest what Mr. Nilson's life is like. What really is troubling him? Find the words which define his "ailment."

2. Of what significance are the similarities of Mr. Nilson and Mr. Tandram in appearance, manner, and situation? What abstractions or qualities does the quince tree seem to represent?

3. "The Japanese Quince" contains little action, but it dramatizes a conflict. Decide exactly what that conflict is. How is it resolved? In a sentence, state the purpose of the story.

All Yankees Are Liars

ERIC KNIGHT 1897–1943

Few modern English authors have lived a more varied life than Eric Knight. He was a man of two cultures—an Anglo-American; for him, going across the Atlantic was almost like going across the street. Knight was born in Yorkshire, in the north of England, but he married an American and lived in this country intermittently. His experiences here and abroad provided a broad background for a writer of fiction. At different periods of his life he was an art student in New York, a factory worker in Manchester, a screen writer in Hollywood, a critic for the Philadelphia *Ledger,* a major in the United States Army, and a soldier in a Canadian regiment in World War I. During World War II he was killed in an airplane crash.

Eric Knight's stories reflect his sympathetic understanding of the lives of ordinary people. His *Song on Your Bugles* and his last novel, *This Above All,* are moving stories about the working people of England; and *The Flying Yorkshireman,* while a delightful fantasy, is also a shrewd appraisal of the

"All Yankees Are Liars" from *Sam Small Flies Again* by Eric Knight. Copyright © 1938 by The Curtis Publishing Co. Reprinted by permission of the Author's Estate.

foibles and strengths of his countrymen. The following story illustrates Knight's ability to weave local color into fiction. Its setting is his native Yorkshire, the characters are village folk, and their dialect and mannerisms are those with which the author was fondly familiar. But the influence of America is also apparent in the story. Knight knew this country, and he proves in humorous fashion that "all Yankees are liars."

> *You can always tell the Irish,*
> *You can always tell the Dutch.*
> *You can always tell a Yankee;*
> *But you cannot tell him much.*

M R. SMITH was pleased with The Spread Eagle. He was pleased with Polkingthorpe Brig. The village was off the beaten track—the truly rural sort of English village the American always wants to see.

The inn was low and rambling, with great sloping roofs. Over the door swung the sign—a darksome bird in a weatherbeaten setting.

Everything justified his decision to take this bicycle trip up into the north—the mullioned[1] windows, the roaring fire, the Yorkshire accents of the men who shuffled over the sanded stone floor of the low-ceilinged room as they played darts. Mr. Smith was almost beginning to understand what they were talking about. During his excellent high tea he had sorted out the four men playing darts. One was Saw Cooper, a farmer; a small old man was referred to as Sam; a young, bright-faced lad who played darts left-handed was Gollicker Pearson; and the fourth, a huge man, was just called Ian.

Mr. Smith watched them play, listening to the endless thwock of the darts in the cork board as he finished his meal. The barmaid, plump, corn-haired, came toward him, her apron rustling stiffly.

"Would there be owt else?"

"No. It was a very good meal." Mr. Smith smiled. He wanted to make the girl talk some more. "Er—what do they do for fun in this place of an evening?"

"Foon?" she repeated. "Well, they sit here—or o' Sat'day neights lots o' fowk goa ovver to Wuxley to t' pictures." She waited. "They gate Boock D'Arcy i' T' Singing Cowboy," she added suggestively.

Mr. Smith had already become acquainted with British cinemas in small towns. Also he was a Southern Californian, and had that familiarity with movies that belongs to all Southern Californians. He had no inclina-

---

[1] *mullioned* (mŭl'yŭnd): windows whose panes are divided by slender vertical bars.

tion to go four miles to see a last year's Class B Western. "No. I think I'll have another ale and sit here," he said.

"If tha'll sit ovver by t' fire, Ah'll bring it to thee theer. Then Ah can clean opp here."

Mr. Smith sat on the bench by the generous fire and nursed his ale. The dart game came to an end with Saw Cooper losing and paying for the round. The men brought their mugs to the fire. Mr. Smith shifted politely. The men, in the presence of a stranger, grew quiet. Mr. Smith decided to put them at ease.

"Pretty chilly for an October evening, isn't it?"

The men considered the remark, as if looking at both sides of it. Finally Saw Cooper spoke.

"Aye," he said.

The others nodded. There was silence, and the five regarded the fire. Then, suddenly, young Gollicker smiled.

"Tha shouldn't heed t' cowd, being a Yankee," he said.

"Ah, but I'm not a Yankee," Mr. Smith said.

They stared at him in disbelief.

"Yankees," explained Mr. Smith, "come from New England."

They looked from Mr. Smith to one another. The big man named Ian took a deep breath.

"Yankees," he said, "coom fro' t' United States."

"Well, yes. New England is a part of the United States," Mr. Smith said. "But it's thousands of miles away from where I live. In fact, believe it or not, I should think you're closer to the Yankees than I am. You see, the United States is a big country. In the part where the Yankees come from, it gets very cold in the winter. Where I am—in Southern California—it never snows. Why, I've never known it to snow there in all my life."

"No snow?" Gollicker breathed.

Mr. Smith smiled. For, after all, he was a Southern Californian—and they were discussing climate. "No snow," he said. "In wintertime we have a bit of a rainy season, but after February it clears, and then it doesn't even rain for nine months—not a drop."

"Noa rain for a nine month—noan at all?" Saw Cooper asked.

"Not a drop. Day after day, the sun comes out, clear skies, never a drop of rain for nine months. Never!"

"Whet do ye graw theer, lad?" Saw asked slyly.

"Lots of things. Truck vegetables, oranges—all kinds of things."

There was a silence again. Big Ian took a breath.

"Orinjis," he said, and then took another breath, "graw i' Spain."

He looked at Mr. Smith so emphatically that Mr. Smith nodded.

"Oh, yes," he said. "They grow in Spain, too, I understand."

"Orinjis," Ian repeated, "graw i' Spain."

That seemed to settle the question. They all looked in the fire in silence. Saw Cooper sniffed.

"Whet else graws theer?"

"Well, I have a ranch there; we grow alfalfa."

"Whet's that off to be?"

"Alfalfa? We use it for hay. It's a desert plant originally, but it thrives in California. We get eight cuttings a year."

"Eight cuttings o' hay a year?"

"Eight cuttings a year."

The little man, Sam, spoke for the first time: "Mister, if it doan't rain for a nine month, how can ye get eight cuttings o' hay a year?"

"Oh, that's easy," Mr. Smith said. "We irrigate the land." He went into a short but conclusive description of irrigating.

"Heh," Saw Cooper said. "Wheer's this here watter coom fro'?"

"In the San Fernando Valley we buy it from the water company, just like you do in your homes."

"Wheer do they get it?"

"From reservoirs."

"If it doan't rain, where's t' reservoys get t' watter?"

"Oh, we pipe it down from five hundred miles north. It rains a lot up there."

"And ye sprinkle t' farming land out o' t' watter tap. How mony acres hesta?"

"It isn't like sprinkling from the tap, of course. I used that to illustrate. The pipes are large—we have fourteen-inch valves on our pipes. We flood the land—cover it right over with water."

Saw looked in the fire. "Does corn graw theer?"

"Well, generally our land is too valuable to put into corn. But it will grow corn fourteen feet high."

They made noises in their throats and shifted their feet.

"Fohteen foot," Saw breathed. "Eigh, ba gum!"

"Mister," Sam said, "once Ah were oop to see t' Firth o' Forth brig. Ah suppose they hev bigger brigs i' Yankeeland?"

Mr. Smith should have touched on the new Oakland bridge, but then, he was a *Southern* Californian.

"We have bridges, but they're building vehicular tunnels under the rivers now."

"Whet for?"

"Well, there's so much motor traffic."

"How mony moatorcars goa through 'em?"

Mr. Smith lit his pipe happily. They seemed quite interested in America.

"I couldn't say. The way they turn 'em out, I should say there's hundreds of thousands."

"How fast do they turn 'em out?" Gollicker asked.

"I don't know. I think they roll out finished at the rate of one every couple of minutes."

"And they goa i' tunnels, not i' brigs?" Sam commented.

"Oh, we have some bridges."

"Big uns, Ah suppose."

"Well," Mr. Smith said modestly, thinking of the Pulaski Skyway coming into New York, "we have some that go right over entire towns. You're practically on one bridge for miles."

Saw Cooper spat in the fire. "How mony fowk is there in all America?"

Mr. Smith didn't know, but he felt expansive. And after all, there was South America, too.

"A quarter of a billion, I should say," he hazarded.

"A quarter of a billion," they repeated. Then they stared at Mr. Smith, and he became aware of their disbelief.

"Wait a moment," he said. "I think a billion is different in America from here. It's a thousand million in America and a million million here, isn't it?"

"A billion," said Ian slowly, "is a billion."

The others nodded, and then Ian stood. The others rose, too.

"Oh—er—wait a minute. Won't you all have a drink with me?" Mr. Smith invited.

"Us is off to play darts for a round—us four," Ian said meaningly.

The other three laughed.

"Ah knew them theer brigs o' thine'd hev to be big," Saw Cooper said as a parting shot as he swung over the bench. "That's so's they'd be able to goa ovver wheat what graws fohteen foot high when ye sprinkle it fro' t' watter tap."

He grinned at the others in victory.

"I didn't say wheat; I said corn," Mr. Smith protested.

"Same thing," Saw snapped.

"It isn't. Wheat grows in an ear. Corn grows on a cob; it has broad long leaves."

"Heh! That's maize," Saw said.

Big Ian stepped between Saw Cooper and Mr. Smith.

"Now, lad," he said flatly, "tha said corn, and Ah heeard thee. Thee and thy orinjis, and farming out o' t' watter tap, and brigs ovver cities, and it nivver rain, and denying th' art a Yankee, and a billion is a billion and yet it ain't. Tha's tripped thysen oop a dozen times, it seems to me. Now, hesta owt to say?"

Mr. Smith looked at Big Ian, standing belligerently with legs widespread and his thumbs in the waistband of his corduroy trousers. He looked round and saw everyone in the inn waiting, silent.

Then a curious thing happened. In that minute the smell of soft-coal smoke and pig-twist tobacco and ale was gone, and instead Mr. Smith was smelling the mixed odor of sun-baked land and citrus blossom and jasmine and eucalyptus trees, just as you smell it on the cool darkness coming across the San Fernando Valley. And he was homesick. Suddenly it felt unreal that he should be so far from home, sitting in an English inn with these men about him. He looked up at the faces, forbidding in their expression of disapproval. And he began to laugh.

It was all so unreal that he laughed until he cried. Every time he looked up he saw the faces, now even more comical in their bewilderment than they had been in their disapproval. They stared at him, and then Big Ian began to laugh.

"Eigh, Ah'll be jiggered!" he roared. "Drat ma buttons if Ah won't!"

It was Mr. Smith's turn to be puzzled now.

Big Ian roared, and suddenly slapped Mr. Smith on the back so heartily that his chin flew up in the air and then banged back on his chest. The others looked on in amazement.

"Why, whet's oop, Ian?" Saw asked.

"Why, ye gowks!" Ian roared. "He's laughing at ye! He's been heving us on! Sitting theer for an hour, keeping his mug straight and telling us the tale! And us swallering it, thinking he was serious!"

"But," Mr. Smith said—"but you don't——"

"Nay, now no moar on it!" Ian roared. "Ye've codded us for fair, and done it champion! Lewk at owd Sam's face!"

The others regarded Ian and scratched their heads and grinned sheepishly, and finally looked at Mr. Smith in admiration.

"But—" Mr. Smith began again.

"Nay, now, ye copped us napping," Ian said, "and here's ma hand on it. Soa we'll hev noa moar—onless ye'd like to tell us whet Yankeeland's rightly like."

Mr. Smith drew a deep breath. "Well, what would you like to hear about?"

"About cowboys," young Gollicker breathed. "Werta ivver a cowboy?"

For a moment Mr. Smith stood on a brink, and then an imp pushed him over.

"Of course I've been a cowboy—naturally," Mr. Smith said. "What would you like to hear about it?"

"Wait a minute," Gollicker said. They all adjusted themselves on the bench. "Now," he went on, "tell us about a roundup—tha knaws, 'Ah'm yeading for t' last roundup,' like Bing Crosby sings."

Mr. Smith held his mental breath and plunged.

"Ah," he said. "A roundup and the life of a cowboy. Up at the crack of dawn, mates, and down to the corral. There you rope your horse——"

"A mustang?" Gollicker asked.

"A mustang," Mr. Smith agreed.

"A wild one off'n the prairies, happen?"

"Indeed a wild one from off the prairies," Mr. Smith agreed. "I see you know America yourself."

Gollicker grinned modestly. "Doan't let me interrupt, measter," he apologized.

Mr. Smith drew another breath. He saw he was up against at least one expert, so he made it very good. Inwardly he thanked fate for what he had hitherto regarded as two entirely misspent weeks on a Nevada dude ranch. He gave them, in more senses than one, a moving picture of the cowboy's life.

When he was done, Gollicker sighed and Big Ian nodded.

"Now," Sam said, "how about them bloody buffalo?"

"Ah, the buffalo," Mr. Smith said. "The thundering herd! The bison! For a while there was danger—or thought to be—that the herds were dying out. But now, I am glad to say—and no doubt you are just as glad to hear—the herds are increasing, and ere long, again the crack of a rifle will bring down a bull in full gallop."

"But how about them bloody Indians?" Saw put in.

Mr. Smith considered the Indians at the station in Santa Fe. They didn't seem at all satisfactory. But he was inspired. He drew himself up.

"You will pardon me if I do not speak of that," he said. "We have not too much love for the paleface who stole our lands. I say 'we,' for my mother was Yellow Blanket, a princess of the Blackfoot tribe. Therefore, let us not speak of the white man and the red man."

He stared into the fire—majestically he hoped.

"Now, see what tha's done?" Ian said to Saw. "Happen it'll learn thee to keep thy yapper shut once in a while. . . . Tha maun excuse him, measter. Tell us about gangsters instead. Didta ivver run into any gangsters?"

"Run into them? Why, how could you help it?" Mr. Smith asked.

Swiftly and graphically he painted for them an America in which here was the town where the bullets of the gangs cracked day and night. Here was the last street, and on it the last house, and beyond that was the trackless prairie where the buffalo thundered, the cowboy rode, and the Indian ever lurked.

As he finished, he looked up. Everyone in the inn was listening. Men had gathered behind him silently. At the bar, the maid leaned on her elbows, entranced.

"Ah, I talk too much," Mr. Smith said.

"Nay, goa on, lad," they said. "Goa on."

"Well, it's dry work. How about a drink?"

"Champion," said Saw.

"Owd on," Big Ian said. "Us'll play darts for a round."

"Now, Ian, if the lad wants to buy——"

"Ah said," Ian repeated, "us'll play darts—onybody that wishes to be in on t' round. And t' loser will pay."

Mr. Smith paid anyhow, for the dart game was trickier than he had thought, and they all seemed to be experts.

He was getting very much better when the barmaid called: "Time, gentlemen, please."

Mr. Smith was sorry. It had been a good evening. They all said good night cheerfully. Big Ian shook him by the hand.

"Well, soa long, lad. We had a champion time. But Ah just want to say, tha didn't fool me when tha were kidding us at first. Tha sees, for one thing, us goas to t' pictures and so us knaws whet America's really like. And then Ah'd allus heeard tell that all Yankees were liars."

"Yes," Mr. Smith said, regarding his conscience, "I did tell some lies."

"Aye, but Ah suppose it's a way ye Yankees hev," Ian said. "But it's all right as long as tha told us t' trewth finally."

YANKEES AND YORKSHIREMEN

1. How does the four-line jingle at the beginning fit the story? What does the name "Yankee" mean as Mr. Smith uses it? as the Yorkshiremen use it?

2. What is the central idea of the story? When do the Yorkshiremen begin to disbelieve Mr. Smith? How does Mr. Smith finally win their favor? How do the Yorkshiremen remind you of people in general?

3. In what part of England is Yorkshire? This story is full of what is usually called "local color"—descriptions of setting and characters and use of dialect that build up an impression of a particular place. Find several examples of local color.

4. How does Knight achieve his humor? Select passages that illustrate his humor.

The Ballroom

WILLIAM SANSOM 1912–

Like some earlier English writers, William Sansom substituted travel for a university degree. He has traveled in Europe; he has lived in France, Germany, Spain, and Hungary. During World War II, he joined the London Fire Service, which helped the city survive the tremendous bombing attacks. Sansom's first book, *Fireman Flower and Other Stories,* reflects wartime London.

After the war Sansom worked as a script writer for a time and then left his job to devote himself entirely to writing. Since then he has enjoyed literary recognition with the publication of short story collections such as *A Contest of Ladies, Among the Dahlias,* and *A Touch of the Sun.* Some of his recent novels are *A Bed of Roses, The Loving Eye,* and *The Cautious Heart.* As a member of the new generation of British storytellers, he has also written for such magazines as *Horizon, New Writing,* and *Cornhill,* all English literary periodicals. In acknowledgment of his literary talent, he has been awarded prizes by the Society of Authors and elected a Fellow of the Royal Society of Literature.

Like Katherine Mansfield and Virginia Woolf of an earlier generation, Sansom prefers to concentrate on the feelings and thoughts of a character over a short period of time rather than to spin out a long narrative. In such stories time seems to stand still while the storyteller probes into the charac-

"The Ballroom" from *A Contest of Ladies* by William Sansom, published in 1956 by The Hogarth Press Ltd. Reprinted by permission of The Hogarth Press Ltd. and Russell & Volkening, Inc.

ter's emotions. He also tries to arouse in us a sense of pity and understanding. See if he succeeds.

STRANGE weather! A warm morning, with all the windows open and the sunlight making a pale fool of the big log fire. Wet and warm in the garden outside, muddy and fresh: and inside the Christmas cards looked like invitations to a summer rout, the holly and mistletoe hung like the morning after some May-Day-night-before, cotton-wool snow looked particularly like cotton-wool and nothing like snow, the tinsel glittered in the sun with the tarnished tang of old seaside souvenirs. Two or three flies Hoovered [1] a Monday buzz about the ceiling and in the garden a red-hot robin stamped its dislike of such an unseasonable Christmas morning.

Snow and ice are seldom to be hoped for. The least that might be expected is a touch of the magic of frost, a winter glitter and a brisk raw bite in the air, something to match the glowing coals and the good rich food. However . . . on that morning there was no hope left, and as Lesseps went to look out over the garden it was in a mood of ill-ease—he felt that he ought to be scrambling the deck-chairs out for an early airing, not thinking of sherry and turkey and the rest of whatever conviviality lay ahead. There was a steam in the air, no wind, and across the hedge at the garden's end the steam thickened to mist above the warm mysterious depths of the Chine. Beyond this lay a wilderness of trees and the ivy-clad walls of Waltham.

The sun struck gold on the topmost windows of this great Victorian house that then belonged to the lady we only knew as "Miss Amery"—and it was perhaps the sudden illumination of a turreted and gabled edifice so in keeping with the idea of an old-fashioned Christmas that led Lesseps once again that morning to wonder about this Miss Amery. The sun struck the topmost windows—and even these had their white blinds drawn—but he knew that in the shadowed wilderness of dripping and overgrown trees and ivy below all the rest of the house would lie in a kind of dead shuttered dusk cut off absolutely from this wide-lit morning. Within the padlocked gates, up the bough-hung drive and under the peeling gables lay a darker world: Miss Amery was what they call a recluse. She had not left the house for fifteen years.

Many the theories. But only one thing is certain about such a secret life, and that is a final uncertainty of anyone getting to know exactly how it is lived. The houses of such solitaries have been examined after

---

[1] *Hoover:* a brand name for a vacuum cleaner.

death—a litter of filth, a wilderness of papers, hoards of money have been found: and once even a house within a house, corridors and rooms lined with the empty tins of a decade, each immaculately shined. But whatever is found, people can only suppose how life was actually lived; nobody *knows,* the germ of the bitter or the radiant secret dies with its conceiver.

So with Miss Amery. But she still lived, and the theories with her. Some said The War. Others that she had always been queer, from a young girl. Others spoke of something that had happened in her childhood. But nobody knew. And few people ever saw her. There were tales that she had occasional guests—once a schoolgirl had been seen in the park: but that might have been any apple-happy intruder of the afternoon.

At all events she was no terrifying figure. No pig-faced woman suffering within her black veil; no wild-eyed brooder over dark religions; no tall, soured châtelaine[1] with the big hands of a stranger. None of these. The few who saw or had seen her, like the postman, talked simply of a little "frail" old lady. Pale eyes, white skin, fragile, timid; a very ordinary picture of lavender and lace.

Yet a vague picture. And on that Christmas Morning, thinking of her all alone somewhere beneath her sunblinded tower—Lesseps suddenly felt a longing to visit her. Don't be a fool, he told himself, she'd hate it. You're just restless. You're just lonely yourself for your white snow and frost.

But the idea persisted. And late that afternoon he excused himself from warm port on the verandah and "went for a walk." As he passed over the Chine bridge he pretended: I'll just get into the grounds and look around. I won't disturb the old girl.

But he never really hesitated; and certainly not on that giddying thin iron bridge that overhung such a sudden rocky drop and its weird wet growth of fern far beneath.

Then the wall of Waltham faced him. Higher than a man, it leaned its old red brickness for as far as he could see to either side: it came from mist and vanished into mist, and this made it seem to go on for ever. It was old, silent, decayed—it kept the eyes from seeing what was beyond, it sat there saying as all walls say: "Keep out." The only sound was the dripping of trees. He felt uneasy. But nevertheless measured its height, the crumbling of its mossed bricks, the inward tilt it took from the roots of trees that would one day overturn its foundation. Would

[1] *châtelaine:* the mistress of a château.

it take his weight? He heard the crash of brick, a sudden thunderclap dying again into the wet silence of the trees. He put his left foot in a crevice, pulled himself up and over, dropped soundlessly on to thick black leaves the other side.

Over. When he had put his foot up, he had felt as guilty and small as a child: now, the deed done and in forbidden territory, he was suddenly instead big as a child feeling itself big as a man, on its mettle. In that deserted overgrown wilderness, even in such quiet, he held his breath and listened. What a different world inside! The sun was sinking—it must have been nearly four o'clock; but those trees were already dark with moss and age, everything creaked and dripped and hung at broken levels, and as he now walked forward in the direction of the house the sky seemed to disappear altogether in a depth of long-fingering arms interlaced above. It was like entering the gloom that masses before a fog in a great town; the air peculiarly still, no fog yet, but all light gone. Yet in its way, at that time, it was preferable to the world outside—this darkness and mystery more matched the mood of Christmas.

He walked on. No twigs snapped; everything too old, rotten, wet. Beneath the trees a thick undergrowth of elder and nettles had grown; he had to snake his way through—once he stopped suddenly, holding his breath: a statue, an eyeless youth in Greek drapery, was watching him from the thicket; mossed and in half-shadow, it stood still as life. He coughed—no echo—and went on. He came up against a huge high bank of overgrown laurel. He had to walk some way to skirt it; it was like a high green wall within the walled garden: but at last he rounded it— and there suddenly was the house itself. He drew back against the laurel. The house accused him with its immense, sudden presence. But then he saw how utterly dead it was—or how deeply asleep. White blinds were drawn over all the upper windows. Creeper hung thick about the lower reaches, a gabled porch and Gothic buttresses, tall stone-framed downstairs windows. From where he stood he could see the rusted bell-pull—and wondered how it could possibly work. Wondering, he found himself going toward it—and then quickly ran the last few yards across the open, weed-grown gravel.

Now he stood in the porch, among wind-blown leaves and littered paper, as if in a deserted wind shelter on a sea front, and looked at that bellpull. It was dead with rust. Thick spider webs, heavy with rotted seed, hung across it. Suddenly he thought, and his stomach dropped— perhaps the old lady was dead? Perhaps no one knows? But then he remembered how groceries and food were still delivered, probably at a back door. They would soon have known in the village. Yet this was a holiday; Christmas is a busy time, the shops had been shut a day already. At the thought again of Christmas it passed absurdly through his mind that if anyone caught him there in the porch he could start singing a carol; but at the same time he decided to go round the house and see if there was a back door that might look more used. But—his mind whispered—with a pile of groceries never taken in?

He never went round.

He held his breath, wondering what so suddenly had happened. Sound? Movement? Something had happened: and everything was changed. But there was no sound, nothing had moved in the porch. What . . . ? And then he realized. The most obvious thing, so obvious that it had passed his notice. All the lights of one of the rooms facing the drive had been turned on—the great dark bank of laurel was now a high pale emerald mass, leaf upon leaf of green and gold, a high theatrical screen of leaf, and across the gravel itself the tall garden windows had thrown their giant rectangular shapes.

Yet no shadow crossed this great new light, no sound echoed its muffling from within the house. It was like an empty theater lit by a dead man's hand.

Lesseps hardly waited.

He moved quickly out of the porch and in again to the wall, creeping like a thief, turning his coat collar up to hide his white shirt, sprung on the toes of his shoes that made no sound on such wet mold, rounding the big buttress until he could squeeze against the stone window frame and peer carefully round, using one eye.

Every chandelier in that room was lit. The windows reached nearly to the ground and all inside, as in a huge glass-case, was light. The floor had been freshly polished and shone with light: tall mirrors on all the walls reflected it further, and the twists and coils of their gilt frames winked and glittered: and then the mirrors reflected each other, one mirror within another within another, until the room receded for ever in corridors of mirror on every side: in each mirror shone a crystal wealth of chandelier, and wherever it struck, either in a leaping of shadows or a red-gilt flaming tongue, there rose and fell the effigy of a great log fire blazing to one end of the room in a richly marbled fireplace. Heavy curtains hung undrawn by the windows. Lesseps' one eye came round by a large gilt-tassel. It must have been the old ballroom.

But old? It was as alive as it had ever been. And in its very center stood a tall Christmas Tree bright with yellow candles. Colored globes caught the fire-shadow, tinsel laced its sparkling snow about the dark branches, and all danced with light; the yellow candles burned steadily upwards, yet sometimes shuddered—it must have been a draught from the fire—leaning afraid all one way, and then as suddenly resuming their solid upward flame.

He stood there held with wonder. It was a magical scene—all polish, wealth, and warmth . . . but empty, no sign of a single person.

And the minutes passed. The last of the red evening sun fell down through the black wet trees outside. Lesseps thought: How exactly like the colored plates in a book of fairy stories, there is no difference, the old red sun casts its strange winter light and the trees become huge, you can still see the drip and drab of ordinary life, but it recedes, light and shadow are really in charge, you're more in an old book than anywhere else. Then he smelled life again, as the sun flashed down and the first sharp nose of a winter's chill envigored the night. Soon he would see his breath.

He peered back into the window. Nobody had come. Nothing had moved but the candles, the fire flames, and the shadows that were always moving. And this motionless moving, this empty liveliness, gave the room more death than if the house had been shut and dark and truly dead; as with a ghost-ship, all sails set, all lights ablaze—empty on an empty ocean; or the shop-window stage of a room, playing the dead life of dummies and never-used furniture, all lights on and nothing, nothing ever to happen. But behind the doors of such rooms people wait: the doors hold back unbelievable crowds waiting to burst in.

And that, then, was what actually happened, unbelievably, exactly in front of Lesseps' one peering eye. So startling him that he drew this back behind the window frame.

Abruptly the room had poured full of children!

A dam of children had burst, it was like that moment in the empty street when a morning of children breaks out of the cinema and the street is stopped with arms and legs and voices whirling and screaming over every inch. He quickly drew back. Where? How? How did they get there . . . ? And all those children had been little girls! Ten, twenty, thirty little girls in white party dresses flooded in through the door! And all had been dressed, he thought, surely alike? All in white, all in sashes alive in the light, blue bows bobbing in each head of curls; all dancing.

He peered round the window frame again. With the air chilling, the window glass was beginning to mist: safe enough, he would never be seen now.

He saw instantly what a mistake he had made—this was after all no room full of girls, it was of course one child only, one child reflected in a dozen mirrors.

And now that one pretty little child, so small and alone among her dozen glittering shadows in so large-lit a hall of a room—the one little child approached on tiptoe the Christmas Tree and bravely, beautifully, dropped a curtsy.

All alone she began to dance.

Lesseps watched charmed and fascinated through the pale mist beading the window. It was growing much colder with the sun down, it was dark now and he shivered out there among the dripping trees—but he only remembered feeling a sense of great gladness and warmth that after all, in that huge lonely shuttered house, the old lady did have her secret friends. Who they might be, he hardly considered—the scene was so warm, friendly, well-lit, a picture of festive content.

Then, as he told us afterwards, a sense of uneasiness grew upon him. He could not say what it was, he tried to push it aside. He thought it was some previous association with the house. Or even his lowered spirits out there in the chill garden. But the feeling persisted, and he began to wonder: had it something to do with such a little girl all alone in so great a room? For as the minutes passed, no one came to be with her— and it began to seem that she, the little one, was the only life in that huge house. A dreadful notion came to him, which he put quickly aside —had the old lady died upstairs and was this child who had come to stay, simply, in her innocence thinking her grand-aunt asleep, dancing on with the fun?

For she never stopped dancing. To and fro, up to the great fireplace, down the polished wood to the mirrors, pirouetting, pointing a toe, weaving her arms into some pretty arabesque,[1] greeting the image of herself in a dozen long mirrors—and always returning, for it was the most special place, to the Christmas Tree.

Lesseps grew more aware—perhaps because it was the central point of her dancing—of that Christmas Tree. It seemed in presence to become taller; and it held now a quiet imminence of movement, the feeling tall wardrobes have, standing so very still and forbidding, that they might at any moment move. . . . He thought: Nonsense. This is only the uneasy memory of old Christmases, old toys, as garish toys can terrify: the

---

[1] *arabesque:* a ballet position in which the dancer bends forward on one leg, extends the corresponding arm horizontally forward, and the other arm and leg backward.

nightmare quality of toys and trees that some children carry with them for ever. And of course, Lesseps concluded, I was such a child. Puppets, golliwogs, even the Happy Family cards, frightened me.

But he felt a sudden wish to get away, to get back behind that bank of wet laurels bathed in their high golden light.

He did the opposite.

He went straight forward and pressed his face against the window.

It was misting now beyond the brightness of the light. He thought he would never be seen. He was holding his breath to see.

But he was seen.

Almost instantly the little girl, in the middle of a pirouette, stopped, stared into his eyes, screamed a hand up to her mouth, and fled back straight into that Christmas Tree.

In a second her dress was blazing.

He had his boot off and was smashing through the glass. The draught of sudden air fanned the flame higher—but he got to her quickly and muffled her in his coat and rolled this poor little bundle on the floor. Then he picked her up and quietly held her in his arms.

She was not badly burned. But she was dead. She must have died of shock.

And then, Lesseps said, his voice was raised to cry for help, to hoarse his wretched stupid sickened heart out—but he never breathed a word . . . for only then did his eyes realize, slowly, the thin blue-veined leg in his hand, the gray-gold hair, the old enameled face—and a mouth set now not in anguish but in sleeping peace, the shade of a smile of childhood dreams on her thin shriveled lips.

A SURPRISE ENDING

1. Did the ending of this story come as a shock to you? The outcome of a story must be made to seem plausible in terms of the information which the author provides. Find clues in the story which helped you to accept the climax.

2. To what extent does the author reveal the personality of Miss Amery? How much does Lesseps really know about her? In what ways are Waltham and Miss Amery alike?

3. Review Lesseps' feelings as he views the ballroom. Describe the emotional impact of the final incident on Lesseps. What specifically appeals to you in this story? What do you learn from "The Ballroom" about the way to end a story?

REACTING TO SUSPENSE

When you are uncertain what will happen next and anxious to find out, you are reacting to an important element of the short story: suspense. What is going to happen to the main character? Can a situation be improved? These and many other questions are in your mind as the writer prepares you for the climax of the action. A story which creates in you this sense of anticipation or suspense will hold your attention. As the British critic E. M. Forster says, the "and then" is what keeps the reader interested. The skillful use of suspense is certainly one way to judge a writer's skill.

The suspense in "The Ballroom" begins almost immediately—in the second paragraph with the garden "in a mood of ill-ease." From that point on, trace the suspense as Sansom builds it: (1) the sudden illumination of Waltham, (2) theories about Miss Amery's life, (3) the decision to visit Miss Amery, (4) scaling the wall of Waltham, (5) entering "that deserted overgrown wilderness," (6) arrival at the house, (7) the turning on of the lights, (8) viewing "a magical scene," (9) watching the dancing child, (10) being seen at the window, (11) entering the blazing room, (12) making a shocking discovery.

The Verger

W. SOMERSET MAUGHAM 1874–

The early life of W. Somerset Maugham (môm) was unhappy. He was born in France of English parents who both died when he was still a boy. Thereafter he went to England to live in the cold, stern atmosphere of his uncle's home. This setting appears in Maugham's novel *Cakes and Ale,* in which he describes a boy like himself: shy, uncertain, afflicted with a stammer, but also imaginative and responsive. Maugham studied in English schools and at the University of Heidelberg. He wanted to be a writer but at the insistence of his uncle studied medicine instead. After a year's internship in the Lambeth slums of London, Maugham suffered an attack of tuberculosis and soon left to travel on the Continent, where he began writing. He worked steadily for years; success did not come easily. In his most famous novel, *Of Human Bondage,* he tells the moving story of a young medical student much like himself.

Somerset Maugham has become perhaps the most accomplished story-

"The Verger" from *The Cosmopolitans* by W. Somerset Maugham. Copyright 1929 by W. Somerset Maugh Reprinted by permission of Doubleday and Company, Inc.; A. P. Watt & Son; William Heinemann Lir and the author.

teller of our time. He has traveled the world over and gathered tales along the way—stories and novels and plays with strange incidents, odd characters, often exotic settings. Possibly one secret of his popularity lies in his stated purpose in writing—entertainment. "Pleasure," he says, "is in itself good." Yet Maugham writes of neither the pleasant nor the pretty. While he does not plead for the poor, he depicts the upper classes with an irony that is often malicious.

THERE had been a christening that afternoon at St. Peter's, Neville Square, and Albert Edward Foreman still wore his verger's[1] gown. He kept his new one, its folds as full and stiff as though it were made not of alpaca but of perennial bronze, for funerals and weddings (St. Peter's, Neville Square, was a church much favored by the fashionable for these ceremonies), and now he wore only his second best. He wore it with complacence; for it was the dignified symbol of his office, and without it (when he took it off to go home) he had the disconcerting sensation of being somewhat insufficiently clad. He took pains with it; he pressed it and ironed it himself. During the sixteen years he had been verger of this church he had had a succession of such gowns; but he had never been able to throw them away when they were worn out, and the complete series, neatly wrapped up in brown paper, lay in the bottom drawer of the wardrobe in his bedroom.

The verger busied himself quietly, replacing the painted wooden cover on the marble font, taking away a chair that had been brought for an infirm old lady, and waited for the vicar to have finished in the vestry so that he could tidy up in there and go home. Presently he saw him walk across the chancel, genuflect in front of the high altar, and come down the aisle; but he still wore his cassock.

"What's he 'anging about for?" the verger said to himself. "Don't 'e know I want my tea?"

The vicar had been but recently appointed, a red-faced, energetic man in his early forties, and Albert Edward still regretted his predecessor, a clergyman of the old school who preached leisurely sermons in a silvery voice and dined out a great deal with his more aristocratic parishioners. He liked things in church to be just so, but he never fussed; he was not like this new man who wanted to have his finger in every pie. But Albert Edward was tolerant. St. Peter's was in a very good neighborhood and the parishioners were a very nice class of people. The new vicar had come

---

[1] *verger:* an employee, or official, who takes care of the interior of a church building and exhibits it to visitors.

from the East End, and he couldn't be expected to fall in all at once with the discreet ways of his fashionable congregation.

"All this 'ustle," said Albert Edward. "But give 'im time; he'll learn."

When the vicar had walked down the aisle so far that he could address the verger without raising his voice more than was becoming in a place of worship, he stopped.

"Foreman, will you come into the vestry for a minute? I have something to say to you."

"Very good, sir."

The vicar waited for him to come up and they walked up the church together.

"A very nice christening, I thought, sir. Funny 'ow the baby stopped cryin' the moment you took him."

"I've noticed they very often do," said the vicar, with a little smile. "After all, I've had a good deal of practice with them."

It was a source of subdued pride to him that he could nearly always quiet a whimpering infant by the manner in which he held it, and he was not unconscious of the amused admiration with which mothers and nurses watched him settle the baby in the crook of his surpliced arm. The verger knew that it pleased him to be complimented on his talent.

The vicar preceded Albert Edward into the vestry. Albert Edward was a trifle surprised to find the two churchwardens there. He had not seen them come in. They gave him pleasant nods.

"Good afternoon, my lord. Good afternoon, sir," he said to one after the other.

They were elderly men, both of them, and they had been churchwardens almost as long as Albert Edward had been verger. They were sitting now at a handsome refectory table that the old vicar had brought many years before from Italy, and the vicar sat down in the vacant chair between them. Albert Edward faced them, the table between him and them, and wondered with slight uneasiness what was the matter. He remembered still the occasion on which the organist had got into trouble and the bother they had had to hush things up. In a church like St. Peter's, Neville Square, they couldn't afford a scandal. On the vicar's red face was a look of resolute benignity, but the others bore an expression that was slightly troubled.

"He's been naggin' them, he 'as," said the verger to himself. "He's jockeyed them into doin' something, but they don't 'alf like it. That's what it is; you mark my words."

But his thoughts did not appear on Albert Edward's clean-cut and

distinguished features. He stood in a respectful but not obsequious attitude. He had been in service before he was appointed to his ecclesiastical
office, but only in very good houses, and his deportment was irreproach-
able. Starting as a page boy in the household of a merchant prince, he
had risen by due degrees from the position of fourth to first footman;
for a year he had been singlehanded butler to a widowed peeress and,
till the vacancy occurred at St. Peter's, butler with two men under him
in the house of a retired ambassador. He was tall, spare, grave, and
dignified. He looked, if not like a duke, at least like an actor of the old
school who specialized in dukes' parts. He had tact, firmness, and self-
assurance. His character was unimpeachable.

The vicar began briskly.

"Foreman, we've got something rather unpleasant to say to you.
You've been here a great many years, and I think his lordship and the
general agree with me that you've fulfilled the duties of your office to the
satisfaction of everybody concerned."

The two churchwardens nodded.

"But a most extraordinary circumstance came to my knowledge the
other day and I felt it my duty to impart it to the churchwardens. I
discovered to my astonishment that you could neither read nor write."

The verger's face betrayed no sign of embarrassment.

"The last vicar knew that, sir," he replied. "He said it didn't make no
difference. He always said there was a great deal too much education
in the world for 'is taste."

"It's the most amazing thing I ever heard," cried the general. "Do you
mean to say that you've been verger of this church for sixteen years and
never learned to read or write?"

"I went into service when I was twelve, sir. The cook in the first place
tried to teach me once; but I didn't seem to 'ave the knack for it, and
then what with one thing and another I never seemed to 'ave the time.
I've never really found the want of it. I think a lot of these young fellows
waste a lot of time readin' when they might be doin' something useful."

"But don't you want to know the news?" said the other churchwarden.
"Don't you ever want to write a letter?"

"No, me lord, I seem to manage very well without. And of late years,
now they've all these pictures in the papers, I get to know what's goin' on
pretty well. Me wife's quite a scholar, and if I want to write a letter she
writes it for me. It's not as if I was a bettin' man."

The two churchwardens gave the vicar a troubled glance and then
looked down at the table.

"Well, Foreman, I've talked the matter over with these gentlemen and they quite agree with me that the situation is impossible. At a church like St. Peter's, Neville Square, we cannot have a verger who can neither read nor write."

Albert Edward's thin, sallow face reddened and he moved uneasily on his feet, but he made no reply.

"Understand me, Foreman, I have no complaint to make against you. You do your work quite satisfactorily. I have the highest opinion both of your character and of your capacity, but we haven't the right to take the risk of some accident that might happen owing to your lamentable ignorance. It's a matter of prudence as well as of principle."

"But couldn't you learn, Foreman?" asked the general.

"No, sir, I'm afraid I couldn't—not now. You see, I'm not as young as I was, and, if I couldn't seem able to get the letters in me 'ead when I was a nipper,[1] I don't think there's much chance of it now."

"We don't want to be harsh with you, Foreman," said the vicar. "But the churchwardens and I have quite made up our minds. We'll give you three months, and if at the end of that time you cannot read and write I'm afraid you'll have to go."

Albert Edward had never liked the new vicar. He'd said from the beginning that they'd made a mistake when they gave him St. Peter's. He wasn't the type of man they wanted with a classy congregation like that. And now he straightened himself a little. He knew his value and he wasn't going to allow himself to be put upon.

"I'm very sorry, sir; I'm afraid it's no good. I'm too old a dog to learn new tricks. I've lived a good many years without knowin' 'ow to read and write, and without wishin' to praise myself—self-praise is no recommendation—I don't mind sayin' I've done my duty in that state of life in which it 'as pleased a merciful providence to place me, and if I *could* learn now I don't know as I'd want to."

"In that case, Foreman, I'm afraid you must go."

"Yes, sir, I quite understand. I shall be 'appy to 'and in my resignation as soon as you've found somebody to take my place."

But when Albert Edward, with his usual politeness, had closed the church door behind the vicar and the two churchwardens, he could not sustain the air of unruffled dignity with which he had borne the blow inflicted upon him, and his lips quivered. He walked slowly back to the vestry and hung up on its proper peg his verger's gown. He sighed as he thought of all the grand funerals and smart weddings it had seen. He

---

[1] *nipper:* English slang for small boy.

tidied everything up, put on his coat, and hat in hand walked down the aisle. He locked the church door behind him. He strolled across the square; but, deep in his sad thoughts, he did not take the street that led him home, where a nice strong cup of tea awaited him—he took the wrong turning.

He walked slowly along. His heart was heavy. He did not know what he should do with himself. He did not fancy the notion of going back to domestic service; after being his own master for so many years—for the vicar and churchwardens could say what they liked; it was he that had run St. Peter's, Neville Square—he could scarcely demean himself by accepting a situation. He had saved a tidy sum, but not enough to live on without doing something; and life seemed to cost more every year. He had never thought to be troubled with such questions. The vergers of St. Peter's, like the popes of Rome, were there for life. He had often thought of the pleasant reference the vicar would make, in his sermon at evensong the first Sunday after his death, to the long and faithful service and the exemplary character of their late verger Albert Edward Foreman.

He sighed deeply. Albert Edward was a nonsmoker and a total abstainer, but with a certain latitude; that is to say, he liked a glass of beer with his dinner and when he was tired he enjoyed a cigarette. It occurred to him now that one would comfort him and, since he did not carry them, he looked about him for a shop where he could buy a packet of Gold Flakes. He did not at once see one and walked on a little. It was a long street, with all sorts of shops in it; but there was not a single one where you could buy cigarettes.

"That's strange," said Albert Edward.

To make sure, he walked right up the street again. No, there was no doubt about it. He stopped and looked reflectively up and down.

"I can't be the only man as walks along this street and wants a fag," he said. "I shouldn't wonder but what a fellow might do very well with a little shop here. Tobacco and sweets, you know."

He gave a sudden start.

"That's an idea," he said. "Strange 'ow things come to you when you least expect it."

He turned, walked home, and had his tea.

"You're very silent this afternoon, Albert," his wife remarked.

"I'm thinkin'," he said.

He considered the matter from every point of view, and next day he went along the street and by good luck found a little shop to let that looked as though it would exactly suit him. Twenty-four hours later he had taken it and, when a month after that he left St. Peter's, Neville Square, forever, Albert Edward Foreman set up in business as a tobacconist and newsagent. His wife said it was a dreadful comedown after being verger of St. Peter's; but he answered that you had to move with the times, the church wasn't what it was, and 'enceforeward he was going to render unto Caesar[1] what was Caesar's. Albert Edward did very well. He did so well that in a year or so it struck him that he might take a second shop and put a manager in. He looked for another long street that hadn't got a tobacconist in it and when he found it, and a shop to let, took it and stocked it. This was a success too. Then it occurred to him that if he could run two he could run half a dozen; so he began walking about London, and whenever he found a long street that had no tobacconist, and a shop to let, he took it. In the course of ten years he had acquired no less than ten shops and he was making money hand over fist. He went round to all of them himself every Monday, collected the week's takings and took them to the bank.

One morning when he was there, paying in a bundle of notes and a heavy bag of silver, the cashier told him that the manager would like to see him. He was shown into an office and the manager shook hands with him.

"Mr. Foreman, I wanted to have a talk to you about the money you've got on deposit with us. D'you know exactly how much it is?"

"Not within a pound or two, sir; but I've got a pretty rough idea."

"Apart from what you paid in this morning, it's a little over thirty thousand pounds. That's a very large sum to have on deposit and I should have thought you'd do better to invest it."

"I wouldn't want to take no risk, sir. I know it's safe in the bank."

"You needn't have the least anxiety. We'll make you out a list of absolutely gilt-edged securities. They'll bring you in a better rate of interest than we can possibly afford to give you."

A troubled look settled on Mr. Foreman's distinguished face.

"I've never 'ad anything to do with stocks and shares and I'd 'ave to leave it all in your 'ands," he said.

The manager smiled.

"We'll do everything. All you'll have to do next time you come in is just to sign the transfers."

"I could do that all right," said Albert uncertainly. "But 'ow should I know what I was signin'?"

"I suppose you can read," said the manager a trifle sharply.

[1] *render unto Caesar:* see Matthew 22:21.

Mr. Foreman gave him a disarming smile.

"Well, sir, that's just it. I can't. I know it sounds funny like, but there it is! I can't read or write—only me name, an' I only learned to do that when I went into business."

The manager was so surprised that he jumped up from his chair.

"That's the most extraordinary thing I ever heard."

"You see, it's like this, sir—I never 'ad the opportunity until it was too late, and then some'ow I wouldn't. I got obstinate like."

The manager stared at him as though he were a prehistoric monster.

"And do you mean to say that you've built up this important business and amassed a fortune of thirty thousand pounds without being able to read or write? Good Lord, man, what would you be now if you had been able to?"

"I can tell you that, sir," said Mr. Foreman, a little smile on his still aristocratic features. "I'd be verger of St. Peter's, Neville Square."

MEMORABLE CHARACTER

1. Why is the conversation of the verger with the vicar and the two churchwardens the big scene in the story? Compare this scene with the final scene between the principal character and the bank manager. Is the verger a changed man at the end of the story? Give reasons for your answer.

2. What part of the story is a flashback? What do you learn of the verger's earlier life? What do you infer about his lifetime's savings as a verger? about his smoking and drinking habits? Notice that a period of ten years is condensed into a single paragraph.

3. The comic spirit of the story does not mean that Maugham is without a serious purpose. What is that purpose?

FOLLOWING CHARACTER DEVELOPMENT

"The Verger" illustrates Maugham's chief interest as a storyteller: characterization. His technique here is an example of what he meant when he said in his book *The Summing Up:* "I think what has chiefly struck me in human beings is their lack of consistency. . . . It has amazed me that the most incongruous traits should exist in the same person and for all that yield a plausible harmony."

The interest in the story you have just read revolves around the verger: what kind of a man he is, what happens to him, and why he acts as he does. There are several ways to suggest character, and Maugham uses many of them to develop the character of Albert Edward Foreman. Character may be revealed by *conversation* and *action*. Recall everything that Foreman says.

Why does Maugham have Foreman talk to himself in a lower-class dialect? In how many places throughout the story does Maugham indicate what is going on in someone's mind by describing what he is doing? Here is one example: "Albert Edward's thin, sallow face reddened and he moved uneasily on his feet, but he made no reply."

One of the verger's two principal actions is his decision *not* to meet the conditions imposed by his superiors. What is his other principal decision, and how do both decisions show his independence as well as his confidence in his own worth?

Character may also be presented, of course, in *direct description*. Find as many short descriptions—phrases or words—as you can that build up your picture of Foreman. Can you find a single statement in the story which might serve to sum up Foreman's character?

Finally, character may often be revealed by showing the *interaction between two persons*. What is the effect of the contrast between the verger and the bank manager? Watching the verger and the manager together, what conclusions can you draw about the extent to which they understand each other?

SUGGESTION FOR WRITING

The topsy-turvy standards found in "The Verger" make us look again at some of our ideas. Is there a necessary connection between learning and virtue? Can an education be used for harmful ends as well as for good? Write your thoughts on one of the following subjects: "Learning Is a Dangerous Thing," "Virtue Is Always Rewarded," "Respect for Our Superiors."

The Doll's House

KATHERINE MANSFIELD 1888–1923

In spite of ill-health and a tragically short life, Katherine Mansfield wrote short stories that won her a secure place in modern English literature. Her real name was Kathleen Beauchamp. Born of a wealthy family in Wellington, New Zealand, she attended Queen's College, London, as a young girl. Her urge to write was great, and on returning to New Zealand she was restless and unhappy. After many conflicts with her domineering father, she returned to London. At first she lived recklessly. Impetuously she married her music teacher and left him almost immediately. An attack of tuberculosis forced her to go to Germany to recuperate, and here she began to write stories. In England once again, she married the editor and critic J. Middleton Murry and became known as a literary reviewer and story writer. But appreciation of her work came too late for her to enjoy. Constantly ill, she spent most of her last years trying to regain her health in the warmer climates of France and Italy. She died at the age of thirty-five while living in France.

In "The Doll's House" one finds the human touch, the keen insight into human nature, and the strong character analysis that are typical of the stories of Katherine Mansfield. Here she condenses the meaning of life into poignant episodes. Her vivid presentation of the situation, her intermingling of pathos and irony, and her sharp contrast of characters reveal her as a deeply emotional writer. Although this story is about children, you will discover that it is not a childish story.

W HEN dear old Mrs. Hay went back to town after staying with the Burnells she sent the children a doll's house. It was so big that the carter and Pat carried it into the courtyard, and there it stayed, propped up on two wooden boxes beside the feed-room door. No harm could come to it; it was summer. And perhaps the smell of paint would have gone off by the time it had to be taken in. For, really, the smell of paint coming from that doll's house ("Sweet of old Mrs. Hay, of course; most sweet and generous!")—but the smell of paint was quite enough to make anyone seriously ill, in Aunt Beryl's opinion. Even before the sacking was taken off. And when it was . . .

There stood the doll's house, a dark, oily, spinach green, picked out with bright yellow. Its two solid little chimneys, glued onto the roof, were painted red and white, and the door, gleaming with yellow varnish, was like a little slab of toffee. Four windows, real windows, were divided into panes by a broad streak of green. There was actually a tiny porch too, painted yellow, with big lumps of congealed paint hanging along the edge.

But perfect, perfect little house! Who could possibly mind the smell? It was part of the joy, part of the newness.

"Open it quickly, someone!"

The hook at the side was stuck fast. Pat pried it open with his penknife, and the whole house front swung back, and—there you were, gazing at one and the same moment into the drawing room and dining room, the kitchen and two bedrooms. That is the way for a house to open! Why don't all houses open like that? How much more exciting than peering through the slit of a door into a mean little hall with a hatstand and two umbrellas! That is—isn't it—what you long to know about a house when you put your hand on the knocker. Perhaps it is the way God opens houses at dead of night when He is taking a quiet turn with an angel. . . .

"O-oh!" The Burnell children sounded as though they were in despair. It was too marvelous; it was too much for them. They had never seen anything like it in their lives. All the rooms were papered. There were pictures on the walls, painted on the paper, with gold frames complete. Red carpet covered all the floors except the kitchen; red plush chairs in the drawing room, green in the dining room; tables, beds with real bed-clothes, a cradle, a stove, a dresser with tiny plates and one big jug. But what Kezia liked more than anything, what she liked frightfully, was the lamp. It stood in the middle of the dining-room table, an exquisite little amber lamp with a white globe. It was even filled all ready for lighting, though, of course, you couldn't light it. But there was something inside that looked like oil, and that moved when you shook it.

The father and mother dolls, who sprawled very stiff as though they had fainted in the drawing room, and their two little children asleep up-stairs, were really too big for the doll's house. They didn't look as though they belonged. But the lamp was perfect. It seemed to smile at Kezia, to say: "I live here." The lamp was real.

The Burnell children could hardly walk to school fast enough the next morning. They burned to tell everybody, to describe, to—well—to boast about their doll's house before the school bell rang.

"I'm to tell," said Isabel, "because I'm the eldest. And you two can join in after. But I'm to tell first."

There was nothing to answer. Isabel was bossy, but she was always right, and Lottie and Kezia knew too well the powers that went with being eldest. They brushed through the thick buttercups at the road edge and said nothing.

"And I'm to choose who's to come and see it first. Mother said I might."

For it had been arranged that while the doll's house stood in the court-yard they might ask the girls at school, two at a time, to come and look. Not to stay to tea, of course, or to come traipsing through the house. But just to stand quietly in the courtyard while Isabel pointed out the beauties, and Lottie and Kezia looked pleased. . . .

But hurry as they might, by the time they had reached the tarred pal-ings of the boys' playground the bell had begun to jangle. They only just had time to whip off their hats and fall into line before the roll was called. Never mind, Isabel tried to make up for it by looking very important and mysterious and by whispering behind her hand to the girls near her: "Got something to tell you at playtime."

Playtime came and Isabel was surrounded. The girls of her class nearly fought to put their arms round her, to walk away with her, to beam flatteringly, to be her special friend. She held quite a court under the huge pine trees at the side of the playground. Nudging, giggling together, the little girls pressed up close. And the only two who stayed outside the ring were the two who were always outside, the little Kelveys. They knew better than to come anywhere near the Burnells.

For the fact was that the school the Burnell children went to was not at all the kind of place their parents would have chosen if there had been any choice. But there was none. It was the only school for miles. And the consequence was all the children in the neighborhood, the Judge's little girls, the doctor's daughters, the storekeeper's children, the milkman's, were forced to mix together. Not to speak of there being an equal number of rude, rough little boys as well. But the line had to be drawn somewhere. It was drawn at the Kelveys. Many of the children, including the Burnells, were not allowed even to speak to them. They walked past the Kelveys with their heads in the air, and as they set the fashion in all matters of behavior, the Kelveys were shunned by everybody. Even the teacher had a special voice for them, and a special smile for the other children when Lil Kelvey came up to her desk with a bunch of dreadfully common-looking flowers.

They were the daughters of a spry, hardworking little washerwoman, who went about from house to house by the day. This was awful enough. But where was Mr. Kelvey? Nobody knew for certain. But everybody said he was in prison. So they were the daughters of a washerwoman and a jailbird. Very nice company for other people's children! And they looked it. Why Mrs. Kelvey made them so conspicuous was hard to understand. The truth was they were dressed in "bits" given to her by the people for whom she worked. Lil, for instance, who was a stout, plain child, with big freckles, came to school in a dress made from a green art-serge tablecloth of the Burnells, with red plush sleeves from the Logans' curtains. Her hat, perched on top of her high forehead, was a grown-up woman's hat, once the property of Miss Lecky, the postmistress. It was turned up at the back and trimmed with a large scarlet quill. What a little guy she looked! It was impossible not to laugh. And her little sister, our Else, wore a long white dress, rather like a nightgown, and a pair of little boy's boots. But whatever our Else wore, she would have looked strange. She was a tiny wishbone of a child, with cropped hair and enormous solemn eyes—a little white owl. Nobody had ever seen her smile; she scarcely ever spoke. She went through life holding on to Lil, with a piece of Lil's skirt screwed up in her hand. Where Lil went our Else followed. In the playground, on the road going to and from school, there was Lil marching in front and our Else holding on behind. Only when she wanted anything, or when she was out of breath, our Else gave Lil a tug, a twitch, and Lil stopped and turned round. The Kelveys never failed to understand each other.

Now they hovered at the edge; you couldn't stop them listening. When the little girls turned round and sneered, Lil, as usual, gave her silly, shamefaced smile, but our Else only looked.

And Isabel's voice, so very proud, went on telling. The carpet made a great sensation, but so did the beds with real bedclothes, and the stove with an oven door.

When she finished, Kezia broke in. "You've forgotten the lamp, Isabel."

"Oh, yes," said Isabel, "and there's a teeny little lamp, all made of yellow glass, with a white globe, that stands on the dining-room table. You couldn't tell it from a real one."

"The lamp's best of all," cried Kezia. She thought Isabel wasn't making half enough of the little lamp. But nobody paid any attention. Isabel was choosing the two who were to come back with them that afternoon and see it. She chose Emmie Cole and Lena Logan. But when the others knew they were all to have a chance, they couldn't be nice enough to Isabel. One by one they put their arms round Isabel's waist and walked her off. They had something to whisper to her, a secret. "Isabel's my friend."

Only the little Kelveys moved away forgotten; there was nothing more for them to hear.

Days passed, and as more children saw the doll's house, the fame of it spread. It became the one subject, the rage. The one question was: "Have you seen Burnells' doll's house? Oh, ain't it lovely!" "Haven't you seen it? Oh, I say!"

Even the dinner hour was given up to talking about it. The little girls sat under the pines eating their thick mutton sandwiches and big slabs of johnnycake spread with butter. While always, as near as they could get, sat the Kelveys, our Else holding on to Lil, listening too, while they chewed their jam sandwiches out of a newspaper soaked with large red blobs. . . .

"Mother," said Kezia, "can't I ask the Kelveys just once?"

At last everybody had seen it except them. On that day the subject rather flagged. It was the dinner hour. The children stood together under the pine trees, and suddenly, as they looked at the Kelveys eating out of their paper, always by themselves, always listening, they wanted to be horrid to them. Emmie Cole started the whisper.

"Lil Kelvey's going to be a servant when she grows up."

"O-oh, how awful!" said Isabel Burnell, and she made eyes at Emmie.

Emmie swallowed in a very meaning way and nodded to Isabel as she'd seen her mother do on those occasions.

"It's true—it's true—it's true," she said.

Then Lena Logan's little eyes snapped. "Shall I ask her?" she whispered.

"Bet you don't," said Jessie May.

"Pooh, I'm not frightened," said Lena. Suddenly she gave a little squeal and danced in front of the other girls. "Watch! Watch me! Watch me now!" said Lena. And sliding, gliding, dragging one foot, giggling behind her hand, Lena went over to the Kelveys.

Lil looked up from her dinner. She wrapped the rest quickly away. Our Else stopped chewing. What was coming now?

"Is it true you're going to be a servant when you grow up, Lil Kelvey?" shrilled Lena.

Dead silence. But instead of answering, Lil only gave her silly, shame-faced smile. She didn't seem to mind the question at all. What a sell for Lena! The girls began to titter.

Lena couldn't stand that. She put her hands on her hips; she shot forward. "Yah, yer father's in prison!" she hissed, spitefully.

This was such a marvelous thing to have said that the little girls rushed away in a body, deeply, deeply excited, wild with joy. Someone found a long rope, and they began skipping. And never did they skip so high, run in and out so fast, or do such daring things as on that morning.

In the afternoon Pat called for the Burnell children with the buggy and they drove home. There were visitors. Isabel and Lottie, who liked visitors, went upstairs to change their pinafores. But Kezia thieved out at the back. Nobody was about; she began to swing on the big white gates of the courtyard. Presently, looking along the road, she saw two little dots. They grew bigger, they were coming toward her. Now she could see that one was in front and one close behind. Now she could see that they were the Kelveys. Kezia stopped swinging. She slipped off the gate as if she was going to run away. Then she hesitated. The Kelveys came nearer, and beside them walked their shadows, very long, stretching right across the road with their heads in the buttercups. Kezia clambered back on the gate; she had made up her mind; she swung out.

"Hullo," she said to the passing Kelveys.

They were so astounded that they stopped. Lil gave her silly smile. Our Else stared.

"You can come and see our doll's house if you want to," said Kezia, and she dragged one toe on the ground. But at that Lil turned red and shook her head quickly.

"Why not?" asked Kezia.

Lil gasped, then she said: "Your ma told our ma you wasn't to speak to us."

"Oh, well," said Kezia. She didn't know what to reply. "It doesn't matter. You can come and see our doll's house all the same. Come on. Nobody's looking."

But Lil shook her head still harder.

"Don't you want to?" asked Kezia.

Suddenly there was a twitch, a tug at Lil's skirt. She turned round. Our Else was looking at her with big, imploring eyes; she was frowning; she wanted to go. For a moment Lil looked at our Else very doubtfully. But then our Else twitched her skirt again. She started forward. Kezia led the way. Like two little stray cats they followed across the courtyard to where the doll's house stood.

"There it is," said Kezia.

There was a pause. Lil breathed loudly, almost snorted; our Else was still as a stone.

"I'll open it for you," said Kezia kindly. She undid the hook and they looked inside.

"There's the drawing room and the dining room, and that's the——"

"Kezia!"

Oh, what a start they gave!

"Kezia!"

It was Aunt Beryl's voice. They turned round. At the back door stood Aunt Beryl, staring as if she couldn't believe what she saw.

"How dare you ask the little Kelveys into the courtyard?" said her cold, furious voice. "You know as well as I do you're not allowed to talk to them. Run away, children, run away at once. And don't come back again," said Aunt Beryl. And she stepped into the yard and shooed them out as if they were chickens.

"Off you go immediately!" she called, cold and proud.

They did not need telling twice. Burning with shame, shrinking together, Lil huddling along like her mother, our Else dazed, somehow they crossed the big courtyard and squeezed through the white gate.

"Wicked, disobedient little girl!" said Aunt Beryl bitterly to Kezia, and she slammed the doll's house to.

The afternoon had been awful. A letter had come from Willie Brent, a terrifying, threatening letter, saying if she did not meet him that evening in Pulman's Bush, he'd come to the front door and ask the reason why! But now that she had frightened those little rats of Kelveys and given Kezia a good scolding, her heart felt lighter. That ghastly pressure was gone. She went back to the house humming.

When the Kelveys were well out of sight of Burnells', they sat down to rest on a big red drainpipe by the side of the road. Lil's cheeks were still burning; she took off the hat with the quill and held it on her knee. Dreamily they looked over the hay paddocks, past the creek, to the group of wattles where Logan's cows stood waiting to be milked. What were their thoughts?

Presently our Else nudged up close to her sister. But now she had forgotten the cross lady. She put out a finger and stroked her sister's quill; she smiled her rare smile.

"I seen the little lamp," she said, softly.

Then both were silent once more.

A STORY OF DEEP FEELING

1. Who notices the little lamp first? What do you think it meant to her? How do the other children regard it? To whom does it also have added meaning? What does the little lamp symbolize?

2. Why did the doll house make the Burnell sisters feel so important? Why are the children cruel to the Kelveys? Are children at this age usually cruel? Why? What truth is the author illustrating here?

ANALYZING MOOD

Mood, not actually an ingredient in the construction of a short story, is somewhat like a filter through which the elements of setting, characters, and action are viewed. Because of Katherine Mansfield's skill in creating an emotional atmosphere or mood, the reader reacts to both the lightheartedness and the pathos which pervade "The Doll's House."

Analyze the change of mood in this story. When the doll's house arrives, the Burnell children are overjoyed. Describe their enthusiasm when they first look at the gift. When does this mood first shift, although momentarily, to a less lighthearted response? Which character helps you to notice this change in emotional attitude? How has Kezia been affected by the doll's house?

The next day on their way to school, the three sisters are joyously anticipating their announcement to their friends. The mood of lightheartedness still pervades the story. But shortly the emotional response changes. Where do you find the definite shift in mood? How are the Kelveys affected by the news?

Notice at this point the intermingling of lightheartedness with that of sadness. How are the elements of pathos then introduced into the story? Recall the incidents which have resulted in a shift in mood. To contrast the mood at the opening of the story with that at the end, do not fail to consider Else's remark, "I seen the little lamp."

SUGGESTION FOR WRITING

Write about a personal incident in which you experienced a change in contrasting moods. You might use happiness and sorrow, love and hate, or anticipation and disappointment. Be sure to show what brought about the change in mood.

The Man of the House

FRANK O'CONNOR 1903–

Frank O'Connor is the pseudonym of Michael O'Donovan. Born in Cork, Ireland, of poor parents, he grew up in that city. Although he left school at an early age, he educated himself further in the public library and began to write poems and essays while still a boy. In the bitter civil war of the 1920's, O'Connor joined the Republicans, who were fighting for an independent and united Ireland. Arrested by the government and imprisoned for a year, he spent his time studying languages and writing. After his release, he became a librarian first in County Cork and then in Dublin. Through this profession he had the welcome opportunity to continue his education and develop as a writer. A former director of the famous Abbey Theatre, O'Connor, who lives in the United States, is today recognized as a scholar, critic, and linguist as well as one of the leading contemporary writers of short stories. He has taught writing at Harvard and Northwestern University, and has published frequently in American magazines. Today he spends time revising the stories for which he wants to be remembered.

O'Connor's Ireland is that of the small shopkeeper, the teacher, and the clerk. His stories, surprisingly varied and original, seem to tell themselves. They follow no single pattern, although most of his tales have a moral or a theme that the reader recognizes as the author's purpose in writing. Following is a good example of O'Connor's lilting Irish-English.

WHEN I woke, I heard my mother coughing, below in the kitchen. She had been coughing for days, but I had paid no attention. We were living on the Old Youghal Road at the time, the old hilly coaching road into East Cork. The coughing sounded terrible. I dressed and went downstairs in my stocking feet, and in the clear morning light I saw her, unaware that she was being watched, collapsed into a little wickerwork armchair, holding her side. She had made an attempt to light the fire, but it had gone against her. She looked so tired and helpless that my heart turned over with compassion. I ran to her.

"Are you all right, Mum?" I asked.

"I'll be all right in a second," she replied, trying to smile. "The old sticks were wet, and the smoke started me coughing."

"Go back to bed and I'll light the fire," I said.

"Ah, how can I, child?" she said anxiously. "Sure, I have to go to work."

"You couldn't work like that," I said. "I'll stop at home from school and look after you."

It's a funny thing about women, the way they'll take orders from anything in trousers, even if it's only ten.

"If you could make yourself a cup of tea, I might be all right later on," she said guiltily, and she rose, very shakily, and climbed back up the stairs. I knew then she must be feeling really bad.

I got more stick out of the coalhole, under the stairs. My mother was so economical that she never used enough, and that was why the fire sometimes went against her. I used a whole bundle, and I soon had the fire roaring and the kettle on. I made her toast while I was about it. I was a great believer in hot buttered toast at all hours of the day. Then I made the tea and brought her up a cup on the tray. "Is that all right?" I asked.

"Would you have a cup of boiling water left?" she asked doubtfully.

" 'Tis too strong," I agreed cheerfully, remembering the patience of the saints in their many afflictions. "I'll pour half of it out."

"I'm an old nuisance," she sighed.

" 'Tis my fault," I said, taking the cup. "I can never remember about tea. Put the shawl round you while you're sitting up. Will I shut the sky-light?"

"Would you be able?" she asked doubtfully.

" 'Tis no trouble," I said, getting the chair to it. "I'll do the messages after."

I had my own breakfast alone by the window, and then I went out and stood by the front door to watch the kids from the road on their way to school.

"You'd better hurry or you'll be killed, Sullivan," they shouted.

"I'm not going," I said. "My mother is sick, and I have to mind the house."

I wasn't a malicious child, by any means, but I liked to be able to take out my comforts and study them by the light of others' misfortunes. Then I heated another kettle of water and cleared up the breakfast things before I washed my face and came up to the attic with my shopping basket, a piece of paper, and a lead pencil.

"I'll do the messages now if you'll write them down," I said. "Would you like me to get the doctor?"

"Ah," said my mother impatiently, "he'd only want to send me to hospital, and how would I go to hospital? You could call in at the chemist's and ask him to give you a good, strong cough bottle."

"Write it down," I said. "If I haven't it written down, I might forget it. And put 'strong' in big letters. What will I get for the dinner? Eggs?"

As boiled eggs were the only dish I could manage, I more or less knew it would be eggs, but she told me to get sausages as well, in case she could get up.

I passed the school on my way. Opposite it was a hill, and I went up a short distance and stood there for ten minutes in quiet contemplation. The schoolhouse and yard and gate were revealed as in a painted picture, detached and peaceful except for the chorus of voices through the opened windows and the glimpse of Danny Delaney, the teacher, passing the front door with his cane behind his back, stealing a glance at the world outside. I could have stood there all day. Of all the profound and simple pleasures of those days, that was the richest.

When I got home, I rushed upstairs and found Minnie Ryan sitting with my mother. She was a middle-aged woman, very knowledgeable, gossipy, and pious.

"How are you, Mum?" I asked.

"Grand," said my mother, with a smile.

"You can't get up today, though," said Minnie Ryan.

"I'll put the kettle on and make a cup of tea for you," I said.

"Sure, I'll do that," said Minnie.

"Ah, don't worry, Miss Ryan," I said lightly. "I can manage it all right."

"Wisha, isn't he very good?" I heard her say in a low voice to my mother.

"As good as gold," said my mother.

"There's not many like that, then," said Minnie. "The most of them that's going now are more like savages than Christians."

In the afternoon, my mother wanted me to run out and play, but I didn't go far. I knew if once I went a certain distance from the house, I was liable to stray into temptation. Below our house, there was a glen, the drill field of the barracks perched high above it on a chalky cliff, and below, in a deep hollow, the millpond and millstream running between wooded hills—the Rockies, the Himalayas, or the Highlands, according to your mood. Once down there, I tended to forget the real world, so I sat on a wall outside the house, running in every half hour to see how the mother was and if there was anything she wanted.

Evening fell; the street lamps were lit, and the paper boy went crying up the road. I bought a paper, lit the lamp in the kitchen and the candle in my mother's attic, and tried to read to her, not very successfully, because I was only at words of one syllable, but I had a great wish to please, and she to be pleased, so we got on quite well, considering.

Later, Minnie Ryan came again, and as she was going, I saw her to the door.

"If she's not better in the morning, I think I'd get the doctor, Hurry," she said, over her shoulder.

"Why?" I asked, in alarm. "Do you think is she worse, Miss Ryan?"

"Ah, I wouldn't say so," she replied with affected nonchalance, "but I'd be frightened she might get pneumonia."

"But wouldn't he send her to hospital, Miss Ryan?"

"Wisha, he mightn't," she said with a shrug, pulling her old shawl about her. "But even if he did, wouldn't it be better than neglecting it? Ye wouldn't have a drop of whiskey in the house?"

"I'll get it," I said at once. I knew what might happen to people who got pneumonia, and what was bound to happen afterward to their children.

"If you could give it to her hot, with a squeeze of lemon in it, it might help to shake it off," said Minnie.

My mother said she didn't want the whiskey, dreading the expense, but

I had got such a fright that I wouldn't be put off. When I went to the public house, it was full of men, who drew aside to let me reach the bar. I had never been in a public house before, and I was frightened.

"Hullo, my old flower," said one man, grinning diabolically at me. "It must be ten years since I seen you last. What are you having?"

My pal, Bob Connell, had told me how he once asked a drunk man for a half crown and the man gave it to him. I always wished I could bring myself to do the same, but I didn't feel like it just then.

"I want a half glass of whiskey for my mother," I said.

"Oh, the thundering ruffian!" said the man. "Pretending 'tis for his mother, and the last time I seen him he had to be carried home."

"I had not," I shouted indignantly. "And 'tis for my mother. She's sick."

"Ah, let the child alone, Johnnie," said the barmaid. She gave me the whiskey, and then, still frightened of the men in the public house, I went off to a shop for a lemon.

When my mother had drunk the hot whiskey, she fell asleep, and I quenched the lights and went to bed, but I couldn't sleep very well. I was regretting I hadn't asked the man in the pub for a half crown. I was wakened several times by the coughing, and when I went into my mother's room her head felt very hot, and she was rambling in her talk. It frightened me more than anything else when she didn't know me, and I lay awake, thinking of what would happen to me if it were really pneumonia.

The depression was terrible when, next morning, my mother seemed not to be any better. I had done all I could do, and I felt helpless. I lit the fire and got her breakfast, but this time I didn't stand at the front door to see the other fellows on their way to school. I should have been too inclined to envy them. Instead, I went over to Minnie Ryan and reported.

"I'd go for the doctor," she said firmly. "Better be sure than sorry."

I had first to go to the house of a Poor Law Guardian, for a ticket to show we couldn't pay. Then I went down to the dispensary, which was in a deep hollow beyond the school. After that I had to go back to ready the house for the doctor. I had to have a basin of water and soap and a clean towel laid out for him, and I had to get the dinner, too.

It was after dinner when he called. He was a fat, loud-voiced man and supposed to be "the cleverest doctor in Cork, if only he'd mind himself." He hadn't been minding himself much that morning, it seemed.

"How are you going to get this now?" he grumbled, sitting on the bed with the prescription pad on his knee. "The only place open is the North Dispensary."

"I'll go, Doctor," I said at once, relieved that he had said nothing about hospital.

" 'Tis a long way," he said, doubtfully. "Do you know where it is?"

"I'll find it," I said.

"Isn't he a great little fellow?" he said to my mother.

"Oh, the best in the world, Doctor!" she said. "A daughter couldn't be better to me."

"That's right," said the doctor. "Look after your mother; she'll be the best for you in the long run. We don't mind them when we have them," he added, to my mother, "and then we spend the rest of our lives regretting it."

I wished he hadn't said that; it tuned in altogether too well with my mood. To make it worse, he didn't even use the soap and water I had laid ready for him.

My mother gave me directions how to reach the dispensary, and I set off with a bottle wrapped in brown paper under my arm. The road led uphill, through a thickly populated poor locality, as far as the barracks, which was perched on the very top of the hill, over the city, and then descended, between high walls, till it suddenly almost disappeared in a stony path, with red brick corporation houses to one side of it, that dropped steeply, steeply, to the valley of the little river, where a brewery stood, and the opposite hillside, a murmuring honeycomb of houses, rose to the gently rounded top, on which stood the purple standstone tower of the cathedral and the limestone spire of Shandon church, on a level with your eye.

It was so wide a view that it was never all lit up together, and the sunlight wandered across it as across a prairie, picking out first a line of roofs with a brightness like snow, and then delving into the depth of some dark street and outlining in shadow figures of climbing carts and straining horses. I leaned on the low wall and thought how happy a fellow could be, looking at that, if he had nothing to trouble him. I tore myself from it with a sigh, slithered without stopping to the bottom of the hill, and climbed up a series of shadowy and stepped lanes around the back of the cathedral, which now seemed enormous. I had a penny, which my mother had given me by way of encouragement, and I made up my mind that when I had done my business, I should go into the cathedral and spend it on a candle to the Blessed Virgin, to make my mother better quick. I felt sure it would be more effective in a really big church like that, so very close to Heaven.

The dispensary was a sordid little hallway with a bench to one side and a window like the one in a railway ticket office at the far end. There was a little girl with a green plaid shawl about her shoulders sitting on the bench. I knocked at the window, and a seedy, angry-looking man opened it. Without waiting for me to finish what I was saying, he grabbed bottle and prescription from me and banged the shutter down again without a word. I waited for a moment and then lifted my hand to knock again.

"You'll have to wait, little boy," said the girl quickly.

"What will I have to wait for?" I asked.

"He have to make it up," she explained. "You might as well sit down."

I did, glad of anyone to keep me company.

"Where are you from?" she asked. "I live in Blarney Lane," she added when I had told her. "Who's the bottle for?"

"My mother," I said.

"What's wrong with her?"

"She have a bad cough."

"She might have consumption," she said thoughtfully. "That's what my sister that died last year had. This is a tonic for my other sister. She have to have tonics all the time. Is it nice where you live?"

I told her about the glen, and then she told me about the river near their place. It seemed to be a nicer place than ours, as she described it. She was a pleasant, talkative little girl, and I didn't notice the time until the window opened again and a red bottle was thrust out.

"Dooley!" shouted the seedy man, and closed the window again.

"That's me," said the little girl. "Yours won't be ready for a good while yet. I'll wait for you."

"I have a penny," I said boastfully.

She waited until my bottle was thrust out, and then she accompanied me as far as the steps leading down to the brewery. On the way, I bought a penny-worth of sweets, and we sat on the other steps, beside the infirmary, to eat them. It was nice there, with the spire of Shandon in shadow behind us, the young trees overhanging the high walls, and the sun, when it came out in great golden blasts, throwing our linked shadows onto the road.

"Give us a taste of your bottle, little boy," she said.

"Why?" I asked. "Can't you taste your own?"

"Mine is awful," she said. "Tonics is awful to taste. You can try it if you like."

I took a taste of it and hastily spat out. She was right; it was awful. After that, I couldn't do less than let her taste mine.

"That's grand," she said enthusiastically, after taking a swig from it. "Cough bottles are nearly always grand. Try it, can't you?"

I did, and saw she was right about that, too. It was very sweet and sticky.

"Give us another," she said excitedly, grabbing at it.

" 'Twill be all gone," I said.

"Erra, 'twon't," she replied with a laugh. "You have gallons of it."

Somehow, I couldn't refuse her. I was swept from my anchorage into an unfamiliar world of spires and towers, trees, steps, shadowy laneways, and little girls with red hair and green eyes. I took a drink myself and gave her another. Then I began to panic. " 'Tis nearly gone," I said. "What am I going to do now?"

"Finish it and say the cork fell out," she replied, and again, as she said it, it sounded plausible enough. We finished the bottle between us, and then, slowly, as I looked at it in my hand, empty as I had brought it, and remembered that I had not kept my word to the Blessed Virgin and had spent her penny on sweets, a terrible despondency swept over me. I had sacrificed everything for the little girl and she didn't even care for me. It was my cough bottle she had coveted all the time. I saw her guile too late. I put my head in my hands and began to cry.

"What are you crying for?" the little girl asked in astonishment.

"My mother is sick, and we're after drinking her medicine," I said.

"Ah, don't be an old crybaby!" she said contemptuously. "You have only to say the cork fell out. Sure, that's a thing could happen to anybody."

"And I promised the Blessed Virgin a candle, and I spent the money on you!" I screamed, and, suddenly grabbing the empty bottle, I ran up the road from her, wailing. Now I had only one refuge and one hope—a miracle. I went back to the cathedral, and, kneeling before the shrine of the Blessed Virgin, I begged her pardon for having spent her penny, and promised her a candle from the next penny I got, if only she would work a miracle and make my mother better before I got back. After that, I crawled miserably homeward, back up the great hill, but now all the light had gone out of the day, and the murmuring hillside had become a vast, alien, cruel world. Besides, I felt very sick. I thought I might be going to die. In one way it would be better.

When I got back into the house, the silence of the kitchen and then the sight of the fire gone out in the grate smote me with the cruel realization that the Blessed Virgin had let me down. There was no miracle, and my mother was still in bed. At once, I began to howl.

"What is it at all, child?" she called in alarm from upstairs.

"I lost the medicine," I bellowed, and rushed up the stairs to throw myself on the bed and bury my face in the clothes.

"Oh, wisha, if that's all that's a trouble to you!" she exclaimed with relief, running her hand through my hair. "Is anything the matter?" she added, after a moment. "You're very hot."

"I drank the medicine," I bawled.

"Ah, what harm?" she murmured soothingly. "You poor, unfortunate child! 'Twas my own fault for letting you go all that way by yourself. And then to have your journey for nothing. Undress yourself now, and you can lie down here."

She got up, put on her slippers and coat, and unlaced my boots while I sat on the bed. But even before she had finished I was fast asleep. I didn't see her dress herself or hear her go out, but some time later I felt a hand on my forehead and saw Minnie Ryan peering down at me, laughing.

"Ah, 'twill be nothing," she said, giving her shawl a pull about her. "He'll sleep it off by morning. The dear knows, Mrs. Sullivan, 'tis you should be in bed."

I knew that was a judgment on me, but I could do nothing about it. Later I saw my mother come in with the candle and her paper, and I smiled up at her. She smiled back. Minnie Ryan might despise me as much as she liked, but there were others who didn't. The miracle had happened, after all.

A STORY WITH A VIEW

1. What does the title "The Man of the House" mean to you after you have finished the story? With what idea is O'Connor mainly concerned?

2. Do you think the boy is a typical child of ten? What incidents in the story help to answer this question? What does the boy mean when he says "I liked to be able to take out my comforts and study them by the light of others' misfortunes"? During the first day of his mother's illness, what was the boy's richest pleasure?

3. Describe the girl that the boy meets at the dispensary. Why is she successful in her plan? What was his "one refuge and one hope"? How do you explain "the miracle" that happened?

READING LIST FOR MODERN SHORT STORIES

Chesterton, G. K., *Father Brown Omnibus*
Fifty stories in which a priest-detective, Father Brown, solves mystery after mystery.

Coppard, A. E., *Collected Tales*
Stories ranging from naturalism to fantasy and symbolism.

Doyle, A. Conan, *The Adventures of Sherlock Holmes*
Some of the best mystery and detective stories by a world favorite.

Galsworthy, John, *Caravan*
Here are the outstanding stories by a master craftsman.

Garrity, Devin A. (editor), *Forty-four Irish Short Stories*
An anthology, from Yeats to Frank O'Connor.

Goodman, Jack (editor), *Fireside Book of Dog Stories*
A dog fancier will enjoy especially the stories by Galsworthy, Kipling, D. H. Lawrence, and Eric Knight.

Mansfield, Katherine, *Short Stories*
Portraits of situations and characters of English life.

O'Connor, Frank, *Stories*
Stories that present the charm and tragedy of everyday life.

O'Faoláin, Seán, *The Man Who Invented Sin*
The essence of Ireland with very real Irishmen transmitted in fifteen stories.

Priestley, J. B., *The Other Place and Other Stories of the Same Sort*
How the supernatural seems to play a part in everyday life is found in all nine stories.

Pritchett, V. S., *The Sailor, Sense of Humour, and Other Stories*
The double lives of middle-class Britishers tormented by changing social forces.

Schweikert, Harry C. (editor), *Short Stories*
Jacobs, Hardy, Conrad, Kipling, Bennett, Barrie, Galsworthy, and Katherine Mansfield are represented with a story and biographical sketch.

Ustinov, Peter, *Add a Dash of Pity*
Eight amusing satires by a playwright, actor, and television personality.

MODERN POETRY

INCLUDED among the poets in this section are A. E. Housman and Dylan Thomas. Now Housman was born in 1859, Dylan Thomas in 1914. So between these two men is a gap of fifty-five years. This is important to remember, for much can happen in the world over a space of fifty-five years. The world that Dylan Thomas knew in his boyhood and youth was very different from the one that Housman knew in the latter half of Victoria's reign. For example, although Housman wrote about young men killed in battle, he grew up in an era of peace, whereas Dylan Thomas, though he wrote little about it, lived in the very shadow of war —total and terrible war.

Even a first quick reading of the work of these two fine and highly original poets reveals at once a profound difference between them as artists. They offer us two quite different kinds of poetry. Housman's "To an Athlete Dying Young" (page 83) has a comparatively simple central theme that we understand at once. The imagery in the sharply chiselled lines, typical of his work, gives his idea a compelling force and a certain haunting beauty. This is the classical manner in poetry; and indeed, Housman, a famous classical scholar, owes much to his study of Greek and Roman poetry.

Turn to Dylan Thomas' magnificent "Do Not Go Gentle into That Good Night" (page 113) and you find something very different, something at once newer and yet at the same time even older. It is newer because, being very modern in its manner (following to some extent the French Symbolist Movement), it depends entirely for its effect on a rapid succession of images, making great demands on the reader's imagination before the poem can be understood and appreciated. And at the same time it is older because Dylan Thomas, not only a Welshman but a very Welsh Welshman, is returning in spirit to the oldest traditions of his people, to the ancient bards and their magical chants. To hear Dylan Thomas read his poetry—and there was no better reader of poetry in our time— was to return with him to this ancient magical tradition. He made your hair stand on end.

Taking Housman and Dylan Thomas for comparison, we have the two extremes, but the difference between them well illustrates the whole modern movement in English poetry, a half century filled with restless experiment and changes in poetical art. There has been both gain and loss, which is of course what always happens when one of the arts is on the move. And the quickest and easiest way to understand what changes have taken place is this—to try to strike a balance between rough estimates of these gains and losses, if the poets will forgive us for dealing with them in bookkeeping terms.

There was first an immense gain in what might be called the subject matter of poetry. When this period began there were still set "poetical" subjects. A poet could write about This but not about That. But the poets in the modern movement felt they could write about anything, that nothing was barred. They were prepared to consider every possible aspect of the world in which they lived. Consequently, there was a sudden and tremendous gain in breadth.

Along with this was a corresponding gain in depth. Just as modern poets ventured into the outer world, so too they delved further into the inner world of the mind and imagination. The new freedom in poetry encouraged them to explore the recesses, no matter how dimly illuminated, of their own being. What they found there could often be communicated only by means of symbolic imagery, if only because these mysterious depths are beyond the reach of conscious thought. This demanded a new attitude on the part of the reader, who could no longer stand away from poetry and ask himself what it meant in terms of conscious thought. The reader had to give himself to the poem and allow it to take possession of him. When I was at school, half a century ago, we had to write paraphrases of poetry. Truly modern poetry cannot be paraphrased. A poem is a poem, existing entirely in its own right, and cannot be turned into anything else without being destroyed.

These gains in breadth, depth, and independence seem very impressive, as indeed they are. It might seem difficult, therefore, to discover what counterbalancing losses there might be. There are losses, however, especially in the relation between poetry and the general reading public. To begin with, the newer poets seem far more obscure and "difficult" than the older ones were. Some of their work suggests a series of riddles, and, although solving riddles can be an entertaining pastime, it seems far removed from the joyful appreciation of poetry. Undoubtedly a great many people, not necessarily stupid, have ceased to read new poetry, preferring to return to older work.

Again, in the change from old to new, there was a definite loss in what can be called the memorable quality of poetry. It is easy to remember given lines of Housman's poetry and very difficult to remember Dylan Thomas', however much we may admire it. And if earlier poetry had often seemed too public in theme and manner, as if written to be declaimed on the steps of the local town hall, now the newer poetry seemed often altogether too private, too much like something muttered among members of a secret society. This too was a loss, reducing the stature and influence of the poet in the community.

One last word. The truly great poet—a man of outstanding genius like W. B. Yeats—cannot be confined within such estimates of gains and losses. He has the good qualities of both the older and newer poets but is free from their respective weaknesses. He can be public and memorable and yet also private, searching, and subtle. He can explore his own inner world without disappearing from the outer world and is able to describe in the market place his most secret and strangest dreams. But this takes us well outside mere literary fashions and movements, for what it demands is original poetic genius.

J. B. P.

A. E. HOUSMAN
1859–1936

Alfred Edward Housman's reputation as a poet rests on the high quality of comparatively few poems. In 1896 he published *A Shropshire Lad,* containing sixty-three simple lyrics. They were the meditations of a young man, many of them tinged with a wistful, ironic, or pessimistic tone, but others filled with the joyousness of a farm boy during springtime in the country. So distinctive was the flavor of these poems that Housman was immediately established as a leader among the new poets of the twentieth century. He did not publish again for twenty-six years. Then an even smaller volume called *Last Poems* appeared. A third volume, *More Poems,* was published by his brother Laurence after the poet's death.

By profession A. E. Housman was a gifted and eminent classical scholar. After leaving Oxford, he worked for ten years in the British patent office, a job which he left in order to become a professor of Latin first at the University of London and later at Cambridge. His carefully wrought lyrics—simple, beautiful, and highly polished—reveal the influence of his life-long interest in classical studies.

Loveliest of Trees

Loveliest of trees, the cherry now
Is hung with bloom along the bough,
And stands about the woodland ride°
Wearing white for Eastertide.

Now, of my three score years and ten,   5
Twenty will not come again,
And take from seventy springs a score,
It only leaves me fifty more.

And since to look at things in bloom
Fifty springs are little room,   10
About the woodlands I will go
To see the cherry hung with snow.

3. *ride:* a road intended for horseback travel. (Notice the small circle after the word that is explained. This sign is used with all the poems in this book to call your attention to each word that is similarly explained. The number of the footnote refers to the line of the poem.)

Far in a Western Brookland

Far in a western brookland
    That bred me long ago
The poplars stand and tremble
    By pools I used to know.

There, in the windless nighttime,   5
    The wanderer, marveling why,
Halts on the bridge to hearken
    How soft the poplars sigh.

He hears: no more remembered
    In fields where I was known,   10
Here I lie down in London
    And turn to rest alone.

"Loveliest of Trees" and "Far in a Western Brookland" from "A Shropshire Lad"—Authorized Edition —from *Complete Poems* by A. E. Housman. Copyright © 1959 by Holt, Rinehart and Winston, Inc. Reprinted by permission of Holt, Rinehart and Winston, Inc. and The Society of Authors as the Literary Representative of the Trustees of the Estate of the late A. E. Housman, and Messrs. Jonathan Cape Limited, publishers of A. E. Housman's *Collected Poems*.

There, by the starlit fences,
    The wanderer halts and hears
My soul that lingers sighing   15
    About the glimmering weirs.

To an Athlete Dying Young

The time you won your town the race
We chaired you through the marketplace;
Man and boy stood cheering by,
And home we brought you shoulder-high.

Today, the road all runners come,   5
Shoulder-high we bring you home,
And set you at your threshold down,
Townsman of a stiller town.

Smart lad, to slip betimes away
From fields where glory does not stay,   10
And early though the laurel grows,
It withers quicker than the rose.

Eyes the shady night has shut
Cannot see the record cut,
And silence sounds no worse than cheers   15
After earth has stopped the ears:

Now you will not swell the rout
Of lads that wore their honors out,
Runners whom renown outran
And the name died before the man.   20

So set, before its echoes fade,
The fleet foot on the sill of shade,
And hold to the low lintel up
The still-defended challenge-cup.

And round that early-laureled head   25
Will flock to gaze the strengthless dead,

"To an Athlete Dying Young" from "A Shropshire Lad"—Authorized Edition—from *Complete Poems* by A. E. Housman. Copyright © 1959 by Holt, Rinehart and Winston, Inc. Reprinted by permission of Holt, Rinehart and Winston, Inc. and The Society of Authors as the Literary Representative of the Trustees of the Estate of the late A. E. Housman, and Messrs. Jonathan Cape Limited, publishers of A. E. Housman's *Collected Poems*.

And find unwithered on its curls
The garland briefer than a girl's.

LYRICS FROM SHROPSHIRE

1. Each of the lyrics expresses a different mood. For each one, state the mood the poet is trying to convey, and in a sentence or two, express the central thought of the poem.

2. Where in these poems do you find sharp contrasts, sometimes wistful, sometimes ironical?

3. Notice that Housman uses a ballad measure. Are these poems ballads? How do they illustrate almost perfectly the usual definition of a lyric poem?

WILLIAM BUTLER YEATS

1865–1939

In contrast to the meager output of Housman, the total output of William Butler Yeats (yāts) is tremendous. This is due partly to patriotic as well as poetic fervor, for Yeats took an active part in the Celtic Renaissance, and he was a senator in the newly established Irish Free State. Much of his poetry was inspired by these two consuming interests. Born in Dublin and educated in London, he lived during his early years with his grandparents in the Irish coastal town of Sligo (slī'gō). Here he became acquainted with Irish folklore, which influenced him greatly throughout his life.

One of the founders of the Irish National Abbey Theater in Dublin, Yeats' special interest was poetic drama. When the theater began to produce realistic prose plays, Yeats proved that he could write effectively in either medium. *The Land of Heart's Desire* is an example of his richly symbolical verse dramas; *The Pot of Broth,* of a successful prose play. Yeats was also an essayist and critic. He is best known, though, for his early lyrics, richly embroidered with metaphors and symbols. In 1923 he received the Nobel Prize for Literature for "his consistently emotional poetry, which in the strictest artistic form expresses a people's spirit."

The Wild Swans at Coole°

The trees are in their autumn beauty,
The woodland paths are dry,
Under the October twilight the water
Mirrors a still sky;
Upon the brimming water among the stones 5
Are nine-and-fifty swans.

The nineteenth autumn has come upon me
Since I first made my count;
I saw, before I had well finished,
All suddenly mount 10
And scatter wheeling in great broken rings
Upon their clamorous wings.

I have looked upon those brilliant creatures,
And now my heart is sore.
All's changed since I, hearing at twilight, 15
The first time on this shore,
The bell-beat of their wings above my head,
Trod with a lighter tread.

Unwearied still, lover by lover,
They paddle in the cold 20
Companionable streams or climb the air;
Their hearts have not grown old;
Passion or conquest, wander where they will,
Attend upon them still.

But now they drift on the still water 25
Mysterious, beautiful;
Among what rushes will they build,
By what lake's edge or pool
Delight men's eyes when I awake some day
To find they have flown away? 30

Title: *Coole* (kōō′lǐ): the estate of Yeats' friend and fellow dramatist Lady
Gregory.

The Lake Isle of Innisfree

The Celtic spirit, with its yearning for the remote, the beautiful, the ideal, is melodiously caught in this poem. Of its origin the author says: "I had still the ambition, formed . . . in my teens, of living in imitation of Thoreau on Innisfree [a little island in Lough Gill, Ireland] . . . and when walking through Fleet Street [London], very homesick, I heard a little tinkle of water and saw a fountain in a shopwindow . . . and began to remember lake water. From the sudden remembrance came my poem, 'Innisfree.'"

I will arise and go now, and go to Innisfree,
   And a small cabin build there, of clay and wattles° made;
Nine bean rows will I have there, a hive for the honeybee,
   And live alone in the bee-loud glade.

And I shall have some peace there, for peace comes dropping slow,   5
   Dropping from the veils of the morning to where the cricket sings;
There midnight's all aglimmer, and noon a purple glow,
   And evening full of the linnet's wings.

I will arise and go now, for always night and day
   I hear lake water lapping with low sounds by the shore;   10
While I stand on the roadway, or on the pavements gray,
   I hear it in the deep heart's core.

2. *wattles:* twigs and pliable rods woven together.

The Fiddler of Dooney

From the earliest days of singers and storytellers, the Irish have held their musicians and poets in high esteem. Although this ballad has a light tone, underneath is the fiddler's strong belief in the sacredness of his important calling.

When I play on my fiddle in Dooney,°
Folk dance like the wave of the sea;
My cousin is priest in Kilvarnet,°
My brother in Moharabuiee.°

1, 3, 4. *Dooney, Kilvarnet, Moharabuiee* (mō·hä·rä·bū·ē′): hamlets on the west coast of Ireland.

I passed my brother and cousin;   5
They read in their books of prayer;
I read in my book of songs
I bought at the Sligo fair.

When we come to the end of time,
To Peter° sitting in state,   10
He will smile on the three old spirits,
But call me first through the gate;

For the good are always the merry,
Save by an evil chance,
And the merry love the fiddle,   15
And the merry love to dance;

And when the folk there spy me,
They will all come up to me,
With "Here is the fiddler of Dooney!"
And dance like a wave of the sea.   20

10. *Peter:* Saint Peter, keeper of the gates of Heaven.

YEATS' POEMS

1. In "The Wild Swans at Coole" at what season of the year and what time of day does the poet describe the swans? What contrast does he feel between himself and the swans after nineteen years?

2. What details in "The Lake Isle of Innisfree" suggest the peace of spirit to be found there? To which poem of Housman's does it have some resemblance in mood?

3. Why does the fiddler of Dooney mention the occupation of his two relatives? Why does he think he will be given preference on entering Heaven? Do you agree with the philosophy in the fourth stanza?

WALTER DE LA MARE
1873–1956

"Walter de la Mare's *Collected Poems* would be my first choice," said a critic once, "if I were to make a present to a child, or a sweetheart, or an old gentleman, or in general, to any happily constituted person. From the first page to the last, one is in the land of poetry, in the atmosphere of genuine folklore, in the age of creative faith."

One would scarcely suspect that the subject of this tribute spent twenty years in the London office of the Anglo-American Oil Company. A grant from the Crown enabled him to withdraw from this prosaic work in 1908 and give free rein to that rare imaginative gift which he displayed in his prose work as well as in his poetry. His *The Memoirs of a Midget* shows a distorted world as seen from the position of a midget—like Gulliver among the giants, only with pathetic rather than satirical effect. His poems for and about children have taken their place as classics beside Stevenson's *A Child's Garden of Verses*. "The Listeners" and "Silver" are De la Mare's most-quoted poems.

The Listeners

The poet takes you into a strange world of echoes and eerie fancies. With details of sound, silence, and light, the desired mood is created and a story suggested.

"Is there anybody there?" said the Traveler,
    Knocking on the moonlit door;
And his horse in the silence champed the grasses
    Of the forest's ferny floor;
And a bird flew up out of the turret,   5
    Above the Traveler's head;
And he smote upon the door again a second time;
    "Is there anybody there?" he said.
But no one descended to the Traveler;
    No head from the leaf-fringed sill   10
Leaned over and looked into his gray eyes,

Where he stood perplexed and still.
But only a host of phantom listeners
    That dwelt in the lone house then
Stood listening in the quiet of the moonlight   15
    To that voice from the world of men;
Stood thronging the faint moonbeams on the dark stair,
    That goes down to the empty hall,
Hearkening in an air stirred and shaken
    By the lonely Traveler's call.   20
And he felt in his heart their strangeness,
    Their stillness answering his cry,
While his horse moved, cropping the dark turf,
    'Neath the starred and leafy sky;
For he suddenly smote on the door, even   25
    Louder, and lifted his head—
"Tell them I came, and no one answered,
    That I kept my word," he said.
Never the least stir made the listeners,
    Though every word he spake   30
Fell echoing through the shadowiness of the still house
    From the one man left awake.
Ay, they heard his foot upon the stirrup,
    And the sound of iron on stone,
And how the silence surged softly backward,   35
    When the plunging hoofs were gone.

Silver

Slowly, silently, now the moon
Walks the night in her silver shoon;
This way, and that, she peers, and sees
Silver fruit upon silver trees;
One by one the casements catch   5
Her beams beneath the silvery thatch;
Couched in his kennel, like a log,
With paws of silver sleeps the dog;
From their shadowy cote the white breasts peep
Of doves in a silver-feathered sleep;   10
A harvest mouse goes scampering by,
With silver claws and a silver eye;
And moveless fish in the water gleam,
By silver reeds in a silver stream.

A Widow's Weeds

Walter de la Mare's imaginative gift touches even the ordinary person. The widow is old; she is dressed in her "weeds," her mourning garments. Sorrow has touched her life. She sows her garden, and it grows. The poet says that "all she has is all she needs."

A poor old Widow in her weeds
Sowed her garden with wild-flower seeds;
Not too shallow, and not too deep,
And down came April—drip—drip—drip.
Up shone May, like gold, and soon   5
Green as an arbour grew leafy June.
And now all summer she sits and sews
Where willow-herb, comfrey, bougloss blows,
Teasel and tansy, meadowsweet,
Campion, toadflax, and rough hawksbit;   10
Brown bee orchis, and Peals of Bells;
Clover, burnet, and thyme she smells;
Like Oberon's° meadows her garden is
Drowsy from dawn till dusk with bees.
Weeps she never, but sometimes sighs,   15
And peeps at her garden with bright brown eyes;
And all she has is all she needs—
A poor old Widow in her weeds.

13. *Oberon* (ō′bĕr·ŏn): in medieval folklore, king of the fairies.

SCENES AND STORIES

1. What is your interpretation of the story which the poet suggests in "The Listeners"? By what details of sight, sound, and silence is the atmosphere created? What is unusual about its rhythm? Contrast the meter of the odd and even lines.

2. "Silver" presents an unusual picture. How many times is the word *silver* used?

3. How would you describe the old lady in "A Widow's Weeds"? What details in the poem help you best to establish a mental image? Explain the significance of line 17.

APPRECIATING FANTASY

De la Mare, a master of fantasy, has a strange freshness of imagination that often carries us into a mysterious and enchanting world. "The Listeners" is marked by its imaginative beauty and excellent craftsmanship. You may read it either of two ways: for the sheer delight of its eerie mystery and haunting music or for the deeper meaning hidden in its strange story.

To appreciate this fantasy fully, you should realize that the poet is concerned with life and universal experience. What does the traveler stand for? He came from the "world of men." He also seems to be expected. Why is his knock unanswered? Who are the listeners? Does the house stand for something? Behind these questions lies the meaning of the fantasy in "The Listeners."

THE POWER OF WORDS

CREATING EFFECT

In "The Listeners" we find a variety of words (e.g., *phantom, lone, quiet, dark*) leading to the climax in the last two lines. In "Silver" effect is created by repeating one word. Of the two methods, is variety or intensity most effective?

G. K. CHESTERTON
1874–1936

The versatile Gilbert Keith Chesterton had many interests, only one of which is represented here. Besides poetry he wrote essays and a series of detective stories. His Father Brown stories, in which a priest-detective is always able to solve the mystery, make absorbing reading.

An energetic and enthusiastic person, Chesterton's first interest was art, and after graduating from art school, he began his career as a reviewer of art books. His manifold activities ranged from art and literature to politics, economics, and philosophy. He traveled and lectured extensively.

In some ways Chesterton resembled Dr. Samuel Johnson. He was large in frame, indifferent to his personal appearance, agile in conversation, prolific in essay writing, and keenly analytic in his studies of writers such as Robert Browning and G. B. Shaw. A writer who thought in terms of contradiction, he is referred to as a master of paradox. You will see examples of this technique in "The World State."

Lepanto

Out of a sixteenth-century battle Chesterton created one of the finest of modern chants. Banging, clanging, colorful, its music beats until we feel in our own pulses the marching song of the mighty host of warriors. This battle was fought in the Gulf of Lepanto (between central and southern Greece) on October 7, 1571. Because the capture of Cyprus by the Turks threatened the end of Venetian trade and even the stability of Spain, Pope Pius V had called for the gathering of a fleet from all the Christian nations. Don John of Austria, a brilliant strategist, was in command of the two hundred and eight vessels of the Christian powers which opposed two hundred and seventy-three small and more poorly equipped Turkish vessels. Both sides depended on galleys manned by prisoners. (This was the last important historical engagement in which galleys were used.) Through their heavier vessels and superior discipline the Christians won the battle, only a few of the Turkish vessels escaping capture or destruction. The Christians lost some eight thousand men; the Turks, more than twenty thousand. Moreover, the Turkish naval power was so broken that it never again threatened the peace of Christian Europe. These historical details are enlivened and glorified by the virile lines of Chesterton's poem.

White founts falling in the Courts of the Sun,
And the Soldan of Byzantium° is smiling as they run;
There is laughter like the fountains in that face of all men feared,
It stirs the forest darkness, the darkness of his beard;
It curls the blood-red crescent, the crescent of his lips;   5
For the inmost sea° of all the earth is shaken with his ships.
They have dared the white republics on the capes of Italy,
They have dashed the Adriatic round the Lion of the Sea,°
And the Pope has cast his arms abroad for agony and loss,

2. *Soldan of Byzantium* (sŏl'dăn . . . bĭ·zăn'shĭ·ŭm): Sultan of Constantinople. 6. *inmost sea:* the Mediterranean. 8. *Lion of the Sea:* The winged lion of St. Mark is the emblem of Venice.

And called the kings of Christendom for swords about the Cross.   10
The cold queen° of England is looking in the glass;
The shadow of the Valois° is yawning at the Mass;
From evening isles fantastical rings faint the Spanish gun,
And the Lord upon the Golden Horn° is laughing in the sun.

Dim drums throbbing, in the hills half heard,   15
Where only on a nameless throne a crownless prince° has stirred,
Where, risen from a doubtful seat and half-attained stall,
The last knight of Europe takes weapons from the wall,
The last and lingering troubadour to whom the bird has sung,
That once went singing southward when all the world was young.   20
In that enormous silence, tiny and unafraid,
Comes up along a winding road the noise of the Crusade.
Strong gongs groaning as the guns boom far,
Don John of Austria is going to the war;
Stiff flags straining in the night blasts cold   25
In the gloom black-purple, in the glint old-gold,
Torchlight crimson on the copper kettledrums,
Then the tuckets,° then the trumpets, then the cannon, and he comes.
Don John laughing in the brave beard curled,
Spurning of his stirrups like the thrones of all the world,   30
Holding his head up for a flag of all the free.
Love light of Spain—hurrah!
Death light of Africa!
Don John of Austria
Is riding to the sea.   35

Mahound° is in his paradise above the evening star;
(*Don John of Austria is going to the war.*)
He moves a mighty turban on the timeless houri's° knees,
His turban that is woven of the sunsets and the seas.
He shakes the peacock gardens as he rises from his ease,   40
And he strides among the treetops and is taller than the trees;
And his voice through all the garden is a thunder sent to bring

11. *cold queen:* Elizabeth of England did not take part in this expedition. 12. *shadow of the Valois* (và'lwà'): Charles IX was nominally King of France, but actually he was in the power of Catherine de Medici, the Duchess of Valois. 14. *Lord upon the Golden Horn:* The Sultan's palace in Constantinople overlooks an arm of the Bosporus called the Golden Horn. 16. *crownless prince:* Don John of Austria. 28. *tuckets:* a flourish of trumpets. 36. *Mahound* (mà·hound'): Mohammed. 38. *timeless houri* (hōō'rĭ): In the Mohammedan paradise, the faithful were rewarded with the companionship of beautiful women (*houris*) throughout eternity.

Black Azrael° and Ariel° and Ammon° on the wing.
Giants and the Genii,
Multiplex of wing and eye, 45
Whose strong obedience broke the sky
When Solomon° was king.
They rush in red and purple from the red clouds of the morn,
From the temples where the yellow gods shut up their eyes in scorn;
They rise in green robes roaring from the green hells of the sea 50
Where fallen skies and evil hues and eyeless creatures be,
On them the sea valves cluster and the gray sea forests curl,
Splashed with a splendid sickness, the sickness of the pearl;
They swell in sapphire smoke out of the blue cracks of the ground—
They gather and they wonder and give worship to Mahound. 55
And he saith, "Break up the mountains where the hermitfolk can hide,
And sift the red and silver sands lest bone of saint abide,
And chase the Giaours° flying night and day, not giving rest,
For that which was our trouble comes again out of the west.
We have set the seal of Solomon on all things under sun, 60
Of knowledge and of sorrow and endurance of things done.
But a noise is in the mountains, in the mountains, and I know
The voice that shook our palaces—four hundred years ago:°
It is he that saith not 'Kismet';° it is he that knows not Fate;
It is Richard,° it is Raymond,° it is Godfrey° at the gate! 65
It is he whose loss is laughter when he counts the wager worth,
Put down your feet upon him, that our peace be on the earth."
For he heard drums groaning and he heard guns jar,
(*Don John of Austria is going to the war.*)
Sudden and still—hurrah! 70
Both from Iberia!°
Don John of Austria
Is gone by Alcalar.

St. Michael's on his Mountain° in the sea roads of the north
(*Don John of Austria is girt and going forth.*) 75
Where the gray seas glitter and the sharp tides shift
And the seafolk labor and the red sails lift.

---

43. *Azrael* (ăz′rȧ·ĕl): the angel of death; *Ariel:* the spirit of the air; *Ammon:* the highest god of the Egyptians. 47. *Solomon:* According to Mohammedan legend, Solomon had a ring inscribed with the name of God which gave him control over demons and genii of the underworld. 58. *Giaours* (jourz): unbelievers; an insulting name used by Mohammedans for anyone not of their faith. 63. *four hundred years ago:* at the time of the early Crusades. 64. *Kismet:* Fate. 65. *Richard, Raymond, Godfrey:* leaders in early Crusades. 71. *Iberia:* Spain. 74. *St. Michael's on his Mountain:* Mont St. Michel, a rocky islet off the coast of France, sacred to St. Michael.

He shakes his lance of iron and he claps his wings of stone;
The noise is gone through Normandy; the noise is gone alone;
The North is full of tangled things and texts and aching eyes,   80
And dead is all the innocence of anger and surprise,
And Christian killeth Christian in a narrow dusty room,
And Christian dreadeth Christ that hath a newer face of doom,
And Christian hateth Mary that God kissed in Galilee—
But Don John of Austria is riding to the sea.   85
Don John calling through the blast and the eclipse
Crying with the trumpet, with the trumpet of his lips,
Trumpet that sayeth *ha!*
   Domino gloria!°
Don John of Austria   90
Is shouting to the ships.
The Pope was in his chapel before day or battle broke,
(*Don John of Austria is hidden in the smoke.*)
The hidden room in man's house where God sits all the year,
The secret window whence the world looks small and very dear.   95
He sees as in a mirror on the monstrous twilight sea
The crescent of his cruel ships whose name is mystery;
They fling great shadows foe-wards, making Cross and Castle° dark;
They veil the plumed lions on the galleys of St. Mark;°
And above the ships are palaces of brown, black-bearded chiefs,   100
And below the ships are prisons, where with multitudinous griefs,
Christian captives° sick and sunless, all a laboring race repines
Like a race in sunken cities, like a nation in the mines.
They are lost like slaves that swat,° and in the skies of morning hung
The stairways of the tallest gods when tyranny was young.   105
They are countless, voiceless, hopeless as those fallen or fleeing on
Before the high Kings' horses in the granite of Babylon.
And many a one grows witless in his quiet room in hell
Where a yellow face looks inward through the lattice of his cell,
And he finds his God forgotten, and he seeks no more a sign—   110
(*But Don John of Austria has burst the battle line!*)
Don John pounding from the slaughter-painted poop,
Purpling all the ocean like a bloody pirate's sloop,
Scarlet running over on the silvers and the golds,
Breaking of the hatches up and bursting of the holds,   115
Thronging of the thousands up that labor under sea
White for bliss and blind for sun and stunned for liberty.

---

89. *Domino gloria* (dō′mǐ·nō glō′rǐ·ȧ): Glory be to God! 98. *Cross and Castle:* the arms of Aragon and of Castile. 99. *galleys of St. Mark:* the Venetian ships. 102. *Christian captives:* galley slaves in the Turkish fleet. 104. *swat:* obsolete form of *sweated.*

Vivat Hispania!°
Domino gloria!
Don John of Austria   120
Has set his people free!

Cervantes° on his galley sets the sword back in the sheath
(*Don John of Austria rides homeward with a wreath.*)
And he sees across a weary land a straggling road in Spain,
Up which a lean and foolish knight° forever rides in vain,   125
And he smiles, but not as Sultans smile, and settles back the blade. . . .
(*But Don John of Austria rides home from the Crusade.*)

118. *Vivat Hispania:* Long live Spain! 122. *Cervantes* (sĕr·văn′tēz): Miguel de
Cervantes (1547–1616), the author of *Don Quixote* (dŏn kwĭk′sŏt), Spain's great
satirical classic. 125. *a lean and foolish knight:* Don Quixote.

The World State

One tendency of Chesterton's prose style is his use of the paradox, an
apparent contradiction of terms that nevertheless throws new light
on the truth. In "The World State" he expresses one of the world's
problems by means of a paradox.

Oh, how I love Humanity,
  With love so pure and pringlish,°
And how I hate the horrid French,
  Who never will be English!

The International Idea,   5
  The largest and the clearest,
Is welding all the nations now,
  Except the one that's nearest.

This compromise has long been known,
  This scheme of partial pardons,   10
In ethical societies
  And small suburban gardens—

The villas and the chapels where
  I learned with little labor
The way to love my fellow man   15
  And hate my next-door neighbor.

2. *pringlish:* a pure invention. What does the word suggest to you?

CHESTERTON'S POETRY

1. Report on the battle of Lepanto as described in a history book. How closely does Chesterton follow actual occurrences?

2. "The World State" shows that it is easier to talk about brotherly love than to practice it. Can you illustrate Chesterton's point from affairs in today's world? in the United States? in your own community?

ANALYZING IDEAS

You will find that it sometimes takes careful review and study to see the order and the form of ideas that a writer is attempting to present. The very dash and surge of "Lepanto" tend to obscure the orderly progress of the thought. A good technique to follow in this and similar cases is to go back and outline the main ideas. Your analysis of "Lepanto" might look like this:

a. The Soldan's arrogant laughter;
b. Rumors of the gathering of the Christian hosts;
c. Mohammed's summons to his helpers;
d. Their arrival and Mohammed's orders to them;
e. The rally of the Christians, forgetful of internal strifes, to the call;
f. The Pope's scrutiny of the battle of the galleys;
g. The thoughts of one combatant—Cervantes.

Complete each scene for color and detail.

JOHN MASEFIELD

1878–

John Masefield has been England's poet laureate since 1930. Interested in common people and everyday concerns, he is a down-to-earth and robust writer.

Orphaned as a child, Masefield was at fourteen apprenticed as a cabin boy on a merchant ship. Between voyages he tramped about in various countries and for several months worked in a New York barroom. Then a reading of Chaucer reawakened in him a childhood love of poetry. He determined to return to England and devote his life to literature. His *Salt-Water Ballads*

(1902) and his later book-length poem *Dauber* struck the keynote of his writing. The tang and terror of the sea, as well as its beauty, were there. His reputation was established with a long poem, *The Everlasting Mercy,* in which a brutal boxer tells of his religious conversion. This poem shocked the public by its frank language and at the same time fascinated readers by its powerful narrative.

During a long life of active writing, Masefield has produced novels, boys' adventure stories, plays, essays, biographies, and accounts of his war experiences; but his poetry tops them all in importance.

In his younger years, Masefield lectured and read his poems in America and was often seen among the literary people of London. At present he leads a retired life at Penbury, Gloucestershire. In person he is gentle, modest, and somewhat shy—quite different from the rough and rugged characters in his poems.

Laugh and Be Merry

Laugh and be merry; remember, better the world with a song,
Better the world with a blow in the teeth of a wrong.
Laugh, for the time is brief, a thread the length of a span,
Laugh and be proud to belong to the old proud pageant of man.

Laugh and be merry; remember, in olden time,   5
God made heaven and earth, for joy He took in a rime,
Made them, and filled them full with the strong red wine of His mirth,
The splendid joy of the stars, the joy of the earth.

So we must laugh and drink from the deep blue cup of the sky,
Join the jubilant song of the great stars sweeping by,   10
Laugh, and battle, and work, and drink of the wine outpoured
In the dear green earth, the sign of the joy of the Lord.

Laugh and be merry together, like brothers akin,
Guesting awhile in the rooms of a beautiful inn,
Glad till the dancing stops, and the life of the music ends.   15
Laugh till the game is played; and be you merry, my friends.

ENGLAND'S POET LAUREATE

From "Laugh and Be Merry" what do you discover about the poet's disposition and philosophy of life? Be specific in your answer.

SIEGFRIED SASSOON

1886–

The terrible toll that World War I took of young poets was not only in the loss of promising young lives but also in the bitterness it left with the survivors. "Let no one from henceforth," said Siegfried Sassoon, "say one word countenancing war." Sassoon was a young man of wealthy family, an Oxford graduate who wrote poetry and loved hunting and music. His life was abruptly changed by military service—as were the lives of hundreds of men. He was made a captain and was later awarded the Military Cross for bravery. His experiences convinced him of the fundamental baseness and futility of war, and his poems painted it with uncompromising realism. Much of Sassoon's writing in the twenties and thirties was milder in tone, but he will probably be best remembered for his invectives against war.

Dreamers

Soldiers are citizens of death's gray land,
    Drawing no dividend from time's tomorrows.
In the great hour of destiny they stand,
    Each with his feuds, and jealousies, and sorrows.
Soldiers are sworn to action; they must win   5
    Some flaming, fatal climax with their lives.
Soldiers are dreamers; when the guns begin
    They think of firelit homes, clean beds, and wives.

I see them in foul dugouts, gnawed by rats,
    And in the ruined trenches, lashed with rain.   10
Dreaming of things they did with balls and bats,
    And mocked by hopeless longing to regain
Bank holidays, and picture shows, and spats,
    And going to the office in the train.

Everyone Sang

The armistice of World War I came on November 11, 1918. Imagine how the sudden news affected soldiers who had gone through four hard years of fighting!

Everyone suddenly burst out singing;
And I was filled with such delight
As prisoned birds must find in freedom
Winging wildly across the white
Orchards and dark green fields; on; on; and out of sight.   5
Everyone's voice was suddenly lifted,
And beauty came like the setting sun.
My heart was shaken with tears, and horror
Drifted away. . . . O, but everyone
Was a bird; and the song was wordless; the singing will never be done.   10

A SOLDIER'S POEMS

1. How does Sassoon show his feeling toward war in "Dreamers"? What does the second line mean? (In the business world, what are dividends?) In what sense do we, in times of peace, draw dividends from the future?

2. How do some of the dreams of these soldiers suggest the difference between the fighters of the two great wars of the twentieth century and those of earlier wars?

3. Is this poem a sonnet? Prove your answer. What do you notice that is unusual about the rhyme scheme?

4. In "Everyone Sang" why is Sassoon's comparison of a soldier with a free-winging bird so appropriate? Why was the song "wordless"? In what way will the singing "never be done"?

RUPERT BROOKE

1887–1915

Rupert Brooke was outstanding among several young poets who died in World War I. "A golden young Apollo," as a friend called him, he started out life with everything in his favor: good looks, a keen mind, athletic prowess, and fine family background (his father was assistant headmaster of the Rugby school). After college he traveled extensively in 1913–14 throughout Europe, America, and the South Seas. When war broke out, he enlisted and was sent to the Dardanelles, but he never reached this destination. Death by blood poisoning overtook him on the way. The little island of Skyros in the Aegean Sea is the "corner of a foreign field that is forever England" which Brooke mentions in his sonnet "The Soldier." The manuscript of this sonnet is kept in the British Museum as a memorial of a whole generation of young men.

Brooke managed to live intensely during his few years, as is shown by the following poem, which lists all the simple things of our common life which gave him especial joy. Through perpetuating them in this much-prized poem, he did indeed "cheat drowsy Death."

The Great Lover

I have been so great a lover: filled my days
So proudly with the splendor of Love's praise,
The pain, the calm, the astonishment,
Desire illimitable, and still content,
And all dear names men use, to cheat despair,   5
For the perplexed and viewless streams that bear
Our hearts at random down the dark of life.
Now, ere the unthinking silence on that strife
Steals down, I would cheat drowsy Death so far,
My night shall be remembered for a star   10
That outshone all the suns of all men's days.
Shall I not crown them with immortal praise
Whom I have loved, who have given me, dared with me
High secrets, and in darkness knelt to see
The inenarrable° godhead of delight?   15
Love is a flame—we have beaconed the world's night;
A city—and we have built it, these and I;
An emperor—we have taught the world to die.
So, for their sakes I loved, ere I go hence,
And the high cause of Love's magnificence,   20
And to keep loyalties young, I'll write those names
Golden forever, eagles, crying flames,
And set them as a banner, that men may know,

15. *inenarrable* (ĭn′ĕ·năr′á·b'l): unspeakable; indescribable.

To dare the generations, burn, and blow
Out on the wind of Time, shining and streaming.   25

These I have loved:
                White plates and cups, clean-gleaming,
Ringed with blue lines; and feathery, fairy dust;
Wet roofs, beneath the lamplight; the strong crust
Of friendly bread; and many-tasting food;
Rainbows; and the blue bitter smoke of wood;   30
And radiant raindrops couching in cool flowers;
And flowers themselves, that sway through sunny hours,
Dreaming of moths that drink them under the moon;
Then, the cool kindliness of sheets, that soon
Smooth away trouble; and the rough male kiss   35
Of blankets; grainy wood; live hair that is
Shining and free; blue-massing clouds; the keen
Unpassioned beauty of a great machine;
The benison of hot water; furs to touch;
The good smell of old clothes; and other such—   40
The comfortable smell of friendly fingers,
Hair's fragrance, and the musty reek that lingers
About dead leaves and last year's ferns—
                        Dear names,
And thousand others throng to me! Royal flames;
Sweet water's dimpling laugh from tap or spring;   45
Holes in the ground; and voices that do sing—
Voices in laughter, too; and body's pain,
Soon turned to peace; and the deep-panting train;
Firm sands; the little dulling edge of foam
That browns and dwindles as the wave goes home;   50
And washen stones, gay for an hour; the cold
Graveness of iron; moist black earthen mold;
Sleep; and high places; footprints in the dew;
And oaks; and brown horse chestnuts, glossy-new;
And new-peeled sticks; and shining pools on grass—   55
All these have been my loves. And these shall pass.
Whatever passes not, in the great hour,
Nor all my passion, all my prayers, have power
To hold them with me through the gate of Death.
They'll play deserter, turn with the traitor breath,   60
Break the high bond we made, and sell Love's trust
And sacramental covenant to the dust.
—Oh, never a doubt but, somewhere, I shall wake,

And give what's left of love again, and make
New friends, now strangers—
                          But the best I've known,   65
Stays here, and changes, breaks, grows old, is blown
About the winds of the world, and fades from brains
Of living men, and dies.
                          Nothing remains.

O dear my loves, O faithless, once again
This one last gift I give: that after men   70
Shall know, and later lovers, far-removed,
Praise you, "All these were lovely"; say, "He loved."

The Soldier

If I should die, think only this of me:
    That there's some corner of a foreign field
That is forever England. There shall be
    In that rich earth a richer dust concealed;
A dust whom England bore, shaped, made aware,   5
    Gave, once, her flowers to love, her ways to roam,
A body of England's, breathing English air,
    Washed by the rivers, blest by suns of home.

And think, this heart, all evil shed away,
    A pulse in the eternal mind, no less   10
        Gives somewhere back the thought by England given;
Her sights and sounds; dreams happy as her day;
    And laughter, learnt of friends; and gentleness,
        In hearts at peace, under an English heaven.

LIFE AND IMMORTALITY

1. Note in "The Great Lover" the keen awareness and the vigorous enthusiasm that the poet brought to the everyday experiences of living. How many of the things listed in the poem would you choose for your personal list of "loves"? What other things would you include?

2. Look through the list to discover some original metaphors, such as the "cool kindliness" of sheets and raindrops "couching" in cool flowers.

3. In "The Soldier" how is the poet's idea of immortality linked with his ideal of patriotism? Why do you think this poem is especially prized? In what way can it be said to have universal appeal, even though the feeling expressed is toward England?

SUGGESTIONS FOR WRITING

1. Write a description of familiar objects or scenes in your life that you would consider your "loves." (If you prefer to try poetry, go ahead.) To give the reader a quick picture of a sympathetic reaction to the thing described, try to use fresh and striking metaphors as Brooke does.

2. The converse of Brooke's theme—things you hate—also makes for natural expression. Which subject—your likes or your dislikes—lends itself best to humorous treatment?

JOHN BETJEMAN
1906–

In 1959 the British literary world claimed John Betjeman (bĕtch′à·măn) as the next poet laureate. This prediction came when the rush for his *Collected Poems,* selling as many as one thousand copies a day, was said to be unmatched since the publication of Byron's *Childe Harold* in 1812.

Born of Quaker parents, Betjeman grew up in London; he was educated at Oxford but failed to get a degree because of an intense dislike for his chief instructor. As an assistant editor of *Architectural Review,* he became known for his wealth of knowledge and appreciation of English places. His guidebooks are described as "glowing." Betjeman describes the English landscape lyrically, sentimentally, and sometimes satirically.

The poet's nostalgia for the Victorian Age is evident. His poetry reveals his dislike for the planned progress of the future. He is interested in small, local, and personal things and asserts, "I write about the things I care about."

Although Betjeman is not chiefly a poet of humor, he at times delights the reader with amusing descriptions of people and scenes. *Slick But Not Streamlined* is a collection of light verse with concrete and witty observations about his country.

As a devoted member of the Anglican Church, Betjeman writes of religion with earnestness and simplicity, and sometimes with a chuckle. At times he can move from mockery to fierce satire. While working at the Ministry of Information during World War II, he wrote the frequently-quoted sardonic prayer which closes with: "But gracious Lord, whate'er shall be, Don't let anyone bomb me."

Today John Betjeman writes book reviews for the London *Daily Telegraph*. He spends most of his time, however, enjoying the countryside around his Berkshire home in Wantage; here, he says, he produces about one poem every six weeks.

The Planster's Vision

Betjeman's love for the past compels him not only to question the desecration of "the old" but also to distrust those who are responsible for planning for "the new." The satire is lacking in cruelty and spite, but Betjeman realistically pictures a state which to him is deplorable.

Cut down that timber! Bells, too many and strong,
  Pouring their music through the branches bare,
  From moon-white church-towers down the windy air
Have pealed the centuries out with Evensong.
Remove those cottages, a huddled throng!   5
  Too many babies have been born in there,
  Too many coffins, bumping down the stair,
Carried the old their garden paths along.

I have a Vision of The Future, chum,
  The workers' flats in fields of soya beans   10
  Tower up like silver pencils, score on score:
And Surging Millions hear the Challenge come
  From microphones in communal canteens
  "No Right! No Wrong! All's perfect, evermore."

Hertfordshire

I had forgotten Hertfordshire,
  The large unwelcome fields of roots
Where with my knickerbockered sire
  I trudged in syndicated shoots;

"The Planster's Vision" and "Hertfordshire" from *Collected Poems* by John Betjeman. Reprinted by permission of John Murray (Publishers) Ltd., and Houghton Mifflin Company.

And that unlucky day when I   5
   Fired by mistake into the ground
Under a Lionel Edwards° sky
   And felt disapprobation round.

The slow drive home by motor-car,
   A heavy Rover Landaulette,°   10
Through Welwyn, Hatfield, Potters Bar,
   Tweed and cigar smoke, gloom and wet:

"How many times must I explain
   The way a boy should hold a gun?"
I recollect my father's pain   15
   At such a milksop for a son.

And now I see these fields once more
   Clothed, thank the Lord, in summer green,
Pale corn waves rippling to a shore
   The shadowy cliffs of elm between,   20

Color-washed cottages reed-thatched
   And weather-boarded water mills,
Flint churches, brick and plaster patched,
   On mildly undistinguished hills—

They still are there. But now the shire   25
   Suffers a devastating change,
Its gentle landscape strung with wire,
   Old places looking ill and strange.

One can't be sure where London ends,
   New towns have filled the fields of root   30
Where father and his business friends
   Drove in the landaulette to shoot;

Tall concrete standards line the lane,
   Brick boxes glitter in the sun:
Far more would these have caused him pain   35
   Than my mishandling of a gun.

7. *Lionel Edwards:* British watercolorist (1878–   ). 10. *Landaulette* (lăn′dô·lĕt′): an automobile having an enclosed rear section with a collapsible roof and an open driver's seat.

LANDSCAPE PAINTER IN WORDS

1. What fears does Betjeman express in "The Planster's Vision"? Why does he seem to dislike planned progress? Where in the poem is there a satirical note? Describe what he foresees as future living conditions. Do you agree with the poet's point of view? Give reasons for your answer.

2. In "Hertfordshire," how many years do you think have elapsed since the incident mentioned by the poet? On revisiting Hertfordshire, what does Betjeman find unchanged? In what ways has the area changed since his boyhood?

SUGGESTION FOR WRITING

Recall a place that you knew well as a child but that has changed considerably in the last five to seven years. How has it changed? What forces have brought about these changes? Write a comparison of this place as you once knew it and as it appears to you now. Include in the composition your reaction to the changes that have occurred.

STEPHEN SPENDER

1909–

At seventeen Stephen Spender had his own printing press and was earning money by printing druggists' labels. Later he put the press to good use in printing his own poems. He did not need to depend on it for an income, however, for his father, a journalist and lecturer at Oxford, was well-to-do. Spender was able to devote himself to poetry and later to literary magazines.

At Oxford he associated with a small group of poets of the "new school," of which W. H. Auden was the leader. In its active life as well as in its poetry, this highly politically and socially conscious group interested itself in the major issues of the day. Spender's emphasis has since changed. Though still concerned with contemporary social and moral problems, today poetry for him has a far broader scope. He is not so satirical as some of the other poets of his generation, nor does he seek poetry as an escape. He thinks that poetry should say to the reader, "This is what life is like. It is even realer, less to be evaded than you thought. But I offer you an example of acceptance and understanding. Now, go back and live!"

The poetry of Brooke and Sassoon is the work of men who experienced World War I. Rupert Brooke's poems sound the note of anticipation of war's terrible price; Siegfried Sassoon gives us the full realization of it. Stephen Spender lived through World War II, during which he worked for the Churchill government. The following poem is from "Part Six 1940–1944: Poems about War" in his *Collected Poems*. An epilogue is usually a speech addressed to the audience after the conclusion of a play. This is a different kind of epilogue. The poet creates a powerful impression of the aftermath of war.

Epilogue to a Human Drama

When pavements were blown up, exposing nerves,
And the gas mains burned blue and gold,
And stucco and brick were pulverized to a cloud
Pungent with smells of mice, dust, garlic, anxiety:
When the reverberant emptied façades   5
Of the West End palaces of commerce
Isolated in a vacuum of silence, suddenly
Cracked and blazed and fell, with the seven-maned
Lions of Wrath licking the stony fragments—

Then the one voice through deserted streets   10
Was the Cassandra° bell which rang and rang and rang
Released at last by Time
To seek those fires that burst through many walls—
Prophetic doom laid bare under the nostrils,
Blood and fire streaming from the stones.   15

London burned with unsentimental dignity
Of resigned kingship: those stores and Churches
Which had glittered century-long in dusty gold
Stood near the throne of domed St. Paul's
Like courtiers round the Royal sainted martyr.   20
August shadows of night
And bursting of concentrated light
Dropped from the skies to paint a final scene
Illuminated agony of frowning stone.

11. *Cassandra* (kă·săn′drà): daughter of Troy; Apollo gave her the gift of prophecy but afterwards, in anger, decreed that no one should believe her prophecies. The word has come to mean any prophetess of evil who is not believed.

Who then can wonder that every word   25
In burning London, stepped out of a play?

On the stage, there were heroes, maidens, fools,
Victims, a Chorus. The heroes were brave,
The fools spat jokes into the skull of death,
The victims waited with the humble patience   30
Of animals trapped behind a wall
For the pickaxes to break, with light and water.
The Chorus assisted, bringing cups of tea,
Praising the heroes, deploring the morals of the wicked,
Underlining punishment, justifying Doom to Truth.   35

The Express

In this poem you can feel the speed and force of a modern express
train.

After the first powerful plain manifesto
The black statement of pistons, without more fuss
But gliding like a queen, she leaves the station.
Without bowing and with restrained unconcern
She passes the houses which humbly crowd outside,   5
The gasworks and at last the heavy page
Of death, printed by gravestones in the cemetery.
Beyond the town there lies the open country
Where, gathering speed, she acquires mystery,
The luminous self-possession of ships on ocean.   10
It is now she begins to sing—at first quite low,
Then loud, and at last with a jazzy madness—
The song of her whistle screaming at curves,
Of deafening tunnels, brakes, innumerable bolts.
And always light, aerial, underneath   15
Goes the elate meter of her wheels.
Steaming through metal landscape on her lines,
She plunges new eras of wild happiness
Where speed throws up strange shapes, broad curves,
And parallels clean like the steel of guns.   20
At last, further than Edinburgh or Rome,
Beyond the crest of the world, she reaches night
Where only a low streamline brightness
Of phosphorus on the tossing hills is white.

Ah, like a comet through flame, she moves entranced   25
Wrapt in her music no bird song, no, nor bough
Breaking with honey buds, shall ever equal.

AN OBSERVER OF MODERN LIFE

1. Describe Spender's feelings toward war as they are expressed in "Epilogue to a Human Drama." What is the toll of war in the city? In what way is the scene a drama for the poet? Compare his reaction to war with that of Brooke and Sassoon.

2. Is the poem "The Express" purely pictorial or does it offer comments on modern living as well? Older poets, like Wordsworth, for example, looked on the railroad as an ugly intrusion on the beauties of nature. What do you think is Spender's view on this matter?

UNDERSTANDING FIGURATIVE LANGUAGE

Did you notice the comparisons that Spender uses in "The Express"? There are fresh combinations of noun and modifier that label accurately what was noted. Some of the comparisons are direct; that is, they are similes beginning with *like,* as in line 3 and line 20. Others are indirect and are worth seeking out, like "the heavy page of death, printed by gravestones" in lines 6–7; "the luminous self-possession of ships" in line 10. Analyze the comparisons made in nearly every line of the poem.

DYLAN THOMAS

1914–1953

Dylan (dĭl'ăn) Thomas is one of the most celebrated poets of the twentieth century. New and dynamic language, remarkably fierce vigor of speech, vibrant imagery, and unusual rhythmical cadences characterize the poetry of this highly talented Welshman. A lecturer at Cambridge said of Dylan Thomas, "He was the most poetical poet of our time. He talked and dressed and behaved and lived like a poet; he was innocent, reckless, flamboyant, and irreverent. And his verse, too, had a romantic wildness about it that even the readers who could make nothing of it recognized as 'poetic.'" His poetry is rich with symbolism and original images. A poet who often demands much of his readers, he has been hailed as the most original and refreshing lyric genius of our time.

Thomas was born in Swansea, a seacoast town in southern Wales. Here he enjoyed a happy childhood, which he writes about in *Quite Early One Morning*, a collection of his prose and poetry. In Part I of this work the prose is especially exuberant in style. Dylan in Welsh means "sea," and he was haunted by it all his life. He lived with his wife and children in the Welsh seacoast village of Laugharne, immortalized in his radio drama *Under Milk Wood*, a play depicting life in a small Welsh village.

Writing documentary films and reading poetry for the British Broadcasting Company gave Thomas some financial security. He was most successful, however, in his American poetry-reading tours. It was while he was on his third tour that he died in New York City at the age of thirty-nine. Not long before his death he published his *Collected Poems 1934–53*. Fortunately, we can still experience the magnificent voice of Dylan Thomas by listening to the recordings he made of many of his writings.

Fern Hill

"Fern Hill," a bright and joyful picture of summer on a Welsh farm, is an echo of Dylan Thomas' youth. Childhood experiences made a deep impression on him. The carefree happiness of a young boy is suggested repeatedly throughout this poem.

Now as I was young and easy under the apple boughs
About the lilting house and happy as the grass was green,
   The night above the dingle° starry,
    Time let me hail and climb
   Golden in the heydays of his eyes,   5
And honored among wagons I was prince of the apple towns
And once below a time I lordly had the trees and leaves
    Trail with daisies and barley
  Down the rivers of the windfall light.

And as I was green and carefree, famous among the barns   10
About the happy yard and singing as the farm was home,
   In the sun that is young once only,
    Time let me play and be
   Golden in the mercy of his means,
And green and golden I was huntsman and herdsman, the calves 15
Sang to my horn, the foxes on the hills barked clear and cold,

3. *dingle:* little valley.

"Fern Hill" from *The Collected Poems of Dylan Thomas.* Copyright © 1957 by New Directions. Reprinted by permission of New Directions, and J. M. Dent & Sons Ltd.

And the sabbath rang slowly
In the pebbles of the holy streams.

All the sun long it was running, it was lovely, the hay
Fields high as the house, the tunes from the chimneys, it was air   20
 And playing, lovely and watery
  And fire green as grass.
 And nightly under the simple stars
As I rode to sleep the owls were bearing the farm away,
All the moon long I heard, blessed among stables, the nightjars°   25
 Flying with the ricks,° and the horses
  Flashing into the dark.

And then to awake, and the farm, like a wanderer white
With the dew, come back, the cock on his shoulder: it was all
 Shining, it was Adam and maiden,   30
  The sky gathered again
 And the sun grew round that very day.
So it must have been after the birth of the simple light
In the first, spinning place, the spellbound horses walking warm
 Out of the whinnying green stable   35
  On to the fields of praise.

And honored among foxes and pheasants by the gay house
Under the new made clouds and happy as the heart was long,
 In the sun born over and over,
  I ran my heedless ways,   40
 My wishes raced through the house high hay
And nothing I cared, at my sky blue trades, that time allows
In all his tuneful turning so few and such morning songs
 Before the children green and golden
  Follow him out of grace,   45

Nothing I cared, in the lamb white days, that time would take me
Up to the swallow thronged loft by the shadow of my hand,
 In the moon that is always rising,
  Nor that riding to sleep
 I should hear him fly with the high fields
And wake to the farm forever fled from the childless land.   50
Oh as I was young and easy in the mercy of his means,
  Time held me green and dying
 Though I sang in my chains like the sea.

  25. *nightjars:* a kind of night bird. 26. *ricks:* haystacks.

Do Not Go Gentle into That Good Night

A defiant attitude toward death is found in the following poem, which Thomas wrote when his father was dying.

Do not go gentle into that good night,
Old age should burn and rave at close of day;
Rage, rage against the dying of the light.

Though wise men at their end know dark is right,
Because their words had worked no lightning they   5
Do not go gentle into that good night.

Good men, the last wave by, crying how bright
Their frail deeds might have danced in a green bay,
Rage, rage against the dying of the light.

Wild men who caught and sang the sun in flight,   10
And learn, too late, they grieved it on its way,
Do not go gentle into that good night.

Grave men, near death, who see with blinding sight
Blind eyes could blaze like meteors and be gay,
Rage, rage against the dying of the light.   15

And you, my father there on the sad height,
Curse, bless, me now with your fierce tears, I pray.
Do not go gentle into that good night.
Rage, rage against the dying of the light.

The Hand That Signed the Paper Felled a City

The hand that signed the paper felled a city;
Five sovereign fingers taxed the breath,
Doubled the globe of dead and halved a country;
These five kings did a king to death.

The mighty hand leads to a sloping shoulder,   5
The finger joints are cramped with chalk;

A goose's quill has put an end to murder
That put an end to talk.

The hand that signed the treaty bred a fever,
And famine grew, and locusts came;   10
Great is the hand that holds dominion over
Man by a scribbled name.

The five kings count the dead but do not soften
The crusted wound nor pat the brow;
A hand rules pity as a hand rules heaven;   15
Hands have no tears to flow.

POEMS OF VIGOR AND SUBTLETY

1. In "Fern Hill" what are the specific scenes and childhood activities which the poet mentions? Do any of them recall experiences you yourself have had?

2. "Fern Hill" is full of striking images and of sounds that are particularly memorable. Select phrases or lines that you like—why are they effective? How does the poet create the mood of exhilaration and joy? What is the thought in the last stanza that changes the mood?

3. What is the poet's central thought in "Do Not Go Gentle into That Good Night"? To whom is he speaking? What do "good night" and "the dying of the light" symbolize? What other symbols in the poem can you interpret? Do you think this poem could have been written by an old man? Explain the reasons for your answer.

4. What does the poet say about the responsibility of a ruler? What results of signing the paper or document are mentioned? Explain the metaphor used for the five fingers of the hand.

APPRECIATING POETIC LANGUAGE

Dylan Thomas was obsessed with words that produce unusual effects. The ordinary person, although he often finds Thomas' play of words puzzling, finds himself responding to the words and phrases which this poet uses in unfamiliar ways. In "Fern Hill" you can find examples of the poet's use of original expressions. What would you normally say instead of "once below a time" (line 7); "all the sun long" (line 19); "all the moon long" (line 25); "riding to sleep" (line 49)?

Thomas' use of metaphor and simile is particularly striking. In "Fern Hill," which is rich in these vivid figures of speech, the poet helps you to see sharp images of what he is describing. Consider the comparisons which are made in

he following: "prince of the apple towns" (line 6); "in the lamb white days"
line 46); "sang in my chains like the sea" (line 54). Do you enjoy seeing
ome common thing in a new way? Find other comparisons in Thomas' poetry
vhich show a fresh use of words. No other poet is better able to use poetic
anguage.

LAURIE LEE

1914-

'n 1960 Laurie Lee gained recognition in the United States when his auto-
)iography, *Edge of Day*, was widely acclaimed. Published a year earlier in
England as *Cider with Rosie*, this work is the delightful story of Lee's boy-
iood in the west of England.

Before the first publication in 1944 of his poems, *The Sun My Monument*,
many of Lee's poems were published in magazines such as *Horizon* and *The
Listener*. Two other collections which followed are *The Blooms of Candles*
1947) and *My Many-Coated Man* (1955).

In much of his writing, Lee seems to be aware of the world's disharmony
and of the necessity to correct its disorder. Both city and country figure in
"Town Owl." "Field of Autumn," in its use of rural rather than urban images,
s perhaps more typical of Lee's poetry.

Town Owl

On eves of cold, when slow coal fires,
rooted in basements, burn and branch,
brushing with smoke the city air;

When quartered moons pale in the sky,
and neons glow along the dark   5
like deadly nightshade on a briar;

Above the muffled traffic then
I hear the owl, and at his note
I shudder in my private chair.

For like an augur he has come   10
to roost among our crumbling walls,
his blooded talons sheathed in fur.

Some secret lure of time it seems
has called him from his country wastes
to hunt a newer wasteland here.   15

And where the candelabra swung,
bright with the dancers' thousand eyes,
now his black, hooded pupils stare,

And where the silk-shoed lovers ran
with dust of diamonds in their hair,   20
he opens now his silent wing,

And, like a stroke of doom, drops down,
and swoops across the empty hall,
and plucks a quick mouse off the stair . . .

Field of Autumn

Slow moves the acid breath of noon
over the copper-coated hill,
slow from the wild crab's bearded breast
the palsied apples fall.

Like colored smoke the day hangs fire,   5
taking the village without sound;
the vulture-headed sun lies low
chained to the violet ground.

The horse upon the rocky height
rolls all the valley in his eye,   10
but dares not raise his foot or move
his shoulder from the fly.

The sheep, snail-backed against the wall,
lifts her blind face but does not know
the cry her blackened tongue gives forth   15
is the first bleat of snow.

'Each bird and stone, each roof and well,
feels the gold foot of autumn pass;
each spider binds with glittering snare
the splintered bones of grass.   20

Slow moves the hour that sucks our life,
slow drops the late wasp from the flower,
the rose tree's thread of scent draws thin—
and snaps upon the air.

IMAGERY AND REALISM

1. What incident does the poet describe in "Town Owl"? See if you can discover a deeper meaning to the poem. Why does the owl come "like an augur" (line 10)? What has happened to the city? Can you attach any significance to the last three lines? Discuss.

2. Contrast the scenery of Lee's "Field of Autumn" with that in Betjeman's "Hertfordshire" (page 105). By what details of sight and sound does Lee create the atmosphere of his poem?

CHARLES CAUSLEY

1917–

Charles Causley—poet, teacher, and broadcaster—was in the communications branch of the Royal Navy during World War II, and a good share of his poems deal with war in one or another of its phases. From 1953–56 he was literary editor of the British Broadcasting Company's West Region radio magazines: *Apollo in the West* and *Signature*. A recent collection of his poetry is entitled *Union Street*.

Causley lived for many years in Cornwall, near the seacoast, and writes of the sea with a lyrical beauty, a clearness, and freshness that has a flavor all its own. He likes to use the ballad form, and in much of his poetry, particularly his later poems, there is a sharp originality in his use of ballad meters. At times, he uses a very strict metrical form as a contrast to the emotion expressed in the poem.

Edith Sitwell, a well-known critic, characterizes "At the British War Cemetery, Bayeux," one of Causley's most powerful war poems, as "magnificent, moving, terrible." In "The Seasons in North Cornwall" are feelings, images, and musical lines not often found today in younger English poets.

At the British War Cemetery, Bayeux°

I walked where in their talking graves
And shirts of earth five thousand lay,
When history with ten feasts of fire
Had eaten the red air away.

I am Christ's boy, I cried, I bear   5
In iron hands the bread, the fishes.°
I hang with honey and with rose
This tidy wreck of all your wishes.

On your geometry of sleep
The chestnut and the fir-tree fly,   10
And lavender and marguerite
Forge with their flowers an English sky.

Turn now toward the belling town
Your jigsaws of impossible bone,
And rising read your rank of snow   15
Accurate as death upon the stone.

About your easy heads my prayers
I said with syllables of clay.
What gift, I asked, shall I bring now
Before I weep and walk away?   20

Take, they replied, the oak and laurel.
Take our fortune of tears and live
Like a spendthrift lover. All we ask
Is the one gift you cannot give.

Title: *Bayeux* (bả·yû′): small community in northwest France. 6. *the bread, the fishes:* (Matthew 14:15–21) parable of the five thousand fed by Jesus with five loaves and two fishes.

"At the British War Cemetery, Bayeux" from *Union Street* by Charles Causley. Reprinted by permission of Rupert Hart-Davis Limited.

The Seasons in North Cornwall

O spring has set off her green fuses
   Down by the Tamar° today,
And careless, like tidemarks, the hedges
   Are bursting with almond and may.

Here lie I, waiting for old summer,   5
   A red face and straw-colored hair has he:
I shall meet him on the road from Marazion°
   And the Mediterranean Sea.

September has flung a spray of rooks
   On the sea chart of the sky,   10
The tall shipmasts crack in the forest
   And the banners of autumn fly.

My room is a bright glass cabin,
   All Cornwall thunders at my door,
And the white ships of winter lie   15
   In the sea roads of the moor.

2. *Tamar* (tä'mĕr): a river in southwest England, flowing between Cornwall and Devonshire. 7. *Marazion:* a small seaport of Cornwall.

A CORNISH POET

1. Describe Causley's feelings toward war in "At the British War Cemetery, Bayeux." Point to references in the poem which suggest World War II. What is the one gift that the poet is unable to give? Compare his reaction to war with that of Brooke, Sassoon, and Spender.

2. In "The Seasons in North Cornwall" how is each season pictured by the poet? What images are especially effective in the poem? Which season do you think Causley prefers? Why?

"The Seasons in North Cornwall" from *Union Street* by Charles Causley. Reprinted by permission of Rupert Hart-Davis Limited.

READING LIST FOR MODERN POETRY

In addition to the following titles, many other anthologies of modern poetry are available. See also the collected works of the poets you have just read.

Cecil, Lord David, and Allen Tate (editors), *Modern Verse in English*
> A reasonably wide choice of poets, with representative selections arranged chronologically. Biographical notes on the fifty-five British poets included.

Cole, William (editor), *Fireside Book of Humorous Poetry*
> This collection includes old favorites, blandly funny poems, and others for more sophisticated taste.

Conquest, Robert (editor), *New Lines*
> The newest group of British poets, who call themselves the New Movement or simply the Movement, has published its own anthology.

Garrity, D. A. (editor), *New Irish Poets*

Gillis, Adolph, and W. R. Benét (editors), *Poems for Modern Youth*
> Easily understood poems.

Ledward, P., and C. Strang (editors), *Poems of This War*
> Poetry of World War II.

Le Gallienne, Richard (editor), *A Modern Book of English Verse*

Lucy, Sean, *T. S. Eliot and the Idea of Tradition*
> An examination of Eliot's influence on those who in turn have influenced him.

Parker, Elinor (editor), *100 More Story Poems*
> The humorous verse of Hillaire Belloc and W. S. Gilbert is especially enjoyable in this volume focusing on narrative poetry.

Sitwell, Dame Edith (editor), *The Atlantic Book of British and American Poetry*
> An anthology prepared by an outstanding poet and critic of poetry.

Untermeyer, Louis (editor), *Modern British Poetry*
> Editions of this comprehensive anthology have been coming out since 1920. Excellent biographical and critical materials are included.

Yeats, W. B. (editor), *The Oxford Book of Modern Verse*

FOR LISTENING

Thomas' "Do Not Go Gentle into That Good Night" has been recorded on *Many Voices 6B*. Spender's "Epilogue to a Human Drama" and Lee's "Field of Autumn" are available on *Many Voices 12A*.

MODERN BIOGRAPHY

Boswell's *Life of Samuel Johnson* is an enduring masterpiece because it gives us everything we want from a biography. It tells what we want to know about the life of a remarkable man; it is a work of art as well—that is, it is deliberately shaped and colored to produce a definite effect; and its detailed scenes and exact dialogue make it as dramatically entertaining as a good novel. There are three different kinds of excellence here, and these are very rarely found together in one biography. What we usually have instead are biographies or pseudo-biographies offering us only one of these virtues.

The supply of what we may call "standard" or "official" biographies continues, simply telling us what we ought to know about the lives of statesmen, famous authors, successful generals, and other important personages. There are plenty of these, to be read casually by the general reader and with greater interest by the historian or literary critic. But few of them make any contribution to literature.

The biography-as-work-of-art is of course far less common. In modern English literature it is chiefly associated with Lytton Strachey, whose *Eminent Victorians* and *Queen Victoria* are extremely successful examples of this form. The witty historian, Philip Guedalla (1889–1944), was not far behind Strachey, though his work is not so well known. A prolific biographer like Hesketh Pearson, with his *Gilbert and Sullivan, Shaw, Oscar Wilde,* and other informative and entertaining biographies, is somewhere between the standard type of biographer and the biographer-as-artist.

A few biographers-as-artists have succeeded not only because of the skill and talent they have brought to their work but also because they were very close, as people, to their subjects. One fascinating example of this kind of biography is the life of her father, the actor Sir Gerald du Maurier, by his daughter, Daphne, (1907–   ), the well-known novelist. Called *Gerald: A Portrait,* it is an intimate, candid, very moving account of a father by his daughter and is probably the best thing Daphne du Maurier has ever written. Oddly enough, a more recent and nearly as successful biography of this kind takes us into the theater too, for it is the life of the playwright, Frederick Lonsdale (1881–1954), also by his daughter.

It is one thing when a genuine biography, like Boswell's, offers us scenes and dialogue as entertaining as those of a good novel, and it is quite another thing when biography and fiction are inextricably mingled in one book. This "biographical fiction" or "fictionalized biography"—and both terms have been often used for it—is a very dubious form, though obviously there is a large public for it, especially in America.

In this type of book, all the more important facts of a man's life may be included, but a great many scenes, together with the dialogue they involve, are simply invented by the author. The result is a doubtful mixture, neither real biography nor out-and-out fiction, and it is all too easy, when composing a book in this fashion, to present a man in such a way that the average reader is sharply prejudiced for or against him. Although the authors of such books may do a great deal of honest research to find as much genuine biographical material as they can, their work should not be classed as biography but as fiction.

The two world wars produced a large crop of diaries, journals, memoirs, and autobiography of all kinds. But in Britain, World War I produced more literature in this form than did World War II, which offered more in quantity but less in quality. Many established English writers have experimented with semiautobiographical books, like Somerset Maugham's *The Summing Up*. But very few have published detailed journals such as Arnold Bennett (1867–1931) did, in three volumes based on his actual diaries. Some years after her death, a selection from Virginia Woolf's diaries was made. But the great autobiography covering, let us say, the last fifty years has still to make its appearance.

J. B. P.

Queen Victoria's Accession

LYTTON STRACHEY 1880–1932

Like a breath of fresh air, Lytton Strachey (lĭt'n strā'chĭ) blew the dust off the dull shelves of biography. "It is perhaps as difficult to write a good life as to live one," he said. "To preserve in a becoming brevity which excludes everything that is redundant, and nothing that is significant—that surely is the first duty of a biographer. The second, no less surely, is to maintain his own freedom of speech." These two duties he followed consistently.

Strachey was a member of a distinguished family; his father, Sir Richard

Strachey, was a general and an Indian administrator, and his cousin John is a writer and a leader in England's Labor party. After his Cambridge days Lytton became a writer of reviews and magazine articles, but his name was little known when in 1918 he published *Eminent Victorians*. In this book he "maintained his freedom of speech" by frank appraisals of four nineteenth-century figures who had become objects of hero worship. By so doing, Strachey launched a new type of biography, which brought forth many imitators. Strachey's reputation was firmly established by *Elizabeth and Essex*, a full-length biography about the sixteenth-century queen and her ill-fated lover. His best-known work is *Queen Victoria*, from which the following selection is taken.

THE NEW QUEEN was almost entirely unknown to her subjects. In her public appearances her mother had invariably dominated the scene. Her private life had been that of a novice in a convent: hardly a human being from the outside world had ever spoken to her; and no human being at all, except her mother and the Baroness Lehzen,[1] had ever been alone with her in a room. Thus it was not only the public at large that was in ignorance of everything concerning her; the inner circles of statesmen and officials and highborn ladies were equally in the dark. When she suddenly emerged from this deep obscurity, the impression that she created was immediate and profound. Her bearing at her first Council filled the whole gathering with astonishment and admiration; the Duke of Wellington, Sir Robert Peel, even the savage Croker, even the cold and caustic Greville[2]—all were completely carried away. Everything that was reported of her subsequent proceedings seemed to be of no less happy augury. Her perceptions were quick, her decisions were sensible, her language was discreet; she performed her royal duties with extraordinary facility. Among the outside public there was a great wave of enthusiasm. Sentiment and romance were coming into fashion; and the spectacle of the little girl-queen, innocent, modest, with fair hair and pink cheeks, driving through her capital, filled the hearts of the beholders with raptures of affectionate loyalty. What, above all, struck everybody with over-

---

[1] *Baroness Lehzen* (lā′tzĕn): Victoria's governess, a clergyman's daughter from Hanover, Germany.

[2] *Duke of Wellington* (1769–1852): victor over Napoleon at the battle of Waterloo, and an important leader of the Conservative party. *Sir Robert Peel* (1788–1850): a leader of the Conservative party and later Prime Minister (1841–46). *Croker:* John Wilson Croker (1780–1857), at this time retired secretary of the Admiralty, prominent member of the Conservative party, and a literary critic. *Greville* (grĕv′il): Charles C. F. Greville (1794–1865), clerk of the council, writer of a famous diary published after his death.

whelming force was the contrast between Queen Victoria and her uncles.[1] The nasty old men, debauched and selfish, pigheaded and ridiculous, with their perpetual burden of debts, confusions, and disreputabilities—they had vanished like the snows of winter, and here at last, crowned and radiant was the spring. Lord John Russell,[2] in an elaborate oration, gave voice to the general sentiment. He hoped that Victoria might prove an Elizabeth without her tyranny, an Anne without her weakness. He asked England to pray that the illustrious Princess who had just ascended the throne with the purest intentions and the justest desires might see slavery abolished, crime diminished, and education improved. He trusted that her people would henceforward derive their strength, their conduct, and their loyalty from enlightened religious and moral principles, and that, so fortified, the reign of Victoria might prove celebrated to posterity and to all the nations of the earth.

Very soon, however, there were signs that the future might turn out to be not quite so simple and roseate as a delighted public dreamed. The "illustrious Princess" might perhaps, after all, have something within her which squared ill with the easy vision of a well-conducted heroine in an edifying storybook. The purest intentions and the justest desires? No doubt; but was that all? To those who watched closely, for instance, there might be something ominous in the curious contour of that little mouth. When, after her first Council, she crossed the anteroom and found her mother waiting for her, she said, "And now, Mamma, am I really and truly Queen?" "You see, my dear, that it is so." "Then, dear Mamma, I hope you will grant me the first request I make to you, as Queen. Let me be by myself for an hour." For an hour she remained in solitude. Then she reappeared, and gave a significant order: her bed was to be moved out of her mother's room. It was the doom of the Duchess of Kent. The long years of waiting were over at last; the moment of a lifetime had come; her daughter was Queen of England; and that very moment brought her own annihilation. She found herself, absolutely and irretrievably, shut off from every vestige of influence, of confidence, of power. She was surrounded, indeed, by all the outward signs of respect and consideration; but that only made the inward truth of her position the more intolerable. Through the mingled formalities of court etiquette and filial duty she could never penetrate to Victoria. She was unable to conceal her disap-

---

[1] *her uncles:* Victoria's father, who died when she was less than a year old, was the Duke of Kent, one of the four sons of George III. Two of these sons became kings as George IV and William IV. When William died in 1837, Victoria was heir to the throne.

[2] *Lord John Russell* (1792–1878): a leader of the Liberal party.

pointment and rage. *"Il n'y a plus d'avenir pour moi,"* she exclaimed to Madame de Lieven; *"je ne suis plus rien."* [1] For eighteen years, she said, this child had been the sole object of her existence, of her thoughts, her hopes, and now—no! she would not be comforted, she had lost everything, she was to the last degree unhappy. Sailing, so gallantly and so pertinaciously, through the buffeting storms of life, the stately vessel, with sails still swelling and pennons flying, had put into harbor at last; to find nothing—a land of bleak desolation.

Within a month of the accession the realities of the new situation assumed a visible shape. The whole royal household moved from Kensington to Buckingham Palace, and, in the new abode, the Duchess of Kent was given a suite of apartments entirely separate from the Queen's. By Victoria herself the change was welcomed, though, at the moment of departure, she could afford to be sentimental. "Though I rejoice to go into B. P. for many reasons," she wrote in her diary, "it is not without feeling of regret that I shall bid adieu forever to this my birthplace, where I have been born and bred, and to which I am really attached!" Her memory lingered for a moment over visions of the past: her sister's wedding, pleasant balls and delicious concerts . . . and there were other recollections. "I have gone through painful and disagreeable scenes here, 'tis true," she concluded, "but still I am fond of the poor old palace."

[Here follows a long discussion of two of the Queen's advisers, Baroness Lehzen and Baron Stockmar, a German doctor who had proved his sagacity as adviser to Victoria's Uncle Leopold, brother of Victoria's mother and king of Belgium.]

With Lehzen to supervise every detail of her conduct, with Stockmar in the next room, so full of wisdom and experience of affairs, with her uncle Leopold's letters, too, pouring out so constantly their stream of encouragements, general reflections, and highly valuable tips, Victoria, even had she been without other guidance, would have stood in no lack of private counselors. But other guidance she had; for all these influences paled before a new star, of the first magnitude, which, rising suddenly upon her horizon, immediately dominated her life.

William Lamb, Viscount Melbourne, was fifty-eight years of age, and had been for the last three years Prime Minister of England. In every outward respect he was one of the most fortunate of mankind. He had been born into the midst of riches, brilliance, and power. Nature had given him beauty and brains; the unexpected death of an elder brother

[1] *Il . . . rien:* "There is no more future for me. I am no longer anything."

brought him wealth, a peerage, and the possibility of high advancement. Bound to succeed, and to succeed easily, he was gifted with so fine a nature that his success became him. His mind, at once supple and copious, his temperament, at once calm and sensitive, enabled him not merely to work, but to live with perfect facility and with the grace of strength. In society he was a notable talker, a captivating companion, a charming man. If one looked deeper, one saw at once that he was not ordinary, that the piquancies of his conversation and his manner—his free-and-easy vaguenesses, his abrupt questions, his lollings and loungings, his innumerable oaths—were something more than an amusing ornament, were the outward manifestations of an individuality that was fundamental. . . .

And now, with old age upon him, his life took a sudden, new, extraordinary turn. He became, in the twinkling of an eye, the intimate adviser and the daily companion of a young girl who had stepped all at once from a nursery to a throne. . . . However, he was used to delicacies, and he met the situation with consummate success. His behavior was from the first moment impeccable. His manner toward the young Queen mingled, with perfect facility, the watchfulness and the respect of a statesman and a courtier with the tender solicitude of a parent. He was at once reverential and affectionate, at once the servant and the guide. At the same time the habits of his life underwent a surprising change. His comfortable, unpunctual days became subject to the unaltering routine of a palace; no longer did he sprawl on sofas; not a single "damn" escaped his lips. The man of the world who had been the friend of Byron and the Regent, the talker whose paradoxes had held Holland House enthralled, the cynic whose ribaldries had enlivened so many deep potations, the lover whose soft words had captivated such beauty and such passion and such wit, might now be seen, evening after evening, talking with infinite politeness to a schoolgirl, bolt upright, amid the silence and the rigidity of court etiquette.

On her side Victoria was instantaneously fascinated by Lord Melbourne. The good report of Stockmar had no doubt prepared the way; Lehzen was wisely propitiated; and the first highly favorable impression was never afterward belied. She found him perfect; and perfect in her sight he remained. Her absolute and unconcealed adoration was very natural; what innocent young creature could have resisted, in any circumstances, the charm and the devotion of such a man? But, in her situation, there was a special influence which gave a peculiar glow to all she felt. After years of emptiness and dullness and suppression she had come suddenly, in the heyday of youth, into freedom and power. She was mistress of herself, of great domains and palaces; she was Queen of England. Responsibilities and difficulties she might have, no doubt, and in heavy measure; but one feeling dominated and absorbed all others—the feeling of joy. Everything pleased her. She was in high spirits from morning till night. Mr. Creevey,[1] grown old now, and very near his end, catching a glimpse of her at Brighton, was much amused, in his sharp fashion, by the ingenuous gaiety of "little Vic."—"A more homely[2] little being you never beheld, when she is at her ease, and she is evidently dying to be always more so. She laughs in real earnest, opening her mouth as wide as it can go, showing not very pretty gums. . . . She eats quite as heartily as she laughs, I think I may say she gobbles. . . . She blushes and laughs every instant in so natural a way as to disarm anybody." But it was not merely when she was laughing or gobbling that she enjoyed herself; the performance of her official duties gave her intense satisfaction. "I really have immensely to do," she wrote in her *Journal* a few days after her accession; "I receive so many communications from my Ministers, but I like it very much." And again, a week later, "I repeat what I said before that I have so many communications from the Ministers, and from me to them, and I get so many papers to sign every day, that I have always a very great deal to do. I delight in this work." Through the girl's immaturity the vigorous predestined tastes of the woman were pushing themselves into existence with eager velocity, with delicious force.

One detail of her happy situation deserves particular mention. Apart from the splendor of her social position and the momentousness of her political one, she was a person of great wealth. As soon as Parliament met, an annuity of £385,000 was settled upon her. When the expenses of her household had been discharged, she was left with £68,000 a year of her own. She enjoyed, besides, the revenues of the Duchy of Lancaster, which amounted annually to over £27,000. The first use to which she put her money was characteristic: she paid off her father's debts. In money matters, no less than in other matters, she was determined to be correct. She had the instincts of a man of business; and she never could have borne to be in a position that was financially unsound.

With youth and happiness gilding every hour, the days passed merrily enough. And each day hinged upon Lord Melbourne. Her diary shows

---

[1] *Mr. Creevey:* Thomas Creevey (1764–1838), well-known London Whig (earlier name for Liberal). His journals give a valuable picture of the late Georgian era.

[2] *homely:* In English usage, this word means informal or unaffected in manners.

us, with undiminished clarity, the life of the young sovereign during the early months of her reign—a life satisfactorily regular, full of delightful business, a life of simple pleasures, mostly physical—riding, eating, dancing—a quick, easy, highly unsophisticated life, sufficient unto itself. The light of the morning is upon it; and, in the rosy radiance, the figure of "Lord M." emerges, glorified and supreme. If she is the heroine of the story, he is the hero; but indeed they are more than hero and heroine, for there are no other characters at all. Lehzen, the Baron, Uncle Leopold, are unsubstantial shadows—the incidental supers of the piece. Her paradise was peopled by two persons, and surely that was enough. One sees them together still, a curious couple, strangely united in those artless pages, under the magical illumination of that dawn of eighty years ago; the polished high fine gentleman with the whitening hair and the whiskers and the thick dark eyebrows and the mobile lips and the big expressive eyes; and beside him the tiny Queen—fair, slim, elegant, active, in her plain girl's dress and little tippet, looking up at him earnestly, adoringly, with eyes blue and projecting, and half-open mouth. So they appear upon every page of the *Journal;* upon every page Lord M. is present, Lord M. is speaking, Lord M. is being amusing, instructive, delightful, and affectionate at once, while Victoria drinks in the honeyed words, laughs till she shows her gums, tries hard to remember, and runs off, as soon as she is left alone, to put it all down. Their long conversations touched upon a multitude of topics. Lord M. would criticize books, throw out a remark or two on the British Constitution, make some passing reflections on human life, and tell story after story of the great people of the eighteenth century. Then there would be business—a dispatch perhaps from Lord Durham in Canada, which Lord M. would read. But first he must explain a little. "He said that I must know that Canada originally belonged to the French, and was only ceded to the English in 1760, when it was taken in an expedition under Wolfe: 'a very daring enterprise,' he said. Canada was then entirely French, and the British only came afterward. . . . Lord M. explained this very clearly (and much better than I have done) and said a good deal more about it. He then read me Durham's dispatch, which is a very long one and took him more than ½ an hour to read. Lord M. read it beautifully with that fine soft voice of his, and with so much expression, so that it is needless to say I was much interested by it." And then the talk would take a more personal turn. Lord M. would describe his boyhood, and she would learn that "he wore his hair long, as all boys then did, till he was 17 (how handsome he must have looked!)." Or she would find out about his queer tastes and habits—

how he never carried a watch, which seemed quite extraordinary. " 'I always ask the servant what o'clock it is, and then he tells me what he likes,' said Lord M." Or, as the rooks wheeled about round the trees, "in a manner which indicated rain," he would say that he could sit looking at them for an hour, and "was quite surprised at my disliking them. . . . Lord M. said, 'The rooks are my delight.' "

The day's routine, whether in London or at Windsor, was almost invariable. The morning was devoted to business and Lord M. In the afternoon the whole court went out riding. The Queen, in her velvet riding habit, and a top hat with a veil draped about the brim, headed the cavalcade; and Lord M. rode beside her. The lively troupe went fast and far, to the extreme exhilaration of Her Majesty. Back in the palace again, there was still time for a little more fun before dinner—a game of battledore and shuttlecock, perhaps, or a romp along the galleries with some children. Dinner came, and the ceremonial decidedly tightened. The gentleman of highest rank sat on the right hand of the Queen; on her left— it soon became an established rule—sat Lord Melbourne. After the ladies had left the dining room, the gentlemen were not permitted to remain behind for very long; indeed, the short time allowed them for their wine drinking formed the subject—so it was rumored—of one of the very few disputes between the Queen and her Prime Minister; but her determination carried the day, and from that moment after-dinner drunkenness began to go out of fashion. When the company was reassembled in the drawing room the etiquette was stiff. For a few moments the Queen spoke in turn to each one of her guests; and during these short uneasy colloquies the aridity of royalty was likely to become painfully evident. One night, Mr. Greville, the Clerk of the Privy Council, was present; his turn soon came; the middle-aged, hard-faced *viveur*[1] was addressed by his young hostess. "Have you been riding today, Mr. Greville?" asked the Queen. "No, Madam, I have not," replied Mr. Greville. "It was a fine day," continued the Queen. "Yes, Madam, a very fine day," said Mr. Greville. "It was rather cold, though," said the Queen. "It was rather cold, Madam," said Mr. Greville. "Your sister, Lady Frances Egerton, rides, I think, doesn't she?" said the Queen. "She does ride sometimes Madam," said Mr. Greville. There was a pause, after which Mr. Greville ventured to take the lead, though he did not venture to change the subject. "Has your Majesty been riding today?" asked Mr. Greville. "Oh, yes, a very long ride," answered the Queen with animation. "Has your Majesty got a nice horse?" said Mr. Greville. "Oh, a very nice horse,"

---

[1] *viveur* (vē·vûr′): one who lives at a fast and reckless pace.

said the Queen. It was over. Her Majesty gave a smile and an inclination of the head, Mr. Greville a profound bow, and the next conversation began with the next gentleman. When all the guests had been disposed of, the Duchess of Kent sat down to her whist, while everybody else was ranged about the round table. Lord Melbourne sat beside the Queen, and talked pertinaciously—very often apropos to the contents of one of the large albums of engravings with which the round table was covered —until it was half-past eleven and time to go to bed.

Occasionally, there were little diversions: the evening might be spent at the opera or at the play. Next morning the royal critic was careful to note down her impressions. "It was Shakespeare's tragedy of *Hamlet,* and we came in at the beginning of it. Mr. Charles Kean (son of old Kean) acted the part of Hamlet, and I must say beautifully. His conception of this very difficult, and I may almost say incomprehensible, character is admirable; his delivery of all the fine long speeches quite beautiful; he is excessively graceful and all his actions and attitudes are good, though not at all goodlooking in face. . . . I came away just as *Hamlet* was over." Later on, she went to see Macready in *King Lear.* The story was new to her; she knew nothing about it, and at first she took very little interest in what was passing on the stage; she preferred to chatter and laugh with the Lord Chamberlain. But, as the play went on, her mood changed; her attention was fixed, and then she laughed no more. Yet she was puzzled; it seemed a strange, a horrible business. What did Lord M. think? Lord M. thought it was a very fine play, but to be sure, "a rough, coarse play, written for those times, with exaggerated characters." "I'm glad you've seen it," he added. But undoubtedly, the evenings which she enjoyed most were those on which there was dancing. She was always ready enough to seize any excuse—the arrival of cousins—a birthday—a gathering of young people—to give the command for that. Then, when the band played, and the figures of the dancers swayed to the music, and she felt her own figure swaying too, with youthful spirits so close on every side—then her happiness reached its height, her eyes sparkled, she must go on and on into the small hours of the morning. For a moment Lord M. himself was forgotten.

The months flew past. The summer was over: "the pleasantest summer I ever passed in my life, and I shall never forget this first summer of my reign." With surprising rapidity, another summer was upon her. The coronation came and went—a curious dream. The antique, intricate, endless ceremonial worked itself out as best it could, like some machine of gigantic complexity which was a little out of order. The small central figure went through her gyrations. She sat; she walked; she prayed; she carried about an orb that was almost too heavy to hold; the Archbishop of Canterbury came and crushed a ring upon the wrong finger, so that she was ready to cry out with the pain; old Lord Rolle tripped up in his mantle and fell down the steps as he was doing homage; she was taken into a side chapel, where the altar was covered with a tablecloth, sandwiches, and bottles of wine; she perceived Lehzen in an upper box and exchanged a smile with her as she sat, robed and crowned, on the Confessor's throne.[1] "I shall ever remember this day as the proudest of my life," she noted. But the pride was soon merged once more in youth and simplicity. When she returned to Buckingham Palace at last she was not tired; she ran up to her private rooms, doffed her splendors, and gave her dog Dash its evening bath.

Life flowed on again with its accustomed smoothness—though, of course, the smoothness was occasionally disturbed. . . .

[1] *the Confessor's throne:* the coronation throne of Edward the Confessor, next to the last of the Saxon kings before the Norman Conquest.

A YOUNG QUEEN

1. What does Victoria's relationship with her mother, as briefly described here, suggest to you about her character? about the demands of being a country's ruler?

2. Summarize your impression of Victoria and Lord Melbourne together. Why did Melbourne appeal to Victoria so greatly? Do you think she would become critical of him as she grew older? Why or why not?

3. In what ways did Victoria show the common sense of a mature woman? In what ways, the lively disposition of a young girl? Can you point out examples of the use of irony in describing her?

4. What do you think of the usual evening activities at the palace? What qualities that we think of as characteristically "Victorian" did they have?

5. What very human touch comes at the end of Victoria's coronation day?

6. The interest of the whole world was centered on the coronation of Elizabeth II of England in June 1953. What reasons can you give for the interest of other nations in this event? How did this coronation differ from that of all preceding monarchs? What parts of the coronation ritual mentioned by Strachey were observed in 1953?

SUGGESTION FOR WRITING

As a project requiring some outside reading, compare and contrast the personalities of Elizabeth I, Victoria, and Elizabeth II on their accession to the throne. Also compare briefly their participation in national affairs.

The Launching of *H.M.S. Pinafore*

HESKETH PEARSON 1887–

After finishing Bedford Grammar School, Pearson "wasted" (as he said) two years as a clerk in a London shipping office. In 1911 he went on the stage, where he remained for many years, except for the brief interval of World War I. Since his theatrical experience brought him in touch with many of the leading producers of the time, it was natural that several subjects of his biographies should have been persons connected with the stage.

In 1931 Pearson gave up acting for writing. He has produced an imposing array of books, mainly biographies, but also some essays of travel and criticism. Among his best-known books are *Tom Paine, G.B.S.: A Full Length Portrait* (George Bernard Shaw), and biographies of Benjamin Disraeli (entitled *Dizzy*) and Sir Walter Scott.

In earlier chapters of his double biography *Gilbert and Sullivan,* Pearson brings out the difference in background of the partners: Gilbert, of the comfortable middle class, with opportunities for attending Oxford and studying law—Sullivan, the son of a poorly paid clarinet player in a theater orchestra. Their particular talents were evident early in life. Gilbert had written fifteen plays by the time he was twenty-five. Sullivan entered the choir of Chapel Royal at twelve years of age and composed madrigals in bed after lights were out. Through scholarships he was able to attend the Royal Academy of Music and the Conservatory at Leipzig, where he began to compose seriously.

In disposition the two men were quite different. Gilbert had a sharp tongue and often "carried a chip on his shoulder." The rehearsals of his plays were sometimes punctuated by his outbursts of temper. On the other hand, the handsome, sweet-tempered Sullivan charmed everyone who met him and was constantly being helped to new opportunities by his friends. He became a great favorite of the royal family and was knighted in 1883 on the recommendation of Prime Minister Gladstone.

Gilbert and Sullivan began their collaboration in 1870 at the suggestion of Richard D'Oyly Carte, a theater manager. *Trial by Jury* was the first of their famous light operas. *H.M.S. Pinafore* was launched in 1877.

JUST BEFORE the end of the year Sullivan received the scenario *H.M.S. Pinafore* from Gilbert, who said: "I have little doubt whatever but that you will be pleased with it." Sullivan was so much pleased with it that, returning home, he began to work on it at once, in spite of the most

"The Launching of *H.M.S. Pinafore*," from *Gilbert and Sullivan* by Hesketh Pearson, published by Hamish Hamilton Ltd. Reprinted by permission of the author.

violent attacks of illness. Throughout the entire period of composition he was racked with pain, and only managed to complete the work between paroxysms of agony which almost left him insensible.

Paroxysms of a different kind were taking place on the stage during rehearsals. Gilbert was already enforcing those methods of production which were to make his name a byword in the profession and revolutionize the art of dramatic presentation. He had learned from Robertson that, in drama, the whole was greater than the part, and he was busy subordinating his actors to the play. He regarded each of his librettos as a composer regards a symphony, which can be wrecked by the playing of a single false note, and he determined from the outset to achieve perfect harmony from his orchestra of actors. Every word had to be said with a certain inflection. Every movement had to be made in a certain manner, every position had to be judged to a square inch, every piece of "business" had to be considered in its relation to the scene. The actors were not allowed, as in the old days, to emerge for an instant from the frame of the picture he was trying to create. They were like chessmen on a board, to be moved at the discretion of the player-producer; they were like marionettes, whose motions were governed by the master; they were the members of a team, under the strict discipline of its captain.

For this reason he preferred his actors to be novices, who could be taught by himself and would not resent the teaching. For this reason, too, he arrived at the first rehearsal with a fairly complete mental picture of all the moves, all the inflections, all the "business," and all the positions of all the actors at every moment of the play. For hour after hour before the commencement of rehearsals, he would sit at his desk with replicas of the scenes on a scale of half an inch to a foot, with blocks of wood three inches high representing the males, two and a half inches high representing the females, and work out every detail of the production. It was not likely therefore that he was going to stand any nonsense from an actor who was solely concerned with his part and who did not mind what happened to the play so long as he made a personal success. At the rehearsals of *Pinafore* a player of the older school refused to repeat for perhaps the fiftieth time a piece of "business" which Gilbert was patiently instructing him to do.

"No, sir, I object," said the actor warmly. "I have been on the stage quite long enough."

"Quite," agreed Gilbert, and dismissed him on the spot.

Gilbert could never see eye-to-eye with people who considered that their proper place was in the center of the stage, and when a lady who was rehearsing the part of Josephine in *Pinafore* pointed out that she had always occupied that position in Italian opera, he remarked:

"Unfortunately this is not Italian opera, but only a low burlesque of the worst possible kind."

The lady continued her career in Italian opera.

Another well-known actress who was cast for a part in *Pinafore* walked out of the theater when she heard that a newcomer with no experience named Jessie Bond was to play in her scenes. Though upsetting at the time, it turned out luckily for Gilbert and Sullivan, as Jessie Bond became one of the most popular Savoy favorites.

Explosions between producer and actors were frequent in the early days, though when Gilbert had gained the complete ascendancy over his actors that had always been his aim, their occurrence was rare. His anger only flashed out when anyone questioned his authority, and his wit was usually confined to such harmless squibs as that recorded by Barrington:

"Cross left on that speech, I think, Barrington, and sit on the skylight over the saloon, pensively," advised Gilbert at a rehearsal of *Pinafore*.

The actor did so, but the stage carpenter had sewn the skylight with packthread and it collapsed under Barrington's fourteen stone.[1]

"That's expensively," remarked Gilbert.

H.M.S. Pinafore was produced on May 25th, 1878, and, its merits apart, caused something of a sensation because of the caricature of W. H. Smith, the publisher, who had recently been appointed First Lord of the Admiralty by Disraeli. For some of the lyrics Gilbert had drawn on the *Bab Ballads,*[2] one of which he adapted for his present purpose. This cutting ridicule of the political game, together with the satire on blatant patriotism in the same opera, reveals a vital aspect of Gilbert's character and explains why he had to wait so long for a knighthood.

It must be repeated that the qualities of wariness and daring were mixed in his nature in about equal proportions; and also, it may be added, stupidity and insight. He was a typical Briton with a streak of genius, possibly the only known example. He could see through a thing, but he could not see around it. He was visited with sudden flashes of reality, but he was not gifted with a steady vision. He had acute perceptions, but no

---

[1] *fourteen stone:* 196 pounds. The British use the unit *stone* (14 pounds) for heavy weights.

[2] *Bab Ballads:* verses written and illustrated by Gilbert for *Fun* magazine in 1869. Cleverly written, they satirize amiably the violence and crime so evident in London at that time. The collection made Gilbert famous as a literary figure.

guiding philosophy. He was a respectable man who made fun of respectability, a sentimentalist who laughed at sentiment, a patriot who ridiculed patriotism. Again and again, at the bidding of some powerful intuition, he exposed a social or national absurdity, but as often as not he failed to see the point of his exposure and fell back upon a piece of conventional claptrap which was equally typical of him. His sudden exhibitions of daring and insight, coupled with his native caution and conventionality, made his work uneven and incalculable, and it was Sullivan's music that rendered it wholly palatable to the Victorians. The Englishman is perhaps the only man in the world who can laugh at himself; add music to the satire and he brings the house down, for music removes the sting of reality. Nevertheless, the chief powers in the land never quite got over the "contempt of court" shown in *Trial by Jury,* the contempt in *Pinafore,* and the continuous digs at authority in the rest of the operas, culminating with the contempt of the Royal Court in *Utopia;* and they took their only possible revenge. The average Englishman laughed, applauded, and whistled the delectable tunes; the important Englishman watched, smiled wryly, and sometimes writhed inwardly.

Owing to the fact that London was visited by a heat wave that summer, the audiences at the Opera Comique varied in size and the directors had periodical fits of panic. They announced the withdrawal of the piece about once a fortnight and canceled the announcement whenever the receipts went up. D'Oyly Carte calmed them to the best of his ability, but both he and the company were kept on tenterhooks for months owing to the nervous condition of his codirectors. Then two things happened to give the show a fillip. Sullivan, who was conducting the Promenade Concerts at Covent Garden, included an arrangement of the *Pinafore* music in one evening's program. It was liked so much that crowds of concertgoers visited the opera, which was running to good houses by the end of August. Next came the news that *Pinafore* had taken New York by storm and was playing to enormous business at no less than eight theaters; and since England was just beginning to model her taste on that of America, and America was just beginning to accept everything English as a model of taste, *Pinafore* soon became the rage in both countries.

Of course it was pirated in America. There was no copyright agreement between the two countries; and unless the author of a play could produce it on the spot, before anyone else could steal it and produce it first, he could whistle for his royalties. American publishers and theatrical managers made fortunes out of *Pinafore* while Gilbert and Sullivan gnashed their teeth in impotence. Adding insult to injury, the Americans put in a number of local "gags," songs about "pants" (which they have an incurable habit of rhyming with "dance")[1] and suchlike unsuitable sallies. Gilbert, Sullivan, and Carte decided that something had to be done about it, and the latter sailed for America to take stock of the situation.

In the summer of that year, a long report from Carte persuaded Gilbert and Sullivan to visit America in order to give their authorized version of *Pinafore* in New York. Before leaving, Sullivan underwent an operation for crushing the stone in the kidney, and received felicitations upon its success from the Prince of Wales and the Duke of Edinburgh. Gilbert was suffering from a different complaint. "I will not have another libretto of mine produced if the Americans are going to steal it," he declared, "not that I need the money so much, but it upsets my digestion."

Reporters swooped down upon them the instant their boat reached New York, and the American public, through the medium of its press, was quickly introduced to the two famous visitors: the librettist, a tall military-looking gentleman, with fair hair, rosy complexion, bright blue eyes, and high massive forehead, who spoke quickly and jerkily in a deep hearty voice; the composer, a short, plump, daintily-clad person, with a thick neck, dark hair and eyes, olive-tinted mobile face, sensuous lips, and tender expression, whose voice was wistful and full of feeling. They were interviewed so thoroughly that Sullivan wondered "Where do all these Americans end?" and Gilbert ceased to wonder. Each of them took pains to make it known that he had done far better work than *Pinafore* unaided by the other. Gilbert said it was a little mortifying to find that a trifle like *Pinafore* should so far exceed in success the plays he held in more serious estimation. Sullivan regretted that his oratorios and other compositions of a more classical and ambitious style had not received the popular approval accorded to *Pinafore*. Neither of them felt unduly flattered when some judge, in an afterdinner speech, hoped they would be brought before him on the charge of being drunk and disorderly, so that he might repay the pleasure *Pinafore* had given him by letting them off. Nor was Gilbert altogether pleased when an American impresario had the bright idea that they might heap up a pile of dollars if only they would prepare an American version of the piece.

"Say now, Mr. Gilbert," said this gentleman, "all you've got to do is to change H.M.S. to U.S.S., pull down the British ensign, hoist the stars

---

[1] *pants:* The British used only the word *trousers,* and pronounced *dance* as *däns,* so that *pants* (pănts) and *dance* (däns) seemed crude.

and stripes, and anchor your ship off Jersey beach. Then, in place of your First Lord of the Admiralty, introduce our navy boss. All the rewriting you'd want would be some new words to Bill Bobstay's song—just let him remain an American instead of an Englishman. Now ain't that a cute notion, sir?"

"Well, yes," replied Gilbert thoughtfully, "perhaps your suggestion is a good one, but I see some difficulties in carrying it out. In the first place I'm afraid I'm not sufficiently versed in your vernacular to translate my original English words. The best I could do would be something like this:

> He is Ameri-can!
>   Though he himself has said it,
>   'Tis not much to his credit,
> That he is Ameri-can!
> For he might have been a Dutchman,
> An Irish, Scotch, or such a man,
> Or perhaps an Englishman!
>   But in spite of hanky-panky,
>   He remains a true-born Yankee,
> A cute Ameri-can."

The impresario was delighted; he swore it would save the situation and set New York ablaze. After a few moments' reflection Gilbert gravely abandoned the notion, on the ground that such words might impair the friendly relations between the two countries.

While Gilbert and Sullivan were rehearsing their opera and being entertained and interviewed until their heads swam, the barrel organs of New York were churning out the tunes of *Pinafore,* the music shops were flooded with its scores, most of the theaters were playing it, and such was the demand for it throughout the States that one paper announced: "At present there are forty-two companies playing *Pinafore* about the country. Companies formed after six p.m. yesterday are not included." The authorized edition of the work appeared on December 1st at the Fifth Avenue Theater and received an ovation. Everyone in the audience was of course already familiar with the airs, but the orchestration, with which the numerous American bands had not troubled their heads, was a revelation. It was greeted as a comparatively new work and it looked as if a ninth company were about to coin money in the city. Gilbert, in his speech before the curtain after the first performance, said: "It has been our purpose to produce something that should be innocent but not imbecile." That was the slogan of the collaborators: clean but clever fun.

FAMOUS COLLABORATORS

1. What differences between Gilbert and Sullivan in appearance and disposition are brought out here? Is it surprising that these two men worked so well together? Discuss.

2. Would you have liked being an actor under Gilbert's direction? If you have had any experience in amateur dramatics, discuss whether actors should be allowed to have some part in the stage direction.

3. Pearson says that some of the songs from *Pinafore* illustrate Gilbert's ridicule of the English ruling classes. What would this have to do with Gilbert's having to "wait so long for a knighthood"? If you have seen other Gilbert and Sullivan operettas, discuss wherein the ridicule lies.

4. What do you think of the proposed American version of *Pinafore?* How do you suppose Americans would have reacted to the words suggested for "He is an Englishman"? Pearson says the English are the only people who can laugh at themselves. If you think Americans also have this faculty, give some examples to prove it.

THE POWER OF WORDS

WORD DISCRIMINATION

Pearson uses five words descriptive of various kinds of humor. A *caricature* is an exaggerated picture in writing or in drawing. It most commonly applies to a person, as the caricature of the First Lord of the Admiralty in *H.M.S. Pinafore. Ridicule* is a more general word. It may be applied to a specific person, an idea, or a whole social system, as in "ridicule of the political game." *Satire* is a special kind of ridicule, employing subtlety and cleverness. This word is also used to describe a type of literature. *Absurdity* applies to the innate quality in something that lays it open to ridicule. (Gilbert exposed national absurdities.) A *sally* is a witty remark. Which of these words can be used as verbs? From which can adjectives be made?

Go Where Glory Waits Thee

FRANK O'CONNOR 1903–

You already know Frank O'Connor ("The Man of the House," page 69) as one of the best contemporary Irish short-story writers. In the following autobiographical selection he tells with dry and subtle humor of his own

"Go Where Glory Waits Thee" by Frank O'Connor. Copyright 1960 by Frank O'Connor. Originally appeared in *The New Yorker.* Reprinted by permission of Harold Matson Co.

fears, disappointments, aspirations, and faith as a young man who discovered that he was to become a writer. Here is an unusual opportunity to learn firsthand of the background and early trials of a man whose work you have studied and to compare O'Connor's treatment in two quite different literary forms. After reading this selection, you may be able to judge how much—and in what ways—O'Connor has drawn upon his own background for "The Man of the House."

Since it first appeared in print, "Go Where Glory Waits Thee" has been published as part of a full-length autobiography entitled *An Only Child*, which was published in 1961 and met with immediate critical acclaim.

ALL I ever wanted from life was an education. Apart from any liking I may have had for it, I knew it was the key to success. Everyone admitted that. They said you could get nowhere without an education. They blamed their own failure in life on the lack of it. You should learn everything, they said, because it all came in useful—every scrap of it. If Father was no more than a casual laborer and never earned more than fourteen or fifteen shillings a week, that was because he hadn't the education like Mr. Moynihan down the road had it. If Mother was only a charwoman who went out every day to work in the big houses on the river in Cork, it was because she hadn't the education, either. So I knew it was up to me to get the education, and, by the Lord, when I did, things were going to be different in the home. Father would have to treat me with proper respect, and Mother, instead of going out to work, would stay at home and look after me. As for me, I'd look after everybody.

But the difficulty was to get started. It seemed to be extremely hard to get an education, or even—at the level on which we lived—to find out what education was. Education, of course, implied nice manners as opposed to coarse ones—I could see that for myself—and I set out to be a polite and good-living boy, which in the main I was, except when the business of getting an education became too much for me and I had to go to confession and tell the priest that I had been disobedient and rude to my parents. Education was also speaking correctly, and I listened with great admiration to the priest on Sunday and then came home and imitated him in front of the mirror. But in moments of depression I realized that these were only the things that went with education, not education itself. The priest not only spoke well but he also knew Latin. Latin was clearly a great part of education, so I got Mother to teach me the Latin hymns she knew, like the "Stabat Mater" and the "Ave Maris Stella," and at intervals I had the excited feeling that I really was getting somewhere at last, but those fits of exultation rarely lasted for more than an evening, and I woke next morning with the foreboding that I was never going to get any education.

All that anybody seemed able to tell you about how you got an education was that you should "stick to the books." Now, I didn't have any books, but I did read comics and boy's weeklies, and I stuck to them with great enthusiasm. I don't mean that I didn't enjoy them for their own sakes, for I did. I lived in a sort of social vacuum between the kids of my own class, who had no ambitions to be educated, and the class above ours —policemen and minor officials—whose sons got educated whether they wanted to or not. The latter lived down the Ballyhooley Road, and the boys gathered at night by the gas lamp. Between them, they produced all those indications of a proper education I learned to recognize from the boy's weeklies—a bicycle, or a stamp album, or a real football, or boxing gloves, or a cricket bat, or occasionally even a copy of *The Boy's Own Paper,* which cost sixpence and had halftone illustrations, as compared with the weeklies I could afford, which cost a penny and only had line drawings. To both of those groups I must have seemed a freak—to the poorer kids because I spoke in what probably sounded like an affected accent, and used strange words I had picked up from my reading and didn't even know how to pronounce; to the others because I was only a ragged laney boy who put on airs and tried to force his company on them. So, though I was a fairly normal child who did his best to fit in with others, the others could never fit in with me, and for a lot of the time I had to live in my fantasy. It wasn't such a bad place to live if only the bottom weren't always falling out of it.

There was nothing exclusive about my approach to the world of make-believe—cops and robbers, cowboys and Indians, sailors and pirates— but more than anything else I loved the penny school stories. I don't think they appealed to me for any snobbish reason, for though English boys might recognize that there were remote originals for such schools, and that being given a hundred lines on the day of a cricket match might be a cruel punishment, and that "playing the game" and "keeping a stiff upper lip" were desirable things socially, with me all this was an act of faith. I had never seen or heard of anything in the least resembling an English public school. The appeal of these stories, which has kept them fresh in my mind to this day, was that the characters were getting an education, and I could watch them at it with the certainty that some of the education was bound to brush off on me. If only the authors had identified the particular hundred lines of Latin that the hero was compelled to write out during the last cricket match of the season, how gladly I would have written them for him! As it was, I had to be content with the odd snatches of Latin and French that emerged from the narrative.

But education was hard. To be properly educated, you had to have a father who didn't drink and a mother who didn't work; you had to have long trousers and a short jacket and a top hat; you had to have footballs and cricket bats and shorts and a suit with white trousers, and the best people had uncles who came to the school in racing cars and tipped them five pounds, a sum of money I had never seen all together, so that they could blow it all in the tuckshop and have a feed in the dormitory after dark. The only rich relative I could get certain tidings of was a patrolman in the Chicago police force, know as Big Tim Fahy. He was a cousin of Mother, and so tall and powerful that Father, who was a six-footer, admitted he felt like a small boy beside him. He had a photograph of him on the sideboard in his uniform, wearing a sword, and the photographs and clippings the Fahys showed us proved that he was highly regarded in Chicago. A man like that would, I thought, go far in the States, and might eventually help me.

Meanwhile, even if you couldn't afford a top hat, you could play cricket with an old piece of board and a raggy ball against a wicket you had chalked on the blank end wall of a block of houses. You could get papers that gave you tips about the Noble Art of Self-Defense and practice a straight left in front of the mirror. You could even abide by the public-school code, and not tell lies, or betray a friend when he'd done something wrong, or yell when you got punished in school. All the boys I knew screamed that their wrist was broken and went back to their desks sobbing and nursing their hand between their knees.

I was always fond of heights, and afterward it struck me that reading was only another form of height. It was a way of looking beyond one's own back yard, and seeing into the neighbors'. Our yard—the real one— had a high back wall, and by early afternoon it had made the whole kitchen dark, but when the evening was fine I climbed the door of the outdoor toilet and onto the top of the wall. It was on a level with the respectable terrace behind ours, which had front gardens and a fine view, and there I sat for hours, on terms of relative equality with the policemen and their children, and watched the opposite hillside that fell headlong toward the valley of the city, with its terraces of tall houses and its crest of dark trees. It was all lit up when our little house was in darkness. In the mornings, the first thing I did when I got up was to put a chair under my attic window and push up the window sash to see the same hillside when it was still in shadow and its colors had the stiffness of early-morning light.

The best place for a good view was the quarry that fell sheer from the neighborhood of the Barrack to the Ballyhooley Road. It was a noisome place, where people dumped their rubbish and gangs of wild kids held stoning matches after school and poor people from lanes around the Barrack poked among the rubbish for treasure; but all that meant nothing to me, and I picked my way through the discarded bully-beef tins and climbed till I found a ledge of rock or a hollow in the quarry face that could be promoted to the rank of a cave, and after carefully placing an old penknife or a heavy stone beside me as a weapon to use against imaginary pursuers, I sat happily surveying the whole neighborhood, from Mayfield Chapel, which rode the extreme top of the hillside on the edge of the open country, to the spire of St. Luke's Church, which lay beneath me, and beyond which, dim in the distance, were the hills at the other side of the River Lee. Lord knows what I should think of it now, but then it seemed to me a wonderful view: the Ballyhooley Road winding up the hill from St. Luke's Cross, with its little houses and their tiny front gardens, and, on the side of the road nearest me, the back yards where the women came to hang out their washing. And all the time the shadow moved with a chill one could almost feel, and the isolated spots of sunlight grew brighter. Up there I felt like some sort of wild bird, secure from everything and observing everything: a horse and cart coming up the road, or a little girl with her skipping rope on the pavement, or an old man staggering along on his stick—all of them unaware of the eagle eyes that watched them from above.

Cork on its hills was full of such spots. Not far from our house was Goulding's Glen, in those days a valley with a stream that led from the clean open country by Ballyvolane to a manure factory in Blackpool where Father worked for a time. It skirted the base of the hill on which the Barrack stood, with the Barrack itself the highest spot, and for hours each day young buglers practiced on the sandy bluff that overlooked the second terrace, known as the Black Patch. Here the British had their rifle range and the local boys played football, and on the third level was the Glen itself, which led from the Big Pond, where we skated in wintertime, past the Mill House, which always looked dank and sinister between its trees, and along by the crimson sluice gates that controlled the factory stream under the steep hills which in those days were still covered in trees. This deep cutting was the first to fill with shadow, and I liked to sit somewhere high up, watching the workmen come home in the evening. Once I began to read, I needed no other landscape for dreaming. It was a pretty dirty hole even then, but for me it contained everything that the books told of—the Rocky Mountains, the Alps, the Castle on the Hill, the Haunted House, and the playing fields of whichever imaginary school I was then reading about.

But whatever the height, whether that of the storybook or the quarry, the eagle had to descend. Even eagles get cold and hungry, and nobody has taught the human eagle to feed off its own heights. Mother would soon be finished work. At some houses she did half a day, which ended at three o'clock, and for which she was paid ninepence or a shilling, and at others she did a whole day, which did not end till six, and for which she was paid one and sixpence. Depending on the humor of the maid she worked for, I might be allowed to call for her half an hour or so before she was finished work. In one house not only was I admitted to the kitchen after school and given my tea, but—if the family was out or on holiday—I was allowed up to the lumber room in the attic, which was filled with old pamphlets, guidebooks, phrase books in German and French, heavenly old dance programs with tassels and tiny pencils, a number of old schoolbooks, including a French primer, and—greatest treasure of all—a text of the Oberammergau Passion Play, in English and German. It was junk that would have meant nothing to almost anyone else in the world, and indeed the maid eventually let me take my pick of it before she cleared it out, but it filled my mind with ravishing glimpse; of how educated people lived, the places they saw, the things they did, and the way they spoke to hotel managers and railway porters. "From which platform does the train start for Köln." "We wish a carriage for non-smokers." "We have two trunks and five bags." "That is for you, young man." It was only another aspect of the vision I had caught in the master bedrooms. In these rooms there were mirrors in which you could see yourself twice over in profile, silver-handled brushes with engraved designs, and curiously shaped bottles that contained hair oil and scents that I experimented with recklessly when Mother's back was turned. Sometimes since then, when I stay in such a house, I wonder what small black face has studied itself in the mirror of the dressing table, what grubby little paw has used the silver-handled brushes to rub in the bay rum, and turn round almost expecting to see a tiny figure dash past me down the stairs toward the kitchen.

So I scampered down the quarry face to the snug suburban road, with its gas lamps and smooth pavements, and went to the tram stop at St. Luke's Cross, where I could be sure Mother would not escape me. In the dusk I sat, swinging my legs on the wall that overlooked the church, afraid to look behind me for fear I might grow dizzy, and when a tram came wheezing up the hill and discharged its load of passengers, I chased the men for cigarette pictures, terrified at the same time that I might miss her, a small, grave figure in a black shawl. Sometimes she had only her day's wages, but occasionally a maid would give her a bit of meat or a slice of apple pie for my supper, and then if she could spare me a penny for a boy's weekly, my day was almost saved. Saved it would be if for any reason Father was working late and we could sit in the dusk over the fire while I explained to her my plans for taking her abroad, and got her to sing for me "Farewell, but Whenever You Welcome the Hour" and "How Dear to Me the Hour When Daylight Dies." She was very fond of "Go Where Glory Waits Thee," and I put up with the rather dull tune for the sake of the words, which were beautiful and held such a personal appeal to myself that I could barely listen to them without tears:

> Go where glory waits thee,
> But while fame elates thee,
>   Oh, then remember me!
> When the praise thou meetest
> To thine ear is sweetest,
>   Oh, still remember me.

But often it was misery to return from the heights. It wasn't only that I might find Father drunk or quarrelsome, or that the rent collector might turn up and take a shilling of what Mother had earned, or that I might be sent for a loaf of bread and be refused it without the money. It was also that sometimes I ran into some happy group of boys amusing themselves at a lamppost, and, drawn by the clublike atmosphere of the pool of light and the shadowy figures, I tried to join them. Everything went well for a minute or two, till I suddenly said something wrong or used a word no one recognized and the whole group began to jeer me and call me "Four-eyes," and I would realize that once again I had been talking the language of the heights.

The trouble was that I was always a little bit of what I had picked up from whatever source—book or picture or glimpse of a different sort of life—always half in and half out of the world of reality, like Moses descending the mountain, or a dreamer waking. I couldn't see a picture of Robin Hood in a storybook but I had to make myself a long bow out of a curtain pole; and when I got a couple of younger kids to assist me at cricket and stood with a make-believe bat before a make-believe wicket, I was always the Dark Horse of the school, emerging to save its honor when all seemed lost. Once when we were playing cricket in the square in front of our house, a policeman came up the road and the others ran home. I didn't run, though I was as scared as they were. I rested on my hurling stick and waited for him to speak. "What do you mean, playing ball on the public street?" he demanded. "Excuse me," I replied politely. "This is not a public street. This square is private property." The bobby was so surprised at being checked by a small spectacled boy with an imitation cricket bat that he let me get away with it. But it wasn't often I got away with it, and sometimes I got in trouble for being cheeky when all I was doing was acting out a part, and at other times I was accused of being a liar when I was still only half in, half out of the dream and telling the truth as best I could; and then I slunk back in tears to my heights and my loneliness.

I couldn't keep from brooding on suffering and injustice, or from making a fool of myself about them. I don't know what age I was when I heard that a wild and handsome boy up the road, whose father beat him savagely, had run away from home and was being searched for by the police. The story was told in whispers. He would eventually be found, people said, and sent to the reformatory. That evening I found him myself, lurking in an alleyway, his long face filthy with tears, and begged him to come home. He would not come, and I would not leave him. At last he agreed to come, on condition that I go with him and plead for him. While I knocked at his door, he stood against the wall, his head down. His elder sister opened the door and I made my little speech. She promised to see that he was not punished, and I went home in a glow of exaltation, feeling that I had saved him from a terrible fate—the fate I was always dreading, of finding myself without a mother and a home. I thought that after this he and I might be friends. When we met again, he wouldn't even look at me but turned away with a sneer, and I knew that his father had beaten him again and that it was all my fault. As a protector of the weak I never was worth much.

As a result of this queer existence, half real and half fantastic, I who was always standing up for truth and justice never learned to fight; I who was always winning games for the school when everything seemed lost never learned to play any game; I who was always swimming flooded rivers to escape my pursuers never could swim at all till I was thirty. I never even got to be an acolyte[1] in the parish church or learned to ride a bicycle. The distance between the dream and the reality, between the private and the public personality, was always too great.

By the time I was fourteen or fifteen, it had become altogether clear

---

[1] *acolyte* (ăk′ô·lĭt): a boy who assists a priest at Mass.

that education was something I could not afford. Not that even then I had any intention of giving it up. I was just looking for a job that would enable me to buy the books from which I could pick up the education myself. So with the rest of the unemployed I went to the newsroom of the Carnegie Library, where on wet days the central heating warmed the perished bodies in the broken boots and made the dirty rags steam and smell. I read carefully through the advertisements and applied for every job that demanded "a smart boy." Sometimes, as a sort of bonus from Providence, I found a new number of *The Times Literary Supplement, The Spectator, The New Statesman,* or *The Studio* free, and I sat there and read reviews of books I would never be able to read and discussions of paintings I would never see, but usually some hungry old man would have toppled asleep over it and I was cheated. The real out-of-works always favored the high-class magazines, at which they were not likely to be disturbed. After a while, I got up and went out and wandered aimlessly round town till hunger or darkness or rain sent me home.

When it became clear that I would never be a priest, Mother's only ambition was for me to become a clerk: someone who would wear a white collar and be called "Mister." Knowing no better but always willing, I went to the Technical School and the School of Commerce at night to learn arithmetic, bookkeeping, and shorthand-typing. Of bookkeeping all I remember is a saying quoted approvingly on the first page of our textbook: "In business there is no such thing as an out-and-out free gift." And the very first thing I was asked to type in the School of Commerce threw me into a fresh fever, for it was Tennyson's "Blow, Bugle, Blow," presented as an example of advanced punctuation. To me it was merely fresh material for fantasy. I also worked hard at a Self-Educator, a big blue book that contained courses in everything, which I had picked up. From my reading I had deduced that German was the real language of culture, and that the greatest of cultured persons was Goethe, so I read Goethe right through in English and studied German out of the Self-Educator to read him in the original. I also made an attempt to learn Greek, which struck me as a very important cultural medium, but as I had never learned the rudiments of grammar in any language, I didn't get far with Greek.

I got my first job through my confessor, a gentle old priest who regarded me as a very saintly boy, and if innocence and sanctity are related, he was probably not so far wrong. The job was in a pious wholesale drapery business, where every single member of the staff seemed to have been recommended by his confessor, but I hated my immediate boss—a small, smug, smooth, greasy man, who tried hard to teach me that whenever he called my name I was instantly to drop whatever I was doing and reply smartly "Yessir." I never minded dropping whatever I was doing, which was usually folding shirts—the two arms neatly across the breast, as if I were laying out a corpse—and I had no objection to calling anybody "sir," but it was several seconds before my armor of daydreaming was penetrated by any voice from outside, and several seconds more before I realized that it was the voice to which I should reply "Yessir;" so at the end of a fortnight I stopped folding shirts and saying yessir and went home to do some more work at Greek. Then I tried a spell in a chemist's shop that was looking for a smart boy, but I soon discovered that I was only wanted to deliver messages. I have a vivid recollection of the end of this job, with myself, a small boy looking up at a tall counter, and a still taller man, refreshed by a visit to the pub next door, looking down at me pityingly and begging me in a thick Dublin accent to get out of this for my own good. There was an even briefer spell at a job printer's. While I was being shown the ropes, the printer asked me if I could spell and I replied airily "Oh, that's my forte!" which was the sort of language we used on the heights and I saw nothing wrong with it. That evening I met the man who had recommended me to the printer, and he repeated my reply with a good deal of laughter, and I realized that as usual I had made a fool of myself. I was so mortified that I never went back. I was sorry about that, because I really was quite good at spelling, and I still think I might have made an excellent typesetter.

I went to the railway as a messenger boy, because I despaired of ever becoming anything better, and, besides, though the hours—eight to seven —were cruelly long for a growing boy, the pay was good—a pound a week—and with money like that coming in I could buy a lot of books and get a lot of education. My job was to assist the invoice and claims clerks, bringing in dockets from the warehouse, and going to the warehouse to inquire for missing goods. All transport companies have colossal claims for missing goods, most of which were not really missing at all but lying around forgotten. Whiskey and tobacco were easy to trace, as they had to be loaded into sealed wagons in the presence of one of the old railway policemen, who recorded them in his book. But nobody took much responsibility for other articles, and it depended on the uncertain memory of checkers whether or not you could find out what had happened to them. A friendly checker could often remember a particular consignment, and if he were in really good humor, find it where it had lain for weeks in a corner, covered by a mountain of fresh merchandise. Usually, nobody remembered anything at all, and you solemnly marked your memorandum or wire with some code word, like "Bison," which signified "Certainly forwarded please say if since received." Back came a wire saying "Moose," meaning that it hadn't been received, and you had to go to the file room, where the dockets were stored, and search through scores of dusty files to find the original docket and the name of the porter or checker who had signed for the goods.

Sheehy and Cremin, the two other tracers, were the sons of railwaymen and protected by their fathers' presence from anything worse than good-natured ragging, but, apart from the patience and kindness of two or three checkers, I had to depend on my wits, which were all but nonexistent. I hated the file room, and when I worked there with Cremin or Sheehy I realized that they found six dockets in the time it took me to find one. I had bad sight, and often failed to see a docket properly, particularly when it was written in the semi-literate scrawl of carters or porters, and even when I should have seen it I was daydreaming, and when I wasn't daydreaming I was harassed by panic, shyness, and ignorance. Sheehy sneered all the time; Cremin sneered only some of the time, because he had a sort of impatient pity for my stupidity, and occasionally, smiling as I bogged myself deeper in some job I couldn't do, he took it from me with a complacent air and did it himself in a moment.

One of my jobs was to answer the telephone, and I did it with such intensity that I could never hear a word the other person said, and usually I was too ashamed to admit that I hadn't understood. When I did admit it, it was worse, for the person at the other end grew furious—a fatal thing to do with me, as it deprives me of the last shred of my wits. The trouble was that I couldn't believe in the telephone or the messages that came by it. I couldn't believe that the missing goods I was supposed to trace had ever existed, or if they had, that their loss meant anything to anybody. All I could believe in was words. I would read the word "unsophisticated" and at once I would want to know what the Irish for it was. In those days I didn't ask to be a writer. All I wanted was to translate, to feel the unfamiliar become familiar, the familiar take on all the mystery of some dark foreign face one glimpsed in the street.

I had taken a checker's discarded notebook from the railway storeroom and, having patiently rubbed out all the pencil notes, begun a poem book of my own. And though I was stupid, I really did care madly about poetry, good and bad, without understanding why I cared. More even than music it is the universal speech, but it is spoken fluently only by those whose existence is already all aflame with emotion, for then the beauty and order of language are the only beauty and order possible. Above all, it is the art of the boy and girl over-burdened by the troubles of their sex and station, for as Jane Austen wistfully noted, poetry can be best appreciated by those who should taste it most sparingly.

It was a strange double life, and small wonder if it comes back to me as hallucination. Each morning when I made my way across the tracks from the passenger station to the goods station, I said good-by to a part of myself, and at seven that evening, when I returned across the dark railway yard and paused in the well-lit passenger station to see the new books in the bookstall, he rejoined me, a boy exactly like myself except that no experience had dinged or dented him.

When my first wretched effort at composition appeared in a boy's paper and word of it got round the office, everyone was astonished, but most of all my boss. Sitting at his high desk with the paper open before him and a frown on his bulgy forehead, he asked, "Did you write this, Native?"

"Yes, sir," I said, feeling sure I had done it again. Everything I did only seemed to get me into fresh trouble.

"Nobody help you?" he asked suspiciously.

"No, sir," I replied warmly, because it looked as though someone else might have fallen under suspicion, and I still hung on to the code of the boy's weeklies and was always prepared to own up sooner than see another suffer.

The frown deepened on his fat face. "Then for God's sake, stick to writing!" he snapped. "You'll never be any good on the Great Southern & Western Railway."

And that, as we used to say in Cork, was one sure five. Looking for models of fine conduct as usual, I had lit on a Left Wing timekeeper, who knew all the Italian operas by heart and made it a point of honor not to take off his cap when speaking to the bosses. Thinking that anyone who knew so much about Italian operas must know the correct thing for other situations, I decided not to take my cap off, either. Even then I should probably have been let off with a reprimand, because my boss realized that I had no self-confidence and went about imitating everybody in the wild hope that I might accidentally strike on the right thing. But with my bad sight, I fell over a hand truck and injured my shin, so that I couldn't walk for weeks. On the railway, bad sight was more serious than bad manners, because it might result in a claim, and transport companies have a thing about claims.

On the Saturday night I was sacked, I read my first paper before the

Gaelic League. It was in Irish, and the subject was Goethe. For me, my whole adolescence is summed up in that extraordinary evening—so much that even yet I can't laugh at it in comfort. I didn't know much about Irish, and I knew practically nothing about Goethe, and that little was wrong. In a truly anthropomorphic spirit, I re-created Goethe in my own image and likeness, as a patriotic young fellow who merely wished to revive the German language, which I considered to have been gravely threatened by the use of French. I drew an analogy between the French culture that dominated eighteenth-century Germany and the English culture by which we in Ireland were dominated.

While I was reading, it was suddenly borne in on me that I no longer had a job, or a penny in the world, or even a home I could return to without humiliation, and that the neighbors would say again, as they had so often said before, that I was mad and a good-for-nothing. And I knew they would be right, for here I was committing myself absolutely and publicly to vague words and vaguer impressions. I could barely control my voice, because the words and impressions no longer mattered. All that mattered to me now was the act of faith, the hope that somewhere, somehow I would be able to prove that I was neither mad nor a good-for-nothing, because now I realized that there was no turning back. I had tossed my cap over the wall of life, and I must follow wherever it had fallen.

A YOUNG IRISHMAN

1. What were O'Connor's reasons as a young boy for wanting an education? How do his reasons differ from what you want from your education? Explain the author's statement that he "lived in a sort of social vacuum." Why did he think that it was hard to get an education?

2. Explain O'Connor's fondness for heights. What do you learn about the neighborhood which the author knew as a boy? What were his favorite pastimes?

3. What does O'Connor's relationship with his mother suggest to you about her character? Explain the significance of "Go where glory waits thee" to the boy and as title of this selection.

4. Do you agree with the author that poetry is the universal speech? Explain. How did he live "a strange double life"? Why did his boss think he should stick to writing? Cite three or four of O'Connor's boyhood experiences which you think really helped him in becoming a writer.

COMPARING WORKS BY THE SAME AUTHOR

What new understanding and appreciation does this selection give you of the short story "The Man of the House" (page 69)? Does the child in "The

Man of the House" seem to have anything in common with O'Connor as a young boy in "Go Where Glory Waits Thee"? What comparisons are you able to make between these two selections—about O'Connor as a writer of fiction and of autobiography?

READING LIST FOR MODERN BIOGRAPHY

Brickhill, Paul, *Reach for the Sky*
> A thrilling account of Douglas Bader, the legless air ace of the Battle of Britain, who was shot down and who escaped from German prisons.

Cecil, Lord David, *Melbourne*
> Queen Victoria's first prime minister, to whom Strachey has already introduced you; one of the best-written biographies of our century.

Hudson, William H., *Far Away and Long Ago*
> The South American boyhood of an Englishman who not only studied nature but could also paint it in colorful words.

* Lee, Laurie, *The Edge of Day*
> A contemporary British poet recounts the story of his childhood in western England.

Maugham, W. Somerset, *The Summing Up*
> The popular Mr. Maugham's observations on himself as a writer and as a man.

Montgomery, Bernard Law, *Montgomery of Alamein*
> Montgomery's autobiography is an important contribution to the history of World War II and to postwar problems.

Pearson, Hesketh, *Merry Monarch: The Life and Likeness of Charles II*
> A modern, lifelike portrait of Charles II as a wise and personable ruler.

——, *Sir Walter Scott, His Life and Personality*
> The romantic life of one of Scotland's greatest poets and novelists, by a major modern biographer.

Pippett, Aileen, *The Moth and the Star*
> An admirer of Virginia Woolf assesses her life and art.

Raverat, Gwen, *Period Piece*
> A granddaughter of Charles Darwin, gifted with a lively style, sketches her famous relatives and describes the life of English young people in the early days of this century.

Tuckerman, Arthur, *The Old School Tie*
> If you want to see the difference between English and American secondary schools, you will enjoy this man's account of his youth.

* Available in *Four English Biographies*, J. B. Priestley and O. B. Davis, eds., (Harcourt, Brace & World, Inc., 1961).

MODERN ESSAYS

THE ESSAY must not be confused with the *article*. The latter belongs to journalism, and its chief purpose is to inform. The article tells you something about the world. The essay, on the other hand, is a literary form and may tell you little or nothing about the world but a great deal about its author. An essay is just as much the expression of a personality as a lyric poem. All good essayists have a very personal manner and style.

By an odd coincidence the essay has best flourished at the beginning of each century: with Bacon early in the seventeenth; Addison and Steele early in the eighteenth; William Hazlitt, Charles Lamb, and Leigh Hunt early in the nineteenth; while the best English essayists of this century, Max Beerbohm, Hilaire Belloc, G. K. Chesterton, Edward Lucas, really belonged to the period ending in 1914.

In the years before 1914, as some of us well remember, essays—real essays, not articles—were regularly published in daily newspapers, which then were still edited for readers who enjoyed good writing. But the leisurely essayist had no place in the later newspapers, which were influenced by the dictates of mass circulation and a standard of taste largely determined by their advertising managers. After World War I, the essayists were restricted to the weekly reviews and monthly magazines, and soon there were fewer and fewer of these. And as the "familiar" (as it was once called) or light essay was always intended for periodical publication first, soon there were fewer and fewer essayists.

But the great tradition was not allowed to die: Robert Lynd, H. M. Tomlinson, and C. E. Montague all produced volumes of essays of enduring merit, and many fine essays were written by authors distinguished in other fields, such as Virginia Woolf, Aldous Huxley, and George Orwell.

The essay, to be successful, demands not only a good writer but also a good reader, somebody with an eye and ear for fine prose and both the taste and leisure to enjoy it. The great mass public for "best sellers" in fiction has never enjoyed essayists. Nevertheless, there has been an interesting development in Britain, thanks to the British Broadcasting Corporation, the noncommercial organization responsible for all radio and half the television of the country. For the essay, which looked as if it might disappear altogether, has had a new lease of life on the air, generally on radio but occasionally on television. Several of the older essayists, notably Max Beerbohm, were able to adapt their art to this new medium, with excellent results. So the essayist may still be with us for some time yet, pleasing a much larger public than the old essayists ever knew.

The essays you will read in this section are both serious and humorous, personal and social, concerned with large issues and the tiny details of ordinary life. They may tell a story; they may discuss a topic; but all express an individual point of view.

J. B. P.

The Pit Mouth

H. M. TOMLINSON 1873–1958

H. M. Tomlinson was born in the East End of London and grew up on the docks of the Thames River, where he mingled with stevedores and sailors from the far corners of the world. At the age of twelve he started to work as a clerk for a shipping company, and though he also began writing at an early age, was unable to secure a more literary job until he was over thirty. After working for a while on the staff of a London newspaper, Tomlinson left England to take a 2,000-mile trip up the Amazon on a tramp steamer of which his brother-in-law was captain. *The Sea and the Jungle* is an exciting travel story of this voyage. Returning to Europe, Tomlinson served as a war correspondent during World War I and worked subsequently on literary magazines. Among his works are *Gallions Reach,* a novel which is largely autobiographical, and *Old Junk,* in which appear some of his best essays.

Christopher Morley has said that reading the best essays of H. M. Tomlinson and surrendering oneself to the "moving music and magic of that prose, so simple and yet so subtle, one wonders whether poetry is not, after all, an inferior and more mechanic form." The following essay is considered one of Tomlinson's best. To witness the Great Barr fire and transmit its significance into words requires both literary skill and genuine compassion.

THERE was Great Barr, idle, still, and quiet. Through the Birmingham suburbs, out into the raw, bleak winter roads between the hedges, quite beyond the big town smoking with its enterprising labors, one approached the village of calamity with some awe and diffidence. You felt you were intruding; that you were a mere gross interloper, coming through curiosity, that was not excused by the compunction you felt, to see the appearance of a place that had tragedy in nearly all its homes. Young

"The Pit Mouth" by H. M. Tomlinson. Reprinted by permission of the Society of Authors as the literary representative of the Estate of the late H. M. Tomlinson.

men streamed by on bicycles in the same direction, groups were hurrying there on foot.

The road rose in a mound to let the railway under, and beyond the far dip was the village, an almost amorphous[1] group of mean red dwellings stuck on ragged fields about the dominant colliery[2] buildings. Three high, slim chimneys were leisurely pouring smoke from the grotesque black skeleton structures above the pits. The road ran by the boundary and was packed with people, all gazing absorbed and quiet into the grounds of the colliery; they were stacked up the hedge banks, and the walls and trees were loaded with boys.

A few empty motorcars of the colliery directors stood about. A carriage horse champed its bit, and the still watchers turned at once to that intrusive sound. Around us a lucid winter landscape (for it had been raining) ran to the distant encompassing hills which lifted like low ramparts of cobalt and amethyst to a sky of luminous saffron and ice green, across which leaden clouds were moving. The country had that hard, coldly radiant appearance which always impresses a sad man as this world's frank expression of its alien disregard; this world not his, on which he has happened, and must endure with his trouble for a brief time.

As I went through the press of people to the colliery gates, the women in shawls turned to me, first with annoyance that their watching should be disturbed, and then with some dull interest. My assured claim to admittance probably made them think I was the bearer of new help outside their little knowledge; and they willingly made room for me to pass. I felt exactly like the interfering fraud I was. What would I not have given then to be made, for a brief hour, a nameless miracle worker.

In the colliery itself was the same seeming apathy. There was nothing to show in that yard, black with soddened cinders and ash muck, where the new red-brick enginehouses stood, that somewhere half a mile beneath our feet were thirty men, their only exit to the outer world barred by a subterranean fire. Nothing showed of the fire but a whitish smoke from a ventilating shaft; and a stranger would not know what that signified. But the women did. Wet with the rain showers, they had been standing watching that smoke all night, and were watching it still, for its unceasing pour to diminish. Constant and unrelenting, it streamed steadily upward, as though it drew its volume from central fires that would never cease.

The doors of the office were thrown open, and three figures emerged. They broke into the listlessness of that dreary place, where nothing

---

[1] *amorphous* (á·môr′fŭs): shapeless.
[2] *colliery* (kŏl′yēr·ĭ): a coal mine.

seemed to be going on, with a sudden real purpose, fast but unhurried, and moved toward the shaft. Three Yorkshire rescue experts—one of them to die later—with the Hamstead manager explaining the path they should follow below with eager seriousness. "Figures of fun!" They had muzzles on their mouths and noses, goggles on their eyes, fantastic helms,[1] and queer cylinders and bags slung about them. As they went up the slope of wet ash, quick and full of purpose, their comical gear and coarse dress became suddenly transfigured; and the silent crowd cheered emotionally that little party of forlorn hope.

They entered the cage, and down they went. Still it was difficult for me to think that we were fronting tragedy, for no danger showed. An hour and more passed in nervous and dismal waiting. There was a signal. Some men ran to the pit head carrying hot bricks and blankets. The doctors took off their coats, and arranged bottles and tinkling apparatus on chairs stuck in the mud. The air smelt of iodoform.[2] A cloth was laid on the ground from the shaft to the enginehouse, and stretchers were placed handy. The women, some carrying infants, broke rank. That quickly uprunning rope was bringing the first news. The rope stopped running and the cage appeared. Only the rescue party came out, one carrying a moribund[3] cat. They knew nothing; and the white-faced women, with hardly repressed hysteria, took again their places by the enginehouse. So we passed that day, watching the place from which came nothing but disappointment. Occasionally a child, too young to know it was adding to its mother's grief, would wail querulously. There came a time when I and all there knew that to go down that shaft was to meet with death. The increasing exhaustion and pouring sweat of the returning rescue parties showed that. Yet the miners who were not selected to go down were angry; they violently abused the favoritism of the officials who would not let all risk their lives.

I have a new regard for my fellows since Great Barr. About you and me there are men like that. There is nothing to distinguish them. They show no signs of greatness. They have common talk. They have coarse ways. They walk with an ugly lurch. Their eyes are not eager. They are not polite. Their clothes are dirty. They live in cheap houses on cheap food. They call you "sir." They are the great unwashed, the mutable[4] many, the common people. The common people! Greatness is as common as that. There are not enough honors and decorations to go round. Talk

---

[1] *helms:* helmets.
[2] *iodoform* (ī·ō′dō·fôrm): a healing and antiseptic dressing for wounds and sores.
[3] *moribund* (mŏr′ĭ·bŭnd): near death.
[4] *mutable:* changeable.

of the soldier! *Vale*[1] to Welsby of Normanton! He was a common miner. He is dead. His fellows were in danger, their wives were white-faced and their children were crying, and he buckled on his harness and went to the assault with no more thought for self than great men have in a great cause; and he is dead. I saw him go to his death. I wish I could tell you of Welsby of Normanton.

I left that place where the starshine was showing the grim skeleton of the shaftwork overhead in the night, and where men moved about below in the indeterminate dark like dismal gnomes. There was a woman whose cry, when Welsby died, was like a challenge.

Next morning, in Great Barr, some blinds were down, the street was empty. Children, who could see no reason about them why their fathers should not return as usual, were playing football by the tiny church. A group of women were still gazing at the grotesque ribs and legs of the pit head staring as though it were a monster without ruth.[2]

[1] *Vale* (vā′lē): farewell.
[2] *ruth:* pity.

A VILLAGE OF CALAMITY

1. What details in the first three paragraphs point to the fact that the author is approaching a "village of calamity"? How do the women at the colliery gates respond to the author? How does he respond to them?

2. Describe the scene at the pit when the author first arrives, when the rescue experts go underground, and when the signal comes from below. What gave Tomlinson a new regard for his fellows? Note the details in the last paragraph which picture Great Barr the next morning. In what respect was the pit head like a monster?

ANALYZING AN AUTHOR'S STYLE

"The Pit Mouth" is more than just a record of what Tomlinson observed at the fire. The tragedy is witnessed by an individual who has a certain attitude toward life; the compassionate way in which he writes about this calamity reflects the man himself.

Imagine that you are to report the pit fire at Great Barr. What are the items of "news value" that you would look for? In addition to his factual reporting, what else characterizes Tomlinson's style of writing? Is the essay written in long or short sentences? Do you notice any relationship between the length of Tomlinson's sentences and what he chooses to say? Can you find examples of unusual word choice and phraseology? Find specific passages that you think illustrate Tomlinson's ability to write effective prose.

SUGGESTION FOR WRITING

After you have discussed the ideas found in "The Pit Mouth" and have analyzed the style of the writer, be ready to write an essay on a scene of tragedy familiar to you. Choose an incident from which you gathered more than simply the items of news value.

Music at Night

ALDOUS HUXLEY 1894–

Aldous Huxley—novelist, essayist, and critic—is the grandson of Thomas Huxley, the eminent Victorian scientist, educator, and writer. On his mother's side, he is the grandnephew of Matthew Arnold, the famous critic, poet, and essayist. Huxley became interested in writing while he was at Eton. His intention of going into medicine was never realized because of eye trouble which left him almost blind.

After several government jobs during World War I, Huxley worked on the staff of the London *Athenaeum* and the *Westminster Gazette,* writing critical essays on drama, art, and music. In 1921 he gave up journalism to support himself by writing; he also traveled extensively in Italy, France, India, and what was then the Dutch East Indies. For special treatment to improve his eyesight, he visited the United States in 1937 and since that time has lived in California. Here he writes fiction, articles and essays, and an occasional motion-picture script. A well-rounded person who is interested in many fields, Huxley has made a special study of Vedanta and other mystic religions, the influence of which is evident in his fiction. In his novels Huxley presents a somewhat exaggerated portrait of the evil tendencies in modern life. In *Point Counter Point,* probably his masterpiece, *Brave New World,* and *Eyeless in Gaza,* these tendencies are shown as extreme forms of perversity. *Brave New World Revisited,* published in 1955, depicts in fictional form Huxley's concept of the world of the future. His imaginative conception has become a contemporary nightmare.

You will find Huxley to be a stimulating essayist. In "Music at Night" he sets down the thoughts which come to him as he listens to a piece of music.

His essay shows him to be a person who possesses a delicate sensitivity to combinations and sequences of sound, a writer who has the ability to translate his impressions into appropriate words. Note the frequent allusions touching on many branches of knowledge. You may wish to investigate some of these references further after finishing the essay.

Moonless, this June night is all the more alive with stars. Its darkness is perfumed with faint gusts from the blossoming lime trees, with the smell of wetted earth and the invisible greenness of the vines. There is silence; but a silence that breathes with the soft breathing of the sea and, in the thin shrill noise of a cricket, insistently, incessantly harps on the fact of its own deep perfection. Far away, the passage of a train is like a long caress, moving gently, with an inexorable gentleness, across the warm living body of the night.

Music, you say; it would be a good night for music. But I have music here in a box, shut up, like one of those bottled djinns[1] in the *Arabian Nights,* and ready at a touch to break out of its prison. I make the necessary mechanical magic, and suddenly, by some miraculously appropriate coincidence (for I had selected the record in the dark, without knowing what music the machine would play), suddenly the introduction to the *Benedictus* in Beethoven's *Missa Solemnis*[2] begins to trace its pattern on the moonless sky.

The *Benedictus.* Blessed and blessing, this music is in some sort the equivalent of the night, of the deep and living darkness, into which, now in a single jet, now in a fine interweaving of melodies, now in pulsing and almost solid clots of harmonious sound, it pours itself, stanchlessly pours itself, like time, like the rising and falling, falling trajectories[3] of a life. It is the equivalent of the night in another mode of being, as an essence is the equivalent of the flowers from which it is distilled.

There is, at least there sometimes seems to be, a certain blessedness lying at the heart of things, a mysterious blessedness, of whose existence occasional accidents or providences (for me, this night is one of them) make us obscurely, or it may be intensely, but always fleetingly, alas, always only for a few brief moments aware. In the *Benedictus* Beethoven gives expression to this awareness of blessedness. His music is the equiv-

---

[1] *djinns* (jĭns): in Mohammedan belief, one of a class of supernatural beings, subject to magic control.

[2] *Beethoven* (bā′tō′vĕn): German composer (1770–1827); *Missa Solemnis* (mĭs′à sŏ·lĕm′nĭs): High Mass.

[3] *trajectories* (trà·jĕk′tō·rĭz): a curve or path which a body describes in space, as a planet or comet in its orbit.

alent of this Mediterranean night, or rather of the blessedness at the heart of the night, of the blessedness as it would be if it could be sifted clear of irrelevance and accident, refined and separated out into its quintessential[1] purity.

"*Benedictus, benedictus* . . ." One after another the voices take up the theme propounded by the orchestra and lovingly meditated through a long and exquisite solo (for the blessedness reveals itself most often to the solitary spirit) by a single violin. "*Benedictus, benedictus* . . ." And then, suddenly, the music dies; the flying djinn has been rebottled. With a stupid insect-like insistence, a steel point rasps and rasps the silence.

At school, when they taught us what was technically known as English, they used to tell us to "express in our own words" some passage from what ever play of Shakespeare was at the moment being rammed, with all its annotations—particularly the annotations—down our reluctant throats. So there we would sit, a row of inky urchins, laboriously translating "now silken dalliance in the wardrobe lies" into "now smart silk clothes lie in the wardrobe," or "To be or not to be" into "I wonder whether I ought to commit suicide or not." When we had finished, we would hand in our papers, and the presiding pedagogue would give us marks, more or less, according to the accuracy with which "our own words" had "expressed" the meaning of the Bard.

He ought, of course, to have given us naught[2] all round with a hundred lines to himself for ever having set us the silly exercise. Nobody's "own words," except those of Shakespeare himself, can possibly "express" what Shakespeare meant. The substance of a work of art is inseparable from its form; its truth and its beauty are two and yet, mysteriously, one. The verbal expression of even a metaphysic[3] or a system of ethics is very nearly as much of a work of art as a love poem. The philosophy of Plato expressed in the "own words" of Jowett[4] is not the philosophy of Plato; nor in the "own words" of, say, Billy Sunday,[5] is the teaching of St. Paul's teaching.

"Our own words" are inadequate even to express the meaning of other words; how much more inadequate, when it is a matter of rendering

[1] *quintessential* (kwĭn'tĕ·sĕn'shăl): highest and most concentrated.
[2] *naught:* zero.
[3] *metaphysic:* here, a theory or philosophy explaining the nature of reality or existence.
[4] *Jowett:* Benjamin Jowett (1817–1893), an English scholar and professor of Greek at Oxford University who wrote what many consider to be the finest translation of the works of the Greek philosopher Plato.
[5] *Billy Sunday:* American evangelist (1862–1935) well known for his conducting of religious revivals.

meanings which have their original expression in terms of music or one of the visual arts! What, for example, does music "say"? You can buy at almost any concert an analytical program that will tell you exactly. Much too exactly; that is the trouble. Every analyst has his own version. Imagine Pharaoh's dream interpreted successively by Joseph, by the Egyptian soothsayers, by Freud, by Rivers, by Adler, by Jung, by Wohlgemuth:[1] it would "say" a great many different things. Not nearly so many, however, as the Fifth Symphony has been made to say in the verbiage[2] of its analysts. Not nearly so many as the Virgin of the Rocks[3] and the Sistine Madonna[4] have no less lyrically said.

Annoyed by the verbiage and this absurd multiplicity of attributed "meanings," some critics have protested that music and painting signify nothing but themselves; that the only things they "say" are things, for example, about modulations and fugues,[5] about color values and three-dimensional forms. That they say anything about human destiny or the universe at large is a notion which these purists dismiss as merely non-sensical.

If the purists were right, then we should have to regard painters and musicians as monsters. For it is strictly impossible to be a human being and not to have views of some kind about the universe at large, very difficult to be a human being and not to express those views, at any rate by implication. Now, it is a matter of observation that painters and musicians are *not* monsters. Therefore . . . The conclusion follows, unescapably.

It is not only in program music[6] and problem pictures[7] that composers and painters express their views about the universe. The purest and most abstract artistic creations can be, in their own peculiar language, as eloquent in this respect as the most deliberately tendentious.[8] . . .

---

[1] *Freud . . . Wohlgemuth:* five famous psychologists whose theories lead to somewhat different explanations of dreams.

[2] *verbiage:* wordiness.

[3] *Virgin of the Rocks:* a tempera panel, now hanging in the Louvre, Paris, painted around 1487 by the celebrated Florentine painter, Leonardo da Vinci.

[4] *Sistine Madonna:* a painting done by Raphael in 1515 for the Church of St. Sixtus at Piacenza, Italy.

[5] *fugue* (fūg): a musical composition in several harmonizing parts which are independent in melody.

[6] *program music:* music inspired by something outside itself, such as a person, place, thing, or a concept of literary, historical, geographical, religious character.

[7] *problem picture:* a picture dealing usually with sociological or philosophical questions.

[8] *tendentious* (tĕn·dĕn′shŭs): argumentative.

The limits of criticism are very quickly reached. When he has said "in his own words" as much, or rather as little, as "own words" can say, the critic can only refer his readers to the original work of art: let them go and see for themselves. Those who overstep the limit are either rather stupid, vain people, who love their "own words" and imagine that they can say in them more than "own words" are able in the nature of things to express. Or else they are intelligent people who happen to be philosophers or literary artists and who find it convenient to make the criticism of other men's work a jumping-off place for their own creativity.

What is true of painting is equally true of music. Music "says" things about the world, but in specifically musical terms. Any attempts to reproduce these musical statements "in our own words" are necessarily doomed to failure. We cannot isolate the truth contained in a piece of music; for it is a beauty-truth and inseparable from its partner. The best we can do is to indicate in the most general terms the nature of the musical beauty-truth under consideration and to refer curious truth-seekers to the original. Thus, the introduction to the *Benedictus* in the *Missa Solemnis* is a statement about the blessedness that is at the heart of things. But this is about as far as "own words" will take us. If we were to start describing in our "own words" exactly what Beethoven felt about this blessedness, how he conceived it, what he thought its nature to be, we should very soon find ourselves writing lyrical nonsense in the style of the analytical program makers. Only music, and only Beethoven's music, and only this particular music of Beethoven, can tell us with any precision what Beethoven's conception of the blessedness at the heart of things actually was. If we want to know, we must listen—on a still June night, by preference, with the breathing of the invisible sea for background, to the music and the scent of lime trees drifting through the darkness, like some exquisite soft harmony apprehended by another sense.

THE POWER OF MUSIC

1. Reread the first paragraph of this essay. What sense impressions contribute to the picture you visualize in this paragraph? Where do you think Huxley was writing?

2. What is the real message of the *Benedictus* for the author?

3. What is the main point that Huxley makes about music in this essay? Do you agree? Why or why not?

CLASS ACTIVITY

Appoint a committee to do research and report to the class on Beethoven's *Missa Solemnis* or on any of the other works of art mentioned in Huxley's essay.

SUGGESTIONS FOR WRITING

1. Select a piece of music, a play, poem, painting, or piece of sculpture which you particularly like and write a composition on how it affects you.

2. Write your thoughts and feelings on one of the following subjects: "The Best Place to Listen to Music," "Why I Like (a certain composer)," "Pictures and Music," "Hearing Poetry Read Aloud."

Shooting an Elephant

GEORGE ORWELL 1903–1950

England lost one of her most original writers in the untimely death of George Orwell. Always a provocative writer, with keen insight into social and political situations, Orwell was a skillful and entertaining novelist as well as an essayist. Because he was so astute a critic of his times, a contemporary called him "the conscience of his generation."

Orwell was born in India, but at an early age was sent to boarding school in England. After finishing his education at Eton, he served briefly with the Imperial Police in Burma. The following essay narrates an exciting incident of his service there and shows how his thinking about world problems was beginning to develop. Greatly concerned with the political and social issues of his day, Orwell stated that it was his aim "to make political writing into an art."

When he decided to become a writer he went to Paris, where he lived through several years of extreme poverty. Just as he began to become known, his health failed him. He died in London from tuberculosis at the age of forty-six. In 1949 he received the *Partisan Review* award for distinguished writing, with a citation for "singular directness and honesty, a scrupulous fidelity to his experience that has placed him in that very valuable clan of the writer who is a witness to his time."

IN MOULMEIN, in lower Burma, I was hated by large numbers of people —the only time in my life that I have been important enough for this to happen to me. I was subdivisional police officer of the town, and in an aimless, petty kind of way an anti-European feeling was very bitter. No one had the guts to raise a riot, but if a European woman went through the bazaars alone somebody would probably spit betel juice over her dress. As a police officer I was an obvious target and was baited whenever it seemed safe to do so. When a nimble Burman tripped me up on the football field and the referee (another Burman) looked the other way, the crowd yelled with hideous laughter. This happened more than once. In the end the sneering yellow faces of young men that met me everywhere, the insults hooted after me when I was at a safe distance, got badly on my nerves. The young Buddhist priests were the worst of all. There were several thousands of them in the town and none of them seemed to have anything to do except stand on street corners and jeer at Europeans.

All this was perplexing and upsetting. For at that time I had already made up my mind that imperialism was an evil thing and the sooner I chucked up my job and got out of it the better. Theoretically—and secretly, of course—I was all for the Burmese and all against their oppressors, the British. As for the job I was doing, I hated it more bitterly than I can perhaps make clear. In a job like that you see the dirty work of Empire at close quarters. The wretched prisoners huddling in the stinking cages of the lockups, the gray, cowed faces of the long-term convicts, the scarred buttocks of men who had been flogged with bamboos—all these oppressed me with an intolerable sense of guilt. But I could get nothing into perspective. I was young and ill-educated and I had to think out my problems in the utter silence that is imposed on every Englishman in the East. I did not know that the British Empire is dying, still less did I know that it is a great deal better than the younger empires that are going to supplant it. All I knew was that I was stuck between my hatred of the empire I served and my rage against the evil-spirited little beasts who tried to make my job impossible. With one part of my mind I thought of the British Raj as an unbreakable tyranny, as something clamped down, in *saecula saeculorum*,[1] upon the will of prostrate peoples; with another part I thought that the greatest joy in the world would be to drive a bayonet into a Buddhist priest's guts. Feelings like these are the normal

---

[1] *saecula* (sĕk′ū·lå) *saeculorum*: forever and ever.

by-product of imperialism; ask any Anglo-Indian official, if you can catch him off duty.

One day something happened which in a roundabout way was enlightening. It was a tiny incident in itself, but it gave me a better glimpse than I had had before of the real nature of imperialism—the real motives for which despotic governments act. Early one morning the subinspector at a police station the other end of the town rang me up on the phone and said that an elephant was ravaging the bazaar. Would I please come and do something about it? I did not know what I could do, but I wanted to see what was happening and I got onto a pony and started out. I took my rifle, an old .44 Winchester and much too small to kill an elephant, but I thought the noise might be useful *in terrorem*.[1] Various Burmans stopped me on the way and told me about the elephant's doings. It was not, of course, a wild elephant, but a tame one which had gone "must."[2] It had been chained up, as tame elephants always are when their attack of "must" is due, but on the previous night it had broken its chain and escaped. Its mahout,[3] the only person who could manage it when it was in that state, had set out in pursuit, but had taken the wrong direction and was now twelve hours' journey away, and in the morning the elephant had suddenly reappeared in the town. The Burmese population had no weapons and were quite helpless against it. It had already destroyed somebody's bamboo hut, killed a cow, and raided some fruit stalls and devoured the stock; also it had met the municipal rubbish van and, when the driver jumped out and took to his heels, had turned the van over and inflicted violences upon it.

The Burmese subinspector and some Indian constables were waiting for me in the quarter where the elephant had been seen. It was a very poor quarter, a labyrinth of squalid huts, thatched with palm leaf, winding all over a steep hillside. I remember it was a cloudy, stuffy morning at the beginning of the rains. We began questioning the people where the elephant had gone and, as usual, failed to get any definite information. That is invariably the case in the East; a story always sounds clear enough at a distance, but the nearer you get to the scene of events the vaguer it becomes. Some of the people said that the elephant had gone in one direction, some said that it had gone in another, some professed not even to have heard of any elephant. I had made up my mind that the whole story was a pack of lies, when I heard yells a little distance away.

---

[1] *in terrorem:* in a case of fright.
[2] *"must":* a condition of dangerous frenzy.
[3] *mahout* (má·hout'): the keeper and driver of an elephant.

There was a loud, scandalized cry of "Go away, child! Go away this instant!" and an old woman with a switch in her hand came round the corner of a hut, violently shooing away a crowd of naked children. Some more women followed, clicking their tongues and exclaiming; evidently there was something the children ought not to have seen. I rounded the hut and saw a man's dead body sprawling in the mud. He was an Indian, a black Dravidian[1] coolie, almost naked, and he could not have been dead many minutes. The people said that the elephant had come suddenly upon him round the corner of the hut, caught him with its trunk, put its foot on his back, and ground him into the earth. This was the rainy season and the ground was soft, and his face had scored a trench a foot deep and a couple of yards long. He was lying on his belly with his arms crucified and head sharply twisted to one side. His face was coated with mud, the eyes wide open, the teeth bared and grinning with an unendurable agony. (Never tell me, by the way, that the dead look peaceful. Most of the corpses I have seen looked devilish.) The friction of the great beast's foot had stripped the skin from his back as neatly as one skins a rabbit. As soon as I saw the dead man I sent an orderly to a friend's house nearby to borrow an elephant rifle. I had already sent back the pony, not wanting it to go mad with fright and throw me if it smelt the elephant.

The orderly came back in a few minutes with a rifle and five cartridges, and meanwhile some Burmans had arrived and told us that the elephant was in the paddy fields[2] below, only a few hundred yards away. As I started forward practically the whole population of the quarter flocked out of the houses and followed me. They had seen the rifle and were all shouting excitedly that I was going to shoot the elephant. They had not shown much interest in the elephant when he was merely ravaging their homes, but it was different now that he was going to be shot. It was a bit of fun to them, as it would be to an English crowd; besides they wanted the meat. It made me vaguely uneasy. I had no intention of shooting the elephant—I had merely sent for the rifle to defend myself if necessary—and it is always unnerving to have a crowd following you. I marched down the hill, looking and feeling a fool, with the rifle over my shoulder and an ever growing army of people jostling at my heels. At the bottom, when you got away from the huts, there was a metaled road and beyond that a miry waste of paddy fields a thousand yards across, not yet plowed but soggy from the first rains and dotted with coarse grass.

[1] *Dravidian* (dră·vĭd'ĭ·ăn): belonging to an ancient race of India, numerous in the south.

[2] *paddy fields:* rice fields.

The elephant was standing eight yards from the road, his left side toward us. He took not the slightest notice of the crowd's approach. He was tearing up bunches of grass, beating them against his knees to clean them, and stuffing them into his mouth.

I had halted on the road. As soon as I saw the elephant I knew with perfect certainty that I ought not to shoot him. It is a serious matter to shoot a working elephant—it is comparable to destroying a huge and costly piece of machinery—and obviously one ought not to do it if it can possibly be avoided. And at that distance, peacefully eating, the elephant looked no more dangerous than a cow. I thought then and I think now that his attack of "must" was already passing off; in which case he would merely wander harmlessly about until the mahout came back and caught him. Moreover, I did not want in the least to shoot him. I decided that I would watch him a little while to make sure that he did not turn savage again, and then go home.

But at that moment I glanced round at the crowd that had followed me. It was an immense crowd, two thousand at the least and growing every minute. It blocked the road for a long distance on either side. I looked at the sea of yellow faces above the garish clothes—faces all happy and excited over this bit of fun, all certain that the elephant was going to be shot. They were watching me as they would watch a conjurer about to perform a trick. They did not like me, but with the magical rifle in my hand I was momentarily worth watching. And suddenly I realized that I would have to shoot the elephant after all. The people expected it of me and I had got to do it; I could feel their two thousand wills pressing me forward irresistibly. And it was at this moment, as I stood there with the rifle in my hands, that I first grasped the hollowness, the futility of the white man's dominion in the East. Here was I, the white man with his gun, standing in front of the unarmed crowd—seemingly the leading actor of the piece; but in reality I was only an absurd puppet pushed to and fro by the will of those yellow faces behind. I perceived in this moment that when the white man turns tyrant it is his own freedom that he destroys. He becomes a sort of hollow, posing dummy, the conventionalized figure of a sahib.[1] For it is the condition of his rule that he shall spend his life in trying to "impress the natives," and so in every crisis he has got to do what the "natives" expect of him. He wears a mask, and his face grows to fit it. I had got to shoot the elephant. I had committed myself to doing it when I sent for the rifle. A sahib has got to act like a sahib; he has got to appear resolute, to know his own mind and do defi-

---

[1] *sahib* (sä′ib): native term for a European gentleman.

nite things. To come all that way, rifle in hand, with two thousand people marching at my heels, and then to trail feebly away, having done nothing —no, that was impossible. The crowd would laugh at me. And my whole life, every white man's in the East, was one long struggle not to be laughed at.

But I did not want to shoot the elephant. I watched him beating his bunch of grass against his knees, with that preoccupied grandmotherly air that elephants have. It seemed to me that it would be murder to shoot him. At that age I was not squeamish about killing animals, but I had never shot an elephant and never wanted to. (Somehow it always seems worse to kill a large animal.) Besides, there was the beast's owner to be considered. Alive, the elephant was worth at least a hundred pounds; dead, he would only be worth the value of his tusks, five pounds, possibly. But I had got to act quickly. I turned to the experienced-looking Burmans who had been there when we arrived, and asked them how the elephant had been behaving. They all said the same thing; he took no notice of you if you left him alone, but he might charge if you went too close to him.

It was perfectly clear to me what I ought to do. I ought to walk up to within, say, twenty-five yards of the elephant and test his behavior. If he charged, I could shoot; if he took no notice of me, it would be safe to leave him until the mahout came back. But I also knew that I was going to do no such thing. I was a poor shot with a rifle and the ground was soft mud into which one would sink at every step. If the elephant charged and I missed him, I should have about as much chance as a toad under a steam roller. But even then I was not thinking particularly of my own skin, only of the watchful yellow faces behind. For at that moment, with the crowd watching me, I was not afraid in the ordinary sense, as I would have been if I had been alone. A white man mustn't be frightened in front of "natives"; and so, in general, he isn't frightened. The thought in my mind was that if anything went wrong those two thousand Burmans would see me pursued, caught, trampled on, and reduced to a grinning corpse like that Indian up the hill. And if that happened it was quite probable that some of them would laugh. That would never do. There was only one alternative. I shoved the cartridges into the magazine and lay down on the road to get a better aim.

The crowd grew very still, and a deep, low, happy sigh, as of people who see the theater curtain go up at last, breathed from innumerable throats. They were going to have their bit of fun after all. The rifle was a beautiful German thing with cross-hair sights. I did not know then that in shooting an elephant one would shoot to cut an imaginary bar running from earhole to earhole. I ought, therefore, as the elephant was sideways on, to have aimed straight at his earhole; actually I aimed several inches in front of this, thinking the brain would be further forward.

When I pulled the trigger I did not hear the bang or feel the kick—one never does when a shot goes home—but I heard the devilish roar of glee that went up from the crowd. In that instant, in too short a time, one would have thought, even for the bullet to get there, a mysterious, terrible change had come over the elephant. He neither stirred nor fell, but every line of his body had altered. He looked suddenly stricken, shrunken, immensely old, as though the frightful impact of the bullet had paralyzed him without knocking him down. At last, after what seemed a long time —it might have been five seconds, I dare say—he sagged flabbily to his knees. His mouth slobbered. An enormous senility seemed to have settled upon him. One could have imagined him thousands of years old. I fired again into the same spot. At the second shot he did not collapse but climbed with desperate slowness to his feet and stood weakly erect, with legs sagging and head drooping. I fired a third time. That was the shot that did for him. You could see the agony of it jolt his whole body and knock the last remnant of strength from his legs. But in falling he seemed for a moment to rise, for as his hind legs collapsed beneath him he seemed to tower upward like a huge rock toppling, his trunk reaching skywards like a tree. He trumpeted for the first and only time. And then down he came, his belly toward me, with a crash that seemed to shake the ground even where I lay.

I got up. The Burmans were already racing past me across the mud. It was obvious that the elephant would never rise again, but he was not dead. He was breathing very rhythmically with long rattling gasps, his great mound of a side painfully rising and falling. His mouth was wide open—I could see far down into caverns of pink throat. I waited a long time for him to die, but his breathing did not weaken. Finally I fired my two remaining shots into the spot where I thought his heart must be. The thick blood welled out of him like red velvet, but still he did not die. His body did not even jerk when the shots hit him, the tortured breathing continued without a pause. He was dying, very slowly and in great agony, but in some world remote from me where not even a bullet could damage him further. I felt that I had got to put an end to that dreadful noise. It seemed dreadful to see the great beast lying there, powerless to move and yet powerless to die, and not even to be able to finish him. I sent back for my small rifle and poured shot after shot into his heart and down his throat. They seemed to make no impression. The tortured gasps continued as steadily as the ticking of a clock.

In the end I could not stand it any longer and went away. I heard later that it took him half an hour to die. Burmans were bringing dahs[1] and baskets even before I left, and I was told they had stripped his body almost to the bones by afternoon.

Afterwards, of course, there were endless discussions about the shooting of the elephant. The owner was furious, but he was only an Indian and could do nothing. Besides, legally I had done the right thing, for a mad elephant has to be killed, like a mad dog, if its owner fails to control it. Among the Europeans, opinion was divided. The older men said I was right, the younger men said it was a shame to shoot an elephant for killing a coolie, because an elephant was worth more than any Coringhee[2] coolie. And afterwards I was very glad that the coolie had been killed; it put me legally in the right and gave me a sufficient pretext for shooting the elephant. I often wondered whether any of the others grasped that I had done it solely to avoid looking a fool.

[1] *dahs* (däz): a large, heavy knife.
[2] *Coringhee* (kô·rĭn'gē).

BRITISH OFFICER IN THE EAST

1. Why was Orwell hated by many people in Burma? In what little ways was this hatred shown? Summarize the author's ideas about imperialism.

2. What characteristics common to human nature everywhere are shown by the Burmese townspeople on hearing that an elephant is to be shot?

3. Why did Orwell think that he should not shoot the elephant? Why did he feel he must do it? What did this paradox show him of the weakness of imperialism?

4. What different opinions were expressed by various people as to whether he should have shot the elephant? How do you feel about this matter?

RECOGNIZING AN AUTHOR'S PURPOSE

To determine the central purpose of the Orwell essay, go beyond the story related and look at this quote from paragraph 2: "I did not know that the British Empire is dying, still less did I know that it is a great deal better than the younger empires that are going to supplant it." Now ask yourself: Why does the incident described become so important to the author? How does a predicament arise from the situation? Is it moral or physical courage which helps solve Orwell's dilemma? Consider your answers to these questions before stating what you think the author's purpose is in "Shooting an Elephant."

CLASS ACTIVITY

Several students may wish to read Orwell's *Animal Farm* and present a report to the class in the form of a panel discussion. Discussion can center on two things: (1) the social and political implications of the book. (2) *Animal Farm* as a twentieth-century satire. Compare the satire in *Animal Farm* with the satire found in the writings of Addison and Steele, Pope, and Swift.

Hours in a Library
VIRGINIA WOOLF 1882–1941

Virginia Woolf was the daughter of Sir Leslie Stephen, a distinguished scholar, critic, and biographer. Throughout her childhood her natural talents were stimulated by association with poets, artists, musicians, and novelists who were friends of her father. After her marriage in 1912 to Leonard Woolf, a London editor, the two set up a hand press for publishing limited editions of modern literature. This venture later developed into a full-fledged publishing house, The Hogarth Press. At their home in the Bloomsbury section of London, the Woolfs were part of the remarkable intellectual circle called the "Bloomsbury Group," which included Lytton Strachey, E. M. Forster, and others in the literary and art world.

It is difficult to say whether Virginia Woolf was more distinguished as a novelist or as an essayist and critic. In fiction, as one of the early advocates of "stream of consciousness" stories, she blazed new trails in technique. Her novels, such as *To the Lighthouse* and *Mrs. Dalloway,* emphasize the psychology and personal motivation of the characters rather than plot. Using some of the methods of the novel, Mrs. Woolf also wrote a unique biography, *Flush.* Here, in telling the story of Elizabeth Barrett's cocker spaniel, she gives a "dog's-eye view" of the famous Browning courtship.

In the essay, Virginia Woolf showed her talent for literary criticism. She was an enthusiastic reader whose interests ranged from medieval to modern literature, and though she could be as scholarly and as discriminating as the best of critics, she preferred to think of herself as the "common reader."

"Hours in a Library" from *Granite and Rainbow* by Virginia Woolf, © 1958 by Leonard Woolf. Reprinted by permission of Leonard Woolf, and Harcourt, Brace & World, Inc.

Some of the authors mentioned in this essay will be familiar to you; others you may want to look up and perhaps sample.

LET US begin by clearing up the old confusion between the man who loves learning and the man who loves reading, and point out that there is no connection whatever between the two. A learned man is a sedentary, concentrated, solitary enthusiast, who searches through books to discover some particular grain of truth upon which he has set his heart. If the passion for reading conquers him, his gains dwindle and vanish between his fingers. A reader, on the other hand, must check the desire for learning at the outset; if knowledge sticks to him well and good, but to go in pursuit of it, to read on a system, to become a specialist or an authority, is very apt to kill what it suits us to consider the more humane passion for pure and disinterested reading.

In spite of all this we can easily conjure up a picture which does service for the bookish man and raises a smile at his expense. We conceive a pale, attenuated [1] figure in a dressing gown, lost in speculation, unable to lift a kettle from the hob,[2] or address a lady without blushing, ignorant of the daily news, though versed in the catalogues of the secondhand booksellers, in whose dark premises he spends the hours of sunlight—a delightful character, no doubt, in his crabbed simplicity, but not in the least resembling that other to whom we would direct attention. For the true reader is essentially young. He is a man of intense curiosity; of ideas; open-minded and communicative, to whom reading is more of the nature of brisk exercise in the open air than of sheltered study; he trudges the high road, he climbs higher and higher upon the hills until the atmosphere is almost too fine to breathe in; to him it is not a sedentary pursuit at all.

But, apart from general statements, it would not be hard to prove by an assembly of facts that the great season for reading is the season between the ages of eighteen and twenty-four. The bare list of what is read then fills the heart of older people with despair. It is not only that we read so many books, but that we had such books to read. If we wish to refresh our memories, let us take down one of those old notebooks which we have all, at one time or another, had a passion for beginning. Most of the pages are blank, it is true; but at the beginning we shall find a certain number very beautifully covered with a strikingly legible handwriting.

---

[1] *attenuated:* thin.
[2] *hob* (hŏb): a projection at the back or side of a fireplace.

Here we have written down the names of great writers in their order of merit; here we have copied out fine passages from the classics; here are lists of books to be read; and here, most interesting of all, lists of books that have actually been read, as the reader testifies with some youthful vanity by a dash of red ink.

The old lists are there to make us smile and perhaps to sigh a little, but we would give much to recall also the mood in which this orgy of reading was done. Happily, this reader was no prodigy, and with a little thought we can most of us recall the stages at least of our own initiation. The books we read in childhood, having purloined [1] them from some shelf supposed to be inaccessible, have something of the unreality and awfulness of a stolen sight of the dawn coming over quiet fields when the household is asleep. Peeping between the curtains we see strange shapes of misty trees which we hardly recognize, though we may remember them all our lives; for children have a strange premonition of what is to come.

But the later reading is quite a different matter. For the first time, perhaps, all restrictions have been removed, we can read what we like; libraries are at our command, and, best of all, friends who find themselves in the same position. For days upon end we do nothing but read. It is a time of extraordinary excitement and exaltation. We seem to rush about recognizing heroes. There is a sort of wonderment in our minds that we ourselves are really doing this, and mixed with it an absurd arrogance and desire to show our familiarity with the greatest human beings who have ever lived in the world. The passion for knowledge is then at its keenest or at least most confident, and we have, too, an intense singleness of mind which the great writers gratify by making it appear that they are at one with us in their estimate of what is good in life. And as it is necessary to hold one's own against some one who has adopted Pope, let us say, instead of Sir Thomas Browne,[2] for a hero, we conceive a deep affection for these men, and feel that we know them not as other people know them, but privately by ourselves. We are fighting under their leadership, and almost in the light of their eyes. So we haunt the old bookshops and drag home folios and quartos, Euripides in wooden boards, and Voltaire in eighty-nine volumes octavo.

But these lists are curious documents, in that they seem to include scarcely any of the contemporary writers. Meredith and Hardy and

---

[1] *purloined:* stolen.

[2] *Sir Thomas Browne* (1605–82): well-known physician, philosopher, and man of letters of the seventeenth century. Author of *Religio Medici*, an exposition of the religious principles of a young, skeptical, and scientifically-minded physician.

Henry James were of course alive when this reader came to them, but they were already accepted among the classics. There is no man of his own generation who influences him as Carlyle, or Tennyson, or Ruskin influenced the young of their day. And this we believe to be very characteristic of youth, for unless there is some admitted giant he will have nothing to do with the smaller men, although they deal with the world he lives in. He will rather go back to the classics, and consort entirely with minds of the very first order. For the time being he holds himself aloof from all the activities of men, and, looking at them from a distance, judges them with superb severity.

Indeed, one of the signs of passing youth is the birth of a sense of fellowship with other human beings as we take our place among them. We should like to think that we keep our standard as high as ever; but we certainly take more interest in the writings of our contemporaries and pardon their lack of inspiration for the sake of something that brings them nearer to us. It is even arguable that we get actually more from the living, although they may be much inferior, than from the dead. In the first place there can be no secret vanity in reading our contemporaries, and the kind of admiration which they inspire is extremely warm and genuine because in order to give way to our belief in them we have often to sacrifice some very respectable prejudice which does us credit. We have also to find our own reasons for what we like and dislike, which acts as a spur to our attention, and is the best way of proving that we have read the classics with understanding.

Thus to stand in a great bookshop crammed with books so new that their pages almost stick together, and the gilt on their backs is still fresh, has an excitement no less delightful than the old excitement of the secondhand bookstall. It is not perhaps so exalted. But the old hunger to know what the immortals thought has given place to a far more tolerant curiosity to know what our own generation is thinking. What do living men and women feel, what are their houses like and what clothes do they wear, what money have they and what food do they eat, what do they love and hate, what do they see of the surrounding world, and what is the dream that fills the spaces of their active lives? They tell us all these things in their books. In them we can see as much both of the mind and of the body of our times as we have eyes for seeing.

When such a spirit of curiosity has fully taken hold of us, the dust will soon lie thick upon the classics unless some necessity forces us to read them. For the living voices are, after all, the ones we understand the best. We can treat them as we treat our equals; they are guessing our riddles, and, what is perhaps more important, we understand their jokes. And we soon develop another taste, unsatisfied by the great—not a valuable taste, perhaps, but certainly a very pleasant possession—the taste for bad books. Without committing the indiscretion of naming names, we know which authors can be trusted to produce yearly (for happily they are prolific) a novel, a book of poems or essays, which affords us indescribable pleasure. We owe a great deal to bad books; indeed, we come to count their authors and their heroes among those figures who play so large a part in our silent life.

Something of the same sort happens in the case of the memoir writers and autobiographers, who have created almost a fresh branch of literature in our age. They are not all of them important people, but strangely enough, only the most important, the dukes and the statesmen, are even really dull. The men and women who set out, with no excuse except perhaps that they saw the Duke of Wellington once, to confide to us their opinions, their quarrels, their aspirations, and their diseases, generally end by becoming, for the time at least, actors in those private dramas with which we beguile our solitary walks and our sleepless hours. Refine all this out of our consciousness and we should be poor indeed. And then there are the books of facts and history, books about bees and wasps and industries and gold mines and Empresses and diplomatic intrigues, about rivers and savages, trade unions, and Acts of Parliament, which we always read and always, alas! forget.

Perhaps we are not making out a good case for a bookshop when we have to confess that it gratifies so many desires which have apparently nothing to do with literature. But let us remember that here we have a literature in the making. From these new books our children will select the one or two by which we shall be known for ever. Here, if we could recognize it, lies some poem, or novel, or history which will stand up and speak with other ages about our age when we lie prone and silent as the crowd of Shakespeare's day is silent and lives for us only in the pages of his poetry.

It is oddly difficult in the case of new books to know which are the real books and what it is that they are telling us, and which are the stuffed books which will come to pieces when they have lain about for a year or two. We can see that there are many books, and we are frequently told that every one can write nowadays. That may be true; yet we do not doubt that at the heart of this immense volubility this flood and foam of language, this irreticence[1] and vulgarity and triviality, there lies the heat

---

[1] *irreticence:* frankness.

of some great passion which only needs the accident of a brain more happily turned than the rest to issue in a shape which will last from age to age. It should be our delight to watch this turmoil, to do battle with the ideas and visions of our own time, to seize what we can use, to kill what we consider worthless, and above all to realize that we must be generous to the people who are giving shape as best they can to the ideas within them.

No age of literature is so little submissive to authority as ours, so free from the dominion of the great; none seems so wayward with its gift of reverence, or so volatile in its experiments. It may well seem, even to the attentive, that there is no trace of school or aim in the work of our poets and novelists. But the pessimist is inevitable, and he shall not persuade us that our literature is dead, or prevent us from feeling how true and vivid a beauty flashes out as the young writers draw together, to form their new vision, the ancient words of the most beautiful of living languages. Whatever we may have learned from reading the classics we need now in order to judge the work of our contemporaries, for whenever there is life in them they will be casting their net out over some unknown abyss to snare new shapes, and we must throw our imaginations after them if we are to accept with understanding the strange gifts they bring back to us.

But if we need all our knowledge of the old writers in order to follow what the new writers are attempting, it is certainly true that we come from adventuring among new books with a far keener eye for the old. It seems that we should now be able to surprise their secrets; to look deep down into their work and see the parts come together, because we have watched the making of new books, and with eyes clear of prejudice can judge more truly what it is that they are doing, and what is good and what bad. We shall find, probably, that some of the great are less venerable than we thought them. Indeed, they are not so accomplished or so profound as some of our own time. But if in one or two cases this seems to be true, a kind of humiliation mixed with joy overcomes us in front of others. Take Shakespeare, or Milton, or Sir Thomas Browne. Our little knowledge of how things are done does not avail us much here, but it does lend an added zest to our enjoyment. Did we ever in our youngest days feel such amazement at their achievement as that which fills us now that we have sifted myriads of words and gone along uncharted ways in search of new forms for our new sensations? New books may be more stimulating and in some ways more suggestive than the old, but they do not give us that absolute certainty of delight which breathes through us when we come back again to *Comus*, or *Lycidas*, *Urn Burial*, or *Antony and Cleopatra*.

Far be it from us to hazard any theory as to the nature of art. It may be that we shall never know more about it than we know by nature, and our longer experience of it teaches us this only—that of all our pleasures those we get from the great artists are indisputably among the best; and more we may not know. But, advancing no theory, we shall find one or two qualities in such works as these which we can hardly expect to find in books made within the span of our lifetime. Age itself may have an alchemy of its own. But this is true: you can read them as often as you will without finding that they have yielded any virtue and left a meaningless husk of words; and there is a complete finality about them. No cloud of suggestions hangs about them teasing us with a multitude of irrelevant ideas. But all our faculties are summoned to the task, as in the great moments of our own experience; and some consecration descends upon us from their hands which we return to life, feeling it more keenly and understanding it more deeply than before.

THE TRUE READER

1. In "Hours in a Library" Virginia Woolf first compares the man who loves learning with the one who loves reading. In what ways does she say they differ? How does she describe the "true reader"? Do you agree with her that "the great season for reading" is "between the ages of eighteen and twenty-four"? Give reasons for your answer.

2. Can you recall your early initiation to books and libraries? Does it compare with that of the author? In what ways does reading change from this first stage? In the opinion of the writer, why do people go back to the classics?

3. Why do we eventually turn to reading contemporary writers? What are the reasons given for this change? How can the taste for bad books be a "pleasant possession"? Explain.

4. What kind of a case does the essayist make for bookshops? In judging today's writers, why is the knowledge of old writers important? Explain: "Age itself may have an alchemy of its own."

SUGGESTION FOR WRITING

Take a look at your reading tastes and determine what kind of a reader you are. Do you read the classics, or the writings of contemporary authors? Have you spent considerable time reading the works of one author in particular?

Do you prefer reading many examples of one type of writing? Decide on a suitable title and write an essay in answer to one of these questions.

A Churchill Sampler

SIR WINSTON CHURCHILL 1874–

We need not await the verdict of history to place Sir Winston Churchill among England's greatest men. His leadership carried England through the darkest period of her entire history—from the summer of 1940 to the autumn of 1941. During this time England stood alone, with a formidable enemy massed across the English Channel ready to attack.

This man who led England through her hour of greatest peril is the descendant of the famous Duke of Marlborough. His father was Lord Randolph Churchill; his mother, a brilliant and beautiful American, was the former Jennie Jerome. Churchill's early career included army service in India, Egypt, and South Africa, and a brief period as a war correspondent. In 1900 he entered the House of Commons as a member of the Conservative party. He was in government service almost continuously from that time until he retired in 1955. At the outbreak of World War II he became First Lord of the Admiralty (the equivalent of our Secretary of the Navy), and in 1940 he was made Prime Minister. Here his magnificent qualities of mind and spirit inspired the English people with the unparalleled courage to fight to victory.

In 1953 Churchill received two notable honors. Queen Elizabeth knighted him and presented him with the Order of the Garter. Later in the year he was awarded the Nobel Prize for Literature for his six volumes of memoirs, *The Second World War*. In 1954, on his eightieth birthday, he was acclaimed by Queen and country as "the greatest living Briton."

All his life, in the midst of a busy public career, Churchill has been a writer. As a young Army officer and later when in government service, he published much nonfiction—on his travels and war experiences, the Marlborough family, and international politics—and one novel. A collection of his speeches during World War II, *Blood, Sweat, and Tears,* takes its title from a sentence in his first speech as Prime Minister, which he delivered just as Hitler was approaching through Holland: "I have nothing to offer but blood, toil, tears, and sweat."

Since his retirement in 1955 he has completed work on the long-contemplated *History of the English-Speaking Peoples: The Birth of Britain* (to 1485), *The New World* (1485–1688), *The Age of Revolution* (1688–1815), and *The Great Democracies* (1815–1900). Sir Winston now divides his time between his home in England and the warm Mediterranean, where one of his hobbies is oil painting.

The Nature of Modern War

In *The Gathering Storm*, Churchill reviews some of his earlier impressions of the world tensions which World War I had failed to settle. This passage (written in 1928) on the meaning of war in our century is significant in the light of what followed. It is still pertinent for readers today in our far-from-peaceful world.

IT WAS NOT until the dawn of the twentieth century of the Christian Era that war began to enter into its kingdom as the potential destroyer of the human race. The organization of mankind into great states and empires, and the rise of nations to full collective consciousness, enabled enterprises of slaughter to be planned and executed upon a scale and with a perseverance never before imagined. All the noblest virtues of individuals were gathered together to strengthen the destructive capacity of the mass. Good finances, the resources of world-wide credit and trade, the accumulation of large capital reserves made it possible to divert for considerable periods the energies of whole peoples to the task of devastation. Democratic institutions gave expression to the will power of millions. Education not only brought the course of the conflict within the comprehension of everyone, but rendered each person serviceable in a high degree for the purpose in hand. The press afforded a means of unification and of mutual stimulation. Religion, having discreetly avoided conflict on the fundamental issues, offered its encouragements and consolations, through all its forms, impartially to all the combatants. Lastly, Science unfolded her treasures and her secrets to the desperate demands of men, and placed in their hand agencies and apparatus almost decisive in their character.

In consequence many novel features presented themselves. Instead of fortified towns being starved, whole nations were methodically subjected, or sought to be subjected, to the process of reduction by famine. The entire population in one capacity or another took part in the war; all were equally the object of attack. The air opened paths along which death and terror could be carried far behind the lines of the actual armies, to women, children, the aged, the sick, who in earlier struggles would perforce have been left untouched. Marvelous organization of railroads, steamships, and motor vehicles placed and maintained tens of millions of men continuously in action. Healing and surgery in their exquisite developments returned them again and again to the shambles. Nothing was wasted that could contribute to the process of waste. The last dying kick was brought into military utility.

But all that happened in the four years of the Great War was only a prelude to what was preparing for the fifth year. The campaign of the year 1919 would have witnessed an immense accession to the powers of destruction. Had the Germans retained the morale to make good their retreat to the Rhine, they would have been assaulted in the summer of 1919 with forces and by methods incomparably more prodigious than any yet employed. Thousands of airplanes would have shattered their cities. Scores of thousands of cannon would have blasted their front. Arrangements were being made to carry simultaneously a quarter of a million men, together with all their requirements, continuously forward across country in mechanical vehicles moving ten or fifteen miles each day. Poison gases of incredible malignity, against which only a secret mask (which the Germans could not obtain in time) was proof, would have stifled all resistance and paralyzed all life on the hostile front subjected to attack. No doubt the Germans too had their plans. But the hour of wrath had passed. The signal of relief was given, and the horrors of 1919 remained buried in the archives of the great antagonists.

The war stopped as suddenly and as universally as it had begun. The world lifted its head, surveyed the scene of ruin, and victors and vanquished alike drew breath. In a hundred laboratories, in a thousand arsenals, factories and bureaus, men pulled themselves up with a jerk, and turned from the task in which they had been absorbed. Their projects were put aside unfinished, unexecuted; but their knowledge was preserved; their data, calculations, and discoveries were hastily bundled together and docketed "for future reference" by the War Office in every country. The campaign of 1919 was never fought; but its ideas go marching along. In every army they are being explored, elaborated, refined, under the surface of peace, and should war come again to the world, it is not with the weapons and agencies prepared for 1919 that it will be fought, but with developments and extensions of these which will be incomparably more formidable and fatal.

It is in these circumstances that we entered upon that period of exhaustion which has been described as Peace. It gives us at any rate an opportunity to consider the general situation. Certain somber facts emerge, solid, inexorable, like the shapes of mountains from drifting mist. It is established that henceforward whole populations will take part in war, all doing their utmost, all subjected to the fury of the enemy. It is established that nations who believe their life is at stake will not be restrained from using any means to secure their existence. It is probable —nay, certain—that among the means which will next time be at their disposal will be agencies and processes of destruction wholesale, unlimited, and perhaps, once launched, uncontrollable.

Mankind has never been in this position before. Without having improved appreciably in virtue or enjoying wiser guidance, it has got into its hands for the first time the tools by which it can unfailingly accomplish its own extermination. That is the point in human destinies to which all the glories and toils of men have at last led them. They would do well to pause and ponder upon their new responsibilities. Death stands at attention, obedient, expectant, ready to serve, ready to shear away the peoples *en masse;* ready, if called on, to pulverize, without hope of repair, what is left of civilization. He awaits only the word of command. He awaits it from a frail, bewildered being, long his victim, now—for one occasion only—his Master.

The Miracle of Dunkirk

On June 4, 1940, Winston Churchill, Prime Minister of Great Britain, stood before the House of Commons to deliver this account of the successful evacuation of some three hundred thousand men of the British Expeditionary Forces. The position of the British Army, trapped on the beaches of northern France with its back to the English Channel, appeared hopeless and tragic. The Belgian Army had already surrendered; the French Army had ceased to be a fighting organization. For the British the choice seemed to be suicidal defense or humiliating surrender. A plan for rescue was hastily conceived. It demanded the concerted effort of all branches of the British armed services, aided by hundreds of volunteers manning small boats of every type. The achievement at Dunkirk has already taken its place among the heroic episodes of history.

THE GERMAN eruption swept like a sharp scythe around the right and rear of the Armies of the north. Eight or nine armored divisions, each of about four hundred armored vehicles of different kinds, but carefully assorted to be complementary and divisible into small self-contained units, cut off all communications between us and the main French Armies. It severed our own communications for food and ammunition, which ran first to Amiens and afterward through Abbeville, and it shoved its way up the coast to Boulogne and Calais and almost to Dunkirk. Behind this armored and mechanized onslaught came a number of German divisions in lorries, and behind them again there plodded comparatively slowly the dull brute mass of the ordinary German Army and German people, always so ready to be led to the trampling down in other lands of liberties and comforts which they have never known in their own land.

I have said this armored scythe-stroke almost reached Dunkirk—almost but not quite. Boulogne and Calais were the scenes of desperate fighting. The Guards defended Boulogne for a while and were then withdrawn by orders from this country. The Rifle Brigade, the 60th Rifles, and the Queen Victoria's Rifles, with a battalion of British tanks and one thousand Frenchmen, in all about four thousand strong, defended Calais to the last. The British Brigadier was given an hour to surrender. He spurned the offer, and four days of intense street fighting passed before silence reigned over Calais, which marked the end of a memorable resistance. Only thirty unwounded survivors were brought off by the Navy, and we do not know the fate of their comrades. Their sacrifice, however, was not in vain. At least two armored divisions, which otherwise would have been turned against the British Expeditionary Force, had to be sent to overcome them. They have added another page to the glories of the light divisions, and the time gained enabled the Gravelines water lines to be flooded and to be held by the French troops.

Thus it was that the port of Dunkirk was kept open. When it was found impossible for the Armies of the north to reopen their communications to Amiens with the main French Armies, only one choice remained. It seemed, indeed, forlorn. The Belgian, British, and French Armies were almost surrounded. Their sole line of retreat was to a single port and to its neighboring beaches. They were pressed on every side by heavy attacks and far outnumbered in the air.

When, a week ago today, I asked the House to fix this afternoon as the occasion for a statement, I feared it would be my hard lot to announce the greatest military disaster in our long history. I thought—and some good judges agreed with me—that perhaps twenty thousand or thirty thousand men might be re-embarked. But it certainly seemed that the whole of the French First Army and the whole of the British Expeditionary Force north of the Amiens-Abbeville gap would be broken up in the open field or else would have to capitulate for lack of food and ammunition. These were the hard and heavy tidings for which I called upon the House and the nation to prepare themselves a week ago. The whole root and core and brain of the British Army, on which and around which we were to build, and are to build, the great British Armies in the later years of the war, seemed about to perish upon the field or to be led into an ignominious and starving captivity. . . .

The enemy attacked on all sides with great strength and fierceness, and their main power, the power of their far more numerous Air Force, was thrown into the battle or else concentrated upon Dunkirk and the beaches. Pressing in upon their narrow exit, both from the east and from the west, the enemy began to fire with cannon upon the beaches by which alone the shipping could approach or depart. They sowed magnetic mines in the channels and seas; they sent repeated waves of hostile aircraft, sometimes more than a hundred strong in one formation, to cast their bombs upon the single pier that remained, and upon the sand dunes upon which the troops had their eyes for shelter. Their U-boats, one of which was sunk, and their motor launches took their toll of the vast traffic which now began. For four days or five days an intense struggle reigned. All their armored divisions—or what was left of them—together with great masses of infantry and artillery, hurled themselves in vain upon the ever-narrowing, ever-contracting appendix within which the British and French Armies fought.

Meanwhile the Royal Navy, with the willing help of countless merchant seamen, strained every nerve to embark the British and Allied troops; 220 light warships and 650 other vessels were engaged. They had to operate upon the difficult coast, often in adverse weather, under an almost ceaseless hail of bombs and an increasing concentration of artillery fire. Nor were the seas, as I have said, themselves free from mines and torpedoes. It was in conditions such as these that our men carried on, with little or no rest, for days and nights on end, making trip after trip across the dangerous waters, bringing with them always men whom they had rescued. The numbers they have brought back are the measure of their devotion and their courage. The hospital ships, which brought off many thousands of British and French wounded, being so plainly marked, were a special target for Nazi bombs; but the men and women on board them never faltered in their duty.

The Royal Air Force, which had already been intervening in the battle, so far as its range would allow, from home bases, now used part of its main metropolitan fighter strength and struck at the German bombers and at the fighters which in large numbers protected them. This struggle was protracted and fierce. Suddenly the scene was cleared; the crash and thunder has for the moment—but only for the moment—died away. A miracle of deliverance, achieved by valor, by perseverance, by perfect discipline, by faultless service, by resource, by skill, by unconquerable fidelity, is manifest to us all. The enemy was hurled back by the retreating British and French troops. He was so roughly handled that he did not hurry their departure seriously. The Royal Air Force engaged the main strength of the German Air Force, and inflicted upon them losses of at least four to one; and the Navy, using nearly one thousand ships of all kinds, carried over three hundred and thirty-five thousand men, French and British, out of the jaws of death and shame, to their native land and to the tasks which lie immediately ahead. We must be very careful not to assign to this deliverance the attributes of a victory. Wars are not won by evacuations. But there was a victory inside this deliverance, which should be noted. It was gained by the Air Force. Many of our soldiers coming back have not seen the Air Force at work; they saw only the bombers which escaped its protective attacks. They underrate its achievements. I have heard much talk of this; that is why I go out of my way to say this. I will tell you about it.

This was a great trial of strength between the British and German Air Forces. Can you conceive a greater objective for the Germans in the air than to make evacuation from these beaches impossible and to sink all these ships which were displayed, almost to the extent of thousands? Could there have been an objective of greater military importance and significance for the whole purpose of the war than this? They tried hard, and they were beaten back; they were frustrated in their task. We got the Army away and they have paid fourfold for any losses which they have inflicted. Very large formations of German airplanes—and we know that they are a very brave race—have turned on several occasions from the attack of one-quarter of their number of the Royal Air Force, and have dispersed in different directions. Twelve airplanes have been hunted by two. One airplane was driven into the water and cast away by the mere charge of a British airplane, which had no more ammunition. All of our types—the Hurricane, the Spitfire, and the new Defiant—and all our pilots have been vindicated as superior to what they have at present to face.

When we consider how much greater would be our advantage in defending the air above this island against an overseas attack, I must say that I find in these facts a sure basis upon which practical and reassuring thoughts may rest. I will pay my tribute to these young airmen. The great French Army was very largely, for the time being, cast back and disturbed by the onrush of a few thousands of armored vehicles. May it not also be that the cause of civilization itself will be defended by the skill and devotion of a few thousand airmen? There never has been, I suppose, in all the world, in all the history of war, such an opportunity for youth. The Knights of the Round Table, the Crusaders, all fall back into the past —not only distant but prosaic; these young men, going forth every morn to guard their native land and all that we stand for, holding in their hands these instruments of colossal and shattering power, of whom it may be said that

> Every morn brought forth a noble chance
> And every chance brought forth a noble knight

deserve our gratitude, as do all of the brave men who, in so many ways and on so many occasions, are ready, and continue ready, to give life and all for their native land.

I return to the Army. In the long series of very fierce battles, now on this front, now on that, fighting on three fronts at once, battles fought by two or three divisions against an equal or somewhat larger number of the enemy, and fought fiercely on some of the old grounds that so many of us knew so well—in these battles our losses in men have exceeded thirty thousand killed, wounded, and missing. I take occasion to express the sympathy of the House to all who have suffered bereavement or who are still anxious. The President of the Board of Trade is not here today. His son has been killed, and many in the House have felt the pangs of affliction in the sharpest form. But I will say this about the missing: we have had a large number of wounded come home safely to this country, but I would say about the missing that there may be very many reported missing who will come back home, someday, in one way or another. In the confusion of this fight it is inevitable that many have been left in positions where honor required no further resistance from them.

Against this loss of over thirty thousand men, we can set a far heavier loss certainly inflicted upon the enemy. But our losses in material are enormous. We have perhaps lost one-third of the men we lost in the opening days of the battle of 21st March, 1918, but we have lost nearly as many guns—nearly one thousand—and all our transport, all the armored vehicles that were with the Army in the north. This loss will impose a further delay on the expansion of our military strength. That expansion had not been proceeding as fast as we had hoped. The best of all we had to give had gone to the British Expeditionary Force; and although they had not the numbers of tanks and some articles of equipment which were desirable, they were a very well and finely equipped Army.

They had the first fruits of all that our industry had to give, and that is gone. And now here is this further delay. How long it will be, how long it will last, depends upon the exertions which we make in this island. An effort the like of which has never been seen in our records is now being made. Work is proceeding everywhere, night and day, Sundays and week-days. Capital and Labor have cast aside their interests, rights, and customs and put them into the common stock. Already the flow of munitions has leaped forward. There is no reason why we should not in a few months overtake the sudden and serious loss that has come upon us, without retarding the development of our general program.

Nevertheless, our thankfulness at the escape of our Army and so many men, whose loved ones have passed through an agonizing week, must not blind us to the fact that what has happened in France and Belgium is a colossal military disaster. The French Army has been weakened; the Belgian Army has been lost; a large part of those fortified lines upon which so much faith had been reposed is gone; many valuable mining districts and factories have passed into the enemy's possession; the whole of the Channel ports are in his hands, with all the tragic consequences that follow from that, and we must expect another blow to be struck almost immediately at us or at France. We are told that Herr Hitler has a plan for invading the British Isles. This has often been thought of before. When Napoleon lay at Boulogne for a year with his flat-bottomed boats and his Grand Army, he was told by someone, "There are bitter weeds in England." There are certainly a great many more of them since the British Expeditionary Force returned.

I would observe that there has never been a period in all these long centuries of which we boast when an absolute guarantee against invasion, still less against serious raids, could have been given to our people. In the days of Napoleon the same wind which would have carried his transports across the Channel might have driven away the blockading fleet. There was always the chance, and it is that chance which has excited and befooled the imaginations of many Continental tyrants. Many are the tales that are told. We are assured that novel methods will be adopted, and when we see the originality of malice, the ingenuity of aggression, which our enemy displays, we may certainly prepare ourselves for every kind of novel stratagem and every kind of brutal and treacherous maneuver. I think that no idea is so outlandish that it should not be considered and viewed with a searching, but at the same time, I hope, with a steady eye. We must never forget the solid assurances of sea power and those which belong to air power if it can be locally exercised.

I have, myself, full confidence that if all do their duty, if nothing is neglected, and if the best arrangements are made, as they are being made, we shall prove ourselves once again able to defend our island home, to ride out the storm of war, and to outlive the menace of tyranny, if necessary for years, if necessary alone. At any rate, that is what we are going to try to do. That is the resolve of His Majesty's Government—every man of them. That is the will of Parliament and the nation. The British Empire and the French Republic, linked together in their cause and in their need, will defend to the death their native soil, aiding each other like good comrades to the utmost of their strength. Even though large tracts of Europe and many old and famous states have fallen or may fall into the grip of the Gestapo and all the odious apparatus of Nazi rule, we shall not flag or fail. We shall go on to the end: we shall fight in France; we shall fight on the seas and oceans; we shall fight with growing confidence and growing strength in the air; we shall defend our island, whatever the cost may be—we shall fight on the beaches; we shall fight on the landing grounds; we shall fight in the fields and in the streets; we shall fight in the hills. We shall never surrender, and even if, which I do not for a moment believe, this island or a large part of it were subjugated and starving, then our Empire beyond the seas, armed and guarded by the British Fleet, would carry on the struggle until, in God's good time, the New World with all its power and might, steps forth to the rescue and the liberation of the old.

Churchill on War and Peace

WHAT General Weygand has called the Battle of France is over. The Battle of Britain is about to begin. Upon this battle depends the survival of Christian civilization. Upon it depends our own British life and the long continuity of our institutions and our empire. The whole fury and might of the enemy must very soon be turned on us. Hitler knows that he will have to break us in this island or lose the war. If we can stand up to him, all Europe may be free, and the life of the world may move forward into broad sunlit uplands. But if we fail, then the whole world, including the United States, including all that we have known and cared for, will sink into the abyss of a new dark age, made more sinister and perhaps more protracted by the light of perverted science. Let us therefore brace ourselves to our duty and so bear ourselves that if the British

Empire and its Commonwealth last for a thousand years, men will still say "This was their finest hour."

(*Speech in the House, June 18, 1940—
the day of the French capitulation.*)

THE PROBLEMS of victory are more agreeable than those of defeat, but they are no less difficult.

(*Speech in the House, November 1942.*)

THE VOICE OF A LEADER

1. Outline the major ways in which, according to Churchill, twentieth-century warfare is different from that of earlier times. Give some specific illustrations of techniques of warfare used in World War I which were quite unlike those used in nineteenth-century wars.

2. The author foresaw great changes in methods of conducting later wars. Give examples of the fulfillment of his prophecy in World War II. What does Churchill's prophecy say to us about current problems?

3. In "The Miracle of Dunkirk" how did the circumstances under which the speech was delivered affect the nature of Churchill's account of what had happened?

4. With a map to help you, study the progress of events so that you can give a clear account of (*a*) the position of the opposing forces, (*b*) the effect of the British and French delaying action at Calais, (*c*) the battle of Dunkirk, (*d*) the co-operative participation of the Royal Navy and the Royal Air Force.

5. To what extent was the prophecy of the closing line fulfilled?

APPRECIATING AN AUTHOR'S STYLE

Being aware of how a man reflects himself in his writing will help you to improve your own writing ability. You already have analyzed the writing of many authors, and by doing so, you have developed an appreciation for those elements which characterize effective written expression.

There are few readers who fail to respond to the style of Sir Winston Churchill, a master of prose. His incisive manner and ready wit lift his style far above that of most men in public life. Study the qualities of Churchill's style by noting (*a*) the directness and clarity of his sentences, (*b*) his use of repetition for emphasis, (*c*) his use of parallel construction and balanced sentences, (*d*) his emotional appeal.

Delight

J. B. PRIESTLEY 1894–

People are always asking me which are my favorites among the many novels, plays, and books of essays I have written. It is only when the question refers strictly to books of essays that I find it easy to answer. My own favorite here is undoubtedly *Delight,* from which the following short pieces have been chosen. Perhaps I like it best because writing it gave me so much pleasure. *Delight* consists entirely of short pieces, like those printed here, and I wrote them not one after the other but at odd times, whenever I felt like doing one. Very few books by experienced professional writers are composed in this random fashion. Generally we just stick at a job until it is done; we cannot afford to write things just when we think we would enjoy writing them. But this is how *Delight* was done, and probably this was the only way it could have been done. In the days when these pieces were written I still had my family living at home or frequently returning home, and when I had done a few of these pieces I would read them aloud in the evenings. I always felt, when writing them, that they should be read aloud, and some years after the book was published I filled two sides of a long-playing record with readings from it. Though books are handier things than records, I hope this particular record can still be obtained, because it does suggest the way I feel these pieces should be read, even by people who are reading to themselves. I have always felt that all good prose should read easily and effectively, have always tried to write through my ear and not my eye. These little *Delight* pieces in particular, however, seem to me to be essentially *spoken* prose, asking to be read aloud. So I hope readers of this volume will try the experiment. If they do not enjoy my pieces, they might at least enjoy the sound of their own voices and find delight that way, which is a good and well-tried way.

J. B. P.

Women and Clothes

WOMEN who say they are indifferent to clothes, like men who say they do not mind what they eat, should be distrusted: there is something wrong. And men who sneer at woman's passionate concern about dress should be banished to the woods. For my part I delight in women when they go into a conference huddle over new clothes. They seem to me then most themselves and the furthest removed from my sex. They are at such times completely in their own world. They are half children, half witches. Note their attitude during these clothes conferences. For example, their absolutely clear-sighted realism about themselves. We chaps always peer at ourselves through a haze of good will. We never believe we are as fat or as thin and bony as other people say we are. The ladies are free of all such illusions. (Notice the direct level glances they give each other on these occasions.) So in their clothes conference, unlike all masculine conferences, there is no clash of illusions. All of them meet on the firm ground of fact. What is known is immediately taken into account: Kate's left shoulder is higher than her right; Meg is very broad across the hips; Phyllis has very short legs. The conference line—and very sensible too—is that we are all imperfect creatures, so how do we make the best of ourselves? (If politicians and their senior officials tried the same line at international conferences, they could change the whole world in a week.) Yet the whole clothes huddle is not simply so much grim realism. There is one grand illusion that they all share and never dream of challenging. It is the belief that out of these clothes, with necessary swaps and alterations, beauty and witchery can emerge, that somewhere here is the beginning of an enchanted life. And I for one find this altogether delightful.

No School Report

WE FATHERS of families have one secret little source of delight that is closed to other men. As we read the school reports upon our children, we realize with a sense of relief that can rise to delight that—thank Heaven—nobody is reporting in this fashion upon us. What a nightmare it would be if our personalities were put through this mincing machine! [1] I can imagine my own report: *"Height and weight at beginning of term —5 feet, 9 inches: 13 stone, 10 pounds. At end of term—5 feet, 8 inches: 14 stone, 2 pounds. Note: Through greed and lack of exercise, J.B. is putting on weight and is sagging. He must get out more and eat and drink less. Conduct—Not satisfactory. J.B. is increasingly irritable, inconsiderate, and unco-operative. He is inclined to blame others for faults in*

---

[1] *mincing machine:* British for *meat grinder.*

himself. He complains of lack of sleep but persists in remaining awake to finish rubbishy detective stories. He smokes far too much, and on several occasions has been discovered smoking in bed. There is no real harm in him but at the present time he tends to be self-indulgent, lazy, vain, and touchy. He should be encouraged to spend some weeks this summer with the Sea Scouts or at a Harvest Camp. *English Language and Literature:* Fair but inclined to be careless. *French:* A disappointing term. *History:* Has not made the progress here that we expected of him. Should read more. *Mathematics:* Very poor. *Art:* Has made some attempts both at oils and water color but shows little aptitude. Has been slack in his Appreciation and did not attend Miss Mulberry's excellent talks on the Italian Primitives.[1] *Music:* Fair, but will not practice. *Natural History:* Still professes an interest but finds it impossible to remember names of birds, butterflies, flowers. Has not joined in the Rambles this term. *Chemistry:* Clearly has no interest in this subject. *Physics:* Poor, though occasionally shows interest. Fails to comprehend basic laws. *Physical Culture:* Sergeant Beefer reports that J.B. has been frequently absent and is obviously far from keen. A bad term. *General Reports:* J.B. is not the bright and helpful member of our little community that he once promised to be. He lacks self-discipline and does not try to cultivate a cheery outlook. There are times when he still exerts himself—e.g., he made a useful contribution to the end of term production of *A Comedy of Errors*—but he tends to be lazy and egoistical. His housemaster has had a talk with him, but I suggest that stronger parental guidance would be helpful, and is indeed necessary." And then I would be asked to see my father, and would find him staring and frowning at this report, and then he would stare and frown at me and would begin asking me, in his deep and rather frightening voice, what on earth was the matter with me. But it can't happen, not this side of the grave. I am knee-deep in the soggy world of graying hair and rotting teeth, of monstrous taxes and overdrafts, of vanishing friends and fading sight; but at least, I can tell myself delightedly, nobody is writing a school report upon me.

[1] *Italian Primitives:* early Italian painters.

Cooking Picnics

LIKE MOST men and unlike nearly all women, those atavistic[1] creatures, I detest picnics. One reason is that I am usually very hungry out in the

[1] *atavistic* (ăt′á·vĭst′ĭk): showing characteristics of remote or primitive ancestors.

open and I dislike the kind of food provided by picnics. Thus, there are few things to eat better than a properly dressed salad in a fine salad bowl, but there are few things less appetizing than an undressed salad out of a paper bag or cardboard box. Then, except for thick slices of ham between thin slices of bread, I have a growing distaste for the whole sandwich family, especially paste, egg, or cheese sandwiches. Again, anything with jam in it or on it is a curse on a summer's day. Finally, there is a peculiarly hard, green, sour little apple that must be grown specially for picnic boxes. Nevertheless, I have delighted in my time—and am not yet past it—in one kind of picnic, namely, the cooking picnic. This is for great souls. The instrumental basis of it is the frying pan. Sausages will do, though steak of course is better. Fried potatoes are essential, and persons whose stomachs shrink from a greasy chip rather underdone should stay at home and nibble health foods. Coffee, which stands up to wood smoke better than tea, is the beverage. The cooking picnic is, I will admit, a smoky job, at least in this damp climate of ours. I have superintended cooking picnics—and I am a natural superintendent on all these occasions—with inflamed and streaming eyes and every sinus wrecked, spluttering and coughing and choking, damning and blasting, glaring at would-be helpful children until they ran away and howled. I have stoked, and fried and stewed and dished out portions until there was nothing left for me but a few bits of greasy muck and a half a cup of coffee grounds. And even my pipe has tasted all wrong in the inferno of wood smoke. Yet I would not have missed a moment of it for a five-pound lunch in a private room on somebody else's expense sheet. Somewhere among the damp obstinate sticks, the dwindling sausages, the vanishing fat, the potatoes that would not brown and the water that would not boil, the billowing smoke on the hillside, the monstrous appetites of the company, there has been delight like a crumb of gold.

THE AUTHOR ASKS SOME QUESTIONS

1. How can you explain what, in "Women and Clothes," I have called women's "absolutely clear-sighted" and "grim realism" about themselves in some respects and their "grand illusion" in another respect?

2. One important ingredient of a sense of humor is the ability to laugh at oneself. Do you think I deserve a better grade in this respect for "No School Report" than I would receive in the subjects listed in my essay? Try writing a humorous report about yourself—not limiting yourself to academic subjects.

3. Do you agree with what I say in "Cooking Picnics" about the relative merits of basket picnics and cooking picnics? How do you account for the fact that some men who never want to cook on the kitchen stove are delighted to cook on an outdoor grill? Why do you think many men enjoy officiating at outdoor cooking occasions?

J. B. P.

SUGGESTION FOR WRITING

Using a light touch with an underlying purpose, write an essay or series of observations or brief comments on some of your own "delights."

READING LIST FOR MODERN ESSAYS

Browsing through the collections of essays in your library is a good way to find entertaining essays. Such books may include the work of both English and American writers as well as essays by writers of many other nationalities.

Bowen, Elizabeth, *A Time in Rome*
> If you have been, or want to go, to Rome, you will be delighted with this beautifully written commentary on the Eternal City.

Cooke, Alistair, *One Man's America*
> A newspaperman, formerly English but now American, takes an inquiring look at our country.

Eliot, T. S., *Selected Essays*
> The poet surveys literature and religion in a classic of modern criticism.

Fairbrother, Nan, *An English Year*
> There is real British flavor in these delightful reflections made around the calendar.

Highet, Gilbert, *People, Places, and Books*
> Mr. Highet, a Scotsman, has recorded his radio talks on the subjects indicated by the title.

Jameson, Robert U. (editor), *Essays Old and New,* 3rd edition
> This collection includes Forster, Leacock, Churchill, Stevenson, and others.

Macaulay, Rose, *Personal Pleasures*
> Akin to the mood of Priestley's *Delight.*

Maugham, W. Somerset, *Points of View*
> Essays, mostly on writers and writing.

Orwell, George, *A Collection of Essays*
> The author discusses books, humor, language, and politics.

Struther, Jan, *A Pocketful of Pebbles*

> The tradition of the informal, personal essay is perpetuated in this "Pocketful," written by the author of *Mrs. Miniver*.

Yeats, William Butler, *Mythologies*

> A collection of revised and rewritten essays based on Irish country beliefs.

FOR LISTENING

A selection from Churchill's speech of June 18, 1940, has been recorded and is available on *Many Voices 6B*. Priestley's "No School Report" is available on *Many Voices 12A*.

MODERN DRAMA

THERE is a simple reason why there are so few periods of really great theater in our whole western world. Too many things have to come right at the very same time. The dramatists must have the right actors, the actors must have the right playhouses, the playhouses must have the right audiences. We must remember that plays exist to be performed, not merely to be read. (Even when you read a play to yourself, try to perform it, to put it on a stage, as you go along.) As soon as a play has to be performed, then some kind of theatrical organization must be there to take charge of the production and to bring in the audience.

The audience is very important. The dramatist shapes his play; the director and his actors shape it too; but the final shaping is done by the audience. The audience is a kind of giant character in any play. Whenever the theater has been great, the audience has been great. At the present time the theater in London and New York is not more than second-rate, but then the audiences are second-rate too.

People should go to see plays as they go to concerts or to picture galleries, to experience some work of dramatic art. Most playgoing in European countries is undertaken in this spirit. But all too often in London and New York people see a play as one item in an evening's long program of celebration, coming between dinner and supper-and-dancing at a night club. The stage to many of these people is not a place where talented players work hard in a difficult art, but a sort of glittering shop window of "glamour." Why have we British and Americans this foolish, rather childish, attitude toward the theater? Perhaps because, unlike Continental people, we are still being influenced by the puritanism of our ancestors, and so secretly expect the theater to be gay and wicked. If we could all go to see the plays of Shakespeare or Shaw in exactly the same spirit in which we go to hear Bach suites or Brahms' symphonies, our drama would soon show some improvement.

POST-ELIZABETHAN DRAMA

The Elizabethan theater reached a height that we have never reached since. The theater of the Restoration and the eighteenth century had their minor triumphs, especially in a type of comedy imitated partly from the French theater (where Molière was the supreme master of comedy) though given a fresher and broader humor, particularly by Farquhar, Goldsmith, and Sheridan. Comedies by these three playwrights still have a place on the English stage.

The nineteenth century is noteworthy chiefly for the failure of the great poets, from Coleridge and Byron to Tennyson and Swinburne, to establish themselves in the theater. Somehow the wonderful fusion of poetry and true drama eluded all their efforts. They did their best, but their best was not good enough; not one of their poetic dramas is performed today.

THE EVOLUTION OF MODERN DRAMA

From the point of view of modern prose drama, a far more important figure is T. W. Robertson (1829–1871), a member of a theatrical family, and an actor himself, who took to playwriting. He had a curious fondness for short titles: *Ours, Caste, School,* and so forth. He was no genius, but he was an extremely successful playwright, with an excellent command of both pathos and humor. He is important because he can be regarded as the father of realism on the English stage. To begin with, his plays themselves were more realistic than other contemporary works. Then he insisted upon realistic scenery, rooms that looked like rooms, gardens that looked like gardens, solid sets in place of the old painted backcloths and wings; and he introduced many realistic effects—falling leaves, whirling snowflakes, and that kind of thing. Finally, instead of having a few days of sketchy rehearsals conducted by the chief actor and the stage manager, he demanded several weeks of careful rehearsing under his own direction. Thus, so far as the London theater is concerned, he became the first director of the modern type.

But it is doubtful if Robertson's innovations, sensible as they seemed at the time, benefited the theater ultimately. His elaborately realistic sets, rooms looking exactly like real rooms, had one grave disadvantage: it took time and money to put them up and take them down. The old scenery consisted of painted cloths that could easily be raised to or lowered from "the flies" (high above the stage, well out of sight of the audience). This meant there was no difficulty about playing one piece on Monday, another on Tuesday, a third on Wednesday, and so on. This was the true "repertory" system, adopted by all great theaters throughout the world. It is true that these theaters now make use of heavy realistic sets, but they do it at enormous expense and so most of them have to be subsidized. However, the use of such sets in the commercial playhouses of London and New York, which are operated to make a profit, brought an end to the repertory system, and put in its place the "long run," in which the play is kept on as long as it shows a profit. The repertory system is much better for dramatists, actors, and audiences.

SHAW, BARRIE, AND GALSWORTHY

Modern realistic prose drama reached its peak during the latter half of the nineteenth century, and curiously enough all three masters of it came from the North. They were Ibsen, Strindberg, and Chekhov. Against these, as outstanding figures of world theater, Britain can offer only Bernard Shaw, the master of modern comedy, whose characteristics are discussed at the end of *Pygmalion.* Contemporary with him in the Edwardian theater—that is, the theater as it was just after the beginning of the century to almost the beginning of World War I—were J. M. Barrie and John Galsworthy. Barrie was immensely popular in Britain and America but never became an important figure in world theater. He is an astonishingly skillful playwright, a wonderful technician, with a whimsical humor and wistful pathos entirely his own, but his themes lack both the depth and the breadth of appeal necessary for world drama. Perhaps his most characteristic and artful piece is *Dear Brutus,* though his *Mary Rose,* too often regarded as being merely sentimental, has unusual psychological depth and subtlety. His *Peter Pan,* marred by sentimentality but glorious in its humor, is one of the few children's classics in the theater. Galsworthy is important in the history of English drama because of his severely realistic method and his handling of social themes, seen at its best perhaps in *The Silver Box,* an early play, and later in *The Skin Game.* But his is a drama entirely devoid of poetry.

IRISH AND SCOTTISH DRAMA

It was across the Irish Sea, in Dublin, that poetry re-entered English-speaking drama. W. B. Yeats, the great poet, and his friend Lady Gregory, herself the author of many excellent plays of peasant life, together created an Irish theater, which had its home, a very modest home, in the small Abbey Theater in Dublin. They were fortunate, first, in finding a number of local actors and actresses of remarkable talent and strong individuality. They were equally fortunate in discovering in John Millington Synge a highly original dramatic genius. Though Synge writes in prose, an elaborate prose based on the speech of the peasants of western Ireland, his genius is essentially poetic. His masterpiece, *The Playboy of the Western World,* defies analysis, being both satirical and romantic, comic and tragic. His one-act *Riders to the Sea* is a good example of his highly individual manner in a tragic key. Much later, the Abbey Theater saw the first productions of Sean O'Casey, not the original genius that Synge was, but a dramatist of great talent, force, and wonderful humor, whose best early work is *Juno and the Paycock.*

After Barrie had done his best work, Scotland was represented during the 1930's and 40's by James Bridie, an unequal dramatist, not always sound in his construction, but one who brought a strong intellect, an original outlook, and something of Shaw's brilliance in debate to the theater. His *Sleeping Clergyman,* in which he makes use of his knowledge of medicine (he had been a doctor), is a good example of his work.

MODERN ENGLISH DRAMA

The London theater has long been attached to what is called "light comedy," rather frivolous witty pieces about people in drawing rooms, for which the unusually polished acting of London players is especially suited. In this particular vein, Somerset Maugham (*The Circle*) and then later, Noel Coward (*Blithe Spirit*) have been notable. Terence Rattigan (*The Browning Version*) began in this easy style but has since broadened his method and added some depth to his plays.

From the late 30's onward, T. S. Eliot has made a gallant but not altogether successful attempt to bring back poetry to the theater, contriving a rather flat, low-toned kind of poetic dialogue that would not seem too far away from ordinary speech. Though some later plays, notably *The Cocktail Party,* were more successful at the box office, it is likely that posterity will recognize an earlier play, *The Family Reunion,* as his best all-round piece of dramatic writing. Christopher Fry (*The Lady's Not for Burning, Venus Observed*) attempts, not without success but with some loss of clarity, a richer poetic style; but though Fry is an experienced man of the theater he tends to be weak on the purely dramatic side of his work. Though other poets, from W. H. Auden to Ronald Duncan, have also attempted poetic drama, no really successful schools of dramatists in this form have been established.

The younger prose dramatists like John Osborne (*Look Back in Anger, The Entertainer*) have a fine ear for effective dialogue and an eye for significant contemporary types of character, but generally they seem to show less interest in and capacity for construction, for the architecture of playwriting, than the older dramatists did. But here they have been encouraged by the younger drama critics, who also tend to be less interested in dramatic form than the older generation of critics.

Both the B.B.C. and the various commercial television networks have shown themselves anxious to use—and, if necessary, to train—new young dramatists who wish to write plays for television. There are signs that a distinct talent for this form—a form quite different from drama for the stage, much more intimate—is beginning to be found among young writers just as it is among young actors and actresses. And here such writers are certain of a vast audience willing to listen to anything they have to say. So drama continues.

J. B. P.

Pygmalion

GEORGE BERNARD SHAW 1856–1950

George Bernard Shaw became a legend in his own lifetime, and his death on November 2, 1950, marked the end of the last of the early pioneers in modern literature. His life spanned almost a century, and he was actively writing drama of a vigorous and original kind almost to the end of his days. Although his sharp tongue and satiric attitude toward conventional thinking made him many enemies, he was generally acknowledged during his last quarter century to be England's greatest living writer.

Shaw was born in Dublin of Irish gentry but from early manhood lived in London. Here he became one of the first socialists in England and served as pamphleteer and speaker for the Fabian Society.

During the eighties and nineties, Shaw became a journalist, writing criticism of music, drama, books, and art for various newspapers. Thus he became known to the literary world. Journalistic criticism fascinated him because it gave him the opportunity to express his ideas to a wide public.

Because he grew disgusted with the poor quality of plays being presented, Shaw began writing plays himself. He interested Ellen Terry, the leading romantic actress of the time, in modern drama; she was the inspiration for several of his plays and a lifelong friend and correspondent.

Like Dr. Samuel Johnson, Shaw was known for the peculiarities of his personality as well as for his literary ability. His active mind was full of theories: he was, for instance, a staunch vegetarian and a great attacker of standard English spelling, leaving, at his death, a large fortune to promote its "reform." But his reputation rests securely on the enduring qualities of his writing, which transcend personal idiosyncrasies. In 1925 he was awarded the Nobel Prize for Literature, and now, several decades later, is still one of the most widely read and admired modern English writers.

Pygmalion, written in 1912, has been a successful play on stage, screen, and television. Shaw took its title from a Greek myth, in which the sculptor Pygmalion carved an ivory statue of a maiden and then fell in love with it. He entreated the goddess Aphrodite for a wife resembling the statue, and she brought the statue to life. Shaw's Pygmalion is Professor Higgins, a phonetician who makes a business as well as a hobby of recording and studying various dialects. Higgins changes the cockney speech of an illiterate, bedraggled flower girl of the London streets into English that is acceptable to the upper classes. But more than that, through the strong influence of her new environment upon her character, a sensitive woman emerges from what had been a "squashed cabbage leaf." You will find that *Pygmalion* is a satire in Shaw's most amusing manner.

In the first act what happens is more important than who the main characters are. Most of these are not even identified by name during the early part of this act. As these persons become increasingly important to the play, however, you will learn to identify them as:

Miss Eynsford Hill, the daughter Clara
Mrs. Eynsford Hill, the mother
Mr. Eynsford Hill, the son Freddy
Eliza Doolittle, the flower girl
Professor Henry Higgins, the note taker and teacher of phonetics
Colonel Pickering, the gentleman and student of Indian dialects.

In the second act, two new characters are introduced:

Mrs. Pearce, Henry Higgins' housekeeper
Alfred Doolittle, Eliza's father.

In the third act, you will meet:

Mrs. Higgins, Henry Higgins' mother

ACT I

Covent Garden[1] at 11:15 P.M. *Torrents of heavy summer rain. Cab whistles blowing frantically in all directions. Pedestrians running for shelter into the market and under the portico[2] of St. Paul's Church, where*

---

[1] *Covent Garden:* a site north of the Strand, London, occupied by the principal fruit, flower, and vegetable market. Covent Garden Theater is the most important place for grand opera in London.

[2] *portico* (pōr′tǐ·kō): a platform with a protecting roof.

there are already several people, among them a lady and her daughter in evening dress. They are all peering out gloomily at the rain, except one man with his back turned to the rest, who seems wholly preoccupied with a notebook in which he is writing busily.

The church clock strikes the first quarter.

THE DAUGHTER (*in the space between the central pillars, close to the one on her left*). I'm getting chilled to the bone. What can Freddy be doing all this time? He's been gone twenty minutes.

THE MOTHER (*on her daughter's right*). Not so long. But he ought to have got us a cab by this.

A BYSTANDER (*on the lady's right*). He won't get no cab not until half-past eleven, missus, when they come back after dropping their theater fares.

THE MOTHER. But we must have a cab. We can't stand here until half-past eleven. It's too bad.

THE BYSTANDER. Well, it ain't my fault, missus.

THE DAUGHTER. If Freddy had a bit of gumption, he would have got one at the theater door.

THE MOTHER. What could he have done, poor boy?

THE DAUGHTER. Other people got cabs. Why couldn't he?

[FREDDY *rushes in out of the rain from the Southampton Street side, and comes between them closing a dripping umbrella. He is a young man of twenty, in evening dress, very wet round the ankles.*]

THE DAUGHTER. Well, haven't you got a cab?

FREDDY. There's not one to be had for love or money.

THE MOTHER. Oh, Freddy, there must be one. You can't have tried.

THE DAUGHTER. It's too tiresome. Do you expect us to go and get one ourselves?

FREDDY. I tell you they're all engaged. The rain was so sudden: nobody was prepared; and everybody had to take a cab. I've been to Charing Cross one way and nearly to Ludgate Circus the other; and they were all engaged.

THE MOTHER. Did you try Trafalgar Square?

FREDDY. There wasn't one at Trafalgar Square.

THE DAUGHTER. Did you try?

FREDDY. I tried as far as Charing Cross Station. Did you expect me to walk to Hammersmith?

THE DAUGHTER. You haven't tried at all.

THE MOTHER. You really are very helpless, Freddy. Go again; and don't come back until you have found a cab.

FREDDY. I shall simply get soaked for nothing.

THE DAUGHTER. And what about us? Are we to stay here all night in this draught, with next to nothing on? You selfish pig—

FREDDY. Oh, very well! I'll go, I'll go.

[*He opens his umbrella and dashes off Strandwards, but comes into collision with a flower girl, who is hurrying in for shelter, knocking her basket out of her hands. A blinding flash of lightning, followed instantly by a rattling peal of thunder, orchestrates the incident.*]

THE FLOWER GIRL. Nah then, Freddy, look why' y' gowin, deah.

FREDDY. Sorry. (*He rushes off.*)

THE FLOWER GIRL (*picking up her scattered flowers and replacing them in the basket*). There's menners f' yer! Te-oo banches o' voylets trod into the mad.[1] (*She sits down on the plinth[2] of the column, sorting her flowers, on the lady's right. She is not at all an attractive person. She is perhaps eighteen, perhaps twenty, hardly older. She wears a little sailor hat of black straw that has long been exposed to the dust and soot of London and has seldom if ever been brushed. Her hair needs washing rather badly: its mousy color can hardly be natural. She wears a shoddy black coat that reaches nearly to her knees and is shaped to her waist. She has a brown skirt with a coarse apron. Her boots are much the worse for wear. She is no doubt as clean as she can afford to be; but compared to the ladies she is very dirty. Her features are no worse than theirs; but their condition leaves something to be desired; and she needs the services of a dentist.*)

THE MOTHER. How do you know that my son's name is Freddy, pray?

THE FLOWER GIRL. Ow, eez ye-ooa san, is e? Wal, fewd dan y' de-ooty bawmz a mather should, eed now bettern to spawl a pore gel's flahrzn than ran awy athaht pyin. Will ye-oo py me f'them?[3]

(*Here, with apologies, this desperate attempt to represent her dialect without a phonetic alphabet must be abandoned as unintelligible outside London.*)

[1] "There is manners for you! Two bunches of violets trod in the mud." The girl speaks with a cockney accent.

[2] *plinth:* (plĭnth): lowest member of the base of a column.

[3] "Oh, he is your son, is he? Well, if you had done your duty by him as a mother should, he would know better than to spoil a poor girl's flowers and then run away without paying. Will you pay me for them?"

THE DAUGHTER. Do nothing of the sort, Mother. The idea!

THE MOTHER. Please allow me, Clara. Have you any pennies?

THE DAUGHTER. No. I've nothing smaller than sixpence.

THE FLOWER GIRL (*hopefully*). I can give you change for a tanner,[1] kind lady.

THE MOTHER (*to Clara*). Give it to me. (*Clara parts reluctantly.*) Now (*to the girl*) this is for your flowers.

THE FLOWER GIRL. Thank you kindly, lady.

THE DAUGHTER. Make her give you the change. These things are only a penny a bunch.

THE MOTHER. Do hold your tongue, Clara. (*To the girl*) You can keep the change.

THE FLOWER GIRL. Oh, thank you, lady.

THE MOTHER. Now tell me how you know that young gentleman's name.

THE FLOWER GIRL. I didn't.

THE MOTHER. I heard you call him by it. Don't try to deceive me.

THE FLOWER GIRL (*protesting*). Who's trying to deceive you? I called him Freddy or Charlie same as you might yourself if you was talking to a stranger and wished to be pleasant. (*She sits down beside her basket.*)

THE DAUGHTER. Sixpence thrown away! Really, Mamma, you might have spared Freddy *that*. (*She retreats in disgust behind the pillar.*)

[*An elderly gentleman of the amiable military type rushes into the shelter, and closes a dripping umbrella. He is in the same plight as* FREDDY, *very wet about the ankles. He is in evening dress, with a light overcoat. He takes the place left vacant by the* DAUGHTER'S *retirement.*]

THE GENTLEMAN. Phew!

THE MOTHER (*to the* GENTLEMAN). Oh, sir, is there any sign of its stopping?

THE GENTLEMAN. I'm afraid not. It started worse than ever about two minutes ago. (*He goes to the plinth beside the* FLOWER GIRL; *puts up his foot on it; and stoops to turn down his trouser end.*)

THE MOTHER. Oh dear! (*She retires sadly and joins her daughter.*)

THE FLOWER GIRL (*taking advantage of the military gentleman's proximity to establish friendly relations with him*). If it's worse, it's a sign it's nearly over. So cheer up, Captain; and buy a flower off a poor girl.

THE GENTLEMAN. I'm sorry. I haven't any change.

---

[1] *tanner:* English slang for a sixpence.

THE FLOWER GIRL. I can give you change, Captain.

THE GENTLEMAN. For a sovereign? I've nothing less.

THE FLOWER GIRL. Garn! [1] Oh do buy a flower off me, Captain. I can change half-a-crown. Take this for tuppence.

THE GENTLEMAN. Now don't be troublesome: there's a good girl. (*Trying his pockets*) I really haven't any change— Stop! Here's three hapence, if that's any use to you. (*He retreats to the other pillar.*)

THE FLOWER GIRL (*disappointed, but thinking three halfpence better than nothing*). Thank you, sir.

THE BYSTANDER (*to the girl*). You be careful; give him a flower for it. There's a bloke[2] here behind taking down every blessed word you're saying. (*All turn to the man who is taking notes.*)

THE FLOWER GIRL (*springing up terrified*). I ain't done nothing wrong by speaking to the gentleman. I've a right to sell flowers if I keep off the curb. (*Hysterically*) I'm a respectable girl. So help me, I never spoke to him except to ask him to buy a flower off me. (*General hubbub, mostly sympathetic to the* FLOWER GIRL *but deprecating[3] her excessive sensibility. Cries of* Don't start hollerin. Who's hurting you? Nobody's going to touch you. What's the good of fussing? Steady on. Easy easy, *etc., come from the elderly staid spectators, who pat her comfortingly. Less patient ones bid her shut her head, or ask her roughly what is wrong with her. A remoter group, not knowing what the matter is, crowd in and increase the noise with question and answer:* What's the row? What's he do? Where is he? A tec[4] taking her down. What! him? Yes! Him over there. Took money off the gentleman, *etc. The* FLOWER GIRL, *distraught and mobbed, breaks through them to the* GENTLEMAN, *crying wildly*) Oh, sir, don't let him charge me. You dunno what it means to me. They'll take away my character and drive me on the streets for speaking to gentlemen. They—

THE NOTE TAKER (*coming forward on her right, the rest crowding after him*). There, there, there, there! Who's hurting you, you silly girl? What do you take me for?

THE BYSTANDER. It's all right; he's a gentleman. Look at his boots. (*Explaining to the* NOTE TAKER) She thought you was a copper's nark, sir.

THE NOTE TAKER (*with quick interest*). What's a copper's nark?

---

[1] *Garn:* expression of disappointment and anger.
[2] *bloke:* slang name for a person.
[3] *deprecating* (dĕp′rē·kā′tĭng): deploring; disapproving.
[4] *tec:* detective.

THE BYSTANDER (*inapt at definition*). It's a—well, it's a copper's nark, as you might say. What else would you call it? A sort of informer.

THE FLOWER GIRL (*still hysterical*). I take my Bible oath I never said a word—

THE NOTE TAKER (*overbearing but good-humored*). Oh, shut up, shut up. Do I look like a policeman?

THE FLOWER GIRL (*far from reassured*). Then what did you take down my words for? How do I know whether you took me down right? You just show me what you've wrote about me. (*The* NOTE TAKER *opens his book and holds it steadily under her nose, though the pressure of the mob trying to read it over his shoulders would upset a weaker man.*) What's that? That ain't proper writing. I can't read that.

THE NOTE TAKER. I can. (*Reads, reproducing her pronunciation exactly*) "Cheer ap, Keptin; n' baw ye flahr orf a pore gel."

THE FLOWER GIRL (*much distressed*). It's because I called him Captain. I meant no harm. (*To the* GENTLEMAN) Oh, sir, don't let him lay a charge agen me for a word like that. You—

THE GENTLEMAN. Charge! I make no charge. (*To the* NOTE TAKER) Really, sir, if you are a detective, you need not begin protecting me against molestation by young women until I ask you. Anybody could see that the girl meant no harm.

THE BYSTANDERS GENERALLY (*demonstrating against police espionage*). Course they could. What business is it of yours? You mind your own affairs. He wants promotion, he does. Taking down people's words! Girl never said a word to him. What harm if she did? Nice thing a girl can't shelter from the rain without being insulted, etc., etc., etc. (*She is conducted by the more sympathetic demonstrators back to her plinth, where she resumes her seat and struggles with her emotion.*)

THE BYSTANDER. He ain't a tec. He's a blooming busybody: that's what he is. I tell you, look at his boots.

THE NOTE TAKER (*turning on him genially*). And how are all your people down at Selsey?

THE BYSTANDER (*suspiciously*). Who told you my people come from Selsey?

THE NOTE TAKER. Never you mind. They did. (*To the girl*) How do you come to be up so far east? You were born in Lisson Grove.

THE FLOWER GIRL (*appalled*). Oh, what harm is there in my leaving Lisson Grove? It wasn't fit for a pig to live in; and I had to pay four-and-six a week. (*In tears*) Oh, boo—hoo—oo—

THE NOTE TAKER. Live where you like; but stop that noise.

THE GENTLEMAN (*to the girl*). Come, come! he can't touch you: you have a right to live where you please.

A SARCASTIC BYSTANDER (*thrusting himself between the* NOTE TAKER *and the* GENTLEMAN). Park Lane, for instance. I'd like to go into the Housing Question with you, I would.

THE FLOWER GIRL (*subsiding into a brooding melancholy over her basket, and talking very low-spiritedly to herself*). I'm a good girl, I am.

THE SARCASTIC BYSTANDER (*not attending to her*). Do you know where *I* come from?

THE NOTE TAKER (*promptly*). Hoxton.

[*Titterings. Popular interest in the* NOTE TAKER'S *performance increases.*]

THE SARCASTIC ONE (*amazed*). Well, who said I didn't? Bly me! You know everything, you do.

THE FLOWER GIRL (*still nursing her sense of injury*). Ain't no call to meddle with me, he ain't.

THE BYSTANDER (*to her*). Of course he ain't. Don't you stand it from him. (*To the* NOTE TAKER) See here! What call have you to know about people what never offered to meddle with you? Where's your warrant?

SEVERAL BYSTANDERS (*encouraged by this seeming point of law*). Yes, where's your warrant?

THE FLOWER GIRL. Let him say what he likes. I don't want to have no truck with him.

THE BYSTANDER. You take us for dirt under your feet, don't you? Catch you taking liberties with a gentleman!

THE SARCASTIC BYSTANDER. Yes, tell *him* where he comes from if you want to go fortune-telling.

THE NOTE TAKER. Cheltenham, Harrow, Cambridge, and India.

THE GENTLEMAN. Quite right. (*Great laughter. Reaction in the* NOTE TAKER'S *favor. Exclamations of* He knows all about it. Told him proper. Hear him tell the toff [1] where he come from? etc.) May I ask, sir, do you do this for your living at a music hall?

THE NOTE TAKER. I've thought of that. Perhaps I shall some day.

[*The rain has stopped; and the persons on the outside of the crowd begin to drop off.*]

THE FLOWER GIRL (*resenting the reaction*). He's no gentleman, he ain't, to interfere with a poor girl.

---

[1] *toff* (tŏf): slang for a dandy.

THE DAUGHTER (*out of patience, pushing her way rudely to the front and displacing the* GENTLEMAN, *who politely retires to the other side of the pillar*). What on earth is Freddy doing? I shall get pneumonia if I stay in this draught any longer.

THE NOTE TAKER (*to himself, hastily making a note of her pronunciation of "monia"*). Earl's Court.

THE DAUGHTER (*violently*). Will you please keep your impertinent remarks to yourself.

THE NOTE TAKER. Did I say that out loud? I didn't mean to. I beg your pardon. Your mother's Epsom, unmistakably.

THE MOTHER (*advancing between her daughter and the* NOTE TAKER). How very curious! I was brought up in Largelady Park, near Epsom.

THE NOTE TAKER (*uproariously amused*). Ha! ha! What a devil of a name! Excuse me. (*To the* DAUGHTER) You want a cab, do you?

THE DAUGHTER. Don't dare speak to me.

THE MOTHER. Oh please, please, Clara. (*Her daughter repudiates her with an angry shrug and retires haughtily*.) We should be so grateful to you, sir, if you found us a cab. (*The* NOTE TAKER *produces a whistle*.) Oh, thank you. (*She joins her daughter*.)

[*The* NOTE TAKER *blows a piercing blast*.]

THE SARCASTIC BYSTANDER. There! I knowed he was a plain-clothes copper.

THE BYSTANDER. That ain't a police whistle. That's a sporting whistle.

THE FLOWER GIRL (*still preoccupied with her wounded feelings*). He's no right to take away my character. My character is the same to me as any lady's.

THE NOTE TAKER. I don't know whether you've noticed it, but the rain stopped about two minutes ago.

THE BYSTANDER. So it has. Why didn't you say so before? And us losing our time listening to your silliness! (*He walks off toward the Strand*.)

THE SARCASTIC BYSTANDER. I can tell where *you* come from. You come from Anwell. Go back there.

THE NOTE TAKER (*helpfully*). *H*anwell.[1]

THE SARCASTIC BYSTANDER (*affecting great distinction of speech*). Thenk you, teacher. Haw haw! So long. (*He touches his hat with mock respect and strolls off*.)

THE FLOWER GIRL. Frightening people like that! How would he like it himself?

---

[1] *Hanwell:* location of a mental hospital.

THE MOTHER. It's quite fine now, Clara. We can walk to a motor bus. Come. (*She gathers her skirts above her ankles and hurries off toward the Strand.*)

THE DAUGHTER. But the cab—(*her mother is out of hearing*). Oh, how tiresome! (*She follows angrily.*)

[*All the rest have gone except the* NOTE TAKER, *the* GENTLEMAN, *and the* FLOWER GIRL, *who sits arranging her basket and still pitying herself in murmurs.*]

THE FLOWER GIRL. Poor girl! Hard enough for her to live without being worrited and chivied.[1]

THE GENTLEMAN (*returning to his former place on the* NOTE TAKER'S *left*). How do you do it, if I may ask?

THE NOTE TAKER. Simply phonetics. The science of speech. That's my profession: also my hobby. Happy is the man who can make a living by his hobby! You can spot an Irishman or a Yorkshireman by his brogue. *I* can place any man within six miles. I can place him within two miles in London. Sometimes within two streets.

THE FLOWER GIRL. Ought to be ashamed of himself, unmanly coward!

THE GENTLEMAN. But is there a living in that?

THE NOTE TAKER. Oh, yes. Quite a fat one. This is an age of upstarts. Men begin in Kentish Town with £80 a year, and end in Park Lane with a hundred thousand. They want to drop Kentish Town; but they give themselves away every time they open their mouths. Now I can teach them—

THE FLOWER GIRL. Let him mind his own business and leave a poor girl—

THE NOTE TAKER (*explosively*). Woman! Cease this detestable boo-hooing instantly, or else seek the shelter of some other place of worship.

THE FLOWER GIRL (*with feeble defiance*). I've a right to be here if I like, same as you.

THE NOTE TAKER. A woman who utters such depressing and disgusting sounds has no right to be anywhere—no right to live. Remember that you are a human being with a soul and the divine gift of articulate speech— that your native language is the language of Shakespeare and Milton and the Bible—and don't sit there crooning like a bilious pigeon.

THE FLOWER GIRL (*quite overwhelmed, looking up at him in mingled wonder and deprecation without daring to raise her head*). Ah-ah-ah-ow-ow-ow-oo!

---

[1] *worrited and chivied:* a cockney expression, meaning worried and tormented.

THE NOTE TAKER (*whipping out his book*). Heavens! what a sound! (*He writes; then holds out the book and reads, reproducing her vowels exactly.*) Ah-ah-ah-ow-ow-ow-oo!

THE FLOWER GIRL (*tickled by the performance, and laughing in spite of herself*). Garn!

THE NOTE TAKER. You see this creature with her curbstone English: the English that will keep her in the gutter to the end of her days. Well, sir, in three months I could pass that girl off as a duchess at an ambassador's garden party. I could even get her a place as lady's maid or shop assistant, which requires better English. That's the sort of thing I do for commercial millionaires. And on the profits of it I do genuine scientific work in phonetics, and a little as a poet on Miltonic lines.

THE GENTLEMAN. I am myself a student of Indian dialects; and—

THE NOTE TAKER (*eagerly*). Are you? Do you know Colonel Pickering, the author of *Spoken Sanscrit?* [1]

THE GENTLEMAN. I *am* Colonel Pickering. Who are you?

THE NOTE TAKER. Henry Higgins, author of *Higgins' Universal Alphabet.* [2]

PICKERING (*with enthusiasm*). I came from India to meet you.

HIGGINS. I was going to India to meet you.

PICKERING. Where do you live?

HIGGINS. 27A Wimpole Street. Come and see me tomorrow.

PICKERING. I'm at the Carlton. Come with me now and let's have a jaw over some supper.

HIGGINS. Right you are.

THE FLOWER GIRL (*to* PICKERING, *as he passes her*). Buy a flower, kind gentleman. I'm short for my lodging.

PICKERING. I really haven't any change. I'm sorry. (*He goes away.*)

HIGGINS (*shocked at the girl's mendacity*). Liar. You said you could change half-a-crown.

THE FLOWER GIRL (*rising in desperation*). You ought to be stuffed with nails, you ought. (*Flinging the basket at his feet*) Take the whole blooming basket for sixpence.

[*The church clock strikes the second quarter.*]

HIGGINS (*hearing in it the voice of God, rebuking him for his Pharisaic* [3]

---

[1] *Sanscrit* (săn′skrĭt): ancient language of the Hindus of India.

[2] *Universal Alphabet:* Shaw is speaking here. He felt that a universal alphabet would help to solve many problems.

[3] *Pharisaic* (făr′ĭ·sā′ĭk): The Pharisees were a group among the ancient Jews known for their formality and strictness. Higgins realizes his strictness of thought and lack of charity toward the flower girl.

want of charity to the poor girl). A reminder. (He raises his hat solemnly; then throws a handful of money into the basket and follows PICKERING.)

THE FLOWER GIRL (*picking up a half-crown*). Ah-ow-ooh! (*Picking up a couple of florins*) Aaah-ow-ooh! (*Picking up several coins*) Aaaaaah-ow-ooh! (*Picking up a half-sovereign*) Aaaaaaaaaaaah-ow-ooh!!!

FREDDY (*springing out of a taxicab*). Got one at last. Hallo! (*To the girl*) Where are the two ladies that were here?

THE FLOWER GIRL. They walked to the bus when the rain stopped.

FREDDY. And left me with a cab on my hands! Damnation!

THE FLOWER GIRL (*with grandeur*). Never mind, young man. I'm going home in a taxi. (*She sails off to the cab. The driver puts his hand behind him and holds the door firmly shut against her. Quite understanding his mistrust, she shows him her handful of money.*) Eightpence ain't no object to me, Charlie. (*He grins and opens the door.*) Angel Court, Drury Lane, round the corner of Micklejohn's oil shop. Let's see how fast you can make her hop it. (*She gets in and pulls the door to with a slam as the taxicab starts.*)

FREDDY. Well, I'm dashed!

MEETING THE CHARACTERS

1. Major characters of a play generally are identified by name when they first appear. Why are the characters not identified in the opening of Act I? Notice what types of people are represented in this act. How would you describe them? How do the mother and her daughter differ in character? What kind of man is Freddy?

2. Why does the crowd stir up a dispute between the flower girl and the note taker? Whose side does the group take? Why? What do you learn about the flower girl that helps you to understand what kind of person she is? How does she react to the sudden possession of money?

3. The flower girl speaks a cockney dialect. Look up "cockney" to determine what kind of dialect it is and what people speak it. Why do you think Shaw includes some speeches written in cockney? What reason does he give for not continuing to write the cockney dialect?

4. Why is the note taker referred to as a detective? What is his profession? What kind of people does he teach? Can you tell what his feelings are toward his pupils? What is his attitude toward the flower girl?

5. What do Higgins, the note taker, and Colonel Pickering, the gentleman, have in common? At this point in the play, try to formulate some idea of the kind of men Higgins and Pickering are. Are they both gentlemen? Give reasons for your answers.

ACT II

Next day at 11 A.M. HIGGINS' *laboratory in Wimpole Street. It is a room on the first floor, looking on the street, and was meant for the drawing room. The double doors are in the middle of the back wall; and persons entering find in the corner to their right two tall file cabinets at right angles to one another against the walls. In this corner stands a flat writing table, on which are a phonograph, a laryngoscope,[1] a row of tiny organ pipes with bellows, a set of lamp chimneys for singing flames with burners attached to a gas plug in the wall by an indiarubber tube, several tuning forks of different sizes, a life-size image of half a human head, showing in section the vocal organs, and a box containing a supply of wax cylinders for the phonograph.*

Further down the room, on the same side, is a fireplace, with a comfortable leather-covered easy chair at the side of the hearth nearest the door, and a coal scuttle. There is a clock on the mantelpiece. Between the fireplace and the phonograph table is a stand for newspapers.

On the other side of the central door, to the left of the visitor, is a cabinet of shallow drawers. On it is a telephone and the telephone directory. The corner beyond, and most of the side wall, is occupied by a grand piano, with the keyboard at the end furthest from the door, and a bench for the player extending the full length of the keyboard. On the piano is a dessert dish heaped with fruit and sweets, mostly chocolates.

The middle of the room is clear. Besides the easy chair, the piano bench, and two chairs at the phonograph table, there is one stray chair. It stands near the fireplace. On the walls, engravings: mostly Piranesis[2] and mezzotint portraits. No paintings.

PICKERING *is seated at the table, putting down some cards and a tuning fork which he has been using.* HIGGINS *is standing up near him, closing two or three file drawers which are hanging out. He appears in the morning light as a robust, vital, appetizing sort of man of forty or thereabouts, dressed in a professional-looking black frock coat with a white linen collar and black silk tie. He is of the energetic, scientific type, heartily, even violently interested in everything that can be studied as a scientific subject, and careless about himself and other people, including their feelings. He is, in fact, but for his years and size, rather like a very impetuous*

---

[1] *laryngoscope* (lă·rĭng′gō·skōp): an instrument for examining the voice.
[2] *Piranesi:* Italian engraver of the eighteenth century.

*baby "taking notice" eagerly and loudly, and requiring almost as much
watching to keep him out of unintended mischief. His manner varies from
genial bullying when he is in a good humor to stormy petulance when
anything goes wrong; but he is so entirely frank and void of malice that he
remains likable even in his least reasonable moments.*

HIGGINS (*as he shuts the last drawer*). Well, I think that's the whole
show.

PICKERING. It's really amazing. I haven't taken half of it in, you know.

HIGGINS. Would you like to go over any of it again?

PICKERING (*rising and coming to the fireplace, where he plants himself
with his back to the fire*). No, thank you; not now. I'm quite done up for
this morning.

HIGGINS (*following him, and standing beside him on his left*). Tired of
listening to sounds?

PICKERING. Yes. It's a fearful strain. I rather fancied myself because
I can pronounce twenty-four distinct vowel sounds, but your hundred and
thirty beat me. I can't hear a bit of difference between most of them.

HIGGINS (*chuckling, and going over to the piano to eat sweets*). Oh,
that comes with practice. You hear no difference at first; but you keep on
listening, and presently you find they're all as different as A from B.
(MRS. PEARCE *looks in; she is* HIGGINS' *housekeeper*.) What's the matter?

MRS. PEARCE (*hesitating, evidently perplexed*). A young woman wants
to see you, sir.

HIGGINS. A young woman! What does she want?

MRS. PEARCE. Well, sir, she says you'll be glad to see her when you
know what she's come about. She's quite a common girl, sir. Very common indeed. I should have sent her away, only I thought perhaps you
wanted her to talk into your machines. I hope I've not done wrong, but
really you see such queer people sometimes—you'll excuse me, I'm sure,
sir—

HIGGINS. Oh, that's all right, Mrs. Pearce. Has she an interesting accent?

MRS. PEARCE. Oh, something dreadful, sir, really. I don't know how
you can take an interest in it.

HIGGINS (*to* PICKERING). Let's have her up. Show her up, Mrs. Pearce.
(*He rushes across to his working table and picks out a cylinder to use on
the phonograph.*)

MRS. PEARCE (*only half resigned to it*). Very well, sir. It's for you to
say. (*She goes downstairs.*)

HIGGINS. This is rather a bit of luck. I'll show you how I make records. We'll set her talking; and I'll take it down first in Bell's Visible Speech; then in broad Romic; and then we'll get her on the phonograph so that you can turn her on as often as you like with the written transcript before you.

MRS. PEARCE (*returning*). This is the young woman, sir.

[*The* FLOWER GIRL *enters in state. She has a hat with three ostrich feathers —orange, sky-blue, and red. She has a nearly clean apron, and the shoddy coat has been tidied a little. The pathos of this deplorable figure, with its innocent vanity and consequential air, touches* PICKER-ING, *who has already straightened himself in the presence of* MRS. PEARCE. *But as to* HIGGINS, *the only distinction he makes between men and women is that when he is neither bullying nor exclaiming to the heavens against some featherweight cross, he coaxes women as a child coaxes its nurse when it wants to get anything out of her.*]

HIGGINS (*brusquely,*[1] *recognizing her with unconcealed disappointment, and at once, babylike, making an intolerable grievance of it*). Why, this is the girl I jotted down last night. She's no use; I've got all the records I want of the Lisson Grove lingo[2]; and I'm not going to waste another cylinder on it. (*To the girl*) Be off with you: I don't want you.

THE FLOWER GIRL. Don't you be so saucy. You ain't heard what I come for yet. (*To* MRS. PEARCE, *who is waiting at the door for further instructions*) Did you tell him I came in a taxi?

MRS. PEARCE. Nonsense, girl! What do you think a gentleman like Mr. Higgins cares what you came in?

THE FLOWER GIRL. Oh, we *are* proud! He ain't above giving lessons, not him. I heard him say so. Well, I ain't come here to ask for any compliment; and if my money's not good enough I can go elsewhere.

HIGGINS. Good enough for what?

THE FLOWER GIRL. Good enough for ye-oo. Now you know, don't you? I'm come to have lessons, I am. And to pay for 'em too; make no mistake.

HIGGINS (*stupefied*). Well!!! (*Recovering his breath with a gasp*) What do you expect me to say to you?

THE FLOWER GIRL. Well, if you was a gentleman, you might ask me to sit down, I think. Don't I tell you I'm bringing you business?

---

[1] *brusquely* (brŭsk′lĭ): abruptly.
[2] *lingo* (lĭng′gō): dialect.

HIGGINS. Pickering, shall we ask this baggage to sit down, or shall we throw her out of the window?

THE FLOWER GIRL (*running away in terror to the piano, where she turns at bay*). Ah-ah-oh-ow-ow-ow-oo! (*Wounded and whimpering*) I won't be called a baggage when I've offered to pay like any lady.

[*Motionless, the two men stare at her from the other side of the room, amazed.*]

PICKERING (*gently*). What is it you want, my girl?

THE FLOWER GIRL. I want to be a lady in a flower shop 'stead of selling at the corner of Tottenham[1] Court Road. But they won't take me unless I can talk more genteel. He said he could teach me. Well, here I am ready to pay him—not asking any favor—and he treats me as if I was dirt.

MRS. PEARCE. How can you be such a foolish ignorant girl as to think you could afford to pay Mr. Higgins?

THE FLOWER GIRL. Why shouldn't I? I know what lessons cost as well as you do, and I'm ready to pay.

HIGGINS. How much?

THE FLOWER GIRL (*coming back to him, triumphant*). Now you're talking! I thought you'd come off it when you saw a chance of getting back a bit of what you chucked at me last night. (*Confidentially*) You'd had a drop in, hadn't you?

HIGGINS (*peremptorily*). Sit down.

THE FLOWER GIRL. Oh, if you're going to make a compliment of it—

HIGGINS (*thundering at her*). Sit down.

MRS. PEARCE (*severely*). Sit down, girl. Do as you're told. (*She places the stray chair near the hearthrug between* HIGGINS *and* PICKERING, *and stands behind it waiting for the girl to sit down.*)

THE FLOWER GIRL. Ah-ah-ah-ow-ow-oo! (*She stands, half rebellious, half bewildered.*)

PICKERING (*very courteous*). Won't you sit down?

LIZA (*coyly*). Don't mind if I do. (*She sits down.* PICKERING *returns to the hearthrug.*)

HIGGINS. What's your name?

THE FLOWER GIRL. Liza Doolittle.

HIGGINS (*declaiming gravely*).

> Eliza, Elizabeth, Betsy and Bess,
> They went to the woods to get a bird's nes':

---

[1] *Tottenham* (tŏt'năm).

PICKERING. They found a nest with four eggs in it:

HIGGINS. They took one apiece, and left three in it.

[*They laugh heartily at their own wit.*]

LIZA. Oh, don't be silly.

MRS. PEARCE. You mustn't speak to the gentleman like that.

LIZA. Well, why won't he speak sensible to me?

HIGGINS. Come back to business. How much do you propose to pay me for the lessons?

LIZA. Oh, I know what's right. A lady friend of mine gets French lessons for eighteenpence an hour from a real French gentleman. Well, you wouldn't have the face to ask me the same for teaching me my own language as you would for French; so I won't give more than a shilling. Take it or leave it.

HIGGINS (*walking up and down the room, rattling his keys and his cash in his pockets*). You know, Pickering, if you consider a shilling, not as a simple shilling, but as a percentage of this girl's income, it works out as fully equivalent to sixty or seventy guineas from a millionaire.

PICKERING. How so?

HIGGINS. Figure it out. A millionaire has about £150 a day. She earns about half-a-crown.

LIZA (*haughtily*). Who told you I only—

HIGGINS (*continuing*). She offers me two-fifths of her day's income for a lesson. Two-fifths of a millionaire's income for a day would be somewhere about £60. It's handsome. By George, it's enormous! It's the biggest offer I ever had.

LIZA (*rising, terrified*). Sixty pounds! What are you talking about? I never offered you sixty pounds. Where would I get—

HIGGINS. Hold your tongue.

LIZA (*weeping*). But I ain't got sixty pounds. Oh—

MRS. PEARCE. Don't cry, you silly girl. Sit down. Nobody is going to touch your money.

HIGGINS. Somebody is going to touch you, with a broomstick, if you don't stop sniveling. Sit down.

LIZA (*obeying slowly*). Ah-ah-ah-ow-oo-o! One would think you was my father.

HIGGINS. If I decide to teach you, I'll be worse than two fathers to you. Here! (*He offers her his silk handkerchief.*)

LIZA. What's this for?

HIGGINS. To wipe your eyes. To wipe any part of your face that feels moist. Remember: that's your handkerchief; and that's your sleeve. Don't mistake the one for the other if you wish to become a lady in a shop.

[LIZA, *utterly bewildered, stares helplessly at him.*]

MRS. PEARCE. It's no use talking to her like that, Mr. Higgins. She doesn't understand you. Besides, you're quite wrong. She doesn't do it that way at all. (*She takes the handkerchief.*)

LIZA (*snatching it*). Here! You give me that handkerchief. He give it to me, not to you.

PICKERING (*laughing*). He did. I think it must be regarded as her property, Mrs. Pearce.

MRS. PEARCE (*resigning herself*). Serve you right, Mr. Higgins.

PICKERING. Higgins, I'm interested. What about the ambassador's garden party? I'll say you're the greatest teacher alive if you make that good. I'll bet you all the expense of the experiment you can't do it. And I'll pay for the lessons.

LIZA. Oh, you are real good. Thank you, Captain.

HIGGINS (*tempted, looking at her*). It's almost irresistible. She's so deliciously low—so horribly dirty—

LIZA (*protesting extremely*). Ah-ah-ah-ah-ow-ow-oo-oo!!! I ain't dirty: I washed my face and hands afore I come, I did.

PICKERING. You're certainly not going to turn her head with flattery, Higgins.

MRS. PEARCE (*uneasy*). Oh, don't say that, sir. There's more ways than one of turning a girl's head; and nobody can do it better than Mr. Higgins, though he may not always mean it. I do hope, sir, you won't encourage him to do anything foolish.

HIGGINS (*becoming excited as the idea grows on him*). What is life but a series of inspired follies? The difficulty is to find them to do. Never lose a chance. It doesn't come every day. I shall make a duchess of this draggle-tailed guttersnipe.

LIZA (*strongly deprecating this view of her*). Ah-ah-ah-ow-ow-oo!

HIGGINS (*carried away*). Yes, in six months—in three if she has a good ear and a quick tongue—I'll take her anywhere and pass her off as anything. We'll start today! now! this moment! Take her away and clean her, Mrs. Pearce. Monkey Brand, if it won't come off any other way. Is there a good fire in the kitchen?

MRS. PEARCE (*protesting*). Yes, but—

HIGGINS (*storming on*). Take all her clothes off and burn them. Ring up Whiteley or somebody for new ones. Wrap her up in brown paper 'til they come.

LIZA. You're no gentleman, you're not, to talk of such things. I'm a good girl, I am; and I know what the like of you are, I do.

HIGGINS. We want none of your Lisson Grove prudery[1] here, young woman. You've got to learn to behave like a duchess. Take her away, Mrs. Pearce. If she gives you any trouble, wallop her.

LIZA (*springing up and running between* PICKERING *and* MRS. PEARCE *for protection*). No! I'll call the police, I will.

MRS. PEARCE. But I've no place to put her.

HIGGINS. Put her in the dustbin.

LIZA. Ah-ah-ah-ow-ow-oo!

PICKERING. Oh come, Higgins! Be reasonable.

MRS. PEARCE (*resolutely*). You *must* be reasonable, Mr. Higgins. Really you must. You can't walk over everybody like this.

[HIGGINS, *thus scolded, subsides. The hurricane is succeeded by a zephyr of amiable surprise.*]

HIGGINS (*with professional exquisiteness of modulation*). *I* walk over everybody! My dear Mrs. Pearce, my dear Pickering, I never had the slightest intention of walking over anyone. All I propose is that we should be kind to this poor girl. We must help her to prepare and fit herself for her new station in life. If I did not express myself clearly it was because I did not wish to hurt her delicacy, or yours.

[LIZA, *reassured, steals back to her chair.*]

MRS. PEARCE (*to* PICKERING). Well, did you ever hear anything like that, sir?

PICKERING (*laughing heartily*). Never, Mrs. Pearce. Never.

HIGGINS (*patiently*). What's the matter?

MRS. PEARCE. Well, the matter is, sir, that you can't take a girl up like that as if you were picking up a pebble on the beach.

HIGGINS. Why not?

MRS. PEARCE. Why not! But you don't know anything about her. What about her parents? She may be married.

---

[1] *prudery* (prōōd'ĕr·ĭ): excessive modesty in speech, behavior, or dress.

LIZA. Garn!

HIGGINS. There! As the girl very properly says, Garn! Married indeed! Don't you know that a woman of that class looks a worn-out drudge of fifty a year after she's married?

LIZA. Who'd marry me?

HIGGINS (*suddenly resorting to the most thrillingly beautiful low tones in his best elocutionary[1] style*). By George, Eliza, the streets will be strewn with the bodies of men shooting themselves for your sake before I've done with you.

MRS. PEARCE. Nonsense, sir. You mustn't talk like that to her.

LIZA (*rising and squaring herself determinedly*). I'm going away. He's off his chump, he is. I don't want no balmies teaching me.

HIGGINS (*wounded in his tenderest point by her insensibility to his elocution*). Oh, indeed! I'm mad, am I? Very well, Mrs. Pearce, you needn't order the new clothes for her. Throw her out.

LIZA (*whimpering*). Nah-ow. You got no right to touch me.

MRS. PEARCE. You see now what comes of being saucy. (*Indicating the door*) This way, please.

LIZA (*almost in tears*). I didn't want no clothes. I wouldn't have taken them. (*She throws away the handkerchief.*) I can buy my own clothes.

HIGGINS (*deftly retrieving the handkerchief and intercepting her on her reluctant way to the door*). You're an ungrateful wicked girl. This is my return for offering to take you out of the gutter and dress you beautifully and make a lady of you.

MRS. PEARCE. Stop, Mr. Higgins. I won't allow it. It's you that are wicked. Go home to your parents, girl; and tell them to take better care of you.

LIZA. I ain't got no parents. They told me I was big enough to earn my own living and turned me out.

MRS. PEARCE. Where's your mother?

LIZA. I ain't got no mother. Her that turned me out was my sixth stepmother. But I done without them. And I'm a good girl, I am.

HIGGINS. Very well, then, what on earth is all this fuss about? The girl doesn't belong to anybody—is no use to anybody but me. (*He goes to* MRS. PEARCE *and begins coaxing.*) You can adopt her, Mrs. Pearce. I'm sure a daughter would be a great amusement to you. Now don't make any more fuss. Take her downstairs, and—

MRS. PEARCE. But what's to become of her? Is she to be paid anything? Do be sensible, sir.

---

[1] *elocutionary* (ĕl′ō·kū′shŭn·ẽr·ĭ): pertaining to the art of public speaking.

HIGGINS. Oh, pay her whatever is necessary. Put it down in the house-keeping book. (*Impatiently*) What on earth will she want with money? She'll have her food and her clothes. She'll only drink if you give her money.

LIZA (*turning on him*). Oh you *are* a brute. It's a lie! Nobody ever saw the sign of liquor on me. (*She goes back to her chair and plants herself there defiantly.*)

PICKERING (*in good-humored remonstrance*). Does it occur to you, Higgins, that the girl has some feelings?

HIGGINS (*looking critically at her*). Oh no, I don't think so. Not any feelings that we need bother about. (*Cheerily*) Have you, Eliza?

LIZA. I got my feelings same as anyone else.

HIGGINS (*to* PICKERING, *reflectively*). You see the difficulty?

PICKERING. Eh? What difficulty?

HIGGINS. To get her to talk grammar. The mere pronunciation is easy enough.

LIZA. I don't want to talk grammar. I want to talk like a lady.

MRS. PEARCE. Will you please keep to the point, Mr. Higgins? I want to know on what terms the girl is to be here. Is she to have any wages? And what is to become of her when you've finished your teaching? You must look ahead a little.

HIGGINS (*impatiently*). What's to become of her if I leave her in the gutter? Tell me that, Mrs. Pearce.

MRS. PEARCE. That's her own business, not yours, Mr. Higgins.

HIGGINS. Well, when I've done with her, we can throw her back into the gutter; and then it will be her own business again; so that's all right.

LIZA. Oh, you've no feeling heart in you: you don't care for nothing but yourself. (*She rises and takes the floor resolutely.*) Here! I've had enough of this. I'm going (*making for the door*). You ought to be ashamed of yourself, you ought.

HIGGINS (*snatching a chocolate cream from the piano, his eyes suddenly beginning to twinkle with mischief*). Have some chocolates, Eliza.

LIZA (*halting, tempted*). How do I know what might be in them? I've heard of girls being drugged by the like of you.

[HIGGINS *whips out his penknife; cuts a chocolate in two; puts one half into his mouth and bolts it; and offers her the other half.*]

HIGGINS. Pledge of good faith, Eliza. I eat one half; you eat the other. (LIZA *opens her mouth to retort; he pops the half chocolate into it.*) You shall have boxes of them, barrels of them, every day. You shall live on them. Eh?

LIZA (*who has disposed of the chocolate after being nearly choked by it*). I wouldn't have ate it, only I'm too ladylike to take it out of my mouth.

HIGGINS. Listen, Eliza. I think you said you came in a taxi.

LIZA. Well, what if I did? I've as good a right to take a taxi as anyone else.

HIGGINS. You have, Eliza; and in future you shall have as many taxis as you want. You shall go up and down and round the town in a taxi every day. Think of that, Eliza.

MRS. PEARCE. Mr. Higgins, you're tempting the girl. It's not right. She should think of the future.

HIGGINS. At her age! Nonsense! Time enough to think of the future when you haven't any future to think of. No, Eliza. Do as this lady does: think of other people's futures; but never think of your own. Think of chocolates, and taxis, and gold, and diamonds.

LIZA. No, I don't want no gold and no diamonds. I'm a good girl, I am. (*She sits down again, with an attempt at dignity.*)

HIGGINS. You shall remain so, Eliza, under the care of Mrs. Pearce. And you shall marry an officer in the Guards, with a beautiful moustache: the son of a marquis, who will disinherit him for marrying you, but will relent when he sees your beauty and goodness—

PICKERING. Excuse me, Higgins; but I really must interfere. Mrs. Pearce is quite right. If this girl is to put herself in your hands for six months for an experiment in teaching, she must understand thoroughly what she's doing.

HIGGINS. How can she? She's incapable of understanding anything. Besides, do any of us understand what we are doing? If we did, would we ever do it?

PICKERING. Very clever, Higgins; but not sound sense. (*To* ELIZA) Miss Doolittle—

LIZA (*overwhelmed*). Ah-ah-ow-oo!

HIGGINS. There! That's all you'll get out of Eliza. Ah-ah-ow-oo! No use explaining. As a military man you ought to know that. Give her her orders; that's what she wants. Eliza, you are to live here for the next six months, learning how to speak beautifully, like a lady in a florist's shop. If you're good and do whatever you're told, you shall sleep in a proper bedroom, and have lots to eat, and money to buy chocolates and take rides in taxis. If you're naughty and idle you will sleep in the back kitchen among the black beetles, and be walloped by Mrs. Pearce with a broomstick. At the end of six months you shall go to Buckingham Palace in a carriage, beautifully dressed. If the King finds out you're not a lady, you will be taken by the police to the Tower of London, where your head will be cut off as a warning to other presumptuous flower girls. If you are not found out, you shall have a present of seven-and-sixpence to start life with as a lady in a shop. If you refuse this offer you will be a most ungrateful and wicked girl; and the angels will weep for you. (*To* PICKERING) Now are you satisfied, Pickering? (*To* MRS. PEARCE) Can I put it more plainly and fairly, Mrs. Pearce?

MRS. PEARCE (*patiently*). I think you'd better let me speak to the girl properly in private. I don't know that I can take charge of her or consent to the arrangement at all. Of course I know you don't mean her any harm; but when you get what you call interested in people's accents, you never think or care what may happen to them or you. Come with me, Eliza.

HIGGINS. That's all right. Thank you, Mrs. Pearce. Bundle her off to the bathroom.

LIZA (*rising reluctantly and suspiciously*). You're a great bully, you are. I won't stay here if I don't like. I won't let nobody wallop me. I never asked to go to Bucknam Palace, I didn't. I was never in trouble with the police, not me. I'm a good girl—

MRS. PEARCE. Don't answer back, girl. You don't understand the gentleman. Come with me. (*She leads the way to the door, and holds it open for* ELIZA.)

LIZA (*as she goes out*). Well, what I say is right. I won't go near the King, not if I'm going to have my head cut off. If I'd known what I was letting myself in for, I wouldn't have come here. I always been a good girl; and I never offered to say a word to him; and I don't owe him nothing; and I don't care; and I won't be put upon; and I have my feeling the same as anyone else—

[MRS. PEARCE *shuts the door; and* ELIZA'S *plaints[1] are no longer audible.* PICKERING *comes from the hearth to the chair and sits astride it with his arms on the back.*]

PICKERING. Excuse the straight question, Higgins. Are you a man of good character where women are concerned?

---

[1] *plaints:* complaints.

HIGGINS (*moodily*). Have you ever met a man of good character where women are concerned?

PICKERING. Yes, very frequently.

HIGGINS (*dogmatically, lifting himself on his hands to the level of the piano, and sitting on it with a bounce*). Well, I haven't. I find that the moment I let a woman make friends with me, she becomes jealous, exacting, suspicious, and a damned nuisance. I find that the moment I let myself make friends with a woman, I become selfish and tyrannical. Women upset everything. When you let them into your life, you find that the woman is driving at one thing and you're driving at another.

PICKERING. At what, for example?

HIGGINS (*coming off the piano restlessly*). Oh, Lord knows! I suppose the woman wants to live her own life, and the man wants to live his; and each tries to drag the other on to the wrong track. One wants to go north and the other south; and the result is that both have to go east, though they both hate the east wind. (*He sits down on the bench at the keyboard.*) So here I am, a confirmed old bachelor, and likely to remain so.

PICKERING (*rising and standing over him gravely*). Come, Higgins! You know what I mean. If I'm to be in this business I shall feel responsible for that girl. I hope it's understood that no advantage is to be taken of her position.

HIGGINS. What! That thing! Sacred, I assure you. (*Rising to explain*) You see, she'll be a pupil; and teaching would be impossible unless pupils were sacred. I've taught scores of American millionairesses how to speak English—the best-looking women in the world. I'm seasoned. They might as well be blocks of wood. I might as well be a block of wood. It's—

[MRS. PEARCE *opens the door. She has* ELIZA'S *hat in her hand.* PICKERING *retires to the easy chair at the hearth and sits down.*]

HIGGINS (*eagerly*). Well, Mrs. Pearce, is it all right?

MRS. PEARCE (*at the door*). I just wish to trouble you with a word, if I may, Mr. Higgins.

HIGGINS. Yes, certainly. Come in. (*She comes forward.*) Don't burn that, Mrs. Pearce. I'll keep it as a curiosity. (*He takes the hat.*)

MRS. PEARCE. Handle it carefully, sir, *please.* I had to promise her not to burn it; but I had better put it in the oven for a while.

HIGGINS (*putting it down hastily on the piano*). Oh! thank you. Well, what have you to say to me?

PICKERING. Am I in the way?

MRS. PEARCE. Not at all, sir. Mr. Higgins, will you please be very particular what you say before the girl?

HIGGINS (*sternly*). Of course. I'm always particular about what I say. Why do you say this to me?

MRS. PEARCE (*unmoved*). No, sir, you're not at all particular when you've mislaid anything or when you get a little impatient. Now it doesn't matter before me. I'm used to it. But you really must not swear before the girl.

HIGGINS (*indignantly*). *I* swear! (*Most emphatically*) I never swear. I detest the habit. What the devil do you mean?

MRS. PEARCE (*stolidly*). That's what I mean, sir. You swear a great deal too much. I don't mind your damning and blasting, and *what* the devil and *where* the devil and *who* the devil—

HIGGINS. Mrs. Pearce, this language from your lips! Really!

MRS. PEARCE (*not to be put off*).—but there is a certain word I must ask you not to use. The girl has just used it herself because the bath was too hot. It begins with the same letter as bath. She knows no better: she learnt it at her mother's knee. But she must not hear it from your lips.

HIGGINS (*loftily*). I cannot charge myself with having ever uttered it, Mrs. Pearce. (*She looks at him steadfastly. He adds, hiding an uneasy conscience with a judicial air*) Except perhaps in a moment of extreme and justifiable excitement.

MRS. PEARCE. Only this morning, sir, you applied it to your boots, to the butter, and to the brown bread.

HIGGINS. Oh, that! Mere alliteration, Mrs. Pearce, natural to a poet.

MRS. PEARCE. Well, sir, whatever you choose to call it, I beg you not to let the girl hear you repeat it.

HIGGINS. Oh, very well, very well. Is that all?

MRS. PEARCE. No, sir. We shall have to be very particular with this girl as to personal cleanliness.

HIGGINS. Certainly. Quite right. Most important.

MRS. PEARCE. I mean not to be slovenly about her dress or untidy in leaving things about.

HIGGINS (*going to her solemnly*). Just so. I intended to call your attention to that. (*He passes on to* PICKERING, *who is enjoying the conversation immensely*). It is these little things that matter, Pickering. Take care of the pence and the pounds will take care of themselves is as true of personal habits as of money. (*He comes to anchor on the hearthrug, with the air of a man in an unassailable position.*)

MRS. PEARCE. Yes, sir. Then might I ask you not to come down to breakfast in your dressing-gown, or at any rate not to use it as a napkin to the extent you do, sir. And if you would be so good as not to eat everything off the same plate, and to remember not to put the porridge saucepan out of your hand on the clean tablecloth, it would be a better example to the girl. You know you nearly choked yourself with a fish-bone in the jam only last week.

HIGGINS (*routed from the hearthrug and drifting back to the piano*). I may do these things sometimes in absence of mind; but surely I don't do them habitually. (*Angrily*) By the way, my dressing-gown smells most damnably of benzine.

MRS. PEARCE. No doubt it does, Mr. Higgins. But if you *will* wipe your fingers—

HIGGINS (*yelling*). Oh very well, very well! I'll wipe them in my hair in future.

MRS. PEARCE. I hope you're not offended, Mr. Higgins.

HIGGINS (*shocked at finding himself thought capable of an unamiable sentiment*). Not at all, not at all. You're quite right, Mrs. Pearce. I shall be particularly careful before the girl. Is that all?

MRS. PEARCE. No, sir. Might she use some of those Japanese dresses you brought from abroad? I really can't put her back into her old things.

HIGGINS. Certainly. Anything you like. Is *that* all?

MRS. PEARCE. Thank you, sir. That's all. (*She goes out.*)

HIGGINS. You know, Pickering, that woman has the most extraordinary ideas about me. Here I am, a shy, diffident sort of man. I've never been able to feel really grown-up and tremendous, like other chaps. And yet she's firmly persuaded that I'm an arbitrary overbearing bossing kind of person. I can't account for it.

[MRS. PEARCE *returns.*]

MRS. PEARCE. If you please, sir, the trouble's beginning already. There's a dustman[1] downstairs, Alfred Doolittle, wants to see you. He says you have his daughter here.

PICKERING (*rising*). Phew! I say! (*He retreats to the hearthrug.*)

HIGGINS (*promptly*). Send the blackguard[2] up.

MRS. PEARCE. Oh, very well, sir. (*She goes out.*)

PICKERING. He may not be a blackguard, Higgins.

HIGGINS. Nonsense. Of course he's a blackguard.

---

[1] *dustman:* a garbage collector.
[2] *blackguard* (blăg′ärd): a scoundrel.

PICKERING. Whether he is or not, I'm afraid we shall have some trouble with him.

HIGGINS (*confidently*). Oh, no. I think not. If there's any trouble he shall have it with me, not I with him. And we are sure to get something interesting out of him.

PICKERING. About the girl?

HIGGINS. No. I mean his dialect.

PICKERING. Oh!

MRS. PEARCE (*at the door*). Doolittle, sir. (*She admits* DOOLITTLE *and retires.*)

[ALFRED DOOLITTLE *is an elderly but vigorous dustman, clad in the costume of his profession, including a hat with a back brim covering his neck and shoulders. He has well-marked and rather interesting features, and seems equally free from fear and conscience. He has a remarkably expressive voice, the result of a habit of giving vent to his feelings without reserve. His present pose is that of wounded honor and stern resolution.*]

DOOLITTLE (*at the door, uncertain which of the two gentlemen is his man*). Professor Higgins?

HIGGINS. Here. Good morning. Sit down.

DOOLITTLE. Morning, Governor. (*He sits down magisterially.*) I come about a very serious matter, Governor.

HIGGINS (*to* PICKERING). Brought up in Hounslow. Mother Welsh, I should think. (DOOLITTLE *opens his mouth, amazed.* HIGGINS *continues*) What do you want, Doolittle?

DOOLITTLE (*menacingly*). I want my daughter, that's what I want. See?

HIGGINS. Of course you do. You're her father, aren't you? You don't suppose anyone else wants her, do you? I'm glad to see you have some spark of family feeling left. She's upstairs. Take her away at once.

DOOLITTLE (*rising, fearfully taken aback*). What!

HIGGINS. Take her away. Do you suppose I'm going to keep your daughter for you?

DOOLITTLE (*remonstrating*). Now, now, look here, Governor. Is this reasonable? Is it fairity to take advantage of a man like this? The girl belongs to me. You got her. Where do I come in? (*He sits down again.*)

HIGGINS. Your daughter had the audacity to come to my house and ask me to teach her how to speak properly so that she could get a place in a flower shop. This gentleman and my housekeeper have been here all the time. (*Bullying him*) How dare you come here and attempt to blackmail me? You sent her here on purpose.

DOOLITTLE (*protesting*). No, Governor.

HIGGINS. You must have. How else could you possibly know that she is here?

DOOLITTLE. Don't take a man up like that, Governor.

HIGGINS. The police shall take you up. This is a plant—a plot to extort money by threats. I shall telephone for the police. (*He goes resolutely to the telephone and opens the directory.*)

DOOLITTLE. Have I asked you for a brass farthing? I leave it to the gentleman here. Have I said a word about money?

HIGGINS (*throwing the book aside and marching down on* DOOLITTLE *with a poser*). What else did you come for?

DOOLITTLE (*sweetly*). Well, what *would* a man come for? Be human, Governor.

HIGGINS (*disarmed*). Alfred! Did you put her up to it?

DOOLITTLE. So help me, Governor, I never did. I take my Bible oath I ain't seen the girl these two months past.

HIGGINS. Then how did you know she was here?

DOOLITTLE (*"most musical, most melancholy"*). I'll tell you, Governor, if you'll only let me get a word in. I'm willing to tell you. I'm wanting to tell you. I'm waiting to tell you.

HIGGINS. Pickering, this chap has a certain natural gift of rhetoric. Observe the rhythm of his native woodnotes wild. "I'm willing to tell you; I'm wanting to tell you; I'm waiting to tell you." Sentimental rhetoric! That's the Welsh strain in him. It also accounts for his mendacity and dishonesty.

PICKERING. Oh, *please,* Higgins. I'm west country myself. (*To* DOOLITTLE) How did you know the girl was here if you didn't send her?

DOOLITTLE. It was like this, Governor. The girl took a boy in the taxi to give him a jaunt. Son of her landlady, he is. He hung about on the chance of her giving him another ride home. Well, she sent him back for her luggage when she heard you was willing for her to stop here. I met the boy at the corner of Long Acre and Endell Street.

HIGGINS. Public house. Yes?

DOOLITTLE. The poor man's club, Governor. Why shouldn't I?

PICKERING. Do let him tell his story, Higgins.

DOOLITTLE. He told me what was up. And I ask you, what was my feelings and my duty as a father? I says to the boy, "You bring me the luggage," I says—

PICKERING. Why didn't you go for it yourself?

DOOLITTLE. Landlady wouldn't have trusted me with it, Governor. She's that kind of woman, you know. I had to give the boy a penny afore he trusted me with it, the little swine. I brought it to her just to oblige you like, and make myself agreeable. That's all.

HIGGINS. How much luggage?

DOOLITTLE. Musical instrument, Governor. A few pictures, a trifle of jewelry, and a bird cage. She said she didn't want no clothes. What was I to think from that, Governor? I ask you as a parent what was I to think?

HIGGINS. So you came to rescue her from worse than death, eh?

DOOLITTLE (*appreciatively: relieved at being so well understood*). Just so, Governor. That's right.

PICKERING. But why did you bring her luggage if you intended to take her away?

DOOLITTLE. Have I said a word about taking her away? Have I now?

HIGGINS (*determinedly*). You're going to take her away, double quick. (*He crosses to the hearth and rings the bell.*)

DOOLITTLE (*rising*). No, Governor. Don't say that. I'm not the man to stand in my girl's light. Here's a career opening for her, as you might say; and—

[MRS. PEARCE *opens the door and awaits orders.*]

HIGGINS. Mrs. Pearce, this is Eliza's father. He has come to take her away. Give her to him. (*He goes back to the piano, with an air of washing his hands of the whole affair.*)

DOOLITTLE. No. This is a misunderstanding. Listen here—

MRS. PEARCE. He can't take her away, Mr. Higgins. How can he? You told me to burn her clothes.

DOOLITTLE. That's right. I can't carry the girl through the streets like a blooming monkey, can I? I put it to you.

HIGGINS. You have put it to me that you want your daughter. Take your daughter. If she has no clothes, go out and buy her some.

DOOLITTLE (*desperate*). Where's the clothes she come in? Did I burn them or did your missus here?

MRS. PEARCE. I am the housekeeper, if you please. I have sent for some clothes for your girl. When they come you can take her away. You can wait in the kitchen. This way, please.

[DOOLITTLE, *much troubled, accompanies her to the door; then hesitates; finally turns confidentially to* HIGGINS.]

DOOLITTLE. Listen here, Governor. You and me is men of the world, ain't we?

HIGGINS. Oh! Men of the world, are we? You'd better go, Mrs. Pearce.

MRS. PEARCE. I think so, indeed, sir. (*She goes, with dignity.*)

PICKERING. The floor is yours, Mr. Doolittle.

DOOLITTLE (*to* PICKERING). I thank you, Governor. (*To* HIGGINS, *who takes refuge on the piano bench, a little overwhelmed by the proximity of his visitor; for* DOOLITTLE *has a professional flavor of dust about him*) Well, the truth is, I've taken a sort of fancy to you, Governor; and if you want the girl, I'm not so set on having her back home again but what I might be open to an arrangement. Regarded in the light of a young woman, she's a fine handsome girl. As a daughter she's not worth her keep; and so I tell you straight. All I ask is my rights as a father; and you're the last man alive to expect me to let her go for nothing; for I can see you're one of the straight sort, Governor. Well, what's a five-pound note to you? And what's Eliza to me? (*He returns to his chair and sits down judicially.*)

PICKERING. I think you ought to know, Doolittle, that Mr. Higgins' intentions are entirely honorable.

DOOLITTLE. Course they are, Governor. If I thought they wasn't, I'd ask fifty.

HIGGINS (*revolted*). Do you mean to say, you callous rascal, that you would sell your daughter for £50?

DOOLITTLE. Not in a general way I wouldn't; but to oblige a gentleman like you I'd do a good deal, I do assure you.

PICKERING. Have you no morals, man?

DOOLITTLE (*unabashed*). Can't afford them, Governor. Neither could you if you was as poor as me. Not that I mean any harm, you know. But if Liza is going to have a bit out of this, why not me too?

HIGGINS (*troubled*). I don't know what to do, Pickering. There can be no question that as a matter of morals it's a positive crime to give this chap a farthing. And yet I feel a sort of rough justice in his claim.

DOOLITTLE. That's it, Governor. That's all I say. A father's heart, as it were.

PICKERING. Well, I know the feeling; but really it seems hardly right—

DOOLITTLE. Don't say that, Governor. Don't look at it that way. What am I, Governors both? I ask you, what am I? I'm one of the undeserving poor, that's what I am. Think of what that means to a man. It means that he's up agen middle class morality all the time. If there's anything going, and I put in for a bit of it, it's always the same story: "You're undeserving; so you can't have it." But my needs is as great as the most deserving widow's that ever got money out of six different charities in one week for the death of the same husband. I don't need less than a deserving man; I need more. I don't eat less hearty than him; and I drink a lot more. I want a bit of amusement, cause I'm a thinking man. I want cheerfulness and a song and a band when I feel low. Well, they charge me just the same for everything as they charge the deserving. What is middle class morality? Just an excuse for never giving me anything. Therefore, I ask you, as two gentlemen, not to play that game on me. I'm playing straight with you. I ain't pretending to be deserving. I'm undeserving; and I mean to go on being undeserving. I like it; and that's the truth. Will you take advantage of a man's nature to do him out of the price of his own daughter what he's brought up and fed and clothed by the sweat of his brow until she's growed big enough to be interesting to you two gentlemen? Is five pounds unreasonable? I put it to you; and I leave it to you.

HIGGINS (*rising, and going over to* PICKERING). Pickering, if we were to take this man in hand for three months, he could choose between a seat in the Cabinet and a popular pulpit in Wales.

PICKERING. What do you say to that, Doolittle?

DOOLITTLE. Not me, Governor, thank you kindly. I've heard all the preachers and all the prime ministers—for I'm a thinking man and game for politics or religion or social reform same as all the other amusements —and I tell you it's a dog's life any way you look at it. Undeserving poverty is my line. Taking one station in society with another, it's—it's— well, it's the only one that has any ginger in it, to my taste.

HIGGINS. I suppose we must give him a fiver.

PICKERING. He'll make a bad use of it, I'm afraid.

DOOLITTLE. Not me, Governor, so help me I won't. Don't you be afraid that I'll save it and spare it and live idle on it. There won't be a penny of it left by Monday. I'll have to go to work same as if I'd never had it. It won't pauperize me, you bet. Just one good spree for myself and the missus, giving pleasure to ourselves and employment to others, and satisfaction to you to think it's not been throwed away. You couldn't spend it better.

HIGGINS (*taking out his pocket book and coming between* DOOLITTLE *and the piano*). This is irresistible. Let's give him ten. (*He offers two notes to the dustman.*)

DOOLITTLE. No, Governor. She wouldn't have the heart to spend ten; and perhaps I shouldn't neither. Ten pounds is a lot of money. It makes a man feel prudent like; and then good-by to happiness. You give me what I ask you, Governor. Not a penny more, and not a penny less.

PICKERING. Why don't you marry that missus of yours? I rather draw the line at encouraging that sort of immorality.

DOOLITTLE. Tell her so, Governor: tell her so. I'm willing. It's me that suffers by it. I've no hold on her. I got to be agreeable to her. I got to give her presents. I got to buy her clothes something sinful. I'm a slave to that woman, Governor, just because I'm not her lawful husband. And she knows it too. Catch her marrying me! Take my advice, Governor: marry Eliza while she's young and don't know no better. If you don't you'll be sorry for it after. If you do, *she'll* be sorry for it after; but better her than you, because you're a man, and she's only a woman and don't know how to be happy anyhow.

HIGGINS. Pickering, if we listen to this man another minute, we shall have no convictions left. (*To* DOOLITTLE) Five pounds I think you said.

DOOLITTLE. Thank you kindly, Governor.

HIGGINS. You're sure you won't take ten?

DOOLITTLE. Not now. Another time, Governor.

HIGGINS (*handing him a five-pound note*). Here you are.

DOOLITTLE. Thank you, Governor. Good morning. (*He hurries to the door, anxious to get away with his booty. When he opens it he is confronted with a dainty and exquisitely clean young Japanese lady in a simple blue cotton kimono printed cunningly with small white jasmine blossoms.* MRS. PEARCE *is with her. He gets out of her way deferentially[1] and apologizes.*) Beg pardon, miss.

THE JAPANESE LADY. Garn! Don't you know your own daughter?

DOOLITTLE			Bly me! it's Eliza!
HIGGINS	}	*exclaiming simultaneously* {	What's that! This!
PICKERING			By Jove!

LIZA. Don't I look silly?

HIGGINS. Silly?

MRS. PEARCE (*at the door*). Now, Mr. Higgins, please don't say anything to make the girl conceited about herself.

---

[1] *deferentially* (dĕf'ẽr·ĕn'shăl·lǐ): respectfully.

HIGGINS (*conscientiously*). Oh! Quite right, Mrs. Pearce. (*To* ELIZA) Yes, damned silly.

MRS. PEARCE. Please, sir.

HIGGINS (*correcting himself*). I mean extremely silly.

LIZA. I should look all right with my hat on. (*She takes up her hat; puts it on; and walks across the room to the fireplace with a fashionable air.*)

HIGGINS. A new fashion, by George! And it ought to look horrible!

DOOLITTLE (*with fatherly pride*). Well, I never thought she'd clean up as good looking as that, Governor. She's a credit to me, ain't she?

LIZA. I tell you, it's easy to clean up here. Hot and cold water on tap, just as much as you like, there is. Woolly towels, there is; and a towel horse so hot, it burns your fingers. Soft brushes to scrub yourself, and a wooden bowl of soap smelling like primroses. Now I know why ladies is so clean. Washing's a treat for them. Wish they saw what it is for the like of me!

HIGGINS. I'm glad the bathroom met with your approval.

LIZA. It didn't. Not all of it, and I don't care who hears me say it. Mrs. Pearce knows.

HIGGINS. What was wrong, Mrs. Pearce?

MRS. PEARCE (*blandly*). Oh, nothing, sir. It doesn't matter.

LIZA. I had a good mind to break it. I didn't know which way to look. But I hung a towel over it, I did.

HIGGINS. Over what?

MRS. PEARCE. Over the looking glass, sir.

HIGGINS. Doolittle, you have brought your daughter up too strictly.

DOOLITTLE. Me! I never brought her up at all, except to give her a lick of a strap now and again. Don't put it on me, Governor. She ain't accustomed to it, you see. That's all. But she'll soon pick up your free-and-easy ways.

LIZA. I'm a good girl, I am; and I won't pick up no free-and-easy ways.

HIGGINS. Eliza, if you say again that you're a good girl, your father shall take you home.

LIZA. Not him. You don't know my father. All he come here for was to touch you for some money to get drunk on.

DOOLITTLE. Well, what else would I want money for? To put into the plate in church, I suppose. (*She puts out her tongue at him. He is so incensed by this that* PICKERING *presently finds it necessary to step between them.*) Don't you give me none of your lip; and don't let me hear you giving this gentleman any of it neither, or you'll hear from me about it. See?

HIGGINS. Have you any further advice to give her before you go, Doolittle? Your blessing, for instance.

DOOLITTLE. No, Governor. I ain't such a mug as to put up my children to all I know myself. Hard enough to hold them in without that. If you want Eliza's mind improved, Governor, you do it yourself with a strap. So long, gentlemen. (*He turns to go.*)

HIGGINS. (*impressively*). Stop. You'll come regularly to see your daughter. It's your duty, you know. My brother is a clergyman, and he could help you in your talks with her.

DOOLITTLE (*evasively*). Certainly. I'll come, Governor. Not just this week, because I have a job at a distance. But later on you may depend on me. Afternoon, gentlemen. Afternoon, ma'am. (*He takes off his hat to* MRS. PEARCE, *who disdains the salutation and goes out. He winks at* HIGGINS, *thinking him probably a fellow-sufferer from* MRS. PEARCE'S *difficult disposition, and follows her.*)

LIZA. Don't you believe the old liar. He'd as soon you set a bulldog on him as a clergyman. You won't see him again in a hurry.

HIGGINS. I don't want to, Eliza. Do you?

LIZA. Not me. I don't want never to see him again, I don't. He's a disgrace to me, he is, collecting dust, instead of working at his trade.

PICKERING. What is his trade, Eliza?

LIZA. Taking money out of other people's pockets into his own. His proper trade's a navvy;[1] and he works at it sometimes too—for exercise—and earns good money at it. Ain't you going to call me Miss Doolittle any more?

PICKERING. I beg your pardon, Miss Doolittle. It was a slip of the tongue.

LIZA. Oh, I don't mind; only it sounded so genteel. I *should* just like to take a taxi to the corner of Tottenham Court Road and get out there and tell it to wait for me, just to put the girls in their place a bit. I wouldn't speak to them, you know.

PICKERING. Better wait 'til we get you something really fashionable.

HIGGINS. Besides, you shouldn't cut your old friends now that you have risen in the world. That's what we call snobbery.

LIZA. You don't call the like of them my friends now, I should hope. They've took it out of me often enough with their ridicule when they had the chance; and now I mean to get a bit of my own back. But if I'm to have fashionable clothes, I'll wait. I should like to have some. Mrs. Pearce says you're going to give me some to wear in bed at night differ-

---

[1] *navvy* (năv′ĭ): an unskilled or common laborer.

ent to what I wear in the daytime; but it do seem a waste of money when you could get something to show. Besides, I never could fancy changing into cold things on a winter night.

MRS. PEARCE (*coming back*). Now, Eliza. The new things have come for you to try on.

LIZA. Ah-ow-oo-oooh! (*She rushes out.*)

MRS. PEARCE (*following her*). Oh, don't rush about like that, girl. (*She shuts the door behind her.*)

HIGGINS. Pickering, we have taken on a stiff job.

PICKERING (*with conviction*). Higgins, we have.

UNDERSTANDING THE CHARACTERS

1. What reason does Eliza give for wanting lessons in speaking? How had she figured the amount she would pay for the instruction? Why does she want Higgins to know that she came in a taxi?

2. Why is Higgins willing to take her? What does Pickering promise to do? How does each man regard Eliza? Find passages that show the differences in their personalities.

3. How does Mrs. Pearce react to Eliza? On what points are Pickering and Mrs. Pearce in agreement? Does their point of view or Higgins' seem more natural to you? What does Higgins mean when he says, "Take care of the pence and the pounds will take care of themselves"?

4. Why does Alfred Doolittle come to see Higgins? How does he feel toward his daughter? What do you learn about Eliza from this visit? Is Doolittle a happy person? Why does he accept five pounds instead of the ten pounds that is offered?

5. Why is Eliza always saying, "I'm a good girl, I am"? Does she have any other virtue to which she can point at this time? Are there any indications that she may have potentialities for growth or change?

ACT III

It is MRS. HIGGINS' *at-home day. Nobody has yet arrived. Her drawing room, in a flat on Chelsea Embankment,*[1] *has three windows looking on the river; and the ceiling is not so lofty as it would be in an older house of the same pretension. The windows are open, giving access to a balcony with flowers in pots. If you stand with your face to the windows, you*

[1] *Chelsea* (chĕl'sĭ) *Embankment:* a metropolitan borough on the north bank of the Thames.

*have the fireplace on your left and the door in the right-hand wall close
to the corner nearest the windows.*

MRS. HIGGINS *was brought up on Morris and Burne-Jones;[1] and her
room, which is very unlike her son's room in Wimpole Street, is not
crowded with furniture and little tables and knick-knacks. In the middle
of the room there is a big ottoman; and this, with the carpet, the Morris
wallpapers, and the Morris chintz window curtains and brocade covers
of the ottoman and its cushions, supply all the ornament, and are much
too handsome to be hidden by odds and ends of useless things. A few
good oil paintings from the exhibitions in the Grosvenor Gallery thirty
years ago (the Burne-Jones, not the Whistler side of them) are on the
walls. The only landscape is a Cecil Lawson on the scale of a Rubens.
There is a portrait of* MRS. HIGGINS *as she was when she defied fashion in
her youth in one of the beautiful Rossettian[2] costumes which, when cari-
catured by people who did not understand, led to the absurdities of popular estheticism in the eighteen-seventies.*

In the corner diagonally opposite the door MRS. HIGGINS, *now over
sixty and long past taking the trouble to dress out of the fashion, sits
writing at an elegantly simple writing table with a bell button within
reach of her hand. There is a Chippendale[3] chair further back in the room
between her and the window nearest her side. At the other side of the
room, further forward, is an Elizabethan chair roughly carved in the taste
of Inigo Jones.[4] On the same side a piano in a decorated case. The
corner between the fireplace and the window is occupied by a divan
cushioned in Morris chintz.*

It is between four and five in the afternoon.

The door is opened violently; and HIGGINS *enters with his hat on.*

MRS. HIGGINS (*dismayed*). Henry (*scolding him*)! What are you doing
here today? It is my at-home day. You promised not to come. (*As he
bends to kiss her, she takes his hat off and presents it to him.*)

HIGGINS. Oh bother! (*He throws the hat down on the table.*)

MRS. HIGGINS. Go home at once.

HIGGINS (*kissing her*). I know, Mother. I came on purpose.

---

[1] *Morris and Burne-Jones:* two members of a flourishing company that under-
took church decoration, carving, stained glass, metalwork, paper-hangings, chintzes,
and carpets.

[2] *Rossettian:* in the simple, flowing style of dress found in Dante Gabriel Rossetti's
paintings.

[3] *Chippendale:* a famous eighteenth-century cabinet maker.

[4] *Inigo Jones:* a seventeenth-century architect and designer.

MRS. HIGGINS. But you mustn't. I'm serious, Henry. You offend all my friends. They stop coming whenever they meet you.

HIGGINS. Nonsense! I know I have no small talk, but people don't mind. (*He sits on the settee.*)

MRS. HIGGINS. Oh! don't they? Small talk indeed! What about your large talk? Really, dear, you mustn't stay.

HIGGINS. I must. I've a job for you. A phonetic job.

MRS. HIGGINS. No use, dear. I'm sorry, but I can't get around your vowels; and though I like to get pretty postcards in your patent shorthand, I always have to read the copies in ordinary writing you so thoughtfully send me.

HIGGINS. Well, this isn't a phonetic job.

MRS. HIGGINS. You said it was.

HIGGINS. Not your part of it. I've picked up a girl.

MRS. HIGGINS. Does that mean that some girl has picked you up?

HIGGINS. Not at all. I don't mean a love affair.

MRS. HIGGINS. What a pity!

HIGGINS. Why?

MRS. HIGGINS. Well, you never fall in love with anyone under forty-five. When will you discover that there are some rather nice-looking young women about?

HIGGINS. Oh, I can't be bothered with young women. My idea of a lovable woman is something as like you as possible. I shall never get into the way of seriously liking young women. Some habits lie too deep to be changed. (*Rising abruptly and walking about, jingling his money and his keys in his trouser pockets*) Besides, they're all idiots.

MRS. HIGGINS. Do you know what you would do if you really loved me, Henry?

HIGGINS. Oh bother! What? Marry, I suppose?

MRS. HIGGINS. No. Stop fidgeting and take your hands out of your pockets. (*With a gesture of despair, he obeys and sits down again.*) That's a good boy. Now tell me about the girl.

HIGGINS. She's coming to see you.

MRS. HIGGINS. I don't remember asking her.

HIGGINS. You didn't. *I* asked her. If you'd known her you wouldn't have asked her.

MRS. HIGGINS. Indeed! Why?

HIGGINS. Well, it's like this. She's a common flower girl. I picked her off the curbstone.

MRS. HIGGINS. And invited her to my at-home!

HIGGINS (*rising and coming to her to coax her*). Oh, that'll be all right. I've taught her to speak properly, and she has strict orders as to her behavior. She's to keep to two subjects: the weather and everybody's health —Fine day and How do you do, you know—and not to let herself go on things in general. That will be safe.

MRS. HIGGINS. Safe! To talk about our health! About our insides! Perhaps about our outsides! How could you be so silly, Henry?

HIGGINS (*impatiently*). Well, she must talk about something. (*He controls himself and sits down again.*) Oh, she'll be all right: don't you fuss. Pickering is in it with me. I've a sort of bet on that I'll pass her off as a duchess in six months. I started on her some months ago; and she's getting on like a house on fire. I shall win my bet. She has a quick ear, and she's been easier to teach than my middle-class pupils because she's had to learn a complete new language. She talks English almost as you talk French.

MRS. HIGGINS. That's satisfactory, at all events.

HIGGINS. Well, it is and it isn't.

MRS. HIGGINS. What does that mean?

HIGGINS. You see, I've got her pronunciation all right; but you have to consider not only *how* a girl pronounces, but *what* she pronounces; and that's where—

[*They are interrupted by the* PARLOR MAID, *announcing guests.*]

THE PARLOR MAID. Mrs. and Miss Eynsford Hill. (*She withdraws.*)

HIGGINS. Oh Lord! (*He rises; snatches his hat from the table; and makes for the door: but before he reaches it his mother introduces him.*)

[MRS. *and* MISS EYNSFORD HILL *are the mother and daughter who sheltered from the rain in Covent Garden. The mother is well-bred, quiet, and has the habitual anxiety of straitened means. The daughter has acquired a gay air of being very much at home in society: the bravado of genteel poverty.*]

MRS. EYNSFORD HILL (*to* MRS. HIGGINS). How do you do? (*They shake hands.*)

MISS EYNSFORD HILL. How d'you do? (*She shakes.*)

MRS. HIGGINS (*introducing*). My son Henry.

MRS. EYNSFORD HILL. Your celebrated son! I have so longed to meet you, Professor Higgins.

HIGGINS (*glumly, making no movement in her direction*). Delighted. (*He backs against the piano and bows brusquely.*)

MISS EYNSFORD HILL (*going to him with confident familiarity*). How do you do?

HIGGINS (*staring at her*). I've seen you before somewhere. I haven't the ghost of a notion where; but I've heard your voice. (*Drearily*) It doesn't matter. You'd better sit down.

MRS. HIGGINS. I'm sorry to say that my celebrated son has no manners. You mustn't mind him.

MISS EYNSFORD HILL (*gaily*). I don't. (*She sits in the Elizabethan chair.*)

MRS. EYNSFORD HILL (*a little bewildered*). Not at all. (*She sits on the ottoman between her daughter and* MRS. HIGGINS, *who has turned her chair away from the writing table.*)

HIGGINS. Oh, have I been rude? I didn't mean to be.

[*He goes to the central window, through which, with his back to the company, he contemplates the river and the flowers in Battersea Park on the opposite bank as if they were a frozen desert.*]

[*The* PARLOR MAID *returns, ushering in* PICKERING.]

THE PARLOR MAID. Colonel Pickering. (*She withdraws.*)

PICKERING. How do you do, Mrs. Higgins?

MRS. HIGGINS. So glad you've come. Do you know Mrs. Eynsford Hill —Miss Eynsford Hill? (*Exchange of bows. The* COLONEL *brings the Chippendale chair a little forward between* MRS. HILL *and* MRS. HIGGINS, *and sits down.*)

PICKERING. Has Henry told you what we've come for?

HIGGINS (*over his shoulder*). We were interrupted, damn it!

MRS. HIGGINS. Oh Henry, Henry, really!

MRS. EYNSFORD HILL (*half rising*). Are we in the way?

MRS. HIGGINS (*rising and making her sit down again*). No, no. You couldn't have come more fortunately. We want you to meet a friend of ours.

HIGGINS (*turning hopefully*). Yes, by George! We want two or three people. You'll do as well as anybody else.

[*The* PARLOR MAID *returns, ushering* FREDDY.]

THE PARLOR MAID. Mr. Eynsford Hill.

HIGGINS (*almost audibly, past endurance*). God of Heaven! another of them.

FREDDY (*shaking hands with* MRS. HIGGINS). Ahdedo?

MRS. HIGGINS. Very good of you to come. (*Introducing*) Colonel Pickering.

FREDDY (*bowing*). Ahdedo?

MRS. HIGGINS. I don't think you know my son, Professor Higgins.

FREDDY (*going to* HIGGINS). Ahdedo?

HIGGINS (*looking at him much as if he were a pickpocket*). I'll take my oath I've met *you* before somewhere. Where was it?

FREDDY. I don't think so.

HIGGINS (*resignedly*). It doesn't matter, anyhow. Sit down.

[*He shakes* FREDDY'S *hand, and almost slings him on to the ottoman with his face to the windows; then comes round to the other side of it.*]

HIGGINS. Well, here we are, anyhow! (*He sits down on the ottoman next to* MRS. EYNSFORD HILL, *on her left.*) And now, what the devil are we going to talk about until Eliza comes?

MRS. HIGGINS. Henry! You are the life and soul of the Royal Society soirées;[1] but really you're rather trying on more commonplace occasions.

HIGGINS. Am I? Very sorry. (*Beaming suddenly*) I suppose I am, you know. (*Uproariously*) Ha, ha!

MISS EYNSFORD HILL (*who considers* HIGGINS *quite eligible matrimonially*). I sympathize. *I* haven't any small talk. If people would only be frank and say what they really think!

HIGGINS (*relapsing into gloom*). Lord forbid!

MRS. EYNSFORD HILL (*taking up her daughter's cue*). But why?

HIGGINS. What they think they ought to think is bad enough, Lord knows; but what they really think would break up the whole show. Do you suppose it would be really agreeable if I were to come out now with what *I* really think?

MISS EYNSFORD HILL (*gaily*). Is it so very cynical?

HIGGINS. Cynical! Who the dickens said it was cynical? I mean it wouldn't be decent.

MRS. EYNSFORD HILL (*seriously*). Oh! I'm sure you don't mean that Mr. Higgins.

HIGGINS. You see, we're all savages, more or less. We're supposed to be civilized and cultured—to know all about poetry and philosophy and art

---

[1] *soirées* (swä·rāz′): evening parties.

and science, and so on; but how many of us know even the meanings of these names? (*To* MISS HILL) What do *you* know of poetry? (*To* MRS. HILL) What do *you* know of science? (*Indicating* FREDDY) What does *he* know of art or science or anything else? What the devil do you imagine I know of philosophy?

MRS. HIGGINS (*warningly*). Or of manners, Henry?

THE PARLOR MAID (*opening the door*). Miss Doolittle. (*She withdraws.*)

HIGGINS (*rising hastily and running to* MRS. HIGGINS). Here she is, Mother. (*He stands on tiptoe and makes signs over his mother's head to* ELIZA *to indicate to her which lady is her hostess.*)

[ELIZA, *who is exquisitely dressed, produces an impression of such remarkable distinction and beauty as she enters that they all rise, quite fluttered. Guided by* HIGGINS' *signals, she comes to* MRS. HIGGINS *with studied grace.*]

LIZA (*speaking with pedantic correctness of pronunciation and great beauty of tone*). How do you do, Mrs. Higgins? (*She gasps slightly in making sure of the H in* HIGGINS, *but is quite successful.*) Mr. Higgins told me I might come.

MRS. HIGGINS (*cordially*). Quite right. I'm very glad indeed to see you.

PICKERING. How do you do, Miss Doolittle?

LIZA (*shaking hands with him*). Colonel Pickering, is it not?

MRS. EYNSFORD HILL. I feel sure we have met before, Miss Doolittle. I remember your eyes.

LIZA. How do you do? (*She sits down on the ottoman gracefully in the place just left vacant by* HIGGINS.)

MRS. EYNSFORD HILL (*introducing*). My daughter Clara.

LIZA. How do you do?

CLARA (*impulsively*). How do you do? (*She sits down on the ottoman beside* ELIZA, *devouring her with her eyes.*)

FREDDY (*coming to their side of the ottoman*). I've certainly had the pleasure.

MRS. EYNSFORD HILL (*introducing*). My son Freddy.

LIZA. How do you do?

[FREDDY *bows and sits down in the Elizabethan chair, infatuated.*]

HIGGINS (*suddenly*). By George, yes! It all comes back to me! (*They stare at him.*) Covent Garden! (*Lamentably*) What a damned thing!

MRS. HIGGINS. Henry, please! (*He is about to sit on the edge of the table*) Don't sit on my writing table; you'll break it.

HIGGINS (*sulkily*). Sorry.

[*He goes to the divan, stumbling into the fender and over the fire irons on his way; extricating himself with muttered imprecations*[1] *and finishing his disastrous journey by throwing himself so impatiently on the divan that he almost breaks it.* MRS. HIGGINS *looks at him, but controls herself and says nothing.*]

[*A long and painful pause ensues.*]

MRS. HIGGINS (*at last, conversationally*). Will it rain, do you think?

LIZA. The shallow depression in the west of these islands is likely to move slowly in an easterly direction. There are no indications of any great change in the barometrical situation.

FREDDY. Ha! ha! how awfully funny!

LIZA. What is wrong with that, young man? I bet I got it right.

FREDDY. Killing!

MRS. EYNSFORD HILL. I'm sure I hope it won't turn cold. There's so much influenza about. It runs right through our whole family regularly every spring.

LIZA (*darkly*). My aunt died of influenza, so they said.

MRS. EYNSFORD HILL (*clicks her tongue sympathetically*)!!!

LIZA (*in the same tragic tone*). But it's my belief they done the old woman in.

MRS. HIGGINS (*puzzled*). Done her in?

LIZA. Y-e-e-es, Lord love you! Why should *she* die of influenza? She come through diphtheria right enough the year before. I saw her with my own eyes. Fairly blue with it, she was. They all thought she was dead; but my father he kept ladling gin down her throat 'til she came to so sudden that she bit the bowl off the spoon.

MRS. EYNSFORD HILL (*startled*). Dear me!

LIZA (*piling up the indictment*[2]). What call would a woman with that strength in her have to die of influenza? What become of her new straw hat that should have come to me? Somebody pinched it; and what I say is, them as pinched it done her in.

MRS. EYNSFORD HILL. What does doing her in mean?

---

[1] *imprecations* (ĭm'prĕ·kā'shŭns): curses.
[2] *indictment* (ĭn·dīt'mĕnt): a statement charging someone with an offense.

HIGGINS (*hastily*). Oh, that's the new small talk. To do a person in means to kill them.

MRS. EYNSFORD HILL (*to* ELIZA, *horrified*). You surely don't believe that your aunt was killed?

LIZA. Do I not! Them she lived with would have killed her for a hatpin, let alone a hat.

MRS. EYNSFORD HILL. But it can't have been right for your father to pour spirits down her throat like that. It might have killed her.

LIZA. Not her. Gin was mother's milk to her. Besides, he'd poured so much down his own throat that he knew the good of it.

MRS. EYNSFORD HILL. Do you mean that he drank?

LIZA. Drank! My word! Something chronic.

MRS. EYNSFORD HILL. How dreadful for you!

LIZA. Not a bit. It never did him no harm what I could see. But then he did not keep it up regular. (*Cheerfully*) On the burst, as you might say, from time to time. And always more agreeable when he had a drop in. When he was out of work, my mother used to give him fourpence and tell him to go out and not come back until he'd drunk himself cheerful and loving-like. There's lots of women has to make their husbands drunk to make them fit to live with. (*Now quite at her ease*) You see, it's like this. If a man has a bit of a conscience, it always takes him when he's sober; and then it makes him low-spirited. A drop of booze just takes that off and makes him happy. (*To* FREDDY, *who is in convulsions of suppressed laughter*) Here! what are you sniggering at?

FREDDY. The new small talk. You do it so awfully well.

LIZA. If I was doing it proper, what was you laughing at? (*To* HIGGINS) Have I said anything I oughtn't?

MRS. HIGGINS (*interposing*). Not at all, Miss Doolittle.

LIZA. Well, that's a mercy, anyhow. (*Expansively*) What I always say is—

HIGGINS (*rising and looking at his watch*). Ahem!

LIZA (*looking round at him; taking the hint; and rising*). Well, I must go. (*They all rise.* FREDDY *goes to the door.*) So pleased to have met you. Good-by. (*She shakes hands with* MRS. HIGGINS.)

MRS. HIGGINS. Good-by.

LIZA. Good-by, Colonel Pickering.

PICKERING. Good-by, Miss Doolittle. (*They shake hands.*)

LIZA (*nodding to the others*). Good-by, all.

FREDDY (*opening the door for her*). Are you walking across the Park, Miss Doolittle? If so—

LIZA. Walk! Not bloody likely. (*Sensation.*) I am going in a taxi. (*She goes out.*)

[PICKERING *gasps and sits down.* FREDDY *goes out on the balcony to catch another glimpse of* ELIZA.]

MRS. EYNSFORD HILL (*suffering from shock*). Well, I really can't get used to the new ways.

CLARA (*throwing herself discontentedly into the Elizabethan chair*). Oh, it's all right, Mamma, quite right. People will think we never go anywhere or see anybody if you are so old-fashioned.

MRS. EYNSFORD HILL. I daresay I am very old-fashioned, but I do hope you won't begin using that expression, Clara. I have got accustomed to hear you talking about men as rotters, and calling everything filthy and beastly, though I do think it horrible and unladylike. But this last is really too much. Don't you think so, Colonel Pickering?

PICKERING. Don't ask me. I've been away in India for several years, and manners have changed so much that I sometimes don't know whether I'm at a respectable dinner table or in a ship's forecastle.

CLARA. It's all a matter of habit. There's no right or wrong in it. Nobody means anything by it. And it's so quaint, and gives such a smart emphasis to things that are not in themselves very witty. I find the new small talk delightful and quite innocent.

MRS. EYNSFORD HILL (*rising*). Well, after that, I think it's time for us to go.

[PICKERING *and* HIGGINS *rise.*]

CLARA (*rising*). Oh, yes! We have three at-homes to go to still. Good-by, Mrs. Higgins. Good-by, Colonel Pickering. Good-by, Professor Higgins.

HIGGINS (*coming grimly at her from the divan, and accompanying her to the door*). Good-by. Be sure you try that small talk at the three at-homes. Don't be nervous about it. Pitch it in strong.

CLARA (*all smiles*). I will. Good-by. Such nonsense, all this early Victorian prudery!

HIGGINS (*tempting her*). Such damned nonsense!

CLARA. Such bloody nonsense!

MRS. EYNSFORD HILL (*convulsively*). Clara!

CLARA. Ha! ha! (*She goes out radiant, conscious of being thoroughly up to date, and is heard descending the stairs in a stream of silvery laughter.*)

FREDDY (*to the heavens at large*). Well, I ask you—(*He gives it up, and comes to* MRS. HIGGINS.) Good-by.

MRS. HIGGINS (*shaking hands*). Good-by. Would you like to meet Miss Doolittle again?

FREDDY (*eagerly*). Yes, I should, most awfully.

MRS. HIGGINS. Well, you know my days.

FREDDY. Yes. Thanks awfully. Good-by. (*He goes out.*)

MRS. EYNSFORD HILL. Good-by, Mr. Higgins.

HIGGINS. Good-by. Good-by.

MRS. EYNSFORD HILL (*to* PICKERING). It's no use. I shall never be able to bring myself to use that word.

PICKERING. Don't. It's not compulsory, you know. You'll get on quite well without it.

MRS. EYNSFORD HILL. Only, Clara is so down on me if I am not positively reeking with the latest slang. Good-by.

PICKERING. Good-by. (*They shake hands.*)

MRS. EYNSFORD HILL (*to* MRS. HIGGINS). You mustn't mind Clara. (PICKERING, *catching from her lowered tone that this is not meant for him to hear, discreetly joins* HIGGINS *at the window.*) We're so poor! And she gets so few parties, poor child! She doesn't quite know. (MRS. HIGGINS, *seeing that her eyes are moist, takes her hand sympathetically and goes with her to the door.*) But the boy is nice. Don't you think so?

MRS. HIGGINS. Oh, quite nice. I shall always be delighted to see him.

MRS. EYNSFORD HILL. Thank you, dear. Good-by. (*She goes out.*)

HIGGINS (*eagerly*). Well? Is Eliza presentable? (*He swoops on his mother and drags her to the ottoman, where she sits down in Eliza's place with her son on her left.*)

[PICKERING *returns to his chair on her right.*]

MRS. HIGGINS. You silly boy, of course she's not presentable. She's a triumph of your art and of her dressmaker's; but if you suppose for a moment that she doesn't give herself away in every sentence she utters, you must be perfectly cracked about her.

PICKERING. But don't you think something might be done? I mean something to eliminate the sanguinary[1] element from her conversation.

MRS. HIGGINS. Not as long as she is in Henry's hands.

HIGGINS (*aggrieved*). Do you mean that *my* language is improper?

---

[1] *sanguinary* (săng'gwĭ·nĕr'ĭ): bloody; a reference to Eliza's use of the slang term "bloody" in her conversation.

MRS. HIGGINS. No, dearest, it would be quite proper—say on a canal barge; but it would not be proper for her at a garden party.

HIGGINS (*deeply injured*). Well I must say—

PICKERING (*interrupting him*). Come, Higgins. You must learn to know yourself. I haven't heard such language as yours since we used to review the volunteers in Hyde Park twenty years ago.

HIGGINS (*sulkily*). Oh, well, if *you* say so, I suppose I don't always talk like a bishop.

MRS. HIGGINS (*quieting Henry with a touch*). Colonel Pickering, will you tell me what is the exact state of things in Wimpole Street?

PICKERING (*cheerfully, as if this completely changed the subject*). Well, I have come to live there with Henry. We work together at my Indian Dialects, and we think it more convenient—

MRS. HIGGINS. Quite so. I know all about that: it's an excellent arrangement. But where does this girl live?

HIGGINS. With us, of course. Where *should* she live?

MRS. HIGGINS. But on what terms? Is she a servant? If not, what is she?

PICKERING (*slowly*). I think I know what you mean, Mrs. Higgins.

HIGGINS. Well, dash me if *I* do! I've had to work at the girl every day for months to get her to her present pitch. Besides, she's useful. She knows where my things are, and remembers my appointments and so forth.

MRS. HIGGINS. How does your housekeeper get on with her?

HIGGINS. Mrs. Pearce? Oh, she's jolly glad to get so much taken off her hands; for before Eliza came, *she* used to have to find things, and remind me of my appointments. But she's got some silly bee in her bonnet about Eliza. She keeps saying "You don't think, sir," doesn't she, Pick?

PICKERING. Yes, that's the formula. "You don't think, sir." That's the end of every conversation about Eliza.

HIGGINS. As if I ever stop thinking about the girl and her confounded vowels and consonants. I'm worn out, thinking about her, and watching her lips and her teeth and her tongue, not to mention her soul, which is the quaintest of the lot.

MRS. HIGGINS. You certainly are a pretty pair of babies, playing with your live doll.

HIGGINS. Playing! The hardest job I ever tackled— Make no mistake about that, Mother. But you have no idea how frightfully interesting it is to take a human being and change her into a quite different human being by creating a new speech for her. It's filling up the deepest gulf that separates class from class and soul from soul.

PICKERING (*drawing his chair closer to* MRS. HIGGINS *and bending over to her eagerly*). Yes, it's enormously interesting. I assure you, Mrs. Higgins, we take Eliza very seriously. Every week—every day almost—there is some new change. (*Closer again*) We keep records of every stage—dozens of gramophone disks and photographs—

HIGGINS (*assailing her at the other ear*). Yes, by George! It's the most absorbing experiment I ever tackled. She regularly fills our lives up, doesn't she, Pick?

PICKERING. We're always talking Eliza.

HIGGINS. Teaching Eliza.

PICKERING. Dressing Eliza.

MRS. HIGGINS. What!

HIGGINS. Inventing new Elizas.

HIGGINS.		You know, she has the most extraordinary quickness of ear:
	[*speaking together*]	
PICKERING.		I assure you, my dear Mrs. Higgins, that girl
HIGGINS.		just like a parrot. I've tried her with every
PICKERING.		is a genius. She can play the piano quite beautifully.
HIGGINS.		possible sort of sound that a human being can make—
PICKERING.		We have taken her to classical concerts and to music
HIGGINS.		Continental dialects, African dialects, Hottentot
PICKERING.		halls; and it's all the same to her: she plays everything
HIGGINS.		clicks, things it took me years to get hold of; and
PICKERING.		she hears right off when she comes home, whether it's
HIGGINS.		she picks them up like a shot, right away, as if she had
PICKERING.		Beethoven and Brahms or Lehar and Lionel Monckton;
HIGGINS.		been at it all her life.
PICKERING.		though six months ago, she'd never as much as touched a piano—

MRS. HIGGINS (*putting her fingers in her ears, as they are by this time shouting one another down with an intolerable noise*). Sh-sh-sh—sh! (*They stop.*)

PICKERING. I beg your pardon. (*He draws his chair back apologetically.*)

HIGGINS. Sorry. When Pickering starts shouting nobody can get a word in edgeways.

MRS. HIGGINS. Be quiet, Henry. Colonel Pickering, don't you realize that when Eliza walked into Wimpole Street, something walked in with her?

PICKERING. Her father did. But Henry soon got rid of him.

MRS. HIGGINS. It would have been more to the point if her mother had. But as her mother didn't something else did.

PICKERING. But what?

MRS. HIGGINS (*unconsciously dating herself by the word*). A problem.

PICKERING. Oh, I see. The problem of how to pass her off as a lady.

HIGGINS. I'll solve that problem. I've half solved it already.

MRS. HIGGINS. No, you two infinitely stupid male creatures! The problem of what is to be done with her afterwards.

HIGGINS. I don't see anything in that. She can go her own way, with all the advantages I have given her.

MRS. HIGGINS. The advantages of that poor woman who was here just now! The manners and habits that disqualify a fine lady from earning her own living without giving her a fine lady's income! Is that what you mean?

PICKERING (*indulgently, being rather bored*). Oh, that will be all right, Mrs. Higgins. (*He rises to go.*)

HIGGINS (*rising also*). We'll find her some light employment.

PICKERING. She's happy enough. Don't you worry about her. Good-by. (*He shakes hands as if he were consoling a frightened child, and makes for the door.*)

HIGGINS. Anyhow, there's no good bothering now. The thing's done. Good-by, Mother. (*He kisses her, and follows* PICKERING.)

PICKERING (*turning for a final consolation*). There are plenty of openings. We'll do what's right. Good-by.

HIGGINS (*to* PICKERING *as they go out together*). Let's take her to the Shakespeare exhibition at Earl's Court.

PICKERING. Yes, let's. Her remarks will be delicious.

HIGGINS. She'll mimic all the people for us when we get home.

PICKERING. Ripping. (*Both are heard laughing as they go downstairs.*)

MRS. HIGGINS (*rises with an impatient bounce, and returns to her work at the writing table. She sweeps a litter of disarranged papers out of her way; snatches a sheet of paper from her stationery case; and tries resolutely to write. At the third line she gives it up; flings down her pen; grips the table angrily and exclaims*). Oh, men! men!! men!!!

PROGRESS AND A PROBLEM

1. How much time has elapsed since the beginning of the experiment? Why does Higgins choose his mother's "at-home" for Eliza's introduction to society? How would you describe the relationship between Higgins and his mother?

2. Point out the differences that you note between Mrs. Higgins and Mrs. Eynsford Hill. Describe the kind of life that Mrs. Eynsford Hill and her children live.

3. How much has Higgins accomplished in his education of Eliza? Compare Eliza now with the girl she was in Acts I and II. How is she received by Mrs. Higgins' guests? Do they recognize her? Does Eliza recognize them?

4. What is Mrs. Higgins' reaction to her son's experiment? How does she regard Eliza? In this act, do you detect a suggestion of a problem that may prove to be important later on? What is it?

ACT IV

The Wimpole Street laboratory. Midnight. Nobody in the room. The clock on the mantelpiece strikes twelve. The fire is not alight; it is a summer night.

Presently HIGGINS *and* PICKERING *are heard on the stairs.*

HIGGINS (*calling down to* PICKERING). I say, Pick. Lock up, will you? I shan't be going out again.

PICKERING. Right. Can Mrs. Pearce go to bed? We don't want anything more, do we?

HIGGINS. Lord, no!

[ELIZA *opens the door and is seen on the lighted landing in opera cloak, brilliant evening dress, and diamonds, with fan, flowers, and all accessories. She comes to the hearth, and switches on the electric lights there. She is tired; her pallor contrasts strongly with her dark eyes and hair; and her expression is almost tragic. She takes off her cloak; puts her fan and flowers on the piano; and sits down on the bench, brooding and silent.* HIGGINS, *in evening dress, with overcoat and hat, comes in, carrying a smoking jacket which he has picked up downstairs. He takes off the hat and overcoat; throws them carelessly on the newspaper stand; disposes of his coat in the same way; puts on the smoking jacket; and throws himself wearily into the easy chair at the hearth.* PICKERING, *similarly attired, comes in. He also takes off his hat and overcoat, and is about to throw them on* HIGGINS' *when he hesitates.*]

PICKERING. I say, Mrs. Pearce will row if we leave these things lying about in the drawing room.

HIGGINS. Oh, chuck them over the bannisters into the hall. She'll find them there in the morning and put them away all right. She'll think we were drunk.

PICKERING. We are, slightly. Are there any letters?

HIGGINS. I didn't look. (PICKERING *takes the overcoats and hats and goes downstairs.* HIGGINS *begins half singing half yawning an air from* La Fanciulla del Golden West.[1] *Suddenly he stops and exclaims*) I wonder where the devil my slippers are!

[ELIZA *looks at him darkly; then rises suddenly and leaves the room.* HIGGINS *yawns again, and resumes his song.* PICKERING *returns, with the contents of the letter box in his hand.*]

PICKERING. Only circulars, and this coroneted billet-doux[2] for you. (*He throws the circulars into the fender, and posts himself on the hearth-rug, with his back to the grate.*)

HIGGINS (*glancing at the billet-doux*). Moneylender. (*He throws the letter after the circulars.*)

[ELIZA *returns with a pair of large down-at-heel slippers. She places them on the carpet before* HIGGINS, *and sits as before without a word.*]

HIGGINS (*yawning again*). Oh Lord! What an evening! What a crew! What a silly tomfoolery! (*He raises his shoe to unlace it, and catches sight of the slippers. He stops unlacing and looks at them as if they had appeared there of their own accord.*) Oh! they're there, are they?

[1] La Fanciulla del Golden West: The Girl of the Golden West, an opera by Puccini.
[2] billet-doux (bĭl'à·dōō'): a love letter.

PICKERING (*stretching himself*). Well, I feel a bit tired. It's been a long day. The garden party, a dinner party, and the opera! Rather too much of a good thing. But you've won your bet, Higgins. Eliza did the trick, and something to spare, eh?

HIGGINS (*fervently*). Thank God it's over!

[ELIZA *flinches violently; but they take no notice of her; and she recovers herself and sits stonily as before.*]

PICKERING. Were you nervous at the garden party? *I* was. Eliza didn't seem a bit nervous.

HIGGINS. Oh, *she* wasn't nervous. I knew she'd be all right. No, it's the strain of putting the job through all these months that has told on me. It was interesting enough at first, while we were at the phonetics; but after that I got deadly sick of it. If I hadn't backed myself to do it I should have chucked the whole thing up two months ago. It was a silly notion. The whole thing has been a bore.

PICKERING. Oh come! The garden party was frightfully exciting. My heart began beating like anything.

HIGGINS. Yes, for the first three minutes. But when I saw we were going to win hands down, I felt like a bear in a cage, hanging about doing nothing. The dinner was worse: sitting gorging there for over an hour, with nobody but a damned fool of a fashionable woman to talk to! I tell you, Pickering, never again for me. No more artificial duchesses. The whole thing has been simple purgatory.

PICKERING. You've never been broken in properly to the social routine. (*Strolling over to the piano*) I rather enjoy dipping into it occasionally myself. It makes me feel young again. Anyhow, it was a great success: an immense success. I was quite frightened once or twice because Eliza was doing it so well. You see, lots of the real people can't do it at all: they're such fools that they think style comes by nature to people in their position, and so they never learn. There's always something professional about doing a thing superlatively well.

HIGGINS. Yes, that's what drives me mad. The silly people don't know their own silly business. (*Rising*) However, it's over and done with; and now I can go to bed at last without dreading tomorrow.

[ELIZA'S *beauty becomes murderous.*]

PICKERING. I think I shall turn in too. Still, it's been a great occasion: a triumph for you. Good night. (*He goes.*)

HIGGINS (*following him*). Good night. (*Over his shoulder, at the door*) Put out the lights, Eliza; and tell Mrs. Pearce not to make coffee for me in the morning. I'll take tea. (*He goes out.*)

[ELIZA *tries to control herself and feel indifferent as she rises and walks across to the hearth to switch off the lights. By the time she gets there she is on the point of screaming. She sits down in* HIGGINS' *chair and holds on hard to the arms. Finally she gives way and flings herself furiously on the floor, raging.*]

HIGGINS (*in despairing wrath outside*). What the devil have I done with my slippers? (*He appears at the door.*)

LIZA (*snatching up the slippers, and hurling them at him one after the other with all her force*). There are your slippers. And there. Take your slippers, and may you never have a day's luck with them!

HIGGINS (*astounded*). What on earth—! (*He comes to her.*) What's the matter? Get up. (*He pulls her up.*) Anything wrong?

LIZA (*breathless*). Nothing wrong—with *you*. I've won your bet for you, haven't I. That's enough for you. *I* don't matter, I suppose.

HIGGINS. *You* won my bet! You! Presumptuous insect! *I* won it. What did you throw those slippers at me for?

LIZA. Because I wanted to smash your face. I'd like to kill you, you selfish brute. Why didn't you leave me where you picked me out of—in the gutter? You thank God it's all over, and that now you can throw me back again there, do you? (*She crisps her fingers frantically.*)

HIGGINS (*looking at her in cool wonder*). The creature is nervous, after all.

LIZA (*gives a suffocated scream of fury, and instinctively darts her nails at his face*)!!

HIGGINS (*catching her wrists*). Ah! would you? Claws in, you cat. How dare you show your temper to me? Sit down and be quiet. (*He throws her roughly into the easy chair.*)

LIZA (*crushed by superior strength and weight*). What's to become of me? What's to become of me?

HIGGINS. How the devil do I know what's to become of you? What does it matter what becomes of you?

LIZA. You don't care. I know you don't care. You wouldn't care if I was dead. I'm nothing to you—not so much as them slippers.

HIGGINS (*thundering*). *Those* slippers.

LIZA (*with bitter submission*). Those slippers. I didn't think it made any difference now.

[*A pause.* ELIZA *hopeless and crushed.* HIGGINS *a little uneasy.*]

HIGGINS (*in his loftiest manner*). Why have you begun going on like this? May I ask whether you complain of your treatment here?

LIZA. No.

HIGGINS. Has anybody behaved badly to you? Colonel Pickering? Mrs. Pearce? Any of the servants?

LIZA. No.

HIGGINS. I presume you don't pretend that *I* have treated you badly?

LIZA. No.

HIGGINS. I am glad to hear it. (*He moderates his tone.*) Perhaps you're tired after the strain of the day. Will you have a glass of champagne? (*He moves toward the door.*)

LIZA. No. (*Recollecting her manners*). Thank you.

HIGGINS (*good-humored again*). This has been coming on you for some days. I suppose it was natural for you to be anxious about the garden party. But that's all over now. (*He pats her kindly on the shoulder. She writhes.*) There's nothing more to worry about.

LIZA. No. Nothing more for *you* to worry about. (*She suddenly rises and gets away from him by going to the piano bench, where she sits and hides her face.*) Oh God! I wish I was dead.

HIGGINS (*staring after her in sincere surprise*). Why? In heaven's name, why? (*Reasonably, going to her*) Listen to me, Eliza. All this irritation is purely subjective.

LIZA. I don't understand. I'm too ignorant.

HIGGINS. It's only imagination. Low spirits and nothing else. Nobody's hurting you. Nothing's wrong. You go to bed like a good girl and sleep it off. Have a little cry and say your prayers. That will make you comfortable.

LIZA. I heard your prayers. "Thank God it's all over!"

HIGGINS (*impatiently*). Well, *don't* you thank God it's all over? Now you are free and can do what you like.

LIZA (*pulling herself together in desperation*). What am I fit for? What have you left me fit for? Where am I to go? What am I to do? What's to become of me?

HIGGINS (*enlightened, but not at all impressed*). Oh *that's* what's worrying you, is it? (*He thrusts his hands into his pockets, and walks about in his usual manner, rattling the contents of his pockets, as if condescending to a trivial subject out of pure kindness.*) I shouldn't bother about it if I were you. I should imagine you won't have much difficulty in settling yourself somewhere or other, though I hadn't quite realized that you were going away. (*She looks quickly at him. He does not look at her, but examines the dessert stand on the piano and decides that he will eat an apple.*) You might marry, you know. (*He bites a large piece out of the apple and munches it noisily.*) You see, Eliza, all men are not confirmed old bachelors like me and the Colonel. Most men are the marrying sort (poor devils!); and you're not bad looking. It's quite a pleasure to look at you sometimes—not now, of course, because you're crying and looking as ugly as the very devil; but when you're all right and quite yourself, you're what I should call attractive. That is, to the people in the marrying line, you understand. You go to bed and have a good nice rest; and then get up and look at yourself in the glass; and you won't feel so cheap.

[ELIZA *again looks at him, speechless, and does not stir. The look is quite lost on him. He eats his apple with a dreamy expression of happiness, as it is quite a good one.*]

HIGGINS (*a genial afterthought occurring to him*). I daresay my mother could find some chap or other who would do very well.

LIZA. We were above that at the corner of Tottenham Court Road.

HIGGINS (*waking up*). What do you mean?

LIZA. I sold flowers. I didn't sell myself. Now you've made a lady of me I'm not fit to sell anything else. I wish you'd left me where you found me.

HIGGINS (*slinging the core of the apple decisively into the grate*). Tosh, Eliza. Don't you insult human relations by dragging all this cant about buying and selling into it. You needn't marry the fellow if you don't like him.

LIZA. What else am I to do?

HIGGINS. Oh, lots of things. What about your old idea of a florist's shop? Pickering could set you up in one. He's lots of money. (*Chuckling*) He'll have to pay for all those togs you have been wearing today; and that, with the hire of the jewelry, will make a big hole in two hundred pounds. Why, six months ago you would have thought it the millennium to have a flower shop of your own. Come! you'll be all right. I must clear off to bed. I'm devilish sleepy. By the way, I came down for something. I forget what it was.

LIZA. Your slippers.

HIGGINS. Oh, yes, of course. You shied them at me. (*He picks them up, and is going out when she rises and speaks to him.*)

LIZA. Before you go, sir—

HIGGINS (*dropping the slippers in his surprise at her calling him Sir*). Eh?

LIZA. Do my clothes belong to me or to Colonel Pickering?

HIGGINS (*coming back into the room as if her question were the very climax of unreason*). What the devil use would they be to Pickering?

LIZA. He might want them for the next girl you pick up to experiment on.

HIGGINS (*shocked and hurt*). Is *that* the way you feel toward us?

LIZA. I don't want to hear anything more about that. All I want to know is whether anything belongs to me. My own clothes were burnt.

HIGGINS. But what does it matter? Why need you start bothering about that in the middle of the night?

LIZA. I want to know what I may take away with me. I don't want to be accused of stealing.

HIGGINS (*now deeply wounded*). Stealing! You shouldn't have said that, Eliza. That shows a want of feeling.

LIZA. I'm sorry. I'm only a common ignorant girl; and in my station I have to be careful. There can't be any feelings between the like of you and the like of me. Please will you tell me what belongs to me and what doesn't?

HIGGINS (*very sulky*). You may take the whole damned houseful if you like. Except the jewels. They're hired. Will that satisfy you? (*He turns on his heel and is about to go in extreme dudgeon.[1]*)

LIZA (*drinking in his emotion like nectar, and nagging him to provoke a further supply*). Stop, please. (*She takes off her jewels.*) Will you take these to your room and keep them safe? I don't want to run the risk of their being missing.

HIGGINS (*furious*). Hand them over. (*She puts them into his hands.*) If these belonged to me instead of to the jeweler, I'd ram them down your ungrateful throat. (*He perfunctorily thrusts them into his pockets, unconsciously decorating himself with the protruding ends of the chains.*)

LIZA (*taking a ring off*). This ring isn't the jeweler's. It's the one you bought me in Brighton. I don't want it now. (HIGGINS *dashes the ring violently into the fireplace, and turns on her so threateningly that she crouches over the piano with her hands over her face, and exclaims*) Don't you hit me.

HIGGINS. Hit you! You infamous creature, how dare you accuse me of such a thing? It is you who have hit me. You have wounded me to the heart.

---

[1] *dudgeon* (dŭj'ŭn): angered feeling.

LIZA (*thrilling with hidden joy*). I'm glad. I've got a little of my own back, anyhow.

HIGGINS (*with dignity, in his finest professional style*). You have caused me to lose my temper—a thing that has hardly ever happened to me before. I prefer to say nothing more tonight. I am going to bed.

LIZA (*pertly*). You'd better leave a note for Mrs. Pearce about the coffee, for she won't be told by me.

HIGGINS (*formally*). Damn Mrs. Pearce; and damn the coffee; and damn you; and damn my own folly in having lavished hard-earned knowledge and the treasure of my regard and intimacy on a heartless guttersnipe. (*He goes out with impressive decorum, and spoils it by slamming the door savagely.*)

[ELIZA *smiles for the first time; expresses her feelings by a wild pantomime in which an imitation of* HIGGINS' *exit is confused with her own triumph; and finally goes down on her knees on the hearthrug to look for the ring.*]

A CRISIS

1. The experiment is finished and Higgins has won his bet. How does he react to his success? What do Higgins and Pickering have to say about the conventional social routine? Do you think that Shaw means this as a criticism of society?

2. Eliza has been silent and brooding, but finally her "beauty becomes murderous." Why? How does Higgins first react to her outburst? What is really bothering her? When had this problem been suggested before? Is Higgins being honest in his response to Eliza? What effect does his response have on Eliza? What adjectives would you use to describe Higgins in this scene?

3. At this point, what do you think Eliza's feelings for Higgins are? Can you justify what she says and what she does? Why do you think Eliza is smiling at the end of the scene?

ACT V

MRS. HIGGINS' *drawing room. She is at her writing table as before. The* PARLOR MAID *comes in.*

THE PARLOR MAID (*at the door*). Mr. Henry, ma'am, is downstairs with Colonel Pickering.

MRS. HIGGINS. Well, show them up.

THE PARLOR MAID. They're using the telephone, ma'am. Telephoning to the police, I think.

MRS. HIGGINS. What!

THE PARLOR MAID (*coming further in and lowering her voice*). Mr. Henry is in a state, ma'am. I thought I'd better tell you.

MRS. HIGGINS. If you had told me that Mr. Henry was not in a state it would have been more surprising. Tell them to come up when they've finished with the police. I suppose he's lost something.

THE PARLOR MAID. Yes, ma'am (*going*).

MRS. HIGGINS. Go upstairs and tell Miss Doolittle that Mr. Henry and the Colonel are here. Ask her not to come down till I send for her.

THE PARLOR MAID. Yes, ma'am.

[HIGGINS *bursts in. He is, as the* PARLOR MAID *has said, in a state.*]

HIGGINS. Look here, Mother! Here's a confounded thing!

MRS. HIGGINS. Yes, dear. Good morning. (*He checks his impatience and kisses her, while the* PARLOR MAID *goes out.*) What is it?

HIGGINS. Eliza's bolted.

MRS. HIGGINS (*calmly continuing her writing*). You must have frightened her.

HIGGINS. Frightened her! Nonsense! She was left last night, as usual, to turn out the lights and all that; and instead of going to bed, she changed her clothes and went right off. Her bed wasn't slept in. She came in a cab for her things before seven this morning, and that fool Mrs. Pearce let her have them without telling me a word about it. What am I to do?

MRS. HIGGINS. Do without, I'm afraid, Henry. The girl has a perfect right to leave if she chooses.

HIGGINS (*wandering distractedly across the room*). But I can't find anything. I don't know what appointments I've got. I'm—(PICKERING *comes in.* MRS. HIGGINS *puts down her pen and turns away from the writing table.*)

PICKERING (*shaking hands*). Good morning, Mrs. Higgins. Has Henry told you? (*He sits down on the ottoman.*)

HIGGINS. What does that fool of an inspector say? Have you offered a reward?

MRS. HIGGINS (*rising in indignant amazement*). You don't mean to say you have set the police after Eliza.

HIGGINS. Of course. What are the police for? What else could we do? (*He sits in the Elizabethan chair.*)

PICKERING. The inspector made a lot of difficulties. I really think he suspected us of some improper purpose.

MRS. HIGGINS. Well, of course he did. What right have you to go to the police and give the girl's name as if she were a thief, or a lost umbrella, or something? Really! (*She sits down again, deeply vexed.*)

HIGGINS. But we want to find her.

PICKERING. We can't let her go like this, you know, Mrs. Higgins. What were we to do?

MRS. HIGGINS. You have no more sense, either of you, than two children. Why—

[*The* PARLOR MAID *comes in and breaks off the conversation.*]

THE PARLOR MAID. Mr. Henry, a gentleman wants to see you very particular. He's been sent on from Wimpole Street.

HIGGINS. Oh, bother! I can't see anyone now. Who is it?

THE PARLOR MAID. A Mr. Doolittle, sir.

PICKERING. Doolittle! Do you mean the dustman?

THE PARLOR MAID. Dustman! Oh no, sir. A gentleman.

HIGGINS (*springing up excitedly*). By George, Pick, it's some relative of hers that she's gone to. Somebody we know nothing about. (*To the* PARLOR MAID) Send him up, quick.

THE PARLOR MAID. Yes, sir. (*She goes.*)

HIGGINS (*eagerly, going to his mother*). Genteel relatives! Now we shall hear something. (*He sits down in the Chippendale chair.*)

MRS. HIGGINS. Do you know any of her people?

PICKERING. Only her father. The fellow we told you about.

THE PARLOR MAID (*announcing*). Mr. Doolittle. (*She withdraws.*)

[DOOLITTLE *enters. He is brilliantly dressed in a new fashionable frock coat, with white waistcoat and gray trousers. A flower in his buttonhole, a dazzling silk hat, and patent leather shoes complete the effect. He is too concerned with the business he has come on to notice* MRS. HIGGINS. *He walks straight to* HIGGINS, *and accosts him with vehement[1] reproach.*]

DOOLITTLE (*indicating his own person*). See here! Do you see this? *You* done this.

[1] *vehement* (vē′ĕ·mĕnt): furious.

HIGGINS. Done what, man?

DOOLITTLE. This, I tell you. Look at it. Look at this hat. Look at this coat.

PICKERING. Has Eliza been buying you clothes?

DOOLITTLE. Eliza! Not she. Not half. Why would she buy me clothes?

MRS. HIGGINS. Good morning, Mr. Doolittle. Won't you sit down?

DOOLITTLE (*taken aback as he becomes conscious that he has forgotten his hostess*). Asking your pardon, ma'am. (*He approaches her and shakes her proffered hand.*) Thank you. (*He sits down on the ottoman, on* PICKERING'S *right.*) I am that full of what has happened to me that I can't think of anything else.

HIGGINS. What the dickens *has* happened to you?

DOOLITTLE. I shouldn't mind if it had only *happened* to me. Anything might happen to anybody and nobody to blame but Providence, as you might say. But this is something that you done to me. Yes, you, Henry Higgins.

HIGGINS. Have you found Eliza? That's the point.

DOOLITTLE. Have you lost her?

HIGGINS. Yes.

DOOLITTLE. You have all the luck, you have. I ain't found her; but she'll find me quick enough now after what you done to me.

MRS. HIGGINS. But what has my son done to you, Mr. Doolittle?

DOOLITTLE. Done to me! Ruined me. Destroyed my happiness. Tied me up and delivered me into the hands of middle class morality.

HIGGINS (*rising intolerantly and standing over* DOOLITTLE). You're raving. You're drunk. You're mad. I gave you five pounds. After that I had two conversations with you, at half-a-crown an hour. I've never seen you since.

DOOLITTLE. Oh! Drunk! am I? Mad! am I? Tell me this. Did you or did you not write a letter to an old blighter in America that was giving five millions to found Moral Reform Societies all over the world, and that wanted you to invent a universal language for him?

HIGGINS. What! Ezra D. Wannafeller! He's dead. (*He sits down again carelessly.*)

DOOLITTLE. Yes, he's dead; and I'm done for. Now did you or did you not write a letter to him to say that the most original moralist at present in England, to the best of your knowledge, was Alfred Doolittle, a common dustman.

HIGGINS. Oh, after your last visit I remember making some silly joke of the kind.

DOOLITTLE. Ah! you may well call it a silly joke. It put the lid on me right enough. Just give him the chance he wanted to show that Americans is not like us: that they recognize and respect merit in every class of life, however humble. Them words is in his blooming will, in which, Henry Higgins, thanks to your silly joking, he leaves me a share in his Predigested Cheese Trust worth three thousand a year on condition that I lecture for his Wannafeller Moral Reform World League as often as they ask me up to six times a year.

HIGGINS. The devil he does! Whew! (*Brightening suddenly*) What a lark!

PICKERING. A safe thing for you, Doolittle. They won't ask you twice.

DOOLITTLE. It ain't the lecturing I mind. I'll lecture them blue in the face, I will, and not turn a hair. It's making a gentleman of me that I object to. Who asked him to make a gentleman of me? I was happy. I was free. I touched pretty nigh everybody for money when I wanted it, same as I touched you, Henry Higgins. Now I am worrited; tied neck and heels; and everybody touches me for money. It's a fine thing for you, says my solicitor. Is it? says I. You mean it's a good thing for you, I say. When I was a poor man and had a solicitor once when they found a pram in the dust cart, he got me off, and got shut of me and got me shut of him as quick as he could. Same with the doctors: used to shove me out of the hospital before I could hardly stand on my legs, and nothing to pay. Now they finds out that I'm not a healthy man and can't live unless they looks after me twice a day. In the house I'm not let do a hand's turn for myself: somebody else must do it and touch me for it. A year ago I hadn't a relative in the world except two or three that wouldn't speak to me. Now I've fifty, and not a decent week's wages among the lot of them. I have to live for others and not for myself. That's middle class morality. *You* talk of losing Eliza. Don't you be anxious: I bet she's on my doorstep by this. She that could support herself easy by selling flowers if I wasn't respectable. And the next one to touch me will be you, Henry Higgins. I'll have to learn to speak middle class language from you, instead of speaking proper English. That's where you'll come in; and I daresay that's what you done it for.

MRS. HIGGINS. But, my dear Mr. Doolittle, you need not suffer all this if you are really in earnest. Nobody can force you to accept this bequest. You can repudiate it. Isn't that so, Colonel Pickering?

PICKERING. I believe so.

DOOLITTLE (*softening his manner in deference to her sex*). That's the tragedy of it, ma'am. It's easy to say chuck it; but I haven't the nerve.

Which of us has? We're all intimidated. Intimidated, ma'am: that's what we are. What is there for me if I chuck it but the workhouse in my old age? I have to dye my hair already to keep my job as a dustman. If I was one of the deserving poor, and had put by a bit, I could chuck it; but then why should I, acause the deserving poor might as well be millionaires for all the happiness they ever has. They don't know what happiness is. But I, as one of the undeserving poor, have nothing between me and the pauper's uniform but this here blasted three thousand a year that shoves me into the middle class. (Excuse the expression, ma'am: you'd use it yourself if you had my provocation.) They've got you every way you turn: it's a choice between the Skilly of the workhouse and the Char Bydis[1] of the middle class; and I haven't the nerve for the workhouse. Intimidated! that's what I am. Broke. Bought up. Happier men than me will call for my dust and touch me for their tip; and I'll look on helpless, and envy them. And that's what your son has brought me to. (*He is overcome by emotion.*)

MRS. HIGGINS. Well, I'm very glad you're not going to do anything foolish, Mr. Doolittle. For this solves the problem of Eliza's future. You can provide for her now.

DOOLITTLE (*with melancholy resignation*). Yes, ma'am. I'm expected to provide for everyone now, out of three thousand a year.

HIGGINS (*jumping up*). Nonsense! He can't provide for her. He shan't provide for her. She doesn't belong to him. I paid him five pounds for her. Doolittle, either you're an honest man or a rogue.

DOOLITTLE (*tolerantly*). A little of both, Henry. Like the rest of us, a little of both.

HIGGINS. Well, you took that money for the girl; and you have no right to take her as well.

MRS. HIGGINS. Henry, don't be absurd. If you want to know where Eliza is, she is upstairs.

HIGGINS (*amazed*). Upstairs!!! Then I shall jolly soon fetch her downstairs. (*He makes resolutely for the door.*)

MRS. HIGGINS (*rising and following him*). Be quiet, Henry. Sit down.

HIGGINS. I—

MRS. HIGGINS. Sit down, dear; and listen to me.

HIGGINS. Oh very well, very well, very well. (*He throws himself un-*

[1] *Skilly . . . Char Bydis:* Doolittle's distortion of Scylla (sĭl'd) and Charybdis (kȧ·rĭb'dĭs), a dangerous rock and whirlpool on either side of a narrow strait between Sicily and Italy. The ancient Greeks personified them as two monsters, and they have come to symbolize two dangers between which it is almost impossible to

graciously on the ottoman, with his face toward the windows.) But I think you might have told us this half an hour ago.

MRS. HIGGINS. Eliza came to me this morning. She passed the night partly walking about in a rage, partly trying to throw herself into the river and being afraid to, and partly in the Carlton Hotel. She told me of the brutal way you two treated her.

HIGGINS (*bounding up again*). What!

PICKERING (*rising also*). My dear Mrs. Higgins, she's been telling you stories. We didn't treat her brutally. We hardly said a word to her; and we parted on particularly good terms. (*Turning on* HIGGINS) Higgins, did you bully her after I went to bed?

HIGGINS. Just the other way about. She threw my slippers in my face. She behaved in the most outrageous way. I never gave her the slightest provocation. The slippers came bang into my face the moment I entered the room—before I had uttered a word. And used perfectly awful language.

PICKERING (*astonished*). But why? What did we do to her?

MRS. HIGGINS. I think I know pretty well what you did. The girl is naturally rather affectionate, I think. Isn't she, Mr. Doolittle?

DOOLITTLE. Very tender-hearted, ma'am. Takes after me.

MRS. HIGGINS. Just so. She had become attached to you both. She worked very hard for you, Henry! I don't think you quite realize what anything in the nature of brain work means to a girl like that. Well, it seems that when the great day of trial came, and she did this wonderful thing for you without making a single mistake, you two sat there and never said a word to her, but talked together of how glad you were that it was all over and how you had been bored with the whole thing. And then you were surprised because she threw your slippers at you! *I* should have thrown the fire irons at you.

HIGGINS. We said nothing except that we were tired and wanted to go to bed. Did we, Pick?

PICKERING (*shrugging his shoulders*). That was all.

MRS. HIGGINS (*ironically*). Quite sure?

PICKERING. Absolutely. Really, that was all.

MRS. HIGGINS. You didn't thank her, or pet her, or admire her, or tell her how splendid she'd been?

HIGGINS (*impatiently*). But she knew all about that. We didn't make speeches to her, if that's what you mean.

PICKERING (*conscience-stricken*). Perhaps we were a little inconsiderate. Is she very angry?

MRS. HIGGINS (*returning to her place at the writing table*). Well, I'm afraid she won't go back to Wimpole Street, especially now that Mr. Doolittle is able to keep up the position you have thrust on her; but she says she is quite willing to meet you on friendly terms and to let bygones be bygones.

HIGGINS (*furious*). Is she, by George? Ho!

MRS. HIGGINS. If you promise to behave yourself, Henry, I'll ask her to come down. If not, go home; for you have taken up quite enough of my time.

HIGGINS. Oh, all right. Very well. Pick, you behave yourself. Let us put on our best Sunday manners for this creature that we picked out of the mud. (*He flings himself sulkily into the Elizabethan chair.*)

DOOLITTLE (*remonstrating*). Now, now, Henry Higgins! have some consideration for my feelings as a middle class man.

MRS. HIGGINS. Remember your promise, Henry. (*She presses the bell-button on the writing table.*) Mr. Doolittle, will you be so good as to step out on the balcony for a moment? I don't want Eliza to have the shock of your news until she has made it up with these two gentlemen. Would you mind?

DOOLITTLE. As you wish, lady. Anything to help Henry to keep her off my hands. (*He disappears through the window.*)

[*The* PARLOR MAID *answers the bell.* PICKERING *sits down in* DOOLITTLE'S *place.*]

MRS. HIGGINS. Ask Miss Doolittle to come down, please.

THE PARLOR MAID. Yes, ma'am. (*She goes out.*)

MRS. HIGGINS. Now, Henry, be good.

HIGGINS. I am behaving myself perfectly.

PICKERING. He is doing his best, Mrs. Higgins.

[*A pause.* HIGGINS *throws back his head; stretches out his legs; and begins to whistle.*]

MRS. HIGGINS. Henry, dearest, you don't look at all nice in that attitude.

HIGGINS (*pulling himself together*). I was not trying to look nice, Mother.

MRS. HIGGINS. It doesn't matter, dear. I only wanted to make you speak.

HIGGINS. Why?

MRS. HIGGINS. Because you can't speak and whistle at the same time.

[HIGGINS *groans. Another very trying pause.*]

HIGGINS (*springing up, out of patience*). Where the devil is that girl? Are we to wait here all day?

[ELIZA *enters, sunny, self-possessed, and giving a staggeringly convincing exhibition of ease of manner. She carries a little workbasket, and is very much at home.* PICKERING *is too much taken aback to rise.*]

LIZA. How do you do, Professor Higgins? Are you quite well?

HIGGINS (*choking*). Am I—(*He can say no more.*)

LIZA. But of course you are. You are never ill. So glad to see you again, Colonel Pickering. (*He rises hastily; and they shake hands.*) Quite chilly this morning, isn't it? (*She sits down on his left. He sits beside her.*)

HIGGINS. Don't you dare try this game on me. I taught it to you, and it doesn't take me in. Get up and come home, and don't be a fool.

[ELIZA *takes a piece of needlework from her basket, and begins to stitch at it, without taking the least notice of this outburst.*]

MRS. HIGGINS. Very nicely put, indeed, Henry. No woman could resist such an invitation.

HIGGINS. You let her alone, Mother. Let her speak for herself. You will jolly soon see whether she has an idea that I haven't put into her head or a word that I haven't put into her mouth. I tell you I have created this thing out of the squashed cabbage leaves of Covent Garden, and now she pretends to play the fine lady with me.

MRS. HIGGINS (*placidly*). Yes, dear; but you'll sit down, won't you?

[HIGGINS *sits down again, savagely.*]

LIZA (*to* PICKERING, *taking no apparent notice of* HIGGINS, *and working away deftly*). Will *you* drop me altogether now that the experiment is over, Colonel Pickering?

PICKERING. Oh, don't. You mustn't think of it as an experiment. It shocks me, somehow.

LIZA. Oh, I'm only a squashed cabbage leaf—

PICKERING (*impulsively*). No.

LIZA (*continuing quietly*).—but I owe so much to you that I should be very unhappy if you forgot me.

PICKERING. It's very kind of you to say so, Miss Doolittle.

LIZA. It's not because you paid for my dresses. I know you are generous to everybody with money. But it was from you that I learned really nice manners, and that is what makes one a lady, isn't it? You see it was so very difficult for me with the example of Professor Higgins always before me. I was brought up to be just like him, unable to control myself, and using bad language on the slightest provocation. And I should never have known that ladies and gentlemen didn't behave like that if you hadn't been there.

HIGGINS. Well!!

PICKERING. Oh, that's only his way, you know. He doesn't mean it.

LIZA. Oh, I didn't mean it either when I was a flower girl. It was only my way. But you see I did it, and that's what makes the difference after all.

PICKERING. No doubt. Still, he taught you to speak; and I couldn't have done that, you know.

LIZA (*trivially*). Of course. That is his profession.

HIGGINS. Damnation!

LIZA (*continuing*). It was just like learning to dance in the fashionable way. There was nothing more than that in it. But do you know what began my real education?

PICKERING. What?

LIZA (*stopping her work for a moment*). Your calling me Miss Doolittle that day when I first came to Wimpole Street. That was the beginning of self-respect for me. (*She resumes her stitching.*) And there were a hundred little things you never noticed, because they came naturally to you. Things about standing up and taking off your hat and opening doors—

PICKERING. Oh, that was nothing.

LIZA. Yes, things that showed you thought and felt about me as if I were something better than a scullery maid; though of course I know you would have been just the same to a scullery maid if she had been let into the drawing room. *You* never took off your boots in the dining room when I was there.

PICKERING. You mustn't mind that. Higgins takes off his boots all over the place.

LIZA. I know. I am not blaming him. It is his way, isn't it? But it made *such* a difference to me that you didn't do it. You see, really and truly, apart from the things anyone can pick up (the dressing and the proper way of speaking, and so on), the difference between a lady and a flower girl is not how she behaves, but how she's treated. I shall always be a flower girl to Professor Higgins, because he always treats me as a flower girl, and always will; but I know I can be a lady to you, because you always treat me as a lady, and always will.

MRS. HIGGINS. Please don't grind your teeth, Henry.

PICKERING. Well, this is really very nice of you, Miss Doolittle.

LIZA. I should like you to call me Eliza, now, if you would.

PICKERING. Thank you. Eliza, of course.

LIZA. And I should like Professor Higgins to call me Miss Doolittle.

HIGGINS. I'll see you damned first.

MRS. HIGGINS. Henry! Henry!

PICKERING (*laughing*). Why don't you slang back at him? Don't stand it. It would do him a lot of good.

LIZA. I can't. I could have done it once; but now I can't go back to it. Last night, when I was wandering about, a girl spoke to me; and I tried to get back into the old way with her, but it was no use. You told me, you know, that when a child is brought to a foreign country, it picks up the language in a few weeks and forgets its own. Well, I am a child in your country. I have forgotten my own language and can speak nothing but yours. That's the real break-off with the corner of Tottenham Court Road. Leaving Wimpole Street finishes it.

PICKERING (*much alarmed*). Oh! but you're coming back to Wimpole Street, aren't you? You'll forgive Higgins?

HIGGINS (*rising*). Forgive! Will she, by George! Let her go. Let her find out how she can get on without us. She will relapse into the gutter in three weeks without me at her elbow.

[DOOLITTLE *appears at the center window. With a look of dignified reproach at* HIGGINS, *he comes slowly and silently to his daughter, who, with her back to the window, is unconscious of his approach.*]

PICKERING. He's incorrigible, Eliza. You won't relapse, will you?

LIZA. No, not now. Never again. I have learnt my lesson. I don't believe I could utter one of the old sounds if I tried. (DOOLITTLE *touches her on her left shoulder. She drops her work, losing her self-possession utterly at the spectacle of her father's splendor*) A-a-a-a-a-ah-ow-ooh!

HIGGINS (*with a crow of triumph*). Aha! Just so. A-a-a-a-ahowooh! A-a-a-a-ahowooh! A-a-a-a-ahowooh! Victory! Victory! (*He throws himself on the divan, folding his arms, and spraddling arrogantly.*)

DOOLITTLE. Can you blame the girl? Don't look at me like that, Eliza. It ain't my fault. I've come into some money.

LIZA. You must have touched a millionaire this time, Dad.

DOOLITTLE. I have. But I'm dressed something special today. I'm going to St. George's, Hanover Square. Your stepmother is going to marry me.

LIZA (*angrily*). You're going to let yourself down to marry that low common woman!

PICKERING (*quietly*). He ought to, Eliza. (*To* DOOLITTLE) Why has she changed her mind?

DOOLITTLE (*sadly*). Intimidated, Governor. Intimidated. Middle class morality claims its victim. Won't you put on your hat, Liza, and come and see me turned off?

LIZA. If the Colonel says I must, I—I'll (*almost sobbing*) I'll demean[1] myself. And get insulted for my pains, like enough.

DOOLITTLE. Don't be afraid. She never comes to words with anyone now, poor woman! Respectability has broke all the spirit out of her.

PICKERING (*squeezing* ELIZA'S *elbow gently*). Be kind to them, Eliza. Make the best of it.

LIZA (*forcing a little smile for him through her vexation*). Oh well, just to show there's no ill feeling. I'll be back in a moment. (*She goes out.*)

DOOLITTLE (*sitting down beside* PICKERING). I feel uncommon nervous about the ceremony, Colonel. I wish you'd come and see me through it.

PICKERING. But you've been through it before, man. You were married to Eliza's mother.

DOOLITTLE. Who told you that, Colonel?

PICKERING. Well, nobody told me. But I concluded—naturally—

DOOLITTLE. No, that ain't the natural way, Colonel. It's only the middle class way. My way was always the undeserving way. But don't say nothing to Eliza. She don't know. I always had a delicacy about telling her.

PICKERING. Quite right. We'll leave it so, if you don't mind.

DOOLITTLE. And you'll come to the church, Colonel, and put me through straight?

PICKERING. With pleasure. As far as a bachelor can.

MRS. HIGGINS. May I come, Mr. Doolittle? I should be very sorry to miss your wedding.

DOOLITTLE. I should indeed be honored by your condescension, ma'am; and my poor old woman would take it as a tremendous com-

---

[1] *demean* (dē·mēn′): lower, degrade.

pliment. She's been very low, thinking of the happy days that are no more.

MRS. HIGGINS (*rising*). I'll order the carriage and get ready. (*The men rise, except* HIGGINS.) I shan't be more than fifteen minutes. (*As she goes to the door* ELIZA *comes in, hatted and buttoning her gloves.*) I'm going to the church to see your father married, Eliza. You had better come in the brougham[1] with me. Colonel Pickering can go on with the bridegroom.

[MRS. HIGGINS *goes out.* ELIZA *comes to the middle of the room between the center window and the ottoman.* PICKERING *joins her.*]

DOOLITTLE. Bridegroom! What a word! It makes a man realize his position, somehow. (*He takes up his hat and goes toward the door.*)

PICKERING. Before I go, Eliza, do forgive him and come back to us.

LIZA. I don't think Papa would allow me. Would you, Dad?

DOOLITTLE (*sad but magnanimous*). They played you off very cunning, Eliza, them two sportsmen. If it had been only one of them, you could have nailed him. But you see, there was two; and one of them chaperoned the other, as you might say. (*To* PICKERING) It was artful of you, Colonel; but I bear no malice. I should have done the same myself. I been the victim of one woman after another all my life; and I don't grudge you two getting the better of Eliza. I shan't interfere. It's time for us to go, Colonel. So long, Henry. See you in St. George's, Eliza. (*He goes out.*)

PICKERING (*coaxing*). Do stay with us, Eliza. (*He follows* DOOLITTLE.)

[ELIZA *goes out on the balcony to avoid being alone with* HIGGINS. *He rises and joins her there. She immediately comes back into the room and makes for the door; but he goes along the balcony quickly and gets his back to the door before she reaches it.*]

HIGGINS. Well, Eliza, you've had a bit of your own back, as you call it. Have you had enough? And are you going to be reasonable? Or do you want any more?

LIZA. You want me back only to pick up your slippers and put up with your tempers and fetch and carry for you.

HIGGINS. I haven't said I wanted you back at all.

---

[1] *brougham* (broom): a light, closed carriage.

LIZA. Oh, indeed. Then what are we talking about?

HIGGINS. About you, not about me. If you come back I shall treat you just as I have always treated you. I can't change my nature, and I don't intend to change my manners. My manners are exactly the same as Colonel Pickering's.

LIZA. That's not true. He treats a flower girl as if she was a duchess.

HIGGINS. And I treat a duchess as if she was a flower girl.

LIZA. I see. (*She turns away composedly, and sits on the ottoman, facing the window.*) The same to everybody.

HIGGINS. Just so.

LIZA. Like father.

HIGGINS (*grinning, a little taken down*). Without accepting the comparison at all points, Eliza, it's quite true that your father is not a snob, and that he will be quite at home in any station of life to which his eccentric destiny may call him. (*Seriously*) The great secret, Eliza, is not having bad manners or good manners or any other particular sort of manners, but having the same manner for all human souls. In short, behaving as if you were in Heaven, where there are no third class carriages, and one soul is as good as another.

LIZA. Amen. You are a born preacher.

HIGGINS (*irritated*). The question is not whether I treat you rudely, but whether you ever heard me treat anyone else better.

LIZA (*with sudden sincerity*). I don't care how you treat me. I don't mind your swearing at me. I don't mind a black eye: I've had one before this. But (*standing up and facing him*) I won't be passed over.

HIGGINS. Then get out of my way, for I won't stop for you. You talk about me as if I were a motor bus.

LIZA. So you are a motor bus. All bounce and go, and no consideration for anyone. But I can do without you; don't think I can't.

HIGGINS. I know you can. I told you you could.

LIZA (*wounded, getting away from him to the other side of the ottoman with her face to the hearth*). I know you did, you brute. You wanted to get rid of me.

HIGGINS. Liar.

LIZA. Thank you. (*She sits down with dignity.*)

HIGGINS. You never asked yourself, I suppose, whether *I* could do without *you*.

LIZA (*earnestly*). Don't you try to get round me. You'll *have* to do without me.

HIGGINS (*arrogant*). I can do without anybody. I have my own soul, my own spark of divine fire. But (*with sudden humility*) I shall miss you, Eliza. (*He sits down near her on the ottoman.*) I have learned something from your idiotic notions. I confess that humbly and gratefully. And I have grown accustomed to your voice and appearance. I like them, rather.

LIZA. Well, you have both of them on your gramophone and in your book of photographs. When you feel lonely without me, you can turn the machine on. It's got no feelings to hurt.

HIGGINS. I can't turn your soul on. Leave me those feelings, and you can take away the voice and the face. They are not you.

LIZA. Oh, you *are* a devil. You can twist the heart in a girl as easy as some could twist her arms to hurt her. Mrs. Pearce warned me. Time and again she has wanted to leave you, and you always got round her at the last minute. And you don't care a bit for her. And you don't care a bit for me.

HIGGINS. I care for life, for humanity; and you are a part of it that has come my way and been built into my house. What more can you or anyone ask?

LIZA. I won't care for anybody that doesn't care for me.

HIGGINS. Commercial principles, Eliza. Like (*reproducing her Covent Garden pronunciation with professional exactness*) s'yollin voylets [selling violets], isn't it?

LIZA. Don't sneer at me. It's mean to sneer at me.

HIGGINS. I have never sneered in my life. Sneering doesn't become either the human face or the human soul. I am expressing my righteous contempt for commercialism. I don't and won't trade in affection. You call me a brute because you couldn't buy a claim on me by fetching my slippers and finding my spectacles. You were a fool! I think a woman fetching a man's slippers is a disgusting sight. Did I ever fetch *your* slippers? I think a good deal more of you for throwing them in my face. No use slaving for me and then saying you want to be cared for. Who cares for a slave? If you come back, come back for the sake of good fellowship; for you'll get nothing else. You've had a thousand times as much out of me as I have out of you; and if you dare to set up your little dog's tricks of fetching and carrying slippers against my creation of a Duchess, Eliza, I'll slam the door in your silly face.

LIZA. What did you do it for if you didn't care for me?

HIGGINS (*heartily*). Why, because it was my job.

LIZA. You never thought of the trouble it would make for me.

HIGGINS. Would the world ever have been made if its maker had been afraid of making trouble? Making life means making trouble. There's only one way of escaping trouble, and that's killing things. Cowards, you notice, are always shrieking to have troublesome people killed.

LIZA. I'm no preacher; I don't notice things like that. I notice that you don't notice me.

HIGGINS (*jumping up and walking about intolerantly*). Eliza! You're an idiot. I waste the treasures of my Miltonic mind by spreading them before you. Once for all, understand that I go my way and do my work without caring twopence what happens to either of us. I am not intimidated, like your father and your stepmother. So you can come back or go to the devil—whichever you please.

LIZA. What am I to come back for?

HIGGINS (*bouncing up on his knees on the ottoman and leaning over it to her*). For the fun of it. That's why I took you on.

LIZA (*with averted face*). And you may throw me out tomorrow if I don't do everything you want me to?

HIGGINS. Yes, and you may walk out tomorrow if I don't do everything *you* want me to.

LIZA. And live with my stepmother?

HIGGINS. Yes, or sell flowers.

LIZA. Oh! if I only *could* go back to my flower basket! I should be independent of both you and father and all the world! Why did you take my independence from me? Why did I give it up? I'm a slave now, for all my fine clothes.

HIGGINS. Not a bit. I'll adopt you as my daughter and settle money on you if you like. Or would you rather marry Pickering?

LIZA (*looking fiercely round at him*). I wouldn't marry *you* if you asked me; and you're nearer my age than what he is.

HIGGINS (*gently*). Than he is; not "than what he is."

LIZA (*losing her temper and rising*). I'll talk as I like. You're not my teacher now.

HIGGINS (*reflectively*). I don't suppose Pickering would, though. He's as confirmed an old bachelor as I am.

LIZA. That's not what I want, and don't you think it. I've always had chaps enough wanting me that way. Freddy Hill writes to me twice and three times a day, sheets and sheets.

HIGGINS (*disagreeably surprised*). Damn his impudence! (*He recoils and finds himself sitting on his heels.*)

LIZA. He has a right to if he likes, poor lad. And he does love me.

HIGGINS (*getting off the ottoman*). You have no right to encourage him.

LIZA. Every girl has a right to be loved.

HIGGINS. What! By fools like that?

LIZA. Freddy's not a fool. And if he's weak and poor and wants me, maybe he'd make me happier than my betters that bully me and don't want me.

HIGGINS. Can he *make* anything of you? That's the point.

LIZA. Perhaps I could make something of him. But I never thought of us making anything of one another; and you never think of anything else. I only want to be natural.

HIGGINS. In short, you want me to be as infatuated about you as Freddy? Is that it?

LIZA. No I don't. That's not the sort of feeling I want from you. And don't you be too sure of yourself or of me. I could have been a bad girl if I'd liked. I've seen more of some things than you, for all your learning. Girls like me can drag gentlemen down to make love to them easy enough. And they wish each other dead the next minute.

HIGGINS. Of course they do. Then what in thunder are we quarreling about?

LIZA (*much troubled*). I want a little kindness. I know I'm a common ignorant girl, and you a book-learned gentleman; but I'm not dirt under your feet. What I done (*correcting herself*) what I did was not for the dresses and the taxis. I did it because we were pleasant together and I come—came—to care for you; not to want you to make love to me, and not forgetting the difference between us, but more friendly like.

HIGGINS. Well, of course. That's just how I feel. And how Pickering feels. Eliza, you're a fool.

LIZA. That's not a proper answer to give me. (*She sinks on the chair at the writing table in tears.*)

HIGGINS. It's all you'll get until you stop being a common idiot. If you're going to be a lady, you'll have to give up feeling neglected if the men you know don't spend half their time sniveling over you and the other half giving you black eyes. If you can't stand the coldness of my sort of life, and the strain of it, go back to the gutter. Work till you are more a brute than a human being; and then cuddle and squabble and drink till you fall asleep. Oh, it's a fine life, the life of the gutter. It's real; it's warm; it's violent. You can feel it through the thickest skin; you can taste it and smell it without any training or any work. Not like Science and Literature and Classical Music and Philosophy and Art. You find me cold, unfeeling, selfish, don't you? Very well. Be off with you to the sort of people you like. Marry some sentimental hog or other with lots of money, and a thick pair of lips to kiss you with and a thick pair of boots to kick you with. If you can't appreciate what you've got, you'd better get what you can appreciate.

LIZA (*desperate*). Oh, you *are* a cruel tyrant. I can't talk to you. You turn everything against me; I'm always in the wrong. But you know very well all the time that you're nothing but a bully. You know I can't go back to the gutter, as you call it, and that I have no real friends in the world but you and the Colonel. You know well I couldn't bear to live with a low common man after you two; and it's wicked and cruel of you to insult me by pretending I could. You think I must go back to Wimpole Street because I have nowhere else to go but father's. But don't you be too sure that you have me under your feet to be trampled on and talked down. I'll marry Freddy, I will, as soon as he's able to support me.

HIGGINS (*sitting down beside her*). Rubbish! You shall marry an ambassador. You shall marry the Governor-General of India or the Lord-Lieutenant of Ireland, or somebody who wants a deputy-queen. I'm not going to have my masterpiece thrown away on Freddy.

LIZA. You think I like you to say that. But I haven't forgot what you said a minute ago, and I won't be coaxed round as if I was a baby or a puppy. If I can't have kindness, I'll have independence.

HIGGINS. Independence? That's middle class blasphemy. We are all dependent on one another, every soul of us on earth.

LIZA (*rising determinedly*). I'll let you see whether I'm dependent on you. If you can preach, I can teach. I'll go and be a teacher.

HIGGINS. What'll you teach, in heaven's name?

LIZA. What you taught me. I'll teach phonetics.

HIGGINS. Ha! ha! ha!

LIZA. I'll offer myself as an assistant to Professor Nepean.

HIGGINS (*rising in a fury*). What! That impostor! That humbug! That toadying ignoramus! Teach him *my* methods! *My* discoveries! You take one step in his direction and I'll wring your neck. (*He lays hands on her.*) Do you hear?

LIZA (*defiantly nonresistant*). Wring away. What do I care? I knew you'd strike me some day. (*He lets her go, stamping with rage at having forgotten himself, and recoils so hastily that he stumbles back into his seat on the ottoman.*) Aha! Now I know how to deal with you. What a fool I was not to think of it before! You can't take away the knowledge you gave me. You said I had a finer ear than you. And I can be civil and kind to people, which is more than you can. Aha! That's done you, Henry Higgins, it has. Now I don't care *that* (*snapping her fingers*) for your bullying and your big talk. I'll advertise it in the papers that your duchess is only a flower girl that you taught, and that she'll teach anybody to be a duchess just the same in six months for a thousand guineas. Oh, when I think of myself crawling under your feet and being trampled on and called names, when all the time I had only to lift up my finger to be as good as you, I could just kick myself.

HIGGINS (*wondering at her*). You impudent hussy, you! But it's better than sniveling; better than fetching slippers and finding spectacles, isn't it? (*Rising*) By George, Eliza, I said I'd make a woman of you; and I have. I like you like this.

LIZA. Yes, you turn round and make up to me now that I'm not afraid of you, and can do without you.

HIGGINS. Of course I do, you little fool. Five minutes ago you were like a millstone round my neck. Now you're a tower of strength, a consort battleship. You and I and Pickering will be three old bachelors together instead of only two men and a silly girl.

[MRS. HIGGINS *returns, dressed for the wedding.* ELIZA *instantly becomes cool and elegant.*]

MRS. HIGGINS. The carriage is waiting, Eliza. Are you ready?

LIZA. Quite. Is the Professor coming?

MRS. HIGGINS. Certainly not. He can't behave himself in church. He makes remarks out loud all the time on the clergyman's pronunciation.

LIZA. Then I shall not see you again, Professor. Good-by. (*She goes to the door.*)

MRS. HIGGINS (*coming to* HIGGINS). Good-by, dear.

HIGGINS. Good-by, Mother. (*He is about to kiss her, when he recollects something.*) Oh, by the way, Eliza, order a ham and a Stilton cheese, will you? And buy me a pair of reindeer gloves, number eights, and a tie to match that new suit of mine, at Eale & Binman's. You can choose the color. (*His cheerful, careless, vigorous voice shows that he is incorrigible.*)

LIZA (*disdainfully*). Buy them yourself. (*She sweeps out.*)

MRS. HIGGINS. I'm afraid you've spoiled that girl, Henry. But never mind, dear. I'll buy you the tie and gloves.

HIGGINS (*sunnily*). Oh, don't bother. She'll buy 'em all right enough. Good-by.

[*They kiss.* MRS. HIGGINS *runs out.* HIGGINS, *left alone, rattles his cash in his pocket; chuckles; and disports himself in a highly self-satisfied manner.*]

AN END AND A BEGINNING

1. Why do you think Eliza goes to Mrs. Higgins? What is Higgins' reaction to Eliza's disappearance?

2. Several months have passed since Alfred Doolittle followed his daughter to Henry Higgins' home. What has happened to him during this interval? How is Higgins responsible for what has happened? Through the character of Doolittle, what is Shaw saying about society?

3. How would you describe Eliza's meeting with Higgins and Pickering? Who is on the defensive? What are Eliza's feelings toward Pickering? Higgins? her father? Find the lines which best illustrate Eliza's feelings. Compare Eliza now with the Eliza in each preceding act. Do you note any changes in Higgins in this final scene?

4. Higgins offers to adopt Eliza as his daughter and settle money on her; what other suggestions does he make? How does she react to each? What do you think Higgins' true feeling for Eliza is?

5. How is the situation at the end of the play the beginning of a new life for Eliza? Shaw ends the play without resolving the dilemma he has posed. What do you think will happen? If you are interested, read Shaw's prose sequel (in *Selected Plays of Bernard Shaw*, Dodd, Mead) in which he tells whom Eliza married, and why.

UNDERSTANDING SHAW'S SATIRE

The humor of George Bernard Shaw always has a touch of satire—a sharp social lash that he uses with superb skill. Satire, a device for exposing and discrediting vice or folly, was used by ancient Roman poets, and it has been developed into an effective and amusing literary art.

Satirists have moved from private animosity, or bitterness toward individuals, to elements in public life with which we all are concerned. All types of literature may be vehicles for satire. The spirit behind satirical writing, while it is always critical, ranges from lighthearted fun to angry denunciation.

1. *Pygmalion* is a satire on the false values of society. What classes is Shaw satirizing? What social standards does he criticize? According to Shaw, what is the most important thing each group or class does not have?

2. Make a list of the different aspects of society that Shaw satirizes in this play. How many of them do you think are justifiably ridiculed? In which instances do you disagree with Shaw's point of view?

3. Review the play, noticing what types of people are represented. For what purposes does Shaw use each of the following characters: Eliza, Higgins, Pickering, Mrs. Higgins, Mrs. Eynsford Hill, Clara, Freddy, Alfred Doolittle, Mrs. Pearce? To what extent are these characters individuals or representatives of types of people? What kind of people did Shaw admire? What kind did he dislike? Give definite evidence in support of your answers.

OTHER PLAYS BY G. B. SHAW

Pygmalion, currently perhaps Shaw's best-known comedy, is but one of the many provocative and entertaining plays written by George Bernard Shaw. Among other Shaw favorites are *Caesar and Cleopatra, The Devil's Disciple, Arms and the Man, Major Barbara, Saint Joan, Back to Methuselah, Heartbreak House, Candida, The Doctor's Dilemma,* and *The Apple Cart.*

Shaw, who questioned many of the institutions and social conventions of his day, delighted in writing "problem plays" in which, using his characters as spokesmen for his own ideas, he put conventional beliefs to the test. He also took great pleasure in shocking his audiences. Discarding the accepted rules of the Victorian theater, Shaw wrote as and about what he pleased, letting the stage serve as a forum for his penetrating and often startling views on a wide variety of subjects.

GBS AS DRAMATIST

Thanks to the stupendous success of *My Fair Lady,* which, squarely based on *Pygmalion,* is one of the most popular musicals ever written, Henry Higgins and Liza Doolittle and her father are easily the most widely known of all the characters that Shaw created. *Pygmalion* is a delightful comedy, typical of its author in many ways. From this play we can learn a good deal about its author and his work.

Pygmalion can be considered one of Shaw's later plays, for he was fifty-six when it was first produced in 1912. One of his reasons for writing it was to provide a fine acting part—that of Liza Doolittle—for Mrs. Patrick Campbell, one of his favorite actresses and a close friend. Mrs. Campbell was a beautiful woman with a thrilling voice and a fiery temperament, and, though no longer a young girl by 1912, she made a sensational hit as Liza.

Although I did not see the original production of the play, I well remember the excitement about Liza's "Not bloody likely." To understand this excitement you must imagine some much stronger word—much more shocking to American ears than "bloody"—being spoken on the stage for the first time. Being by this time an old hand in the theater, Shaw of course had carefully calculated the effect this particular word would produce.

SHAW'S LITERARY BEGINNINGS

Shaw did not begin his career by writing plays. First he wrote several novels. Very queer novels they are too, full of ideas, like everything he ever wrote, but not really satisfying as fiction. Then he was for some time a music critic—he had a good knowledge of music and was particularly fond of the operas of Mozart. After this he turned to the theater and wrote dramatic criticism for many newspapers and magazines.

Shaw's dramatic criticism, which he published later in volume form, is among the best ever written. In the 1890's, when Shaw was a critic, the London theater appealed chiefly to fashionable audiences, and most of the plays it produced were thin, light comedies about fashionable people, broad farces, and sentimental-romantic costume plays. For nearly all of these, Shaw had sharp contempt. He complained, wittily rather than bitterly, that the English theater was almost entirely lacking in ideas and offered little or nothing to an intelligent playgoer.

But whether it has ideas or not, the theater is still the theater. To capture and maintain the interest of the audience, it depends upon dramatic situations and effects. Although Shaw might have despised nearly all the plays he had to review, he learned a great deal from them about how to achieve dramatic effects. He learned how to take an audience by surprise, how to compel it to applaud or burst into a shout of laughter. Most of Shaw's effects are anything but subtle—he was never afraid of downright clowning—but no audiences can resist them. Indeed, they are mostly foolproof old devices.

One of the most obvious of them, which never fails if properly contrived, is the unexpected entrance of a character dressed in a surprising way. Two very effective examples of this dramatic device are the entrance of Liza, fashionably dressed, in Act III, and a similar entrance by her father, no longer a dustman, in Act V. These are typical of Shaw's broadly theatrical method, based on his knowledge of audiences, which in a comedy need to be visually as well as intellectually amused. But of course there is a lot more in Shaw than this, for he is also essentially a dramatist of ideas and debate. To understand how he came to be such a dramatist, we must take another look at his life.

Shaw was born in Dublin, a charming but untidy city. His father was a wholesale merchant on the Dublin Corn Exchange; his mother, who finally left her husband to earn her living in London, was a gifted musician. A proud and sensitive youth, Shaw reacted violently against his early surroundings, with their Bohemian sloppiness, drink, and easy emotionalism. After this reaction he became not only a good deal of a puritan in his style of living but also a lover of order, authority, and discipline—anything that compelled people to lead sensible and decent lives.

After settling in London and becoming active with the Fabians, a newly founded political society, Shaw learned through his work with them to speak fluently and wittily in public, and for years he seized every opportunity to address any kind of audience and to engage in public debate with any opponent. All this public speaking and debating, all these audiences, were later of immense service to him in the theater.

SHAVIAN DRAMATIC COMEDY

Shaw's special achievement in the theater was to create a type of comedy all his own. The basis of it, in spite of those broadly dramatic effects we have already noted, was debate. Shaw's characters are always arguing about ideas and indeed only stop when some touch of drama, some piece of broad clowning, takes hold of the scene just when the audience might be bored. He was fascinated by opera, and as he wrote his plays he thought of them as operas of talk—first, perhaps, a duet, then a trio, then a quartet—only instead of singing, the characters eloquently express their various points of view and are busy arguing.

Here I must point out that although Shaw is a master comic dramatist, perhaps the greatest since Molière, he has been a very bad influence on younger dramatists, who have produced all too many boring and unsuccessful plays just because they were trying to copy his methods. For the Shaw comedy of debate demands a Shaw to write it. Nobody else has his particular touch or is able to create his special atmosphere.

There are good reasons why this is so. To begin with, Shaw had a lot of strongly held opinions on all manner of subjects. Then, as we have seen, he had enjoyed years of experience in public debating about these opinions. Very eloquent and witty speeches came naturally to him. In addition, as we have also seen, he had learned all the tricks, in and out of the theater, to keep audiences amused. Finally, he was never deeply emotionally involved with most of his opinions, and his natural good humor gave his plays a sunny atmosphere very valuable to comedy.

All this indicates how Shaw could make an effective comedy out of themes that would defeat any other dramatist. He does just this in *Pygmalion,* which is a kind of Cinderella story created out of an unusual combination of elements: his keen interest in phonetics and language, his opinion of the English class structure of society, and his insight into various modes of life—that of the working class, the idly fashionable, the ultra-respectable middle class, and the new classless kind of life led by enthusiastic research scientists, represented here by Higgins. Nobody else but Shaw could have combined these peculiar and seemingly unpromising elements into a brilliant comedy.

SHAVIAN CHARACTERS

People who do not enjoy Shaw always tell us that he cannot really create character, as a dramatist ought to be able to do, that all his characters talk alike, as if they were all Shaw himself. But this is simply not true. Although Shaw does not have the astounding range of a supreme master of the drama like Shakespeare, he is able to create convincing and amusing characters quite different from himself. In *Pygmalion,* for instance, there may be a good deal of Shaw himself in Higgins, but Doolittle and Pickering are very different from Shaw, and Doolittle especially is a wonderfully effective comic character. His women are more limited in range, it is true, for the tolerant, amused, wise type of woman, represented here by Higgins' mother, appears in play after play. As for Liza herself, although a brilliant actress could dazzle us into accepting her, she is not altogether convincing.

In a long afterword to *Pygmalion,* Shaw explains at length that Liza and Higgins remained close friends but that she married Freddy, who finally assisted her in running a flower shop. Here, in my view, Shaw deliberately refused to behave like more conventional dramatists, and he did so really to his own disadvantage. For it is obvious in Act V that Liza is in love with Higgins. Shaw's determination that nothing shall come of it, in the usual theatrical style of "the happy ending," does not belong to him as a creative dramatist but stems from his more superficial role as an anti-romantic, unconventional, paradoxical thinker. Liza's protest against being regarded not as a person but as the mere subject of an experiment —a protest many of us are ready to echo and applaud in these later days of ceaseless scientific experiments—is real enough, but the depth of feeling behind her protest is not truly represented in the play's final action. Cinderella should marry the prince, even if he is crazy about phonetics and twenty years older than she.

Nevertheless, in *Pygmalion* we have merely one helping—of fun, character, argument, insight, wisdom—from the huge feast that this great Irishman, the finest master of comedy in the modern age, has left us. It enchants us in the theater, where Shaw, like a true dramatist, belongs, and it keeps us amused and happy as readers. We should take advantage of this wonderful gift and be grateful.

J. B. P.

The Old Lady Shows Her Medals

JAMES M. BARRIE 1860–1937

No English writer has given more widespread delight to all ages and nations than the creator of *Peter Pan,* James M. Barrie. With Mary Martin as Peter Pan, this perennial favorite has been produced on Broadway and televised in color. While he excelled as a dramatist, Barrie is also known as a story writer and a novelist.

J. M. Barrie began life in a little Lowland village, referred to on the map as Kirriemuir, but known as Thrums to Barrie fans. After receiving his master's degree from the University of Edinburgh when he was twenty-two, Barrie left Scotland for England. When far away from his village and homesick, he recorded the amusing situations and racy speech of his old neighbors in *A Window in Thrums.* But fame shied away from him, and he said later that for three years he kept body and soul together with coffee and penny buns. Thrums won him rewards in the end, however. Many short stories and three novels based on village life brought him enthusiastic readers.

When his best-known novel, *The Little Minister,* was made into a successful play, Barrie turned to the stage. With a fertile imagination, he was able to toss off play after play. Among his most popular comedies are *Quality Street, The Admirable Crichton,* and *What Every Woman Knows.*

In 1913 Barrie was knighted by King George V for his marked contribution to British life and letters. His own University of Edinburgh presented him with a degree of Doctor of Letters in 1922 and made him Chancellor in 1930.

The following short play, set in London during the days of World War I, is typical of Barrie in many ways. It shows Scottish characters, in whose portrayal Barrie excelled. It blends humor and pathos, as do most of his plays. It contains the storylike and lengthy stage directions—in which playwright talks to reader—which are a trademark of Barrie plays. It shows Barrie's sympathetic portrayal of people in the humblest ranks of society and illustrates the comment made about him that "his magic touch has ennobled and endeared the common things of life."

Characters

MRS. DOWEY

MRS. TWYMLEY

MRS. HAGGERTY

MRS. MICKLEHAM

THE REVEREND MR. WILLINGS

PRIVATE K. DOWEY

Three nice old ladies and a criminal, who is even nicer, are discussing the war over a cup of tea. The criminal, who is the hostess, calls it a dish of tea, which shows that she comes from Caledonia,[1] but that is not her crime.

They are all London charwomen,[2] but three of them, including the hostess, are what are called professionally "charwomen and" or simply "ands." An "and" is also a caretaker when required; her name is entered as such in ink in a registry book, financial transactions take place across a counter between her and the registrar, and altogether she is of a very different social status from one who, like MRS. HAGGERTY, *is a charwoman but nothing else.* MRS. HAGGERTY, *though present, is not at the party by invitation; having seen* MRS. DOWEY *buying the winkles,[3] she followed her downstairs—and so has shuffled into the play and sat down in it against our wish. We would remove her by force, or at least print her name in small letters, were it not that she takes offense very readily and says that nobody respects her. So, as you have slipped in, you can sit there,* MRS. HAGGERTY; *but keep quiet.*

There is nothing doing at present in the caretaking way for MRS.

[1] *Caledonia* (kăl'ĕ·dōn'yà): Scotland.
[2] *charwomen:* cleaning women.
[3] *winkles:* small shellfish.

DOWEY, *our hostess; but this does not damp[1] her, caretaking being only to such as she an extra financially and a halo socially. If she had the honor of being served with an income-tax paper she would probably fill in one of the nasty little compartments with the words "Trade—charring. Profession (if any)—caretaking." This home of hers (from which, to look after your house, she makes, occasionally, temporary departures in great style, escorting a barrow) is in one of those what-care-I streets that you discover only when you have lost your way; on discovering them your duty is to report them to the authorities who immediately add them to the map of London. That is why we are now reporting Friday Street. We shall call it, in the rough sketch drawn for tomorrow's press, "Street in which the criminal resided"; and you will find* MRS. DOWEY'S *home therein marked with an X.*

Her abode really consists of one room, but she maintains that there are two; so, rather than argue, let us say that there are two. The other one has no window, and she could not swish her old skirts in it without knocking something over; its grandest display is of tin pans and crockery on top of a dresser which has a lid to it; you have but to whip off the utensils and raise the lid, and, behold, a bath with hot and cold. MRS. DOWEY *is very proud of this possession, and when she shows it off, as she does perhaps too frequently, she first signs to you with closed fist (funny old thing that she is) to approach softly. She then tiptoes to the dresser and pops off the lid, as if to take the bath unawares. Then she sucks her lips, and is modest if you have the grace to do the exclamations.*

In the real room is a bed, though that is putting the matter too briefly. The fair way to begin, if you love MRS. DOWEY, *is to say to her that it is a pity she has no bed. If she is in her best form she will chuckle, and agree that the want of a bed tries her sore; she will keep you on the hooks, so to speak, as long as she can; and then, with that mouselike movement again, she will suddenly spring the bed on you. You thought it was a wardrobe, but she brings it down from the wall, and lo, a bed. There is nothing else in her abode (which we now see to contain four rooms—kitchen, pantry, bedroom, and bathroom) that is absolutely a surprise; but it is full of "bits," every one of which has been paid ready money for and gloated over and tended until it has become part of its owner. Genuine Doweys, the dealers might call them, though there is probably nothing in the place except the bed that would fetch half-a-crown.*

---

[1] *damp:* as used here, discourage.

Her home is in the basement, so that the view is restricted to the lower half of persons passing overhead beyond the area stairs. Here at the window MRS. DOWEY *sometimes sits of a summer evening gazing, not sentimentally at a flowerpot which contains one poor bulb, nor yearningly at some tiny speck of sky, but with unholy relish at holes in stockings, and the like, which are revealed to her from her point of vantage. You, gentle reader, may flaunt by, thinking that your finery awes the street; but* MRS. DOWEY *can tell (and does) that your soles are in need of neat repair.*

Also, lower parts being as expressive as the face to those whose view is thus limited, she could swear to scores of the passers-by in a court of law.

These four lively old codgers are having a good time at the tea table, and wit is flowing free. As you can see by their everyday garments, and by their pails and mops (which are having a little tea party by themselves in the corner), it is not a gathering by invitations stretching away into yesterday. It is a purely informal affair, so much more attractive—don't you think?—than banquets elaborately prearranged. You know how they come about, especially in wartime. Very likely MRS. DOWEY *met* MRS. TWYMLEY *and* MRS. MICKLEHAM *quite casually in the street, and meant to do no more than pass the time of day; then, naturally enough, the word camouflage[1] was mentioned and they got heated, but in the end* MRS. TWYMLEY *apologized; then, in the odd way in which one thing leads to another, the winkleman appeared, and* MRS. DOWEY *remembered that she had that pot of jam and that* MRS. MICKLEHAM *had stood treat last time; and soon they were all three descending the area stairs, followed cringingly by the* HAGGERTY WOMAN.

They have been extremely merry, and never were four hard-worked old ladies who deserved it better. All a woman can do in wartime they do daily and cheerfully, just as their menfolk are doing it at the Front; and now, with the mops and pails laid aside, they sprawl gracefully at ease. There is no intention on their part to consider peace terms until a decisive victory has been gained in the field (Sarah Ann Dowey), until the Kaiser is put to the rightabout (Emma Mickleham) and singing very small (Amelia Twymley).

At this tea party the lady who is to play the part of MRS. DOWEY *is sure to want to suggest that our heroine has a secret sorrow; namely, the crime. But you should see us knocking that idea out of her head!* MRS.

---

[1] *camouflage* (kăm′ŏŏ·fläzh): in the old ladies' time, a new and exciting word. It refers to various ways of disguising military equipment or installations.

DOWEY *knows she is a criminal, but, unlike the actress, she does not know that she is about to be found out; and she is, to put it bluntly in her own Scotch way, the merriest of the whole clamjamfry. She presses more tea on her guests, but they wave her away from them in the pretty manner of ladies who know that they have already had more than enough.*

MRS. DOWEY. Just one more winkle, Mrs. Mickleham?

[*Indeed there is only one more. But* MRS. MICKLEHAM *indicates politely that if she took this one it would have to swim for it. The* HAGGERTY WOMAN *takes it long afterward when she thinks, erroneously, that no one is looking.* MRS. TWYMLEY *is sulking. Evidently someone has contradicted her. Probably the* HAGGERTY WOMAN.]

MRS. TWYMLEY. I say it is so.

THE HAGGERTY WOMAN. I say it may be so.

MRS. TWYMLEY. I suppose I ought to know: me that has a son a prisoner in Germany. (*She has so obviously scored that all good feeling seems to call upon her to end here. But she continues, rather shabbily.*) Being the only lady present that has that proud misfortune.

[*The others are stung.*]

MRS. DOWEY. My son is fighting in France.

MRS. MICKLEHAM. Mine is wounded in two places.

THE HAGGERTY WOMAN. Mine is at Salonaiky.[1]

[*The absurd pronunciation of this uneducated person moves the others to mirth.*]

MRS. DOWEY. You'll excuse us, Mrs. Haggerty, but the correct pronunciation is Salonikky.

THE HAGGERTY WOMAN (*to cover her confusion*). I don't think. (*She feels that even this does not prove her case.*) And I speak as one that has War Savings Certificates.

MRS. TWYMLEY. We all have them.

[*The* HAGGERTY WOMAN *whimpers, and the other guests regard her with unfeeling disdain.*]

[1] *Salonaiky:* her mispronunciation of Salonika (săl'ō·nē′kȧ), Greece, where a great naval battle took place in World War I.

MRS. DOWEY (*to restore cheerfulness*). Oh, it's a terrible war.

ALL (*brightening*). It is. You may say so.

MRS. DOWEY (*encouraged*). What I say is, the men is splendid; but I'm none so easy about the staff. That's your weak point, Mrs. Mickleham.

MRS. MICKLEHAM (*on the defense, but determined to reveal nothing that might be of use to the enemy*). You may take it from me, the staff's all right.

MRS. DOWEY. And very relieved I am to hear you say it.

[*It is here that the* HAGGERTY WOMAN *has the remaining winkle.*]

MRS. MICKLEHAM. You don't understand properly about trench warfare. If I had a map—

MRS. DOWEY (*wetting her finger to draw lines on the table*). That's the river Sommy.[1] Now, if we had barrages here—

MRS. TWYMLEY. Very soon you would be enfilided.[2] Where's your supports, my lady?

[MRS. DOWEY *is damped.*]

MRS. MICKLEHAM. What none of you grasps is that this is a artillery war—

THE HAGGERTY WOMAN (*strengthened by the winkle*). I say that the word is Salonaiky.

[*The others purse their lips.*]

MRS. TWYMLEY (*with terrible meaning*). We'll change the subject. Have you seen this week's *Fashion Chat*? (*She has evidently seen and devoured it herself, and even licked up the crumbs.*) The gabardine with accordion pleats has quite gone out.

MRS. DOWEY (*her old face sparkling*). My sakes! You tell me?

MRS. TWYMLEY (*with the touch of haughtiness that comes of great topics*). The plain smock has come in again, with silk lacing, giving that charming chic effect.

MRS. DOWEY. Oho!

MRS. MICKLEHAM. I must say I was always partial to the straight line

---

[1] *Sommy:* her mispronunciation of the French river Somme (sôm), a scene of many conflicts in World War I.

[2] *enfilided:* her mispronunciation of enfiladed (ĕn'fĭ·lād'ĕd), a military term meaning "raked by gunfire."

(*thoughtfully regarding the want of line in* MRS. TWYMLEY'S *person*) though trying to them as is of too friendly a figure.

[*It is here that the* HAGGERTY WOMAN'S *fingers close unostentatiously upon a piece of sugar.*]

MRS. TWYMLEY (*sailing into the empyrean*[1]). Lady Dolly Kanister was seen conversing across the railings in a dainty *de jou*.[2]

MRS. DOWEY. Fine would I have liked to see her.

MRS. TWYMLEY. She is equally popular as maid, wife, and munition worker. Her two children is inset.[3] Lady Pops Babington was married in a tight tulle.

MRS. MICKLEHAM. What was her going-away dress?

MRS. TWYMLEY. A champagny cream velvet with dreamy corsage. She's married to Colonel the Honorable Chingford—"Snubs," they called him at Eton.

THE HAGGERTY WOMAN (*having disposed of the sugar*). Very likely he'll be sent to Salonaiky.

MRS. MICKLEHAM. Wherever he is sent, she'll have the same tremors as the rest of us. She'll be as keen to get the letters wrote with pencils as you or me.

MRS. TWYMLEY. Them pencil letters!

MRS. DOWEY (*in her sweet Scotch voice, timidly, afraid she may be going too far*). And women in enemy lands gets those pencil letters and then stop getting them, the same as ourselves. Let's occasionally think of that.

[*She has gone too far. Chairs are pushed back.*]

THE HAGGERTY WOMAN. I ask you!

MRS. MICKLEHAM. That's hardly language, Mrs. Dowey.

MRS. DOWEY (*scared*). Kindly excuse. I swear to death I'm none of your pacifists.

MRS. MICKLEHAM. Freely granted.

MRS. TWYMLEY. I've heard of females that have no male relations, and so they have no man-party at the wars. I've heard of them, but I don't mix with them.

---

[1] *empyrean* (ĕm′pĭ·rē′ăn): the highest part of heaven.

[2] *de jou* (dĕ zho͞o): a dress "for play" (French).

[3] *inset:* Pictures of Lady Kanister's two children were apparently inserted into the larger picture of her.

MRS. MICKLEHAM. What can the likes of us have to say to them? It's not their war.

MRS. DOWEY (*wistfully*). They are to be pitied.

MRS. MICKLEHAM. But the place for them, Mrs. Dowey, is within doors with the blinds down.

MRS. DOWEY (*hurriedly*). That's the place for them.

MRS. MICKLEHAM. I saw one of them today buying a flag. I thought it was very impudent of her.

MRS. DOWEY (*meekly*). So it was.

MRS. MICKLEHAM (*trying to look modest with indifferent success*). I had a letter from my son, Percy, yesterday.

MRS. TWYMLEY. Alfred sent me his photo.

THE HAGGERTY WOMAN. Letters from Salonaiky is less common.

[*Three bosoms heave, but not, alas,* MRS. DOWEY'S. *Nevertheless she doggedly knits her lips.*]

MRS. DOWEY (*the criminal*). Kenneth writes to me every week. (*There are exclamations. The dauntless old thing holds aloft a packet of letters.*) Look at this. All his.

[*The* HAGGERTY WOMAN *whimpers.*]

MRS. TWYMLEY. Alfred has little time for writing, being a bombardier.

MRS. DOWEY (*relentlessly*). Do your letters begin "Dear mother"?

MRS. TWYMLEY. Generally.

MRS. MICKLEHAM. Invariable.

THE HAGGERTY WOMAN. Every time.

MRS. DOWEY (*delivering the knockout blow*). Kenneth's begin "Dearest mother."

[*No one can think of the right reply.*]

MRS. TWYMLEY (*doing her best*). A short man, I should say, judging by yourself. (*She ought to have left it alone.*)

MRS. DOWEY. Six feet two—and a half.

[*The gloom deepens.*]

MRS. MICKLEHAM (*against her better judgment*). A kilty, did you tell me?

MRS. DOWEY. Most certainly. He's in the famous Black Watch.

THE HAGGERTY WOMAN (*producing her handkerchief*). The Surrey Rifles is the famousest.

MRS. MICKLEHAM. There you and the King disagrees, Mrs. Haggerty. His choice is the Buffs, same as my Percy's.

MRS. TWYMLEY (*magnanimously*). Give me the R.H.A.[1] and you can keep all the rest.

MRS. DOWEY. I'm sure I have nothing to say against the Surreys and the R.H.A. and Buffs; but they are just breeches regiments, I understand.

THE HAGGERTY WOMAN. We can't all be kilties.

MRS. DOWEY (*crushingly*). That's very true.

MRS. TWYMLEY (*it is foolish of her, but she can't help saying it*). Has your Kenneth great hairy legs?

MRS. DOWEY. Tremendous.

[*The wicked woman, but let us also say "Poor Sarah Ann Dowey." For, at this moment, enter Nemesis.[2] In other words, the less important part of a clergyman appears upon the stair.*]

MRS. MICKLEHAM. It's the reverent gent!

MRS. DOWEY (*little knowing what he is bringing her*). I see he has had his boots heeled.

[*It may be said of MR. WILLINGS that his happy smile always walks in front of him. This smile makes music of his life; it means that once again he has been chosen, in his opinion, as the central figure in romance. No one can well have led a more drab existence, but he will never know it; he will always think of himself, humbly though elatedly, as the chosen of the gods. Of him must it have been originally written that adventures are for the adventurous. He meets them at every street corner. For instance, he assists an old lady off a bus and asks her if he can be of any further help. She tells him that she wants to know the way to Maddox the butcher's. Then comes the kind, triumphant smile; it always comes first, followed by its explanation, "I was there yesterday!" This is the merest sample of the adventures that keep MR. WILLINGS up to the mark.*]

[*Since the war broke out, his zest for life has become almost terrible. He can scarcely lift a newspaper and read of a hero without remembering*

---

[1] *Black Watch, Surrey Rifles, Buffs,* and *R.H.A.:* well-known British army regiments.

[2] *Nemesis* (nĕm'ĕ·sĭs): avenging fate (Greek mythology).

that he knows someone of the same name. The Soldiers' Rest he is connected with was once a china emporium, and—mark my words— he had bought his tea service at it. Such is life when you are in the thick of it. Sometimes he feels that he is part of a gigantic spy drama. In the course of his extraordinary comings and goings he meets with Great Personages, of course, and is the confidential recipient of secret news. Before imparting the news he does not, as you might expect, first smile expansively; on the contrary, there comes over his face an awful solemnity, which, however, means the same thing. When divulging the names of the personages, he first looks around to make sure that no suspicious character is about, and then, lowering his voice, tells you, "I had that from Mr. Farthing himself—he is the secretary of the Bethnal Green Branch—H'sh . . ."

[*There is a commotion about finding a worthy chair for "the reverent," and there is also some furtive pulling down of sleeves; but he stands surveying the ladies through his triumphant smile. This amazing man knows that he is about to score again.*]

MR. WILLINGS (*waving aside the chairs*). I thank you. But not at all. Friends, I have news.

MRS. MICKLEHAM. News?

THE HAGGERTY WOMAN. From the Front?

MRS. TWYMLEY. My Alfred, sir?

[*They are all grown suddenly anxious—all except the hostess, who knows that there can never be any news from the Front for her.*]

MR. WILLINGS. I tell you at once that all is well. The news is for Mrs. Dowey.

MRS. DOWEY (*she stares*). News for me?

MR. WILLINGS. Your son, Mrs. Dowey—he has got five days' leave.

[*She shakes her head slightly, or perhaps it only trembles a little on its stem.*]

Now, now, good news doesn't kill.

MRS. TWYMLEY. We're glad, Mrs. Dowey.

MRS. DOWEY. You're sure?

MR. WILLINGS. Quite sure. He has arrived.

MRS. DOWEY. He is in London?

MR. WILLINGS. He is. I have spoken to him.

MRS. MICKLEHAM. You lucky woman.

[*They might see that she is not looking lucky, but experience has told them how differently these things take people.*]

MR. WILLINGS (*marveling more and more as he unfolds his tale*). Ladies, it is quite a romance. I was in the . . . (*He looks around cautiously, but he knows that they are all to be trusted.*) . . . in the Church Army quarters in Central Street, trying to get on the track of one or two of our missing men. Suddenly my eyes—I can't account for it— but suddenly my eyes alighted on a Highlander seated rather drearily on a bench, with his kit at his feet.

THE HAGGERTY WOMAN. A big man?

MR. WILLINGS. A great brawny fellow.

[*The* HAGGERTY WOMAN *groans.*]

"My friend," I said at once, "welcome back to Blighty." [1] I make a point of calling it Blighty. "I wonder," I said, "if there is anything I can do for you?" He shook his head "What regiment?" I asked (*Here* MR. WILLINGS *very properly lowers his voice to a whisper.*) "Black Watch, 5th Battalion," he said. "Name?" I asked. "Dowey," he said.

MRS. MICKLEHAM. I declare. I do declare.

MR. WILLINGS (*showing how the thing was done, with the help of a chair*). I put my hand on his shoulder as it might be thus. "Kenneth Dowey," I said, "I know your mother."

MRS. DOWEY (*wetting her lips*). What did he say to that?

MR. WILLINGS. He was incredulous. Indeed, he seemed to think I was balmy. But I offered to bring him straight to you. I told him how much you had talked to me about him.

MRS. DOWEY. Bring him here!

MRS. MICKLEHAM. I wonder he needed to be brought.

MR. WILLINGS. He had just arrived, and was bewildered by the great city. He listened to me in the taciturn Scotch way, and then he gave a curious laugh.

MRS. TWYMLEY. Laugh?

MR. WILLINGS (*whose wild life has brought him into contact with the strangest people*). The Scotch, Mrs. Twymley, express their emotions differently from us. With them tears signify a rollicking mood, while merriment denotes that they are plunged in gloom. When I had finished he said at once, "Let us go and see the old lady."

---

[1] *Blighty* (blī'tĭ): British slang for home, much used by soldiers.

MRS. DOWEY (*backing, which is the first movement she has made since he began his tale*). Is he—coming?

MR. WILLINGS (*gloriously*). He has come. He is up there. I told him I thought I had better break the joyful news to you.

[*Three women rush to the window.* MRS. DOWEY *looks at her pantry door, but perhaps she remembers that it does not lock on the inside. She stands rigid, though her face has gone very gray.*]

MRS. DOWEY. Kindly get them to go away.

MR. WILLINGS. Ladies, I think this happy occasion scarcely requires you. (*He is not the man to ask of woman a sacrifice that he is not prepared to make himself.*) I also am going instantly.

[*They all survey* MRS. DOWEY, *and understand—or think they understand.*]

MRS. TWYMLEY (*pail and mop in hand*). I would thank none for their company if my Alfred was at the door.

MRS. MICKLEHAM (*similarly burdened*). The same from me. Shall I send him down, Mrs. Dowey?

[*The old lady does not hear her. She is listening, terrified, for a step on the stairs.*]

Look at the poor, joyous thing, sir. She has his letters in her hand.

[*The three women go.* MR. WILLINGS *puts a kind hand on* MRS. DOWEY'S *shoulder. He thinks he so thoroughly understands the situation.*]

MR. WILLINGS. A good son, Mrs. Dowey, to have written to you so often.

[*Our old criminal quakes, but she grips the letters more tightly.* PRIVATE DOWEY *descends.*]

Dowey, my friend, there she is, waiting for you, with your letters in her hand.

DOWEY (*grimly*). That's great.

[MR. WILLINGS *ascends the stair without one backward glance, like the good gentleman he is; and the* DOWEYS *are left together, with nearly the whole room between them. He is a great rough chunk of Scotland, howked out of her not so much neatly as liberally; and in his Black Watch uniform, all caked with mud, his kit and nearly all his worldly possessions on his back, he is an apparition scarcely less fearsome (but so much less ragged) than those ancestors of his who trotted with Prince Charlie[1] to Derby. He stands silent, scowling at the old lady, daring her to raise her head; and she would like very much to do it, for she longs to have a first glimpse of her son. When he does speak, it is to jeer at her.]*

DOWEY. Do you recognize your loving son, missis?

[*"Oh, the fine Scotch tang of him," she thinks.*]

MRS. DOWEY (*trembling*). I'm pleased you wrote so often. (*"Oh, but he's raised,"* [2] *she thinks.*)

[*He strides toward her, and seizes the letters roughly.*]

DOWEY. Let's see them.

[*There is a string round the package and he unties it, and examines the letters at his leisure with much curiosity. The envelopes are in order, all addressed in pencil to* MRS. DOWEY, *with the proud words "Opened by Censor" on them. But the letter paper inside contains not a word of writing.*]

DOWEY. Nothing but blank paper! Is this your writing in pencil on the envelope? (*She nods, and he gives the matter further consideration.*) The covey[3] told me you were a charwoman. So I suppose you picked the envelopes out of wastepaper baskets, or such like, and then changed the addresses?

[*She nods again; still she dare not look up, but she is admiring his legs. When, however, he would cast the letters into the fire, she flames up with sudden spirit. She clutches them.*]

MRS. DOWEY. Don't burn them letters, mister.
DOWEY. They're not real letters.
MRS. DOWEY. They're all I have.
DOWEY (*returning to irony*). I thought you had a son?

---

[1] *Prince Charlie:* the Young Pretender to the British throne in the eighteenth century.
[2] *raised:* annoyed.
[3] *covey* (kŭv'ĭ): slang for *fellow.*

MRS. DOWEY. I never had a man nor a son nor anything. I just call myself Missis to give me a standing.

DOWEY. Well, it's past my seeing through.

[*He turns to look for some explanation from the walls. She gets a peep at him at last. Oh, what a grandly set-up man! Oh, the stride of him. Oh, the noble rage of him. Oh, Samson had been like this before that woman took him in hand.*[1]]

DOWEY (*whirling round on her*). What made you do it?

MRS. DOWEY. It was everybody's war, mister, except mine. (*She beats her arms.*) I wanted it to be my war too.

DOWEY. You'll need to be plainer. And yet I'm d——d if I care to hear you, you lying old trickster.

[*The words are merely what were to be expected, and so are endurable; but he has moved toward the door.*]

MRS. DOWEY. You're not going already, mister?

DOWEY. Yes, I just came to give you an ugly piece of my mind.

MRS. DOWEY (*holding out her arms longingly*). You haven't gave it to me yet.

DOWEY. You have a cheek!

MRS. DOWEY (*giving further proof of it*). You wouldn't drink some tea?

DOWEY. Me! I tell you I came here for the one purpose of blazing away at you.

[*It is such a roaring negative that it blows her into a chair. But she is up again in a moment, is this spirited old lady.*]

MRS. DOWEY. You could drink the tea while you was blazing away There's winkles.

DOWEY. Is there? (*He turns interestedly toward the table, but his proud Scots character checks him—which is just as well, for what she should have said was that there had been winkles.*) Not me. You're just a common rogue. (*He seats himself far from the table.*) Now, then, out with it. Sit down! (*She sits meekly; there is nothing she would not do for him.*) As you char, I suppose you are on your feet all day.

MRS. DOWEY. I'm more on my knees.

---

[1] *Samson . . . in hand:* In the Bible, Samson was betrayed to his enemies by Delilah, who sheared his hair—the source of his strength—while he slept.

DOWEY. That's where you should be to me.

MRS. DOWEY. Oh, mister. I'm willing.

DOWEY. Stop it. Go on, you accomplished liar.

MRS. DOWEY. It's true that my name is Dowey.

DOWEY. It's enough to make me change mine.

MRS. DOWEY. I've been charring and charring and charring as far back as I mind. I've been in London this twenty years.

DOWEY. We'll skip your early days. I have an appointment.

MRS. DOWEY. And then when I was old the war broke out.

DOWEY. How could it affect you?

MRS. DOWEY. Oh, mister, that's the thing. It didn't affect me. It affected everybody but me. The neighbors looked down on me. Even the posters, on the walls, of the woman saying "Go, my boy," leered at me. I sometimes cried by myself in the dark. You won't have a cup of tea?

DOWEY. No.

MRS. DOWEY. Suddenlike the idea came to me to pretend I had a son.

DOWEY. You depraved old limmer! [1] But what in the name of Old Nick made you choose me out of the whole British Army?

MRS. DOWEY (*giggling*). Maybe, mister, it was because I like you best.

DOWEY. Now, now, woman.

MRS. DOWEY. I read one day in the papers, "In which he was assisted by Private K. Dowey, 5th Battalion, Black Watch."

DOWEY (*flattered*). Did you, now! Well, I expect that's the only time I was ever in the papers.

MRS. DOWEY (*trying it on again*). I didn't choose you for that alone. I read a history of the Black Watch first, to make sure it was the best regiment in the world.

DOWEY. Anybody could have told you that. (*He is moving about now in better humor, and meeting the loaf in his stride, he cuts a slice from it. He is hardly aware of this, but* MRS. DOWEY *knows.*) I like the Scotch voice of you, woman. It drumbles on like a hill burn. [2]

MRS. DOWEY. Prosen Water runs by where I was born. Maybe it teached me to speak, mister.

DOWEY. Canny, woman, canny.

MRS. DOWEY. I read about the Black Watch's ghostly piper that plays proudly when the men of the Black Watch do well, and prouder when they fall.

DOWEY. There's some foolish story of that kind. (*He has another care-*

---

[1] *limmer:* Scotch for rascal.
[2] *burn:* Scotch for brook.

less slice off the loaf.) But you couldn't have been living here at that time
or they would have guessed. I suppose you flitted? [1]

MRS. DOWEY. Yes, it cost me eleven and sixpence.

DOWEY. How did you guess the *K* in my name stood for Kenneth?

MRS. DOWEY. Does it?

DOWEY. Umpha.

MRS. DOWEY. An angel whispered it to me in my sleep.

DOWEY. Well, that's the only angel in the whole black business. (*He
chuckles.*) You little thought I would turn up! (*Wheeling suddenly on
her*) Or did you?

MRS. DOWEY. I was beginning to weary for a sight of you, Kenneth.

DOWEY. What word was that?

MRS. DOWEY. Mister.

[*He helps himself to butter, and she holds out the jam pot to him; but he
haughtily rejects it. Do you think she gives in now? Not a bit of it. He
returns to sarcasm.*]

DOWEY. I hope you're pleased with me now you see me.

MRS. DOWEY. I'm very pleased. Does your folk live in Scotland?

DOWEY. Glasgow.

MRS. DOWEY. Both living?

DOWEY. Ay.

MRS. DOWEY. Is your mother terrible proud of you?

DOWEY. Naturally.

MRS. DOWEY. You'll be going to them?

DOWEY. After I've had a skite[2] in London first.

MRS. DOWEY (*sniffing*). So she is in London.

DOWEY. Who?

MRS. DOWEY. Your young lady.

DOWEY. Are you jealyous?

MRS. DOWEY. Not me.

DOWEY. You needna be. She's a young thing.

MRS. DOWEY. You surprises me. A beauty, no doubt?

DOWEY. You may be sure. (*He tries the jam.*) She's a titled person. She
is equally popular as maid, wife, and munition worker.

[MRS. DOWEY *remembers Lady Dolly Kanister, so familiar to readers of
fashionable gossip, and a very leery expression indeed comes into her
face.*]

[1] *flitted:* moved.
[2] *skite:* a good time, or "fling."

MRS. DOWEY. Tell me more about her, man.

DOWEY. She has sent me a lot of things, especially cakes, and a worsted waistcoat, with a loving message on the enclosed card.

[*The old lady is now in a quiver of excitement. She loses control of her arms, which jump excitedly this way and that.*]

MRS. DOWEY. You'll try one of my cakes, mister?

DOWEY. Not me.

MRS. DOWEY. They're of my own making.

DOWEY. No, I thank you.

[*But with a funny little run she is in the pantry and back again. She pushes a cake before him, at sight of which he gapes.*]

MRS. DOWEY. What's the matter? Tell me, oh, tell me, mister!

DOWEY. That's exactly the kind of cake that her ladyship sends me.

[MRS. DOWEY *is now a very glorious old character indeed.*]

MRS. DOWEY. Is the waistcoat right, mister? I hope the Black Watch colors pleased you.

DOWEY. What-at! Was it you?

MRS. DOWEY. I daredna give my own name, you see, and I was always reading hers in the papers.

[*The badgered man looms over her, terrible for the last time.*]

DOWEY. Woman, is there no getting rid of you!

MRS. DOWEY. Are you angry?

[*He sits down with a groan.*]

DOWEY. Oh, hell! Give me some tea.

[*She rushes about preparing a meal for him, every bit of her wanting to cry out to every other bit, "Oh, glory, glory, glory!" For a moment she hovers behind his chair. "Kenneth!" she murmurs. "What?" he asks, no longer aware that she is taking a liberty. "Nothing," she says. "Just Kenneth," and is off gleefully for the tea caddy. But when his tea is poured out, and he has drunk a saucerful, the instinct of self-preservation returns to him between two bites.*]

DOWEY. Don't you be thinking, missis, for one minute that you have got me.

MRS. DOWEY. No, no.

[*On that understanding he unbends.*]

DOWEY. I have a theater tonight, followed by a randy-dandy.[1]

MRS. DOWEY. Oho! Kenneth, this is a queer first meeting!

DOWEY. It is, woman—oh, it is—(*guardedly*)—and it's also a last meeting.

MRS. DOWEY. Yes, yes.

DOWEY. So here's to you—you old mop and pail. *Ave atque vale.*

MRS. DOWEY. What's that?

DOWEY. That means Hail and Farewell.

MRS. DOWEY. Are you a scholar?

DOWEY. Being Scotch, there's almost nothing I don't know.

MRS. DOWEY. What was you to trade?

DOWEY. Carter, glazier, orraman,[2] any rough jobs.

MRS. DOWEY. You're a proper man to look at.

DOWEY. I'm generally admired.

MRS. DOWEY. She's an enviable woman.

DOWEY. Who?

MRS. DOWEY. Your mother.

DOWEY. Eh? Oh, that was just protecting myself from you. I have neither father nor mother nor wife nor grandmama. (*Bitterly*) This party never even knew who his proud parents were.

MRS. DOWEY. Is that—(*gleaming*)—is that true?

DOWEY. It's gospel.

MRS. DOWEY. Heaven be praised!

DOWEY. Eh? None of that! I was a fool to tell you. But don't think you can take advantage of it. Pass the cake.

MRS. DOWEY. I daresay it's true we'll never meet again, Kenneth, but —but if we do, I wonder where it will be?

DOWEY. Not in this world.

MRS. DOWEY. There's no telling—(*leering ingratiatingly*)—it might be at Berlin.

DOWEY. Tod, if I ever get to Berlin, I believe I'll find you there waiting for me!

---

[1] *randy-dandy:* a noisy frolic.
[2] *orraman:* one who does odd jobs.

MRS. DOWEY. With a cup of tea for you in my hand.

DOWEY. Yes, and (*heartily*) very good tea too.

[*He has partaken heavily; he is now in high good humor.*]

MRS. DOWEY. Kenneth, we could come back by Paris!

DOWEY. All the ladies likes to go to Paris.

MRS. DOWEY. Oh, Kenneth, Kenneth, if just once before I die I could be fitted for a Paris gown with dreamy corsage!

DOWEY. You're all alike, old covey. We have a song about it. (*He sings*):

> Mrs. Gill is very ill,
>   Nothing can improve her
> But to see the Tuileries[1]
> And waddle through the Louvre.[2]

[*No song ever had a greater success.* MRS. DOWEY *is doubled up with mirth. When she comes to—when they both come to, for they are a pair of them—she cries:*]

MRS. DOWEY. You must learn me that (*and off she goes in song also*):

> Mrs. Dowey's very ill,
>   Nothing can improve her.

DOWEY. Stop!

> But dressed up in a Paris gown
>   To waddle through the Louvre.

[*They fling back their heads. She points at him; he points at her.*]

MRS. DOWEY (*ecstatically*). Hairy legs!

[*A mad remark, which brings him to his senses; he remembers who and what she is.*]

DOWEY. Mind your manners! (*Rising*) Well, thank you for my tea. I must be stepping.

[*Poor* MRS. DOWEY, *he is putting on his kit.*]

---

[1] *Tuileries* (twē'lĕr·ĭz): famous royal palace in Paris.
[2] *Louvre* (lōō'vr'): famous art gallery connected with the Tuileries.

MRS. DOWEY. Where are you living?

DOWEY. (*He sighs.*) That's the question. But there's a place called The Hut, where some of the 2nd Battalion are. They'll take me in. Beggars— (*bitterly*)—can't be choosers.

MRS. DOWEY. Beggars?

DOWEY. I've never been here before. If you knew (*a shadow comes over him*) what it is to be in such a place without a friend. I was crazy with glee, when I got my leave, at the thought of seeing London at last; but after wandering its streets for four hours, I would almost have been glad to be back in the trenches.

[*"If you knew," he has said, but indeed the old lady knows.*]

MRS. DOWEY. That's my quandorum¹ too, Kenneth.

[*He nods sympathetically.*]

DOWEY. I'm sorry for you, you poor old body (*shouldering his kit*) but I see no way out for either of us.

MRS. DOWEY (*cooing*). Do you not?

DOWEY. Are you at it again!

[*She knows that it must be now or never. She has left her biggest guns for the end. In her excitement she is rising up and down on her toes.*]

MRS. DOWEY. Kenneth, I've heard that the thing a man on leave longs for more than anything else is a bed with sheets, and a bath.

DOWEY. You never heard anything truer.

MRS. DOWEY. Go into that pantry, Kenneth Dowey, and lift the dresser top, and tell me what you see.

[*He goes. There is an awful stillness. He returns, impressed.*]

DOWEY. It's a kind of a bath!

MRS. DOWEY. You could do yourself there pretty, half at a time.

DOWEY. Me?

MRS. DOWEY. There's a woman through the wall that would be very willing to give me a shakedown till your leave is up.

DOWEY. (*He snorts.*) Oh, is there!

[*She has not got him yet, but there is still one more gun.*]

MRS. DOWEY. Kenneth, look!

¹ *quandorum:* Mrs. Dowey's way of saying *quandary*, or *predicament*.

[*With these simple words she lets down the bed. She says no more; an effect like this would be spoiled by language. Fortunately he is not made of stone. He thrills.*]

DOWEY. Gosh! That's the dodge we need in the trenches.

MRS. DOWEY. That's your bed, Kenneth.

DOWEY. Mine? (*He grins at her.*) You queer old divert.[1] What can make you so keen to be burdened by a lump like me?

MRS. DOWEY. He! he! he! he!

DOWEY. I tell you, I'm the commonest kind of man.

MRS. DOWEY. I'm just the commonest kind of old wifie myself.

DOWEY. I've been a kick-about all my life, and I'm no great shakes at the war.

MRS. DOWEY. Yes, you are. How many Germans have you killed?

DOWEY. Just two for certain, and there was no glory in it. It was just because they wanted my shirt.

MRS. DOWEY. Your shirt?

DOWEY. Well, they said it was their shirt.

MRS. DOWEY. Have you took prisoners?

DOWEY. I once took half a dozen, but that was a poor affair too.

MRS. DOWEY. How could one man take half a dozen?

DOWEY. Just in the usual way. I surrounded them.

MRS. DOWEY. Kenneth, you're just my ideal.

DOWEY. You're easily pleased. (*He turns again to the bed.*) Let's see how the thing works. (*He kneads the mattress with his fist, and the result is so satisfactory that he puts down his kit.*) Old lady, if you really want me, I'll bide.

MRS. DOWEY. Oh oh! oh! oh!

[*Her joy is so demonstrative that he has to drop a word of warning.*]

DOWEY. But mind you, I don't accept you as a relation. For your personal glory you can go on pretending to the neighbors, but the best I can say for you is that you're on your probation. I'm a cautious character, and we must see how you'll turn out.

MRS. DOWEY. Yes, Kenneth.

DOWEY. And now, I think, for that bath. My theater begins at six-thirty. A cove I met on a bus is going with me.

---

[1] *divert* (dǐ'vŭrt): slang for an odd or different person.

MRS. DOWEY. (*She is a little alarmed.*) You're sure you'll come back?

DOWEY. Yes, yes. (*Handsomely*) I leave my kit in pledge.

MRS. DOWEY. You won't liquor up too freely, Kenneth?

DOWEY. You're the first (*chuckling*) to care whether I do or not. (*Nothing she has said has pleased the lonely man so much as this.*) I promise. Tod, I'm beginning to look forward to being wakened in the morning by hearing you cry, "Get up, you lazy swine." I've kind of envied men that had womenfolk with the right to say that.

[*He is passing to the bathroom when a diverting notion strikes him.*]

MRS. DOWEY. What is it, Kenneth?

DOWEY. The theater. It would be showier if I took a lady.

[MRS. DOWEY *feels a thumping at her breast.*]

MRS. DOWEY. Kenneth, tell me this instant what you mean. Don't keep me on the dumps.

[*He turns her around.*]

DOWEY. No, it couldn't be done.

MRS. DOWEY. Was it me you were thinking of?

DOWEY. Just for the moment (*regretfully*) but you have no style.

[*She catches hold of him by the sleeve.*]

MRS. DOWEY. Not in this, of course. But, oh, Kenneth, if you saw me in my merino! [1] It's laced up the back in the very latest.

DOWEY. Hum (*doubtfully*) but let's see it.

[*It is produced from a drawer, to which the old lady runs with almost indecent haste. The connoisseur examines it critically.*]

DOWEY. Looks none so bad. Have you a bit of chiffon for the neck? It's not bombs nor Kaisers nor Tipperary that men in the trenches think of; it's chiffon.

MRS. DOWEY. I swear I have, Kenneth. And I have a bangle,[2] and a muff, and gloves.

DOWEY. Ay, ay. (*He considers.*) Do you think you could give your face less of a homely look?

---

[1] *merino:* a fine, soft wool fabric.
[2] *bangle:* bracelet.

MRS. DOWEY. I'm sure I could.

DOWEY. Then you can have a try. But, mind you, I promise nothing. All will depend on the effect.

[*He goes into the pantry, and the old lady is left alone. Not alone, for she is ringed round by entrancing hopes and dreadful fears. They beam on her and jeer at her; they pull her this way and that. With difficulty she breaks through them and rushes to her pail, hot water, soap, and a looking glass.*

[*Our last glimpse of her for this evening shows her staring—not discontentedly—at her soft old face, licking her palm, and pressing it to her hair. Her eyes are sparkling.*]

[*One evening a few days later* MRS. TWYMLEY *and* MRS. MICKLEHAM *are in* MRS. DOWEY'S *house, awaiting that lady's return from some fashionable dissipation. They have undoubtedly been discussing the war, for the first words we catch are:*]

MRS. MICKLEHAM. I tell you flat, Amelia, I bows no knee to junkerdom.[1]

MRS. TWYMLEY. Sitting here by the fire, you and me, as one to another, what do you think will happen after the war? Are we to go back to being as we were?

MRS. MICKLEHAM. Speaking for myself, Amelia, not me. The war has wakened me up to a understanding of my own importance that is really astonishing.

MRS. TWYMLEY. Same here. Instead of being the poor worms the like of you and me thought we was, we turns out to be visible departments of a great and haughty empire.

[*They are well under way, and with a little luck we might now hear their views on various passing problems of the day, such as the neglect of science in our public schools. But in comes the* HAGGERTY WOMAN, *and spoils everything. She is attired, like them, in her best; but the effect of her is that her clothes have gone out for a walk, leaving her at home.*]

MRS. MICKLEHAM (*with deep distaste*). Here's that submarine again.

[*The* HAGGERTY WOMAN *cringes to them, but gets no encouragement.*]

THE HAGGERTY WOMAN. It's a terrible war.

---

[1] *junkerdom:* the junkers, Prussian nobility; here means Germany's might.

MRS. TWYMLEY. Is that so?

THE HAGGERTY WOMAN. I wonder what will happen when it ends?

MRS. MICKLEHAM. I have no idea.

[*The intruder produces her handkerchief, but does not use it. After all, she is in her best.*]

THE HAGGERTY WOMAN. Are they not back yet?

[*Perfect ladies must reply to a direct question.*]

MRS. MICKLEHAM. No. (*Icily*) We have been waiting this half-hour. They are at the theater again.

THE HAGGERTY WOMAN. You tell me! I just popped in with an insignificant present for him, as his leave is up.

MRS. TWYMLEY. The same errand brought us.

THE HAGGERTY WOMAN. My present is cigarettes.

[*They have no intention of telling her what their presents are, but the secret leaps from them.*]

MRS. MICKLEHAM. So is mine.

MRS. TWYMLEY. Mine too.

[*Triumph of the* HAGGERTY WOMAN. *But it is short-lived.*]

MRS. MICKLEHAM. Mine has gold tips.

MRS. TWYMLEY. So has mine.

THE HAGGERTY WOMAN (*need not say a word. You have only to look at her to know that her cigarettes are not gold-tipped. She tries to brazen it out, which is so often a mistake.*) What care I? Mine is Exquisytos.

[*No wonder they titter.*]

MRS. MICKLEHAM. Excuse us, Mrs. Haggerty—if that's your name—but the word is Exquiseetos.

THE HAGGERTY WOMAN. Much obliged! (*Weeps.*)

MRS. MICKLEHAM. I think I heard a taxi.

MRS. TWYMLEY. It will be her third this week.

[*They peer through the blind. They are so excited that rank is forgotten.*]

THE HAGGERTY WOMAN. What is she in?

MRS. MICKLEHAM. A new astrakhan[1] jacket he gave her, with Venus sleeves.

THE HAGGERTY WOMAN. Has she sold her gabardine coat?

MRS. MICKLEHAM. Not her! She has them both at the theater, warm night though it is. She's wearing the astrakhan—and carrying the gabardine, flung carelesslike over her arm.

THE HAGGERTY WOMAN. I saw her strutting about with him yesterday, looking as if she thought the two of them made a procession.

MRS. TWYMLEY. Hsh! (*Peeping*) Strike me dead—if she's not coming mincing down the stair, hooked on his arm!

[*Indeed it is thus that* MRS. DOWEY *enters. Perhaps she had seen shadows lurking on the blind, and at once hooked on to* KENNETH *to impress the visitors. She is quite capable of it.*

[*Now we see what Kenneth saw that afternoon five days ago when he emerged from the bathroom and found the old trembler awaiting his inspection. Here are the muff and the gloves and the chiffon, and such a kind old bonnet that it makes you laugh at once. I don't know how to describe it; but it is trimmed with a kiss, as bonnets should be when the wearer is old and frail. We must take the merino for granted until she steps out of the astrakhan. She is dressed up to the nines; there is no doubt about it. Yes, but is her face less homely? Above all, has she style? The answer is in a stout affirmative. Ask Kenneth. He knows. Many a time he has had to go behind a door to roar hilariously at the old lady. He has thought of her as a lark to tell his mates about by and by; but for some reason that he cannot fathom, he knows now that he will never do that.*]

MRS. DOWEY (*affecting surprise*). Kenneth, we have visitors!

DOWEY. Your servant, ladies.

[*He is no longer mud-caked and dour. A very smart figure is this Private Dowey; and he winks engagingly at the visitors, like one who knows that for jolly company you cannot easily beat charwomen. The pleasantries that he and they have exchanged this week! The sauce he has given them. The wit of* MRS. MICKLEHAM'S *retorts. The badinage[2] of*

---

[1] *astrakhan:* the fur of Persian lambs which is used in jackets and coats.
[2] *badinage:* playful banter or joking.

MRS. TWYMLEY. *The neat giggles of the* HAGGERTY WOMAN. *There has been nothing like it since you took the countess in to dinner.*]

MRS. TWYMLEY. We should apologize. We're not meaning to stay.

MRS. DOWEY. You are very welcome. Just wait (*the ostentation of this!*) till I get out of my astrakhan—and my muff—and my gloves—and (*It is the bonnet's turn now*) my Excelsior.

[*At last we see her in the merino—a triumph.*]

MRS. MICKLEHAM. You've given her a glory time, Mr. Dowey.

DOWEY. It's her that has given it to me, missis.

MRS. DOWEY. Hey! hey! hey! hey! He just pampers me. (*Waggling her fists*) The Lord forgive us, but, this being the last night, we had a sit-down supper at a restaurant! (*Vehemently*) I swear by God that we had champagny wine. (*There is a dead stillness, and she knows very well what it means; she has even prepared for it.*) And to them as doubts my word—here's the cork. (*She places the cork, in its lovely gold drapery, upon the table.*)

MRS. MICKLEHAM. I'm sure!

MRS. TWYMLEY. I would thank you, Mrs. Dowey, not to say a word against my Alfred.

MRS. DOWEY. Me!

DOWEY. Come, come, ladies! (*In the masterful way that is so hard for women to resist*) If you say another word, I'll kiss the lot of you.

[*There is a moment of pleased confusion.*]

MRS. MICKLEHAM. Really, them sodgers!

THE HAGGERTY WOMAN. The kilties is the worst!

MRS. TWYMLEY (*heartily*). I'm sure we don't grudge you your treats, Mrs. Dowey; and sorry we are that this is the end.

DOWEY. Yes, it's the end. (*With a troubled look at his old lady*) I must be off in ten minutes.

[*The little soul is too gallant to break down in company. She hurries into the pantry and shuts the door.*]

MRS. MICKLEHAM. Poor thing! But we must run, for you'll be having some last words to say to her.

DOWEY. I kept her out long on purpose so as to have less time to say them in. (*He more than half wishes that he could make a bolt to a public house.*[1])

MRS. TWYMLEY. It's the best way. (*In the important affairs of life there is not much that anyone can teach a charwoman.*) Just a mere nothing—to wish you well, Mr. Dowey.

[*All three present him with the cigarettes.*]

MRS. MICKLEHAM. A scraping, as one might say.

THE HAGGERTY WOMAN (*enigmatically*[2]). The heart is warm, though it may not be gold-tipped.

DOWEY. You bricks!

THE LADIES. Good luck, cocky.

DOWEY. The same to you. And if you see a sodger man up there in a kilt, he is one that is going back with me. Tell him not to come down, but—but to give me till the last minute, and then to whistle.

[*It is quite a grave man who is left alone, thinking what to do next. He tries a horse laugh, but that proves of no help. He says "Hell!" to himself, but it is equally ineffective. Then he opens the pantry door and calls.*]

DOWEY. Old lady.

[*She comes timidly to the door, her hand up as if to ward off a blow.*]

MRS. DOWEY. Is it time?

[*An encouraging voice answers her.*]

DOWEY. No, no, not yet. I've left word for Dixon to whistle when go I must.

MRS. DOWEY. All is ended.

DOWEY. Now, then, you promised to be gay. We were to help one another.

MRS. DOWEY. Yes, Kenneth.

DOWEY. It's bad for me, but it's worse for you.

MRS. DOWEY. The men have medals to win, you see.

DOWEY. The women have their medals, too. (*He knows she likes him to order her about, so he tries it again.*) Come here. No, I'll come to

_____

[1] *public house:* a tavern or bar.
[2] *enigmatically:* in a puzzling, or obscure, way.

you. (*He stands gaping at her wonderingly. He has no power of words, nor does he quite know what he would like to say.*) God!

MRS. DOWEY. What is it, Kenneth?

DOWEY. You're a woman.

MRS. DOWEY. I had near forgot it.

[*He wishes he was at the station with Dixon. Dixon is sure to have a bottle in his pocket. They will be roaring a song presently. But in the meantime—there is that son business. Blethers,[1] the whole thing, of course—or mostly blethers. But it's the way to please her.*]

DOWEY. Have you noticed you have never called me son?

MRS. DOWEY. Have I noticed it! I was feared, Kenneth. You said I was on probation.

DOWEY. And so you were. Well, the probation's ended. (*He laughs uncomfortably.*) The like of me! But if you want me you can have me.

MRS. DOWEY. Kenneth, will I do?

DOWEY (*artfully gay*). Woman, don't be so forward. Wait till I have proposed.

MRS. DOWEY. Propose for a mother?

DOWEY. What for no? (*In the grand style*) Mrs. Dowey, you queer carl,[2] you spunky tiddy, have I your permission to ask you the most important question a neglected orphan can ask of an old lady?

[*She bubbles with mirth. Who could help it, the man has such a way with him!*]

MRS. DOWEY. None of your sauce, Kenneth.

DOWEY. For a long time, Mrs. Dowey, you cannot have been unaware of my sonnish feelings for you.

MRS. DOWEY. Wait till I get my mop to you—

DOWEY. And if you're not willing to be my mother, I swear I'll never ask another. (*The old divert pulls him down to her and strokes his hair.*) Was I a well-behaved infant, Mother?

MRS. DOWEY. Not you, sonny—you were a rampaging rogue.

DOWEY. Was I slow in learning to walk?

MRS. DOWEY. The quickest in our street. He! he! he! (*She starts up.*) Was that the whistle?

---

[1] *Blethers:* nonsense.
[2] *carl:* fellow or person.

DOWEY. No, no. See here. In taking me over you have, in a manner of speaking, joined the Black Watch.

MRS. DOWEY. I like to think that, Kenneth.

DOWEY. Then you must behave so that the ghost piper can be proud of you. 'Tion! (*She stands bravely at attention.*) That's the style. Now listen. I've sent in your name as being my nearest of kin, and your allowance will be coming to you weekly in the usual way.

MRS. DOWEY. Hey! hey! hey! Is it wicked, Kenneth?

DOWEY. I'll take the responsibility for it in both worlds. You see, I want you to be safeguarded in case anything hap—

MRS. DOWEY. Kenneth!

DOWEY. 'Tion! Have no fear. I'll come back, covered with mud and medals. Mind you have that cup of tea waiting for me.

[*He is listening for the whistle. He pulls her onto his knee.*]

MRS. DOWEY. Hey! hey! hey! hey!

DOWEY. What fun we'll have writing to one another! Real letters this time!

MRS. DOWEY. Yes.

DOWEY. It would be a good plan if you began the first letter as soon as I've gone.

MRS. DOWEY. I will.

DOWEY. I hope Lady Dolly will go on sending me cakes.

MRS. DOWEY. You may be sure.

[*He ties his scarf round her neck.*]

DOWEY. You must have been a bonny thing when you were young.

MRS. DOWEY. Away with you!

DOWEY. That scarf sets you fine.

MRS. DOWEY. Blue was always my color.

[*The whistle sounds.*]

DOWEY. Old lady, you are what Blighty means to me now.

[*She hides in the pantry again. She is out of sight of us, but she does something that makes* PRIVATE DOWEY *take off his bonnet. Then he shoulders his equipment and departs. That is he laughing coarsely with Dixon.*]

We have one last glimpse of the old lady—a month or two after Kenneth's death in action. It would be rosemary to us to see her in her black dress, of which she is very proud; but let us rather peep at her in the familiar garments that make a third to her mop and pail. It is early morning, and she is having a look at her medals before setting off on the daily round. They are in a drawer with the scarf covering them, and on the scarf a piece of lavender. First the black frock, which she carries in her arms like a baby. Then her War Savings Certificates, Kenneth's bonnet, a thin packet of real letters, and the famous champagne cork. She kisses the letters, but she does not blub over them. She strokes the dress, and waggles her head over the certificates and presses the bonnet to her cheeks, and rubs the tinsel of the cork carefully with her apron. She is a tremulous old 'un; yet she exults, for she owns all these things and also the penny flag on her breast. She puts them away in the drawer, the scarf over them, the lavender on the scarf. Her air of triumph well becomes her. She lifts the pail and the mop, and slouches off gamely to the day's toil.

INTERPRETER OF CHARACTER

1. How do Barrie's stage directions differ from the usual stage directions? How do they affect your interest in the play? How do they affect your understanding of the characters? How would they help actors? How might they hinder them?

2. Point out bits of humor in the opening conversation among the charwomen, especially their discussion of fashions. What apparently unimportant details of this discussion later prove to have bearing on the plot? When do you first realize the nature of Mrs. Dowey's "crime"?

3. Show how each character in the play is made different in personality even though the part is very minor. What do you learn about British "class society" from this play?

4. Trace the steps in Kenneth's change of attitude. Is it made convincing? What are the most telling points in winning him over?

5. Study Mrs. Dowey's character carefully. What leads her to commit her "crime"? How would you characterize her feelings at the end of the play as she looks over her "medals"? In what way does she deserve them?

REPORTING AND DRAMATIZATION

1. In a panel or general discussion examine the contrast between the mother-son relationship in *Pygmalion* and *The Old Lady Shows Her Medals*.

2. Act all or certain chosen parts of *The Old Lady Shows Her Medals*. Discuss how you would handle on the stage the short last scene for which there is no dialogue. How would you indicate the lapse of time? the fact that Kenneth has been killed? Would you try to supply any speech whatever for this scene? Why or why not?

READING LIST FOR MODERN DRAMA

Barrie, Sir James M., *Representative Plays*
A good selection of Barrie's best.

Coward, Noel, *Plays*
Social satires by the dramatist considered the best of his generation in England.

Eliot, T. S., *The Confidential Clerk*
A provocative play in blank verse about a financier whose aspirations are thwarted.

Fry, Christopher, *The Dark Is Light Enough*
The value of human life and the error in using violence to redress wrong are the main themes of this three-act verse play.

Maugham, W. Somerset, *Quartet*
Four Maugham short stories with their screenplays by R. C. Sheriff.

O'Casey, Sean, *Selected Plays*
Among these eight plays which the author wants to survive him are *The Shadow of a Gunman, Juno and the Paycock,* and *The Plough and the Stars.*

Priestley, J. B., *Wonderful World of the Theater*
An attractive, illustrated history of the theater.

Rattigan, Terence, *The Winslow Boy*
A dramatic study of the effects of a long court trial on a middle-class family.

Shaw, George Bernard, *Plays*
Witty dramas promoting the rule of the goddess Reason.

Synge, John, *Complete Plays*
A collection of intense plays by a playwright who celebrated his native land, Ireland, in lyric beauty.

Wilde, Oscar, *Plays*
Sophisticated comedies of manners by a wit.

FOR LISTENING

The first half of Act II of Shaw's *Pygmalion* has been recorded and is available on *Many Voices 6B*.

THE MODERN NOVEL

Typhoon

JOSEPH CONRAD (1857–1924)

The writer who called himself Joseph Conrad can perhaps be considered the oddest figure in English literature. Everything about him is unexpected. He was born in Poland (then under Russian rule) in 1857; his real name was Jozef Teodor Konrad Korzeniowski; his father was a man of letters and a fervent patriot who was banished from Poland in 1862 by the Russian government. By the time Conrad (as we must call him) was twelve, both his parents were dead, probably victims of the anxieties and miseries of exile. He was then brought up by an uncle in Cracow, and while still in his teens made his way to Marseilles (he spoke French fluently) because he wanted to go to sea. In 1878 he signed on an English ship, and then stayed in the British merchant service, eventually taking British nationality. In 1886 he passed his final examinations to become a "ship's master." For the next eight years he was a master mariner, sailing mostly in tropical seas. He then retired from the sea to become a professional writer, married, and settled first in France and then in southern England. He struggled hard for many years, not only to write the sort of books he wanted to write, but to earn a bare living for himself and his family. His reputation grew slowly but surely during the later 1890's and early 1900's, but he enjoyed no popular success until 1914, when the influential American publisher, F. N. Doubleday, made up his mind that Conrad's new novel, *Chance,* would be a hit. After that, until his death in 1924, Conrad no longer had to worry about money and he enjoyed enormous prestige, perhaps greater in Britain and America than that of any other novelist of his time.

So much for the facts. Now let us consider what a strange story this is. A young Pole, brought up far from the sea, knowing nothing about it, becomes determined—against much opposition—to be a sailor. We are told that when Conrad was still a young boy, his father was translating into Polish that tremendous romantic tale, Victor Hugo's *Toilers of the Sea,* and that the boy, reading aloud one chapter after another crammed with adventure, fell in love with this strange seafaring life. And here we may note that something of this romantic attitude towards the sea, this far inland view of it as a kind of symbol of what is remote and strange, fascinating and magical, remained with Conrad. The small Polish boy's wonder at this distant magical element never entirely vanished from his mind.

Nineteenth-century Poles, exiled from their own country (like Chopin, for example), were immediately attracted to France rather than England. For one thing, the foreign language most of them knew was French, not English; for another, it was in France that they found most of their fellow exiles. Now it would not have seemed unusually odd if Conrad had stayed with French ships and had finally left them to write in French, being well acquainted as he was with the language and literature of France. But not only did he decide to serve in English ships, he also decided to write in English, a language he could not even begin to speak, let alone write, until he was twenty.

Yet he became in the end, in spite of poverty, obscurity, neglect, and illness, not only a good English novelist but one of the greatest of his time. And—though some critics always had reservations, declaring that his essential manner in prose remained French—he was enthusiastically praised as a stylist, a writer with extraordinary descriptive powers, able to find words (always after much toil) to convey to sensitive English readers the many-colored splendor, the beauty and mystery, of the seascapes and landscapes he remembered from his voyages. And this, nobody can deny, is very odd indeed. His is a unique case.

Moreover, what fascinated him in much of his story-telling was the peculiarly English character, remote from Polish or French characteristics, of the sailors he preferred to describe—men like MacWhirr in *Typhoon,* apparently dull, unimaginative, obviously unromantic, in whom Conrad discovered some remarkable qualities that seemed to him to typify Man himself defying that huge, dangerous element, the sea, and facing the chances, the threats, the ultimate menace of his destiny on this earth. No English writer has come closer to understanding the typical English sea captain or engineer of the later Victorian era, when British tramp steamers went rolling round the seven seas, than this Polish-born stylist. The final and the finest word about these vanished seamen belongs to Conrad.

He was entirely unlike them himself, except in his seagoing experience. He was intensely imaginative, a kind of poet, and at heart a romantic, though of a hard, not soft, sort. No wonder he was hard; his life at sea, mostly serving in small ships in remote places, had not been easy; he had known years of struggle, poverty, and disappointment as a writer, and when at last he knew prosperity he did not bask in it but regarded it with some irony. Most important of all, probably, was his childhood experience of sharing his parents' life as exiles. He was by temperament an aristocrat, aloof and ironical, and always tending to pessimism, whether brooding over his own life or over the whole existence of our species on this planet. He was the very opposite of the enthusiastic reformer, the progressive, the forward-looker, the man who believes that when a few changes have been made everything will be wonderful. Conrad dismissed such easy optimistic beliefs with contempt.

He felt—and his experiences in childhood and youth, his life at sea, his bitter struggle to establish himself as a writer, all confirmed this feeling—he felt that men worthy of the name always found themselves matched against terrible odds, that what in the end carried them through, not to any "happy-ever-afterwards" but to some satisfaction and enjoyment of their own manhood, were a few simple old-fashioned virtues—courage, endurance, a sense of integrity and of their worth and honor as men. To this idea, this recurring theme, we shall return in *Typhoon: An Afterword.*

J. B. P.

CHAPTER ONE

Captain MAC WHIRR, of the steamer *Nan-Shan,* had a physiognomy[1] that, in the order of material appearances, was the exact counterpart of his mind: it presented no marked characteristics of firmness or stupidity; it had no pronounced characteristics whatever; it was simply ordinary, irresponsive, and unruffled.

The only thing his aspect might have been said to suggest, at times, was bashfulness; because he would sit, in business offices ashore, sunburnt and smiling faintly, with downcast eyes. When he raised them, they were perceived to be direct in their glance and of blue color. His hair was fair and extremely fine, clasping from temple to temple the bald dome of his skull in a clamp as of fluffy silk. The hair of his face, on the contrary, carroty and flaming, resembled a growth of copper wire clipped short to the line of the lip; while, no matter how close he shaved, fiery metallic gleams passed, when he moved his head, over the surface of his cheeks. He was rather below the medium height, a bit round-shouldered, and so sturdy of limb that his clothes always looked a shade too tight for his arms and legs. As if unable to grasp what is due to the difference of latitudes, he wore a brown bowler hat, a complete suit of a brownish hue, and clumsy black boots. These harbor togs gave to his thick figure an air of stiff and uncouth smartness. A thin silver watch chain looped his waistcoat, and he never left his ship for the shore without clutching in his powerful, hairy fist an elegant umbrella of the very best quality, but generally unrolled. Young Jukes, the chief mate, attending his commander to the gangway, would sometimes venture to say, with the greatest gentleness, "Allow me, sir"—and possessing himself of the umbrella deferentially, would elevate the ferule, shake the folds, twirl a neat furl in a jiffy, and hand it back; going through the perform-

---

[1] *physiognomy* (fĭz′ĭ·ŏg′nŏ·mĭ): facial appearance.

ance with a face of such portentous gravity that Mr. Solomon Rout, the chief engineer, smoking his morning cigar over the skylight, would turn away his head in order to hide a smile. "Oh! aye! The blessed gamp.[1] . . . Thank 'ee, Jukes, thank 'ee," would mutter Captain MacWhirr heartily, without looking up.

Having just enough imagination to carry him through each successive day, and no more, he was tranquilly sure of himself; and from the very same cause he was not in the least conceited. It is your imaginative superior who is touchy, overbearing, and difficult to please; but every ship Captain MacWhirr commanded was the floating abode of harmony and peace. It was, in truth, as impossible for him to take a flight of fancy as it would be for a watchmaker to put together a chronometer[2] with nothing except a two-pound hammer and a whipsaw in the way of tools. Yet the uninteresting lives of men so entirely given to the actuality of the bare existence have their mysterious side. It was impossible in Captain MacWhirr's case, for instance, to understand what under heaven could have induced that perfectly satisfactory son of a petty grocer in Belfast to run away to sea. And yet he had done that very thing at the age of fifteen. It was enough, when you thought it over, to give you the idea of an immense, potent, and invisible hand thrust into the ant heap of the earth, laying hold of shoulders, knocking heads together, and setting the unconscious faces of the multitude towards inconceivable goals and in undreamt-of directions.

His father never really forgave him for this undutiful stupidity. "We could have got on without him," he used to say later on, "but there's the business. And he an only son, too!" His mother wept very much after his disappearance. As it had never occurred to him to leave word behind, he was mourned over for dead till, after eight months, his first letter arrived from Talcahuano.[3] It was short, and contained the statement: "We had very fine weather on our passage out." But evidently, in the writer's mind, the only important intelligence was to the effect that his captain had, on the very day of writing, entered him regularly on the ship's articles as Ordinary Seaman. "Because I can do the work," he explained. The mother again wept copiously, while the remark, "Tom's an ass," expressed the emotions of the father. He was a corpulent man,

---

[1] *gamp:* a large umbrella, like the one carried by Mrs. Gamp in Dickens' *Martin Chuzzlewit.*

[2] *chronometer* (krō·nŏm′ĕ·tēr): the kind of highly accurate timepiece commonly used on ships.

[3] *Talcahuano* (Täl′kä·wä′nō): a port in Chile.

with a gift for sly chaffing, which to the end of his life he exercised in his intercourse with his son, a little pityingly, as if upon a half-witted person.

MacWhirr's visits to his home were necessarily rare, and in the course of years he dispatched other letters to his parents, informing them of his successive promotions and of his movements upon the vast earth. In these missives could be found sentences like this: "The heat here is very great." Or: "On Christmas day at 4 P.M. we fell in with some icebergs." The old people ultimately became acquainted with a good many names of ships, and with the names of the skippers who commanded them—with the names of Scots and English shipowners—with the names of seas, oceans, straits, promontories—with outlandish names of lumber ports, of rice ports, of cotton ports—with the names of islands—with the name of their son's young woman. She was called Lucy. It did not suggest itself to him to mention whether he thought the name pretty. And then they died.

The great day of MacWhirr's marriage came in due course, following shortly upon the great day when he got his first command.

All these events had taken place many years before the morning when, in the chartroom of the steamer *Nan-Shan,* he stood confronted by the fall of a barometer he had no reason to distrust. The fall— taking into account the excellence of the instrument, the time of the year, and the ship's position on the terrestrial globe—was of a nature ominously prophetic; but the red face of the man betrayed no sort of inward disturbance. Omens were as nothing to him, and he was unable to discover the message of a prophecy till the fulfillment had brought it home to his very door. "That's a fall, and no mistake," he thought. "There must be some uncommonly dirty weather knocking about."

The *Nan-Shan* was on her way from the southward to the treaty port of Fu-chau, with some cargo in her lower holds and two hundred Chinese coolies returning to their village homes in the province of Fo-kien, after a few years of work in various tropical colonies. The morning was fine, the oily sea heaved without a sparkle, and there was a queer white misty patch in the sky like a halo of the sun. The foredeck, packed with Chinamen, was full of somber clothing, yellow faces, and pigtails, sprinkled over with a good many naked shoulders, for there was no wind and the heat was close. The coolies lounged, talked, smoked, or stared over the rail; some, drawing water over the side, sluiced each other; a few slept on hatches, while several small parties of six sat on their heels surrounding iron trays with plates of rice and tiny teacups;

and every single Celestial[1] of them was carrying with him all he had in the world—a wooden chest with a ringing lock and brass on the corners, containing the savings of his labors: some clothes of ceremony, sticks of incense, a little opium maybe, bits of nameless rubbish of conventional value, and a small hoard of silver dollars, toiled for in coal lighters, won in gambling houses or in petty trading, grubbed out of earth, sweated out in mines, on railway lines, in deadly jungle, under heavy burdens—amassed patiently, guarded with care, cherished fiercely.

A cross swell had set in from the direction of Formosa Channel about ten o'clock, without disturbing these passengers much, because the *Nan-Shan,* with her flat bottom, rolling chocks on bilges,[2] and great breadth of beam, had the reputation of an exceptionally steady ship in a seaway. Mr. Jukes, in moments of expansion on shore, would proclaim loudly that the "old girl was as good as she was pretty." It would never have occurred to Captain MacWhirr to express his favorable opinion so loud or in terms so fanciful.

She was a good ship, undoubtedly, and not old either. She had been built in Dumbarton[3] less than three years before, to the order of a firm of merchants in Siam—Messrs. Sigg and Son. When she lay afloat, finished in every detail and ready to take up the work of her life, the builders contemplated her with pride.

"Sigg has asked us for a reliable skipper to take her out," remarked one of the partners; and the other, after reflecting for a while, said: "I think MacWhirr is ashore just at present." "Is he? Then wire him at once. He's the very man," declared the senior, without a moment's hesitation.

Next morning MacWhirr stood before them unperturbed, having traveled from London by the midnight express after a sudden but undemonstrative parting with his wife. She was the daughter of a superior couple who had seen better days.

"We had better be going together over the ship, Captain," said the senior partner; and the three men started to view the perfections of the *Nan-Shan* from stem to stern, and from her keelson[4] to the trucks[5] of her two stumpy pole masts.

---

[1] *celestial:* the Chinese thought of themselves as Celestials or "sons of Heaven."

[2] *rolling chocks on bilges* (now called *bilge keels*): long strips of metal or wood extending from both sides of a ship below the water line, used to check rolling.

[3] *Dumbarton:* a city in Scotland, well-known as a ship-building center.

[4] *keelson:* a structure running lengthwise through a ship, used to stiffen the frame. It is usually fastened to the keel.

[5] *trucks:* small wooden disks at the tops of masts, used to hold signal flags.

Captain MacWhirr had begun by taking off his coat, which he hung on the end of a steam windlass[1] embodying all the latest improvements.

"My uncle wrote of you favorably by yesterday's mail to our good friends—Messrs. Sigg, you know—and doubtless they'll continue you out there in command," said the junior partner. "You'll be able to boast of being in charge of the handiest boat of her size on the coast of China, Captain," he added.

"Have you? Thank 'ee," mumbled vaguely MacWhirr, to whom the view of a distant eventuality could appeal no more than the beauty of a wide landscape to a purblind tourist; and his eyes happening at the moment to be at rest upon the lock of the cabin door, he walked up to it, full of purpose, and began to rattle the handle vigorously, while he observed, in his low, earnest voice, "You can't trust the workmen nowadays. A brand-new lock, and it won't act at all. Stuck fast. See? See?"

As soon as they found themselves alone in their office across the yard: "You praised that fellow up to Sigg. What is it you see in him?" asked the nephew, with faint contempt.

"I admit he has nothing of your fancy skipper about him, if that's what you mean," said the elder man, curtly. "Is the foreman of the joiners[2] on the Nan-Shan outside? . . . Come in, Bates. How is it that you let Tait's people put us off with a defective lock on the cabin door? The Captain could see directly he set eye on it. Have it replaced at once. The little straws, Bates . . . the little straws. . . ."

The lock was replaced accordingly and a few days afterwards the Nan-Shan steamed out to the East, without MacWhirr having offered any further remark as to her fittings, or having been heard to utter a single word hinting at pride in his ship, gratitude for his appointment, or satisfaction at his prospects.

With a temperament neither loquacious nor taciturn he found very little occasion to talk. There were matters of duty, of course—directions, orders, and so on; but the past being to his mind done with, and the future not there yet, the more general actualities of the day required no comment—because facts can speak for themselves with overwhelming precision.

Old Mr. Sigg liked a man of few words, and one that "you could be sure would not try to improve upon his instructions." MacWhirr satisfying these requirements, was continued in command of the Nan-Shan

---

[1] *windlass:* a device for hauling, consisting of a barrel around which the hoisting rope is wound.

[2] *joiners:* carpenters.

and applied himself to the careful navigation of his ship in the China seas. She had come out on a British register, but after some time Messrs. Sigg judged it expedient to transfer her to the Siamese flag.

At the news of the contemplated transfer Jukes grew restless, as if under a sense of personal affront. He went about grumbling to himself, and uttering short scornful laughs. "Fancy having a ridiculous Noah's Ark elephant in the ensign of one's ship," he said once at the engine-room door. "Dash me if I can stand it: I'll throw up the billet.[1] Don't it make *you* sick, Mr. Rout?" The chief engineer only cleared his throat with the air of a man who knows the value of a good billet. The first morning the new flag floated over the stern of the *Nan-Shan* Jukes stood looking at it bitterly from the bridge. He struggled with his feelings for a while, and then remarked, "Queer flag for a man to sail under, sir."

"What's the matter with the flag?" inquired Captain MacWhirr. "Seems all right to me." And he walked across to the end of the bridge to have a good look.

"Well, it looks queer to me," burst out Jukes, greatly exasperated, and flung off the bridge.

Captain MacWhirr was amazed at these manners. After a while he stepped quietly into the chartroom and opened his International Signal Codebook at the plate where the flags of all the nations are correctly figured in gaudy rows. He ran his finger over them, and when he came to Siam he contemplated with great attention the red field and the white elephant. Nothing could be more simple; but to make sure he brought the book out on the bridge for the purpose of comparing the colored drawing with the real thing at the flagstaff astern. When next Jukes, who was carrying on the duty that day with a sort of suppressed fierceness, happened on the bridge, his commander observed:

"There's nothing amiss with that flag."

"Isn't there?" mumbled Jukes, falling on his knees before a deck locker and jerking therefrom viciously a spare lead line.

"No. I looked up the book. Length twice the breadth and the elephant exactly in the middle. I thought the people ashore would know how to make the local flag. Stands to reason. You were wrong, Jukes. . . ."

"Well, sir," began Jukes, getting up excitedly, "all I can say——" He fumbled for the end of the coil of line with trembling hands.

"That's all right." Captain MacWhirr soothed him, sitting heavily

[1] *billet:* professional appointment or job.

on a little canvas folding stool he greatly affected. "All you have to do is to take care they don't hoist the elephant upside down before they get quite used to it."

Jukes flung the new lead line over on the foredeck with a loud "Here you are, bo'sun—don't forget to wet it thoroughly," and turned with immense resolution towards his commander; but Captain MacWhirr spread his elbows on the bridge rail comfortably.

"Because it would be, I suppose, understood as a signal of distress," he went on. "What do you think? That elephant there, I take it, stands for something in the nature of the Union Jack in the flag. . . ."

"Does it!" yelled Jukes, so that every head on the *Nan-Shan*'s decks looked towards the bridge. Then he sighed, and with sudden resignation: "It would certainly be a distressful sight," he said meekly.

Later in the day he accosted the chief engineer with a confidential, "Here, let me tell you the old man's latest."

Mr. Solomon Rout (frequently alluded to as Long Sol, Old Sol, or Father Rout), from finding himself almost invariably the tallest man on board every ship he joined, had acquired the habit of a stooping, leisurely condescension. His hair was scant and sandy, his flat cheeks were pale, his bony wrists and long scholarly hands were pale, too, as though he had lived all his life in the shade.

He smiled from on high at Jukes and went on smoking and glancing about quietly, in the manner of a kind uncle lending an ear to the tale of an excited schoolboy. Then, greatly amused but impassive, he asked: "And did you throw up the billet?"

"No," cried Jukes, raising a weary, discouraged voice above the harsh buzz of the *Nan-Shan*'s friction winches. All of them were hard at work, snatching slings of cargo, high up, to the end of long derricks, only, as it seemed, to let them rip down recklessly by the run. The cargo chains groaned in the gins,[1] clinked on coamings,[2] rattled over the side; and the whole ship quivered, with her long gray flanks smoking in wreaths of steam. "No," cried Jukes, "I didn't. What's the good? I might just as well fling my resignation at this bulkhead.[3] I don't believe you can make a man like that understand anything. He simply knocks me over."

At that moment Captain MacWhirr, back from the shore, crossed the deck, umbrella in hand, escorted by a mournful, self-possessed

---

[1] *gins:* machines for hauling or moving heavy weights.
[2] *coamings:* raised pieces of wood or metal around hatches.
[3] *bulkhead:* the wall of a shipboard compartment.

Chinaman walking behind in paper-soled silk shoes, and who also carried an umbrella.

The master of the *Nan-Shan,* speaking just audibly and gazing at his boots as his manner was, remarked that it would be necessary to call at Fu-chau this trip, and desired Mr. Rout to have steam up tomorrow afternoon at one o'clock sharp. He pushed back his hat to wipe his forehead, observing at the same time that he hated going ashore anyhow; while overtopping him Mr. Rout, without deigning a word, smoked austerely, nursing his right elbow in the palm of his left hand. Then Jukes was directed in the same subdued voice to keep the forward 'tween deck clear of cargo. Two hundred coolies were going to be put down there. The Bun Hin Company were sending that lot home. Twenty-five bags of rice would be coming off in a sampan[1] directly, for stores. All seven-years'-men they were, said Captain MacWhirr, with a camphorwood chest to every man. The carpenter should be set to work nailing three-inch battens along the deck below, fore and aft, to keep these boxes from shifting in a seaway. Jukes had better look to it at once. "D'ye hear, Jukes?" This Chinaman here was coming with the ship as far as Fu-chau—a sort of interpreter he would be. Bun Hin's clerk he was, and wanted to have a look at the space. Jukes had better take him forward. "D'ye hear, Jukes?"

Jukes took care to punctuate these instructions in proper places with the obligatory "Yes, sir," ejaculated without enthusiasm. His brusque "Come along, John; make look see" set the Chinaman in motion at his heels.

"Wanchee look see, all same look see can do," said Jukes, who having no talent for foreign languages mangled the very pidgin-English cruelly. He pointed at the open hatch. "Catchee number one piecie place to sleep in. Eh?"

He was gruff, as became his racial superiority, but not unfriendly. The Chinaman, gazing sad and speechless into the darkness of the hatchway, seemed to stand at the head of a yawning grave.

"No catchee rain down there—savvy?" pointed out Jukes. "Suppose all'ee same fine weather, one piecie coolie-man come topside," he pursued, warming up imaginatively. "Make so—Phooooo!" He expanded his chest and blew out his cheeks. "Savvy, John? Breathe—fresh air. Good. Eh? Washee him piecie pants, chow-chow topside—see, John?"

With his mouth and hands he made exuberant motions of eating rice

---

[1] *sampan:* a small Chinese or Japanese sailing vessel.

and washing clothes; and the Chinaman, who concealed his distrust of this pantomime under a collected demeanor tinged by a gentle and refined melancholy, glanced out of his almond eyes from Jukes to the hatch and back again. "Velly good," he murmured, in a disconsolate undertone, and hastened smoothly along the decks, dodging obstacles in his course. He disappeared, ducking low under a sling of ten dirty gunny bags full of some costly merchandise and exhaling a repulsive smell.

Captain MacWhirr meantime had gone on the bridge and into the chartroom, where a letter, commenced two days before, awaited termination. These long letters began with the words, "My darling wife," and the steward, between the scrubbing of the floors and the dusting of chronometer boxes, snatched at every opportunity to read them. They interested him much more than they possibly could the woman for whose eye they were intended; and this for the reason that they related in minute detail each successive trip of the *Nan-Shan*.

Her master, faithful to facts, which alone his consciousness reflected, would set them down with painstaking care upon many pages. The house in a northern suburb to which these pages were addressed had a bit of garden before the bow windows, a deep porch of good appearance, colored glass with imitation lead frame in the front door. He paid five-and-forty pounds a year for it, and did not think the rent too high, because Mrs. MacWhirr (a pretentious person with a scraggy neck and a disdainful manner) was admittedly ladylike, and in the neighborhood considered as "quite superior." The only secret of her life was her abject terror of the time when her husband would come home to stay for good. Under the same roof there dwelt also a daughter called Lydia and a son, Tom. These two were but slightly acquainted with their father. Mainly, they knew him as a rare but privileged visitor, who of an evening smoked his pipe in the dining room and slept in the house. The lanky girl, upon the whole, was rather ashamed of him; the boy was frankly and utterly indifferent in a straightforward, delightful, unaffected way manly boys have.

And Captain MacWhirr wrote home from the coast of China twelve times every year, desiring quaintly to be "remembered to the children," and subscribing himself "your loving husband," as calmly as if the words so long used by so many men were, apart from their shape, worn-out things, and of a faded meaning.

The China seas north and south are narrow seas. They are seas full of everyday, eloquent facts, such as islands, sandbanks, reefs, swift and changeable currents—tangled facts that nevertheless speak to a seaman in clear and definite language. Their speech appealed to Captain MacWhirr's sense of realities so forcibly that he had given up his stateroom below and practically lived all his days on the bridge of his ship, often having his meals sent up, and sleeping at night in the chartroom. And he indited there his home letters. Each of them, without exception, contained the phrase, "The weather has been very fine this trip," or some other form of a statement to that effect. And this statement, too, in its wonderful persistence, was of the same perfect accuracy as all the others they contained.

Mr. Rout likewise wrote letters; only no one on board knew how chatty he could be pen in hand, because the chief engineer had enough imagination to keep his desk locked. His wife relished his style greatly. They were a childless couple, and Mrs. Rout, a big, high-bosomed, jolly woman of forty, shared with Mr. Rout's toothless and venerable mother a little cottage near Teddington. She would run over her correspondence, at breakfast, with lively eyes, and scream out interesting passages in a joyous voice at the deaf old lady, prefacing each extract by the warning shout, "Solomon says!" She had the trick of firing off Solomon's utterances also upon strangers, astonishing them easily by the unfamiliar text and the unexpectedly jocular vein of these quotations. On the day the new curate[1] called for the first time at the cottage, she found occasion to remark, "As Solomon says: 'the engineers that go down to the sea in ships behold the wonders of sailor nature' "; when a change in the visitor's countenance made her stop and stare.

"Solomon.[2]. . . Oh! . . . Mrs. Rout," stuttered the young man, very red in the face, "I must say . . . I don't. . . ."

"He's my husband," she announced in a great shout, throwing herself back in the chair. Perceiving the joke, she laughed immoderately with a handkerchief to her eyes, while he sat wearing a forced smile, and, from his inexperience of jolly women, fully persuaded that she must be deplorably insane. They were excellent friends afterwards; for, absolving her from irreverent intention, he came to think she was a very worthy person indeed; and he learned in time to receive without flinching other scraps of Solomon's wisdom.

---

[1] *curate:* a clergyman, usually the assistant to the rector of a parish.
[2] *Solomon:* The new curate obviously thinks that Mrs. Rout is referring to the Biblical Solomon.

"For my part," Solomon was reported by his wife to have said once, "give me the dullest ass for a skipper before a rogue. There is a way to take a fool; but a rogue is smart and slippery." This was an airy generalization drawn from the particular case of Captain MacWhirr's honesty, which, in itself, had the heavy obviousness of a lump of clay. On the other hand, Mr. Jukes, unable to generalize, unmarried, and unengaged, was in the habit of opening his heart after another fashion to an old chum and former shipmate, actually serving as second officer on board an Atlantic liner.

First of all he would insist upon the advantages of the Eastern trade, hinting at its superiority to the Western ocean service. He extolled the sky, the seas, the ships, and the easy life of the Far East. The *Nan-Shan,* he affirmed, was second to none as a sea boat.

"We have no brassbound uniforms, but then we are like brothers here," he wrote. "We all mess together and live like fighting cocks. . . . All the chaps of the black-squad [1] are as decent as they make that kind, and old Sol, the Chief, is a dry stick. We are good friends. As to our old man, you could not find a quieter skipper. Sometimes you would think he hadn't sense enough to see anything wrong. And yet it isn't that. Can't be. He has been in command for a good few years now. He doesn't do anything actually foolish, and gets his ship along all right without worrying anybody. I believe he hasn't brains enough to enjoy kicking up a row. I don't take advantage of him. I would scorn it. Outside the routine of duty he doesn't seem to understand more than half of what you tell him. We get a laugh out of this at times; but it is dull, too, to be with a man like this—in the long run. Old Sol says he hasn't much conversation. Conversation! O Lord! He never talks. The other day I had been yarning under the bridge with one of the engineers, and he must have heard us. When I came up to take my watch, he steps out of the chartroom and has a good look all round, peeps over at the sidelights, glances at the compass, squints upwards at the stars. That's his regular performance. By-and-by he says: 'Was that you talking just now in the port alleyway?' 'Yes, sir.' 'With the third engineer?' 'Yes, sir.' He walks off to starboard, and sits under the dodger [2] on a little campstool of his, and for half an hour perhaps he makes no sound, except that I heard him sneeze once. Then after a while I hear him getting up over there, and he strolls across to port,

---

[1] *black-squad:* the engineering officers.

[2] *dodger:* a canvas or wood screen used to protect lookouts from spray.

where I was. 'I can't understand what you can find to talk about,' says he. 'Two solid hours. I am not blaming you. I see people ashore at it all day long, and then in the evening they sit down and keep at it over the drinks. Must be saying the same things over and over again. I can't understand.'

"Did you ever hear anything like that? And he was so patient about it. It made me quite sorry for him. But he is exasperating, too, sometimes. Of course one would not do anything to vex him even if it were worth while. But it isn't. He's so jolly innocent that if you were to put your thumb to your nose and wave your fingers at him he would only wonder gravely to himself what got into you. He told me once quite simply that he found it very difficult to make out what made people always act so queerly. He's too dense to trouble about, and that's the truth."

Thus wrote Mr. Jukes to his chum in the Western ocean trade, out of the fullness of his heart and the liveliness of his fancy.

He had expressed his honest opinion. It was not worth while trying to impress a man of that sort. If the world had been full of such men, life would have probably appeared to Jukes an unentertaining and unprofitable business. He was not alone in his opinion. The sea itself, as if sharing Mr. Jukes' good-natured forbearance, had never put itself out to startle the silent man, who seldom looked up, and wandered innocently over the waters with the only visible purpose of getting food, raiment, and houseroom for three people ashore. Dirty weather he had known, of course. He had been made wet, uncomfortable, tired, in the usual way, felt at the time and presently forgotten. So that upon the whole he had been justified in reporting fine weather at home. But he had never been given a glimpse of immeasurable strength and of immoderate wrath, the wrath that passes exhausted but never appeased—the wrath and fury of the passionate sea. He knew it existed, as we know that crime and abominations exist; he had heard of it as a peaceable citizen in a town hears of battles, famines, and floods, and yet knows nothing of what these things mean—though, indeed, he may have been mixed up in a street row, have gone without his dinner once, or been soaked to the skin in a shower. Captain MacWhirr had sailed over the surface of the oceans as some men go skimming over the years of existence to sink gently into a placid grave, ignorant of life to the last, without ever having been made to see all it may contain of perfidy, of violence, and of terror. There are on sea and land such men thus fortunate—or thus disdained by destiny or by the sea.

CHAPTER TWO

Observing the steady fall of the barometer, Captain MacWhirr thought, "There's some dirty weather knocking about." This is precisely what he thought. He had had an experience of moderately dirty weather—the term dirty as applied to the weather implying only moderate discomfort to the seaman. Had he been informed by an indisputable authority that the end of the world was to be finally accomplished by a catastrophic disturbance of the atmosphere, he would have assimilated the information under the simple idea of dirty weather, and no other, because he had no experience of cataclysms, and belief does not necessarily imply comprehension. The wisdom of his country had pronounced by means of an Act of Parliament that before he could be considered as fit to take charge of a ship he should be able to answer certain simple questions on the subject of circular storms such as hurricanes, cyclones, typhoons; and apparently he had answered them, since he was now in command of the *Nan-Shan* in the China seas during the season of typhoons. But if he had answered he remembered nothing of it. He was, however, conscious of being made uncomfortable by the clammy heat. He came out on the bridge, and found no relief to this oppression. The air seemed thick. He gasped like a fish, and began to believe himself greatly out of sorts.

The *Nan-Shan* was plowing a vanishing furrow upon the circle of the sea that had the surface and the shimmer of an undulating piece of gray silk. The sun, pale and without rays, poured down leaden heat in a strangely indecisive light, and the Chinamen were lying prostrate about the decks. Their bloodless, pinched, yellow faces were like the faces of bilious invalids. Captain MacWhirr noticed two of them especially, stretched out on their backs below the bridge. As soon as they had closed their eyes they seemed dead. Three others, however, were quarreling barbarously away forward; and one big fellow, half naked, with herculean shoulders, was hanging limply over a winch; another, sitting on the deck, his knees up and his head drooping sideways in a girlish attitude, was plaiting his pigtail with infinite languor depicted in his whole person and in the very movement of his fingers. The smoke struggled with difficulty out of the funnel, and instead of streaming away spread itself out like an infernal sort of cloud, smelling of sulphur and raining soot all over the decks.

"What the devil are you doing there, Mr. Jukes?" asked Captain MacWhirr.

This unusual form of address, though mumbled rather than spoken, caused the body of Mr. Jukes to start as though it had been prodded under the fifth rib. He had had a low bench brought on the bridge, and, sitting on it with a length of rope curled about his feet and a piece of canvas stretched over his knees, was pushing a sail needle vigorously. He looked up, and his surprise gave to his eyes an expression of innocence and candor.

"I am only roping some of that new set of bags we made last trip for whipping up[1] coals," he remonstrated, gently. "We shall want them for the next coaling, sir."

"What became of the others?"

"Why, worn out of course, sir."

Captain MacWhirr, after glaring down irresolutely at his chief mate, disclosed the gloomy and cynical conviction that more than half of them had been lost overboard, "if only the truth was known," and retired to the other end of the bridge. Jukes, exasperated by this unprovoked attack, broke the needle at the second stitch, and dropping his work got up and cursed the heat in a violent undertone.

The propeller thumped, the three Chinamen forward had given up squabbling very suddenly, and the one who had been plaiting his tail clasped his legs and stared dejectedly over his knees. The lurid sunshine cast faint and sickly shadows. The swell ran higher and swifter every moment, and the ship lurched heavily in the smooth, deep hollows of the sea.

"I wonder where that beastly swell comes from," said Jukes aloud, recovering himself after a stagger.

"Northeast," grunted the literal MacWhirr, from his side of the bridge. "There's some dirty weather knocking about. Go and look at the glass." [2]

When Jukes came out of the chartroom, the cast of his countenance had changed to thoughtfulness and concern. He caught hold of the bridge rail and stared ahead.

The temperature in the engine room had gone up to a hundred and seventeen degrees. Irritated voices were ascending through the skylight and through the fiddle of the stokehold in a harsh and resonant uproar, mingled with angry clangs and scrapes of metal, as if men with limbs

[1] *whipping up:* hoisting.
[2] *glass:* the barometer.

of iron and throats of bronze had been quarreling down there. The second engineer was falling foul of the stokers for letting the steam go down. He was a man with arms like a blacksmith, and generally feared; but that afternoon the stokers were answering him back recklessly, and slammed the furnace doors with the fury of despair. Then the noise ceased suddenly, and the second engineer appeared, emerging out of the stokehold streaked with grime and soaking wet like a chimney sweep coming out of a well. As soon as his head was clear of the fiddle[1] he began to scold Jukes for not trimming properly the stokehold ventilators; and in answer Jukes made with his hands deprecatory soothing signs meaning: "No wind—can't be helped—you can see for yourself." But the other wouldn't hear reason. His teeth flashed angrily in his dirty face. He didn't mind, he said, the trouble of punching their blanked heads down there, blank his soul, but did the condemned sailors think you could keep steam up in the godforsaken boilers simply by knocking the blanked stokers about? No, by George! You had to get some draft, too—may he be everlastingly blanked for a swab-headed deck hand if you didn't! And the chief, too, rampaging before the steam gauge and carrying on like a lunatic up and down the engine room ever since noon. What did Jukes think he was stuck up there for, if he couldn't get one of his decayed, good-for-nothing deck cripples to turn the ventilators to the wind?

The relations of the "engine room" and the "deck" of the *Nan-Shan* were, as is known, of a brotherly nature; therefore Jukes leaned over and begged the other in a restrained tone not to make a disgusting ass of himself; the skipper was on the other side of the bridge. But the second declared mutinously that he didn't care a rap who was on the other side of the bridge, and Jukes, passing in a flash from lofty disapproval into a state of exaltation, invited him in unflattering terms to come up and twist the beastly things to please himself, and catch such wind as a donkey of his sort could find. The second rushed up to the fray. He flung himself at the port ventilator as though he meant to tear it out bodily and toss it overboard. All he did was to move the cowl round a few inches, with an enormous expenditure of force, and seemed spent in the effort. He leaned against the back of the wheelhouse, and Jukes walked up to him.

"Oh, Heavens!" ejaculated the engineer in a feeble voice. He lifted his eyes to the sky, and then let his glassy stare descend to meet the

---

[1] *fiddle:* the raised rim around the hatch.

horizon that, tilting up to an angle of forty degrees, seemed to hang on a slant for a while and settled down slowly. "Heavens! Phew! What's up, anyhow?"

Jukes, straddling his long legs like a pair of compasses, put on an air of superiority. "We're going to catch it this time," he said. "The barometer is tumbling down like anything, Harry. And you trying to kick up that silly row. . . ."

The word "barometer" seemed to revive the second engineer's mad animosity. Collecting afresh all his energies, he directed Jukes in a low and brutal tone to shove the unmentionable instrument down his gory throat. Who cared for his crimson barometer? It was the steam—the steam—that was going down; and what between the firemen going faint and the chief going silly, it was worse than a dog's life for him; he didn't care a tinker's curse how soon the whole show was blown out of the water. He seemed on the point of having a cry, but after regaining his breath he muttered darkly, "I'll faint them," and dashed off. He stopped upon the fiddle long enough to shake his fist at the unnatural daylight, and dropped into the dark hole with a whoop.

When Jukes turned, his eyes fell upon the rounded back and the big red ears of Captain MacWhirr, who had come across. He did not look at his chief officer but said at once, "That's a very violent man, that second engineer."

"Jolly good second, anyhow," grunted Jukes. "They can't keep up steam," he added, rapidly, and made a grab at the rail against the coming lurch.

Captain MacWhirr, unprepared, took a run and brought himself up with a jerk by an awning stanchion.[1]

"A profane man," he said, obstinately. "If this goes on, I'll have to get rid of him the first chance."

"It's the heat," said Jukes. "The weather's awful. It would make a saint swear. Even up here I feel exactly as if I had my head tied up in a woolen blanket."

Captain MacWhirr looked up. "D'ye mean to say, Mr. Jukes, you ever had your head tied up in a blanket? What was that for?"

"It's a manner of speaking, sir," said Jukes, stolidly.

"Some of you fellows do go on! What's that about saints swearing? I wish you wouldn't talk so wild. What sort of saint would that be that would swear? No more saint than yourself, I expect. And what's a blanket got to do with it—or the weather either. . . . The heat does not make

[1] *stanchion:* upright support.

me swear—does it? It's filthy bad temper. That's what it is. And what's the good of your talking like this?"

Thus Captain MacWhirr expostulated against the use of images in speech, and at the end electrified Jukes by a contemptuous snort, followed by words of passion and resentment: "I'll fire him out of the ship if he don't look out."

And Jukes, incorrigible, thought: "Goodness me! Somebody's put a new inside to my old man. Here's temper, if you like. Of course it's the weather; what else? It would make an angel quarrelsome—let alone a saint."

All the Chinamen on deck appeared at their last gasp.

At its setting the sun had a diminished diameter and an expiring brown, rayless glow, as if millions of centuries elapsing since the morning had brought it near its end. A dense bank of cloud became visible to the northward; it had a sinister dark olive tint and lay low and motionless upon the sea, resembling a solid obstacle in the path of the ship. She went floundering towards it like an exhausted creature driven to its death. The coppery twilight retired slowly, and the darkness brought out overhead a swarm of unsteady, big stars, that, as if blown upon, flickered exceedingly and seemed to hang very near the earth. At eight o'clock Jukes went into the chartroom to write up the ship's log.

He copied neatly out of the rough book the number of miles, the course of the ship, and in the column for "wind" scrawled the word "calm" from top to bottom of the eight hours since noon. He was exasperated by the continuous, monotonous rolling of the ship. The heavy inkstand would slide away in a manner that suggested perverse intelligence in dodging the pen. Having written in the large space under the head of "Remarks" "Heat very oppressive," he stuck the end of the penholder in his teeth, pipe fashion, and mopped his face carefully.

"Ship rolling heavily in a high cross swell," he began again, and commented to himself, "Heavily is no word for it." Then he wrote: "Sunset threatening, with a low bank of clouds to N. and E. Sky clear overhead."

Sprawling over the table with arrested pen, he glanced out of the door, and in that frame of his vision he saw all the stars flying upwards between the teakwood jambs on a black sky. The whole lot took flight together and disappeared, leaving only a blackness flecked with white flashes, for the sea was as black as the sky and speckled with foam afar. The stars that had flown to the roll came back on the return swing of the ship, rushing downwards in their glittering multitude, not of fiery points, but enlarged to tiny disks brilliant with a clear wet sheen.

Jukes watched the flying big stars for a moment, and then wrote: "8 P.M. Swell increasing. Ship laboring and taking water on her decks. Battened down the coolies for the night. Barometer still falling." He paused, and thought to himself, "Perhaps nothing whatever'll come of it." And then he closed resolutely his entries: "Every appearance of a typhoon coming on."

On going out he had to stand aside, and Captain MacWhirr strode over the doorstep without saying a word or making a sign.

"Shut the door, Mr. Jukes, will you?" he cried from within.

Jukes turned back to do so, muttering ironically: "Afraid to catch cold, I suppose." It was his watch below, but he yearned for communion with his kind; and he remarked cheerily to the second mate: "Doesn't look so bad, after all—does it?"

The second mate was marching to and fro on the bridge, tripping down with small steps one moment and the next climbing with difficulty the shifting slope of the deck. At the sound of Jukes' voice he stood still, facing forward, but made no reply.

"Hallo! That's a heavy one," said Jukes, swaying to meet the long roll till his lowered hand touched the planks. This time the second mate made in his throat a noise of an unfriendly nature.

He was an oldish, shabby little fellow, with bad teeth and no hair on his face. He had been shipped in a hurry in Shanghai, that trip when the second officer brought from home had delayed the ship three hours in port by contriving (in some manner Captain MacWhirr could never understand) to fall overboard into an empty lighter lying alongside, and had to be sent ashore to the hospital with concussion of the brain and a broken limb or two.

Jukes was not discouraged by the unsympathetic sound. "The Chinamen must be having a lovely time of it down there," he said. "It's lucky for them the old girl has the easiest roll of any ship I've even been in. There now! This one wasn't so bad."

"You wait," snarled the second mate.

With his sharp nose, red at the tip, and his thin pinched lips, he always looked as though he were raging inwardly; and he was concise in his speech to the point of rudeness. All his time off duty he spent in his cabin with the door shut, keeping so still in there that he was supposed to fall asleep as soon as he had disappeared; but the man who came in to wake him for his watch on deck would invariably find him with his eyes wide open, flat on his back in the bunk, and glaring irritably from a soiled pillow. He never wrote any letters, did not seem to hope for news from

anywhere; and though he had been heard once to mention West Hartle-
pool, it was with extreme bitterness, and only in connection with the extortionate charges of a boardinghouse. He was one of those men who are
picked up at need in the ports of the world. They are competent enough,
appear hopelessly hard up, show no evidence of any sort of vice, and
carry about them all the signs of manifest failure. They come aboard on
an emergency, care for no ship afloat, live in their own atmosphere of
casual connection amongst their shipmates who know nothing of them,
and make up their minds to leave at inconvenient times. They clear out
with no words of leave-taking in some godforsaken port other men would
fear to be stranded in, and go ashore in company of a shabby sea chest,
corded like a treasure box, and with an air of shaking the ship's dust off
their feet.

"You wait," he repeated, balanced in great swings with his back to
Jukes, motionless and implacable.

"Do you mean to say we are going to catch it hot?" asked Jukes with
boyish interest.

"Say? . . . I say nothing. You don't catch me," snapped the little
second mate, with a mixture of pride, scorn, and cunning, as if Jukes'
question had been a trap cleverly detected. "Oh, no! None of you here
shall make a fool of me if I know it," he mumbled to himself.

Jukes reflected rapidly that this second mate was a mean little beast,
and in his heart he wished poor Jack Allen had never smashed himself up
in the coal lighter. The far-off blackness ahead of the ship was like another night seen through the starry night of the earth—the starless night
of the immensities beyond the created universe, revealed in its appalling
stillness through a low fissure in the glittering sphere of which the earth
is the kernel.

"Whatever there might be about," said Jukes, "we are steaming straight
into it."

"*You've* said it," caught up the second mate, always with his back to
Jukes. "You've said it, mind—not I."

"Oh, go to Jericho!" said Jukes, frankly; and the other emitted a triumphant little chuckle.

"You've said it," he repeated.

"And what of that?"

"I've known some real good men get into trouble with their skippers
for saying a sight less," answered the second mate feverishly. "Oh, no!
You don't catch me."

"You seem deucedly anxious not to give yourself away," said Jukes, completely soured by such absurdity. "I wouldn't be afraid to say what I think."

"Aye, to me! That's no great trick. I am nobody, and well I know it."

The ship, after a pause of comparative steadiness, started upon a series of rolls, one worse than the other, and for a time Jukes, preserving his equilibrium, was too busy to open his mouth. As soon as the violent swinging had quieted down somewhat, he said: "This is a bit too much of a good thing. Whether anything is coming or not I think she ought to be put head on to that swell. The old man is just gone in to lie down. Hang me if I don't speak to him."

But when he opened the door of the chartroom he saw his captain reading a book. Captain MacWhirr was not lying down: he was standing up with one hand grasping the edge of the bookshelf and the other holding open before his face a thick volume. The lamp wriggled in the gimbals,[1] the loosened books toppled from side to side on the shelf, the long barometer swung in jerky circles, the table altered its slant every moment. In the midst of all this stir and movement Captain MacWhirr, holding on, showed his eyes above the upper edge, and asked, "What's the matter?"

"Swell getting worse, sir."

"Noticed that in here," muttered Captain MacWhirr. "Anything wrong?"

Jukes, inwardly disconcerted by the seriousness of the eyes looking at him over the top of the book, produced an embarrassed grin.

"Rolling like old boots," he said, sheepishly.

"Aye! Very heavy—very heavy. What do you want?"

At this Jukes lost his footing and began to flounder.

"I was thinking of our passengers," he said, in the manner of a man clutching at a straw.

"Passengers?" wondered the Captain, gravely. "What passengers?"

"Why, the Chinamen, sir," explained Jukes, very sick of this conversation.

"The Chinamen! Why don't you speak plainly? Couldn't tell what you meant. Never heard a lot of coolies spoken of as passengers before. Passengers, indeed! What's come to you?"

Captain MacWhirr, closing the book on his forefinger, lowered his arm and looked completely mystified. "Why are you thinking of the Chinamen, Mr. Jukes?" he inquired.

---

[1] *gimbals:* moving holders which allow a lamp to remain upright when the ship tilts.

Jukes took a plunge, like a man driven to it. "She's rolling her decks full of water, sir. Thought you might put her head on perhaps—for a while. Till this goes down a bit—very soon, I dare say. Head to the eastward. I never knew a ship roll like this."

He held on in the doorway, and Captain MacWhirr, feeling his grip on the shelf inadequate, made up his mind to let go in a hurry, and fell heavily on the couch.

"Head to the eastward?" he said, struggling to sit up. "That's more than four points off her course."

"Yes, sir. Fifty degrees. . . . Would just bring her head far enough round to meet this. . . ."

Captain MacWhirr was now sitting up. He had not dropped the book, and he had not lost his place.

"To the eastward?" he repeated, with dawning astonishment. "To the . . . Where do you think we are bound to? You want me to haul a full-powered steamship four points off her course to make the Chinamen comfortable! Now, I've heard more than enough of mad things done in the world—but this. . . . If I didn't know you, Jukes, I would think you were in liquor. Steer four points off. . . . And what afterwards? Steer four points over the other way, I suppose, to make the course good. What put it into your head that I would start to tack a steamer as if she were a sailing ship?"

"Jolly good thing she isn't," threw in Jukes, with bitter readiness. "She would have rolled every blessed stick out of her this afternoon."

"Aye! And you just would have had to stand and see them go," said Captain MacWhirr, showing a certain animation. "It's a dead calm, isn't it?"

"It is, sir. But there's something out of the common coming, for sure."

"Maybe. I suppose you have a notion I should be getting out of the way of that dirt," said Captain MacWhirr, speaking with the utmost simplicity of manner and tone, and fixing the oilcloth on the floor with a heavy stare. Thus he noticed neither Jukes' discomfiture nor the mixture of vexation and astonished respect on his face.

"Now, here's this book," he continued with deliberation, slapping his thigh with the closed volume. "I've been reading the chapter on the storms there."

This was true. He had been reading the chapter on the storms. When he had entered the chartroom, it was with no intention of taking the book down. Some influence in the air—the same influence, probably, that caused the steward to bring without orders the Captain's sea boots and oilskin coat up to the chartroom—had as it were guided his hand to the shelf; and without taking the time to sit down he had waded with a conscious effort into the terminology of the subject. He lost himself amongst advancing semicircles, left- and right-hand quadrants, the curves of the tracks, the probable bearing of the center, the shifts of wind and the readings of barometer. He tried to bring all these things into a definite relation to himself, and ended by becoming contemptuously angry with such a lot of words and with so much advice, all head work and supposition, without a glimmer of certitude.

"It's the maddest thing, Jukes," he said. "If a fellow was to believe all that's in there, he would be running most of his time all over the sea trying to get behind the weather."

Again he slapped his leg with the book; and Jukes opened his mouth, but said nothing.

"Running to get behind the weather! Do you understand that, Mr. Jukes? It's the maddest thing!" ejaculated Captain MacWhirr, with pauses, gazing at the floor profoundly. "You would think an old woman had been writing this. It passes me. If that thing means anything useful, then it means that I should at once alter the course away, away to the devil somewhere, and come booming down on Fu-chau from the northward at the tail of this dirty weather that's supposed to be knocking about in our way. From the north! Do you understand, Mr. Jukes? Three hundred extra miles to the distance, and a pretty coal bill to show. I couldn't bring myself to do that if every word in there was gospel truth, Mr. Jukes. Don't you expect me. . . ."

And Jukes, silent, marveled at this display of feeling and loquacity.

"But the truth is that you don't know if the fellow is right, anyhow. How can you tell what a gale is made of till you get it? He isn't aboard here, is he? Very well. Here he says that the center of them things bears eight points off the wind; but we haven't got any wind, for all the barometer falling. Where's his center now?"

"We will get the wind presently," mumbled Jukes.

"Let it come, then," said Captain MacWhirr, with dignified indignation. "It's only to let you see, Mr. Jukes, that you don't find everything in books. All these rules for dodging breezes and circumventing the winds of heaven, Mr. Jukes, seem to me the maddest thing, when you come to look at it sensibly."

He raised his eyes, saw Jukes gazing at him dubiously, and tried to illustrate his meaning.

"About as queer as your extraordinary notion of dodging the ship head to sea, for I don't know how long, to make the Chinamen comfortable; whereas all we've got to do is to take them to Fu-chau, being timed to get there before noon on Friday. If the weather delays me—very well. There's your logbook to talk straight about the weather. But suppose I went swinging off my course and came in two days late, and they asked me: 'Where have you been all that time, Captain?' What could I say to that? 'Went around to dodge the bad weather,' I would say. 'It must've been bad,' they would say. 'Don't know,' I would have to say; 'I've dodged clear of it.' See that, Jukes? I have been thinking it all out this afternoon."

He looked up again in his unseeing, unimaginative way. No one had ever heard him say so much at one time. Jukes, with his arms open in the doorway, was like a man invited to behold a miracle. Unbounded wonder was the intellectual meaning of his eye, while incredulity was seated in his whole countenance.

"A gale is a gale, Mr. Jukes," resumed the Captain, "and a full-powered steamship has got to face it. There's just so much dirty weather knocking about the world, and the proper thing is to go through it with none of what old Captain Wilson of the *Melita* calls 'storm strategy.' The other day ashore I heard him hold forth about it to a lot of shipmasters who came in and sat at a table next to mine. It seemed to me the greatest nonsense. He was telling them how he outmaneuvered, I think he said, a terrific gale, so that it never came nearer than fifty miles to him. A neat piece of headwork he called it. How he knew there was a terrific gale fifty miles off beats me altogether. It was like listening to a crazy man. I would have thought Captain Wilson was old enough to know better."

Captain MacWhirr ceased for a moment, then said, "It's your watch below, Mr. Jukes?"

Jukes came to himself with a start. "Yes, sir."

"Leave orders to call me at the slightest change," said the Captain. He reached up to put the book away, and tucked his legs upon the couch. "Shut the door so that it don't fly open, will you? I can't stand a door banging. They've put a lot of rubbishy locks into this ship, I must say."

Captain MacWhirr closed his eyes.

He did so to rest himself. He was tired, and he experienced that state of mental vacuity which comes at the end of an exhaustive discussion that has liberated some belief matured in the course of meditative years. He had indeed been making his confession of faith, had he only known it; and its effect was to make Jukes, on the other side of the door, stand scratching his head for a good while.

Captain MacWhirr opened his eyes.

He thought he must have been asleep. What was that loud noise? Wind? Why had he not been called? The lamp wriggled in its gimbals, the barometer swung in circles, the table altered its slant every moment; a pair of limp sea boots with collapsed tops went sliding past the couch. He put out his hand instantly, and captured one.

Jukes' face appeared in a crack of the door: only his face, very red, with staring eyes. The flame of the lamp leaped, a piece of paper flew up, a rush of air enveloped Captain MacWhirr. Beginning to draw on the boot, he directed an expectant gaze at Jukes' swollen, excited features.

"Came on like this," shouted Jukes, "five minutes ago . . . all of a sudden."

The head disappeared with a bang, and a heavy splash and patter of drops swept past the closed door as if a pailful of melted lead had been flung against the house. A whistling could be heard now upon the deep vibrating noise outside. The stuffy chartroom seemed as full of drafts as a shed. Captain MacWhirr collared the other sea boot on its violent passage along the floor. He was not flustered, but he could not find at once the opening for inserting his foot. The shoes he had flung off were scurrying from end to end of the cabin, gamboling playfully over each other like puppies. As soon as he stood up he kicked at them viciously, but without effect.

He threw himself into the attitude of a lunging fencer, to reach after his oilskin coat; and afterwards he staggered all over the confined space while he jerked himself into it. Very grave, straddling his legs far apart, and stretching his neck, he started to tie deliberately the strings of his sou'-wester[1] under his chin, with thick fingers that trembled slightly. He went through all the movements of a woman putting on her bonnet before a glass, with a strained, listening attention, as though he had expected every moment to hear the shout of his name in the confused clamor that had suddenly beset his ship. Its increase filled his ears while he was getting ready to go out and confront whatever it might mean. It was tumultuous and very loud—made up of the rush of the wind, the crashes of the sea, with that prolonged deep vibration of the air, like the roll of an immense and remote drum beating the charge of the gale.

He stood for a moment in the light of the lamp, thick, clumsy, shapeless in his panoply of combat, vigilant and red-faced.

"There's a lot of weight in this," he muttered.

---

[1] *sou'wester:* a canvas hat with a flap at the back.

As soon as he attempted to open the door the wind caught it. Clinging to the handle, he was dragged out over the doorstep, and at once found himself engaged with the wind in a sort of personal scuffle whose object was the shutting of that door. At the last moment a tongue of air scurried in and licked out the flame of the lamp.

Ahead of the ship he perceived a great darkness lying upon a multitude of white flashes; on the starboard beam a few amazing stars drooped, dim and fitful, above an immense waste of broken seas, as if seen through a mad drift of smoke.

On the bridge a knot of men, indistinct and toiling, were making great efforts in the light of the wheelhouse windows that shone mistily on their heads and backs. Suddenly darkness closed upon one pane, then on another. The voices of the lost group reached him after the manner of men's voices in a gale, in shreds and fragments of forlorn shouting snatched past the ear. All at once Jukes appeared at his side, yelling, with his head down.

"Watch—put in—wheelhouse shutters—glass—afraid—blow in."

Jukes heard his commander upbraiding.

"This—come—anything—warning—call me."

He tried to explain, with the uproar pressing on his lips.

"Light air—remained—bridge—sudden—northeast—could turn—thought—you—sure—hear."

They had gained the shelter of the weather cloth, and could converse with raised voices, as people quarrel.

"I got the hands along to cover up all the ventilators. Good job I had remained on deck. I didn't think you would be asleep, and so . . . What did you say, sir? What?"

"Nothing," cried Captain MacWhirr. "I said—all right."

"By all the powers! We've got it this time," observed Jukes in a howl.

"You haven't altered her course?" inquired Captain MacWhirr, straining his voice.

"No, sir. Certainly not. Wind came out right ahead. And here comes the head sea."

A plunge of the ship ended in a shock as if she had landed her forefoot upon something solid. After a moment of stillness a lofty flight of sprays drove hard with the wind upon their faces.

"Keep her at it as long as we can," shouted Captain MacWhirr.

Before Jukes had squeezed the salt water out of his eyes all the stars had disappeared.

CHAPTER THREE

Jukes was as ready a man as any half dozen young mates that may be caught casting a net upon the waters; and though he had been somewhat taken aback by the startling viciousness of the first squall, he had pulled himself together on the instant, had called out the hands and had rushed them along to secure such openings about the deck as had not been already battened down earlier in the evening. Shouting in his fresh, stentorian voice, "Jump, boys, and bear a hand!" he led in the work, telling himself the while that he had "just expected this."

But at the same time he was growing aware that this was rather more than he had expected. From the first stir of the air felt on his cheek the gale seemed to take upon itself the accumulated impetus of an avalanche. Heavy sprays enveloped the Nan-Shan from stem to stern, and instantly in the midst of her regular rolling she began to jerk and plunge as though she had gone mad with fright.

Jukes thought, "This is no joke." While he was exchanging explanatory yells with his captain, a sudden lowering of the darkness came upon the night, falling before their vision like something palpable. It was as if the masked lights of the world had been turned down. Jukes was uncritically glad to have his captain at hand. It relieved him as though that man had, by simply coming on deck, taken most of the gale's weight upon his shoulders. Such is the prestige, the privilege, and the burden of command.

Captain MacWhirr could expect no relief of that sort from anyone on earth. Such is the loneliness of command. He was trying to see, with that watchful manner of a seaman who stares into the wind's eye as if into the eye of an adversary, to penetrate the hidden intention and guess the aim and force of the thrust. The strong wind swept at him out of a vast obscurity; he felt under his feet the uneasiness of his ship, and he could not even discern the shadow of her shape. He wished it were not so; and very still he waited, feeling stricken by a blind man's helplessness.

To be silent was natural to him, dark or shine. Jukes, at his elbow, made himself heard yelling cheerily in the gusts, "We must have got the worst of it at once, sir." A faint burst of lightning quivered all round, as if flashed into a cavern—into a black and secret chamber of the sea, with a floor of foaming crests.

It unveiled for a sinister, fluttering moment a ragged mass of clouds hanging low, the lurch of the long outlines of the ship, the black figures of men caught on the bridge, heads forward, as if petrified in the act of butting. The darkness palpitated down upon all this, and then the real thing came at last.

It was something formidable and swift, like the sudden smashing of a vial of wrath. It seemed to explode all round the ship with an overpowering concussion and a rush of great waters, as if an immense dam had been blown up to windward. In an instant the men lost touch of each other. This is the disintegrating power of a great wind: it isolates one from one's kind. An earthquake, a landslip, an avalanche, overtake a man incidentally, as it were—without passion. A furious gale attacks him like a personal enemy, tries to grasp his limbs, fastens upon his mind, seeks to rout his very spirit out of him.

Jukes was driven away from his commander. He fancied himself whirled a great distance through the air. Everything disappeared—even, for a moment, his power of thinking; but his hand had found one of the rail stanchions. His distress was by no means alleviated by an inclination to disbelieve the reality of this experience. Though young, he had seen some bad weather, and had never doubted his ability to imagine the worst; but this was so much beyond his powers of fancy that it appeared incompatible with the existence of any ship whatever. He would have been incredulous about himself in the same way, perhaps, had he not been so harassed by the necessity of exerting a wrestling effort against a force trying to tear him away from his hold. Moreover, the conviction of not being utterly destroyed returned to him through the sensations of being half-drowned, bestially shaken, and partly choked.

It seemed to him he remained there precariously alone with the stanchion for a long, long time. The rain poured on him, flowed, drove in sheets. He breathed in gasps; and sometimes the water he swallowed was fresh and sometimes it was salt. For the most part he kept his eyes shut tight, as if suspecting his sight might be destroyed in the immense flurry of the elements. When he ventured to blink hastily, he derived some moral support from the green gleam of the starboard light shining feebly upon the flight of rain and sprays. He was actually looking at it when its ray fell upon the uprearing sea which put it out. He saw the head of the wave topple over, adding the mite of its crash to the tremendous uproar raging around him, and almost at the same instant the stanchion was wrenched away from his embracing arms. After a crushing thump on his back he found himself suddenly afloat and borne upwards. His first irresistible notion was that the whole China Sea had climbed on the bridge. Then, more sanely, he concluded himself gone overboard. All the time he was being tossed, flung, and rolled in great volumes of water, he kept on repeating mentally, with the utmost precipitation, the words: "My God! My God! My God! My God!"

All at once, in a revolt of misery and despair, he formed the crazy resolution to get out of that. And he began to thresh about with his arms and legs. But as soon as he commenced his wretched struggles he discovered that he had become somehow mixed up with a face, an oilskin coat, somebody's boots. He clawed ferociously all these things in turn, lost them, found them again, lost them once more, and finally was himself caught in the firm clasp of a pair of stout arms. He returned the embrace closely round a thick solid body. He had found his captain.

They tumbled over and over, tightening their hug. Suddenly the water let them down with a brutal bang; and stranded against the side of the wheelhouse, out of breath and bruised, they were left to stagger up in the wind and hold on where they could.

Jukes came out of it rather horrified, as though he had escaped some unparalleled outrage directed at his feelings. It weakened his faith in himself. He started shouting aimlessly to the man he could feel near him in that fiendish blackness, "Is it you, sir? Is it you, sir?" till his temples seemed ready to burst. And he heard in answer a voice, as if crying far away, as if screaming to him fretfully from a very great distance, the one word "Yes!" Other seas swept again over the bridge. He received them defenselessly right over his bare head, with both his hands engaged in holding.

The motion of the ship was extravagant. Her lurches had an appalling helplessness: she pitched as if taking a header into a void, and seemed to find a wall to hit every time. When she rolled she fell on her side headlong, and she would be righted back by such a demolishing blow that Jukes felt her reeling as a clubbed man reels before he collapses. The gale howled and scuffled about gigantically in the darkness, as though the entire world were one black gully. At certain moments the air streamed against the ship as if sucked through a tunnel with a concentrated solid force of impact that seemed to lift her clean out of the water and keep her up for an instant with only a quiver running through her from end to end. And then she would begin her tumbling again as if dropped back into a boiling caldron. Jukes tried hard to compose his mind and judge things coolly.

The sea, flattened down in the heavier gusts, would uprise and overwhelm both ends of the *Nan-Shan* in snowy rushes of foam, expanding wide, beyond both rails, into the night. And on this dazzling sheet, spread under the blackness of the clouds and emitting a bluish glow, Captain MacWhirr could catch a desolate glimpse of a few tiny specks black as ebony, the tops of the hatches, the battened companions, the heads of the covered winches, the foot of a mast. This was all he could see of his ship. Her middle structure, covered by the bridge which bore him, his mate, the closed wheelhouse where a man was steering shut up with the fear of being swept overboard together with the whole thing in one great crash— her middle structure was like a half-tide rock awash upon a coast. It was like an outlying rock with the water boiling up, streaming over, pouring off, beating round—like a rock in the surf to which shipwrecked people cling before they let go—only it rose, it sank, it rolled continuously, without respite and rest, like a rock that should have miraculously struck adrift from a coast and gone wallowing upon the sea.

The *Nan-Shan* was being looted by the storm with a senseless, destructive fury: trysails torn out of the extra gaskets, double-lashed awnings blown away, bridge swept clean, weather cloths burst, rails twisted, light screens smashed—and two of the boats had gone already. They had gone unheard and unseen, melting, as it were, in the shock and smother of the wave. It was only later, when, upon the white flash of another high sea hurling itself amidships, Jukes had a vision of two pairs of davits[1] leaping black and empty out of the solid blackness, with one overhauled fall [2] flying and an iron-bound block[3] capering in the air, that he became aware of what had happened within about three yards of his back.

He poked his head forward, groping for the ear of his commander. His lips touched it—big, fleshy, very wet. He cried in an agitated tone, "Our boats are going now, sir."

And again he heard that voice, forced and ringing feebly, but with a penetrating effect of quietness in the enormous discord of noises, as if sent out from some remote spot of peace beyond the black wastes of the gale; again he heard a man's voice—the frail and indomitable sound that can be made to carry an infinity of thought, resolution and purpose, that shall be pronouncing confident words on the last day, when heavens fall, and justice is done—again he heard it, and it was crying to him, as if from very, very far—"All right."

He thought he had not managed to make himself understood. "Our boats—I say boats—the boats, sir! Two gone!"

---

[1] *davits:* the stationary cranes on which ships' boats are hoisted and held.
[2] *fall:* hoisting tackle of the davit.
[3] *block:* a heavy pulley; part of the davit tackle

The same voice, within a foot of him and yet so remote, yelled sensibly, "Can't be helped."

Captain MacWhirr had never turned his face, but Jukes caught some more words on the wind.

"What can—expect—when hammering through—such——. Bound to leave—something behind—stands to reason."

Watchfully Jukes listened for more. No more came. This was all Captain MacWhirr had to say; and Jukes could picture to himself rather than see the broad squat back before him. An impenetrable obscurity pressed down upon the ghostly glimmers of the sea. A dull conviction seized upon Jukes that there was nothing to be done.

If the steering gear did not give way, if the immense volumes of water did not burst the deck in or smash one of the hatches, if the engines did not give up, if way could be kept on the ship against this terrific wind, and she did not bury herself in one of these awful seas, of whose white crests alone, topping high above her bows, he could now and then get a sickening glimpse—then there was a chance of her coming out of it. Something within him seemed to turn over, bringing uppermost the feeling that the *Nan-Shan* was lost.

"She's done for," he said to himself, with a surprising mental agitation, as though he had discovered an unexpected meaning in this thought. One of these things was bound to happen. Nothing could be prevented now, and nothing could be remedied. The men on board did not count, and the ship could not last. This weather was too impossible.

Jukes felt an arm thrown heavily over his shoulders; and to this overture he responded with great intelligence by catching hold of his captain round the waist.

They stood clasped thus in the blind night, bracing each other against the wind, cheek to cheek and lip to ear, in the manner of two hulks lashed stem to stern together.

And Jukes heard the voice of his commander hardly any louder than before, but nearer, as though, starting to march athwart[1] the prodigious rush of the hurricane, it had approached him, bearing that strange effect of quietness like the serene glow of a halo.

"D'ye know where the hands got to?" it asked, vigorous and evanescent at the same time, overcoming the strength of the wind, and swept away from Jukes instantly.

Jukes didn't know. They were all on the bridge when the real force of the hurricane struck the ship. He had no idea where they had crawled to.

---

[1] *athwart:* in opposition to.

Under the circumstances they were nowhere, for all the use that could be made of them. Somehow the Captain's wish to know distressed Jukes.

"Want the hands, sir?" he cried, apprehensively.

"Ought to know," asserted Captain MacWhirr. "Hold hard."

They held hard. An outburst of unchained fury, a vicious rush of the wind absolutely steadied the ship; she rocked only, quick and light like a child's cradle, for a terrific moment of suspense, while the whole atmosphere, as it seemed, streamed furiously past her, roaring away from the tenebrous[1] earth.

It suffocated them, and with eyes shut they tightened their grasp. What from the magnitude of the shock might have been a column of water running upright in the dark, butted against the ship, broke short, and fell on her bridge, crushingly, from on high, with a dead burying weight.

A flying fragment of that collapse, a mere splash, enveloped them in one swirl from their feet over their heads, filling violently their ears, mouths and nostrils with salt water. It knocked out their legs, wrenched in haste at their arms, seethed away swiftly under their chins; and opening their eyes they saw the piled-up masses of foam dashing to and fro amongst what looked like the fragments of a ship. She had given way as if driven straight in. Their panting hearts yielded, too, before the tremendous blow; and all at once she sprang up again to her desperate plunging, as if trying to scramble out from under the ruins.

The seas in the dark seemed to rush from all sides to keep her back where she might perish. There was hate in the way she was handled, and a ferocity in the blows that fell. She was like a living creature thrown to the rage of a mob: hustled terribly, struck at, borne up, flung down, leaped upon. Captain MacWhirr and Jukes kept hold of each other, deafened by the noise, gagged by the wind; and the great physical tumult beating about their bodies brought, like an unbridled display of passion, a profound trouble to their souls. One of those wild and appalling shrieks that are heard at times passing mysteriously overhead in the steady roar of a hurricane, swooped, as if borne on wings, upon the ship, and Jukes tried to outscream it.

"Will she live through this?"

The cry was wrenched out of his breast. It was as unintentional as the birth of a thought in the head, and he heard nothing of it himself. It all became extinct at once—thought, intention, effort—and of his cry the inaudible vibration added to the tempest waves of the air.

He expected nothing from it. Nothing at all. For indeed what answer

---

[1] *tenebrous:* (tĕn'ē·brŭs): dark, gloomy.

could be made? But after a while he heard with amazement the frail and resisting voice in his ear, the dwarf sound, unconquered in the giant tumult.

"She may!"

It was a dull yell, more difficult to seize than a whisper. And presently the voice returned again, half submerged in the vast crashes, like a ship battling against the waves of an ocean.

"Let's hope so!" it cried—small, lonely and unmoved, a stranger to the visions of hope or fear; and it flickered into disconnected words: "Ship . . . This . . . Never—— Anyhow . . . for the best." Jukes gave it up.

Then, as if it had come suddenly upon the one thing fit to withstand the power of a storm, it seemed to gain force and firmness for the last broken shouts:

"Keep on hammering . . . builders . . . good men. . . . And chance it . . . engines. . . . Rout . . . good man."

Captain MacWhirr removed his arm from Jukes' shoulders, and thereby ceased to exist for his mate, so dark it was; Jukes, after a tense stiffening of every muscle, would let himself go limp all over. The gnawing of profound discomfort existed side by side with an incredible disposition to somnolence,[1] as though he had been buffeted and worried into drowsiness. The wind would get hold of his head and try to shake it off his shoulders; his clothes, full of water, were as heavy as lead, cold and dripping like an armor of melting ice: he shivered—it lasted a long time; and with his hands closed hard on his hold, he was letting himself sink slowly into the depths of bodily misery. His mind became concentrated upon himself in an aimless, idle way, and when something pushed lightly at the back of his knees he nearly, as the saying is, jumped out of his skin.

In the start forward he bumped the back of Captain MacWhirr who didn't move; and then a hand gripped his thigh. A lull had come, a menacing lull of the wind, the holding of a stormy breath—and he felt himself pawed all over. It was the boatswain. Jukes recognized these hands, so thick and enormous that they seemed to belong to some new species of man.

The boatswain had arrived on the bridge, crawling on all fours against the wind, and had found the chief mate's legs with the top of his head. Immediately he crouched and began to explore Jukes' person upwards with prudent, apologetic touches, as became an inferior.

He was an ill-favored, undersized, gruff sailor of fifty, coarsely hairy,

---

[1] *somnolence:* sleepiness.

short-legged, long-armed, resembling an elderly ape. His strength was immense; and in his great lumpy paws, bulging like brown boxing gloves on the end of furry forearms, the heaviest objects were handled like playthings. Apart from the grizzled pelt on his chest, the menacing demeanor and the hoarse voice, he had none of the classical attributes of his rating. His good nature almost amounted to imbecility: the men did what they liked with him, and he had not an ounce of initiative in his character, which was easy-going and talkative. For these reasons Jukes disliked him; but Captain MacWhirr, to Jukes' scornful disgust, seemed to regard him as a first-rate petty officer.

He pulled himself up by Jukes' coat, taking that liberty with the greatest moderation, and only so far as it was forced upon him by the hurricane.

"What is it, bos'un, what is it?" yelled Jukes, impatiently. What could that fraud of a bos'un want on the bridge? The typhoon had got on Jukes' nerves. The husky bellowings of the other, though unintelligible, seemed to suggest a state of lively satisfaction. There could be no mistake. The old fool was pleased with something.

The boatswain's other hand had found some other body, for in a changed tone he began to inquire: "Is it you, sir? Is it you, sir?" The wind strangled his howls.

"Yes!" cried Captain MacWhirr.

CHAPTER FOUR

ALL that the boatswain, out of a superabundance of yells, could make clear to Captain MacWhirr was the bizarre intelligence that "All them Chinamen in the fore 'tween deck have fetched away, sir."

Jukes to leeward [1] could hear these two shouting within six inches of his face, as you may hear on a still night half a mile away two men conversing across a field. He heard Captain MacWhirr's exasperated "What? What?" and the strained pitch of the other's hoarseness. "In a lump . . . seen them myself. . . . Awful sight, sir . . . thought . . . tell you."

Jukes remained indifferent, as if rendered irresponsible by the force of the hurricane, which made the very thought of action utterly vain. Besides, being very young, he had found the occupation of keeping his

---

[1] *leeward:* the place farthest from the point from which the wind is blowing. (The opposite of *windward*.)

heart completely steeled against the worst so engrossing that he had come to feel an overpowering dislike towards any other form of activity whatever. He was not scared; he knew this because, firmly believing he would never see another sunrise, he remained calm in that belief.

These are the moments of do-nothing heroics to which even good men surrender at times. Many officers of ships can no doubt recall a case in their experience when just such a trance of confounded stoicism[1] would come all at once over a whole ship's company. Jukes, however, had no wide experience of men or storms. He conceived himself to be calm—inexorably calm; but as a matter of fact he was daunted; not abjectly, but only so far as a decent man may, without becoming loathsome to himself.

It was rather like a forced-on numbness of spirit. The long, long stress of a gale does it; the suspense of the interminably culminating catastrophe; and there is a bodily fatigue in the mere holding on to existence within the excessive tumult; a searching and insidious fatigue that penetrates deep into a man's breast to cast down and sadden his heart, which is incorrigible, and of all the gifts of the earth—even before life itself—aspires to peace.

Jukes was benumbed much more than he supposed. He held on—very wet, very cold, stiff in every limb; and in a momentary hallucination of swift visions (it is said that a drowning man thus reviews all his life) he beheld all sorts of memories altogether unconnected with his present situation. He remembered his father, for instance: a worthy businessman, who at an unfortunate crisis in his affairs went quietly to bed and died forthwith in a state of resignation. Jukes did not recall these circumstances, of course, but remaining otherwise unconcerned he seemed to see distinctly the poor man's face; a certain game of nap[2] played when quite a boy in Table Bay on board a ship, since lost with all hands; the thick eyebrows of his first skipper; and without any emotion, as he might years ago have walked listlessly into her room and found her sitting there with a book, he remembered his mother—dead, too, now—the resolute woman, left badly off, who had been very firm in his bringing up.

It could not have lasted more than a second, perhaps not so much. A heavy arm had fallen about his shoulders; Captain MacWhirr's voice was speaking his name into his ear.

"Jukes! Jukes!"

He detected the tone of deep concern. The wind had thrown its weight

---

[1] *stoicism:* the quality of being indifferent to pleasure or pain, good or ill, which was characteristic of the ancient Greek *Stoic* philosophers.

[2] *nap:* a card game popular among sailors.

on the ship, trying to pin her down amongst the seas. They made a clean breach over her, as over a deep-swimming log; and the gathered weight of crashes menaced monstrously from afar. The breakers flung out of the night with a ghostly light on their crests—the light of sea foam that in a ferocious, boiling-up pale flash showed upon the slender body of the ship the toppling rush, the downfall, and the seething mad scurry of each wave. Never for a moment could she shake herself clear of the water; Jukes, rigid, perceived in her motion the ominous sign of haphazard floundering. She was no longer struggling intelligently. It was the beginning of the end; and the note of busy concern in Captain MacWhirr's voice sickened him like an exhibition of blind and pernicious folly.

The spell of the storm had fallen upon Jukes. He was penetrated by it, absorbed by it; he was rooted in it with a rigor of dumb attention. Captain MacWhirr persisted in his cries, but the wind got between them like a solid wedge. He hung round Jukes' neck as heavy as a millstone, and suddenly the sides of their heads knocked together.

"Jukes! Mr. Jukes, I say!"

He had to answer that voice that would not be silenced. He answered in the customary manner: ". . . Yes, sir."

And directly, his heart, corrupted by the storm that breeds a craving for peace, rebelled against the tyranny of training and command.

Captain MacWhirr had his mate's head fixed firm in the crook of his elbow, and pressed it to his yelling lips mysteriously. Sometimes Jukes would break in, admonishing hastily: "Look out, sir!" or Captain Mac-Whirr would bawl an earnest exhortation to "Hold hard, there!" and the whole black universe seemed to reel together with the ship. They paused. She floated yet. And Captain MacWhirr would resume his shouts. ". . . Says . . . whole lot . . . fetched away. . . . Ought to see . . . what's the matter."

Directly the full force of the hurricane had struck the ship, every part of her deck became untenable; and the sailors, dazed and dismayed, took shelter in the port alleyway under the bridge. It had a door aft, which they shut; it was very black, cold, and dismal. At each heavy fling of the ship they would groan all together in the dark, and tons of water could be heard scuttling about as if trying to get at them from above. The boat-swain had been keeping up a gruff talk, but a more unreasonable lot of men, he said afterwards, he had never been with. They were snug enough there, out of harm's way, and not wanted to do anything, either; and yet they did nothing but grumble and complain peevishly like so many sick kids. Finally, one of them said that if there had been at least some light to see each other's noses by, it wouldn't be so bad. It was making him crazy, he declared, to lie there in the dark waiting for the blamed hooker to sink.

"Why don't you step outside, then, and be done with it at once?" the boatswain turned on him.

This called up a shout of execration. The boatswain found himself overwhelmed with reproaches of all sorts. They seemed to take it ill that a lamp was not instantly created for them out of nothing. They would whine after a light to get drowned by—anyhow! And though the unreason of their revilings was patent—since no one could hope to reach the lamp room, which was forward—he became greatly distressed. He did not think it was decent of them to be nagging at him like this. He told them so, and was met by general contumely. He sought refuge, therefore, in an embittered silence. At the same time their grumbling and sighing and muttering worried him greatly, but by-and-by it occurred to him that there were six globe lamps hung in the 'tween deck, and that there could be no harm in depriving the coolies of one of them.

The *Nan-Shan* had an athwartship[1] coal bunker, which, being at times used as cargo space, communicated by an iron door with the fore 'tween deck. It was empty then, and its manhole was the foremost one in the alleyway. The boatswain could get in, therefore, without coming out on deck at all; but to his great surprise he found he could induce no one to help him in taking off the manhole cover. He groped for it all the same, but one of the crew lying in his way refused to budge.

"Why, I only want to get you that blamed light you are crying for," he expostulated, almost pitifully.

Somebody told him to go and put his head in a bag. He regretted he could not recognize the voice, and that it was too dark to see; otherwise, as he said, he would have put a head on *that* son of a sea cook, anyway, sink or swim. Nevertheless, he had made up his mind to show them he could get a light, if he were to die for it.

Through the violence of the ship's rolling, every movement was dangerous. To be lying down seemed labor enough. He nearly broke his neck dropping into the bunker. He fell on his back, and was sent shooting helplessly from side to side in the dangerous company of a heavy iron bar—a coal trimmer's slice probably—left down there by somebody. This thing made him as nervous as though it had been a wild beast. He could not see it, the inside of the bunker coated with coal dust being perfectly and impenetrably black; but he heard it sliding and clattering,

---

[1] *athwartship:* running from one side of the ship to the other.

and striking here and there, always in the neighborhood of his head. It seemed to make an extraordinary noise, too—to give heavy thumps as though it had been as big as a bridge girder. This was remarkable enough for him to notice while he was flung from port to starboard and back again, and clawing desperately the smooth sides of the bunker in the endeavor to stop himself. The door into the 'tween deck not fitting quite true, he saw a thread of dim light at the bottom.

Being a sailor, and a still active man, he did not want much of a chance to regain his feet; and as luck would have it, in scrambling up he put his hand on the iron slice, picking it up as he rose. Otherwise he would have been afraid of the thing breaking his legs, or at least knocking them down again. At first he stood still. He felt unsafe in this darkness that seemed to make the ship's motion unfamiliar, unforeseen, and difficult to counteract. He felt so much shaken for a moment that he dared not move for fear of "taking charge again." He had no mind to get battered to pieces in that bunker.

He had struck his head twice; he was dazed a little. He seemed to hear yet so plainly the clatter and bangs of the iron slice flying about his ears that he tightened his grip to prove to himself he had it there safely in his hand. He was vaguely amazed at the plainness with which down there he could hear the gale raging. Its howls and shrieks seemed to take on, in the emptiness of the bunker, something of the human character, of human rage and pain—being not vast but infinitely poignant. And there were, with every roll, thumps, too—profound, ponderous thumps, as if a bulky object of five-ton weight or so had got play in the hold. But there was no such thing in the cargo. Something on deck? Impossible. Or alongside? Couldn't be.

He thought all this quickly, clearly, competently, like a seaman, and in the end remained puzzled. This noise, though, came deadened from outside, together with the washing and pouring of water on deck above his head. Was it the wind? Must be. It made down there a row like the shouting of a big lot of crazed men. And he discovered in himself a desire for a light, too—if only to get drowned by—and a nervous anxiety to get out of that bunker as quickly as possible.

He pulled back the bolt: the heavy iron plate turned on its hinges; and it was as though he had opened the door to the sounds of the tempest. A gust of hoarse yelling met him: the air was still; and the rushing of water overhead was covered by a tumult of strangled, throaty shrieks that produced an effect of desperate confusion. He straddled his legs the whole width of the doorway and stretched his neck. And at first he perceived only what he had come to seek: six small yellow flames swinging violently on the great body of the dusk.

It was stayed [1] like the gallery of a mine, with a row of stanchions in the middle, and crossbeams overhead, penetrating into the gloom ahead—indefinitely. And to port there loomed, like the caving in of one of the sides, a bulky mass with a slanting outline. The whole place, with the shadows and the shapes, moved all the time. The boatswain glared: the ship lurched to starboard, and a great howl came from that mass that had the slant of fallen earth.

Pieces of wood whizzed past. Planks, he thought, inexpressibly startled, and flinging back his head. At his feet a man went sliding over, open-eyed, on his back, straining with uplifted arms for nothing: and another came bounding like a detached stone with his head between his legs and his hands clenched. His pigtail whipped in the air; he made a grab at the boatswain's legs, and from his opened hand a bright white disk rolled against the boatswain's foot. He recognized a silver dollar, and yelled at it with astonishment. With a precipitated sound of trampling and shuffling of bare feet, and with guttural cries, the mound of writhing bodies piled up to port detached itself from the ship's side and, sliding, inert and struggling, shifted to starboard, with a dull, brutal thump. The cries ceased. The boatswain heard a long moan through the roar and whistling of the wind; he saw an inextricable confusion of heads and shoulders, naked soles kicking upwards, fists raised, tumbling backs, legs, pigtails, faces.

"Good Lord!" he cried, horrified, and banged-to the iron door upon this vision.

This was what he had come on the bridge to tell. He could not keep it to himself; and on board ship there is only one man to whom it is worth while to unburden yourself. On his passage back the hands in the alleyway swore at him for a fool. Why didn't he bring that lamp? What the devil did the coolies matter to anybody? And when he came out, the extremity of the ship made what went on inside of her appear of little moment.

At first he thought he had left the alleyway in the very moment of her sinking. The bridge ladders had been washed away, but an enormous sea filling the afterdeck floated him up. After that he had to lie on his stomach for some time, holding to a ringbolt, getting his breath now and then, and swallowing salt water. He struggled farther on his hands and knees, too frightened and distracted to turn back. In this way he reached the after-

[1] *stayed*: supported.

part of the wheelhouse. In that comparatively sheltered spot he found the second mate. The boatswain was pleasantly surprised—his impression being that everybody on deck must have been washed away a long time ago. He asked eagerly where the Captain was.

The second mate was lying low, like a malignant little animal under a hedge.

"Captain? Gone overboard, after getting us into this mess." The mate, too, for all he knew or cared. Another fool. Didn't matter. Everybody was going by-and-by.

The boatswain crawled out again into the strength of the wind; not because he much expected to find anybody, he said, but just to get away from "that man." He crawled out as outcasts go to face an inclement world. Hence his great joy at finding Jukes and the Captain. But what was going on in the 'tween deck was to him a minor matter by that time. Besides, it was difficult to make yourself heard. But he managed to convey the idea that the Chinamen had broken adrift together with their boxes, and that he had come up on purpose to report this. As to the hands, they were all right. Then, appeased, he subsided on the deck in a sitting posture, hugging with his arms and legs the stand of the engine-room telegraph[1]—an iron casting as thick as a post. When that went, why, he expected he would go, too. He gave no more thought to the coolies.

Captain MacWhirr had made Jukes understand that he wanted him to go down below—to see.

"What am I to do then, sir?" And the trembling of his whole wet body caused Jukes' voice to sound like bleating.

"See first . . . Bos'un . . . says . . . adrift."

"That bos'un is a confounded fool," howled Jukes, shakily.

The absurdity of the demand made upon him revolted Jukes. He was as unwilling to go as if the moment he had left the deck the ship were sure to sink.

"I must know . . . can't leave. . . ."

"They'll settle, sir."

"Fight . . . bos'un says they fight. . . . Why? Can't have . . . fighting . . . board ship. . . . Much rather keep you here . . . case. . . . I should . . . washed overboard myself. . . . Stop it . . . some

[1] *engine-room telegraph:* a device for sending orders from the bridge to the engine room.

way. You see and tell me . . . through engine-room tube. Don't want you . . . come up here . . . too often. Dangerous . . . moving about . . . deck."

Jukes, held with his head in chancery,[1] had to listen to what seemed horrible suggestions.

"Don't want . . . you get lost . . . so long . . . ship isn't. . . . Rout . . . Good man . . . Ship . . . may . . . through this . . . all right yet."

All at once Jukes understood he would have to go.

"Do you think she may?" he screamed.

But the wind devoured the reply, out of which Jukes heard only the one word, pronounced with great energy ". . . Always. . . ."

Captain MacWhirr released Jukes, and bending over the boatswain, yelled, "Get back with the mate." Jukes only knew that the arm was gone off his shoulders. He was dismissed with his orders—to do what? He was exasperated into letting go his hold carelessly, and on the instant was blown away. It seemed to him that nothing could stop him from being blown right over the stern. He flung himself down hastily, and the boatswain, who was following, fell on him.

"Don't you get up yet, sir," cried the boatswain. "No hurry!"

A sea swept over. Jukes understood the boatswain to splutter that the bridge ladders were gone. "I'll lower you down, sir, by your hands," he screamed. He shouted also something about the smokestack being as likely to go overboard as not. Jukes thought it very possible, and imagined the fires out, the ship helpless. . . . The boatswain by his side kept on yelling. "What? What is it?" Jukes cried distressfully; and the other repeated, "What would my old woman say if she saw me now?"

In the alleyway, where a lot of water had got in and splashed in the dark, the men were still as death, till Jukes stumbled against one of them and cursed him savagely for being in the way. Two or three voices then asked, eager and weak, "Any chance for us, sir?"

"What's the matter with you fools?" he said brutally. He felt as though he could throw himself down amongst them and never move any more. But they seemed cheered; and in the midst of obsequious warnings, "Look out! Mind that manhole lid, sir," they lowered him into the bunker. The boatswain tumbled down after him, and soon as he had picked himself up he remarked, "She would say, 'Serve you right, you old fool, for going to sea.'"

---

[1] *in chancery:* in a wrestler's headlock.

The boatswain had some means, and made a point of alluding to them frequently. His wife—a fat woman—and two grown-up daughters kept a greengrocer's shop in the East End of London.

In the dark, Jukes, unsteady on his legs, listened to a faint thunderous patter. A deadened screaming went on steadily at his elbow, as it were; and from above the louder tumult of the storm descended upon these near sounds. His head swam. To him, too, in that bunker, the motion of the ship seemed novel and menacing, sapping his resolution as though he had never been afloat before.

He had half a mind to scramble out again; but the remembrance of Captain MacWhirr's voice made this impossible. His orders were to go and see. What was the good of it, he wanted to know. Enraged, he told himself he would see—of course. But the boatswain, staggering clumsily, warned him to be careful how he opened that door; there was a blamed fight going on. And Jukes, as if in great bodily pain, desired irritably to know what the devil they were fighting for.

"Dollars! Dollars, sir. All their rotten chests got burst open. Blamed money skipping all over the place, and they are tumbling after it head over heels—tearing and biting like anything. A regular little hell in there."

Jukes convulsively opened the door. The short boatswain peered under his arm.

One of the lamps had gone out, broken perhaps. Rancorous, guttural cries burst out loudly on their ears, and a strange panting sound, the working of all these straining breasts. A hard blow hit the side of the ship: water fell above with a stunning shock, and in the forefront of the gloom, where the air was reddish and thick, Jukes saw a head bang the deck violently, two thick calves waving on high, muscular arms twined round a naked body, a yellow face, open-mouthed and with a set wild stare, look up and slide away. An empty chest clattered turning over; a man fell head first with a jump, as if lifted by a kick; and farther off, indistinct, others streamed like a mass of rolling stones down a bank, thumping the deck with their feet and flourishing their arms wildly. The hatchway ladder was loaded with coolies swarming on it like bees on a branch. They hung on the steps in a crawling, stirring cluster, beating madly with their fists the underside of the battened hatch, and the head-long rush of the water above was heard in the intervals of their yelling. The ship heeled over more, and they began to drop off: first one, then two, then all the rest went away together, falling straight off with a great cry.

Jukes was confounded. The boatswain, with gruff anxiety, begged him, "Don't you go in there, sir."

The whole place seemed to twist upon itself, jumping incessantly the while; and when the ship rose to a sea Jukes fancied that all these men would be shot upon him in a body. He backed out, swung the door to, and with trembling hands pushed at the bolt. . . .

As soon as his mate had gone Captain MacWhirr, left alone on the bridge, sidled and staggered as far as the wheelhouse. Its door being hinged forward, he had to fight the gale for admittance, and when at last he managed to enter, it was with an instantaneous clatter and a bang, as though he had been fired through the wood. He stood within, holding on to the handle.

The steering gear leaked steam, and in the confined space the glass of the binnacle[1] made a shiny oval of light in a thin white fog. The wind howled, hummed, whistled, with sudden booming gusts that rattled the doors and shutters in the vicious patter of sprays. Two coils of lead line and a small canvas bag hung on a long lanyard [2] swung wide off, and came back clinging to the bulkheads. The gratings underfoot were nearly afloat; with every sweeping blow of a sea, water squirted violently through the cracks all round the door, and the man at the helm had flung down his cap, his coat, and stood propped against the gear casing in a striped cotton shirt open on his breast. The little brass wheel in his hands had the appearance of a bright and fragile toy. The cords of his neck stood hard and lean, a dark patch lay in the hollow of his throat, and his face was still and sunken as in death.

Captain MacWhirr wiped his eyes. The sea that had nearly taken him overboard had, to his great annoyance, washed his sou'wester hat off his bald head. The fluffy, fair hair, soaked and darkened, resembled a mean skein of cotton threads festooned round his bare skull. His face, glistening with sea water, had been made crimson with the wind, with the sting of sprays. He looked as though he had come off sweating from before a furnace.

"You here?" he muttered, heavily.

The second mate had found his way into the wheelhouse some time before. He had fixed himself in a corner with his knees up, a fist pressed against each temple; and this attitude suggested rage, sorrow, resignation, surrender, with a sort of concentrated unforgiveness. He said mournfully and defiantly, "Well, it's my watch below now: ain't it?"

---

[1] *binnacle:* a stationary lighted box in which the ship's compass is set.
[2] *lanyard:* a piece of rope.

The steam gear clattered, stopped, clattered again, and the helmsman's eyeballs seemed to project out of a hungry face as if the compass card behind the binnacle glass had been meat. God knows how long he had been left there to steer, as if forgotten by all his shipmates. The bells had not been struck; there had been no reliefs; the ship's routine had gone down wind; but he was trying to keep her head north-northeast. The rudder might have been gone for all he knew, the fires out, the engines broken down, the ship ready to roll over like a corpse. He was anxious not to get muddled and lose control of her head, because the compass card swung far both ways, wriggling on the pivot, and sometimes seemed to whirl right around. He suffered from mental stress. He was horribly afraid, also, of the wheelhouse going. Mountains of water kept on tumbling against it. When the ship took one of her desperate dives the corners of his lips twitched.

Captain MacWhirr looked up at the wheelhouse clock. Screwed to the bulkhead, it had a white face on which the black hands appeared to stand quite still. It was half-past one in the morning.

"Another day," he muttered to himself.

The second mate heard him, and lifting his head as one grieving amongst ruins, "You won't see it break," he exclaimed. His wrists and his knees could be seen to shake violently. "No, by God! You won't. . . ."

He took his face again between his fists.

The body of the helmsman had moved slightly, but his head didn't budge on his neck—like a stone head fixed to look one way from a column. During a roll that all but took his booted legs from under him, and in the very stagger to save himself, Captain MacWhirr said austerely, "Don't you pay any attention to what that man says." And then, with an indefinable change of tone, very grave, he added, "He isn't on duty."

The sailor said nothing.

The hurricane boomed, shaking the little place, which seemed airtight; and the light of the binnacle flickered all the time.

"You haven't been relieved," Captain MacWhirr went on, looking down. "I want you to stick to the helm, though, as long as you can. You've got the hang of her. Another man coming here might make a mess of it. Wouldn't do. No child's play. And the hands are probably busy with a job down below. . . . Think you can?"

The steering gear leaped into an abrupt short clatter; stopped, smoldering like an ember; and the still man, with a motionless gaze, burst out, as if all the passion in him had gone into his lips: "By Heaven, sir! I can steer forever if nobody talks to me."

"Oh! aye! All right. . . ." The Captain lifted his eyes for the first time to the man, ". . . Hackett."

And he seemed to dismiss this matter from his mind. He stooped to the engine-room speaking tube, blew in, and bent his head. Mr. Rout below answered, and at once Captain MacWhirr put his lips to the mouthpiece.

With the uproar of the gale around him he applied alternately his lips and his ear, and the engineer's voice mounted to him, harsh and as if out of the heat of an engagement. One of the stokers was disabled, the others had given in, the second engineer and the donkeyman[1] were firing up. The third engineer was standing by the steam valve. The engines were being tended by hand. How was it above?

"Bad enough. It mostly rests with you," said Captain MacWhirr. Was the mate down there yet? No? Well, he would be presently. Would Mr. Rout let him talk through the speaking tube?—through the deck speaking tube, because he—the Captain was going out again on the bridge directly. There was some trouble amongst the Chinamen. They were fighting, it seemed. Couldn't allow fighting anyhow. . . .

Mr. Rout had gone away, and Captain MacWhirr could feel against his ear the pulsation of the engines, like the beat of the ship's heart. Mr. Rout's voice down there shouted something distantly. The ship pitched headlong, the pulsation leaped with a hissing tumult, and stopped dead. Captain MacWhirr's face was impassive, and his eyes were fixed aimlessly on the crouching shape of the second mate. Again Mr. Rout's voice cried out in the depths, and the pulsating beats recommenced, with slow strokes —growing swifter.

Mr. Rout had returned to the tube. "It don't matter much what they do," he said, hastily; and then, with irritation, "She takes these dives as if she never meant to come up again."

"Awful sea," said the Captain's voice from above.

"Don't let me drive her under," barked Solomon Rout up the pipe.

"Dark and rain. Can't see what's coming," uttered the voice. "Must— keep—her—moving—enough to steer—and chance it," it went on to state distinctly.

"I am doing as much as I dare."

"We are—getting—smashed up—a good deal up here," proceeded the

---

[1] *donkeyman:* mechanic in charge of the deck or "donkey" engines used to power cargo cranes and davits.

voice mildly. "Doing—fairly well, though. Of course, if the wheelhouse should go. . . ."

Mr. Rout, bending an attentive ear, muttered peevishly something under his breath.

But the deliberate voice up there became animated to ask: "Jukes turned up yet?" Then, after a short wait, "I wish he would bear a hand. I want him to be done and come up here in case of anything. To look after the ship. I am all alone. The second mate's lost. . . ."

"What?" shouted Mr. Rout into the engine room, taking his head away. Then up the tube he cried, "Gone overboard?" and clapped his ear to.

"Lost his nerve," the voice from above continued in a matter-of-fact tone. "Awkward circumstance."

Mr. Rout, listening with bowed neck, opened his eyes wide at this. However, he heard something like the sounds of a scuffle and broken exclamations coming down to him. He strained his hearing; and all the time Beale, the third engineer, with his arms uplifted, held between the palms of his hands the rim of a little black wheel projecting at the side of a big copper pipe. He seemed to be poising it above his head, as though it were a correct attitude in some sort of game.

To steady himself, he pressed his shoulder against the white bulkhead, one knee bent, and a sweat rag tucked in his belt hanging on his hip. His smooth cheek was begrimed and flushed, and the coal dust on his eyelids, like the black penciling of a make-up, enhanced the liquid brilliance of the whites, giving to his youthful face something of a feminine, exotic and fascinating aspect. When the ship pitched he would with hasty movements of his hands screw hard at the little wheel.

"Gone crazy," began the Captain's voice suddenly in the tube. "Rushed at me. . . . Just now. Had to knock him down. . . . This minute. You heard, Mr. Rout?"

"The devil!" muttered Mr. Rout. "Look out, Beale!"

His shout rang out like the blast of a warning trumpet between the iron walls of the engine room. Painted white, they rose high into the dusk of the skylight, sloping like a roof; and the whole lofty space resembled the interior of a monument, divided by floors of iron grating, with lights flickering at different levels, and a mass of gloom lingering in the middle, within the columnar stir of machinery under the motionless swelling of the cylinders. A loud and wild resonance, made up of all the noises of the hurricane, dwelt in the still warmth of the air. There was in it the smell of hot metal, of oil, and a slight mist of steam. The blows of the sea seemed to traverse it in an unringing, stunning shock, from side to side.

Gleams, like pale long flames, trembled upon the polish of metal; from the flooring below the enormous crankheads emerged in their turns with a flash of brass and steel—going over; while the connecting rods, big-jointed, like skeleton limbs, seemed to thrust them down and pull them up again with an irresistible precision. And deep in the half-light other rods dodged deliberately to and fro, crossheads nodded, disks of metal rubbed smoothly against each other, slow and gentle, in a commingling of shadows and gleams.

Sometimes all those powerful and unerring movements would slow down simultaneously, as if they had been the functions of a living organism, stricken suddenly by the blight[1] of languor; and Mr. Rout's eyes would blaze darker in his long sallow face. He was fighting this fight in a pair of carpet slippers. A short shiny jacket barely covered his loins, and his white wrists protruded far out of the tight sleeves, as though the emergency had added to his stature, had lengthened his limbs, augmented his pallor, hollowed his eyes.

He moved, climbing high up, disappearing low down, with a restless, purposeful industry, and when he stood still, holding the guardrail in front of the starting gear, he would keep glancing to the right at the steam gauge, at the water gauge, fixed upon the white wall in the light of a swaying lamp. The mouths of two speaking tubes gaped stupidly at his elbow, and the dial of the engine-room telegraph resembled a clock of large diameter, bearing on its face curt words instead of figures. The grouped letters stood out heavily black, around the pivot head of the indicator, emphatically symbolic of loud exclamations: AHEAD, ASTERN, SLOW, HALF, STAND BY; and the fat black hand pointed downwards to the word FULL, which, thus singled out, captured the eye as a sharp cry secures attention.

The wood-encased bulk of the low-pressure cylinder, frowning portly from above, emitted a faint wheeze at every thrust, and except for that low hiss the engines worked their steel limbs headlong or slow with a silent, determined smoothness. And all this, the white walls, the moving steel, the floor plates under Solomon Rout's feet, the floors of iron grating above his head, the dusk and the gleams, uprose and sank continuously, with one accord, upon the harsh wash of the waves against the ship's side. The whole loftiness of the place, booming hollow to the great voice

[1] *blight:* a withering or wasting disease.

of the wind, swayed at the top like a tree, would go over bodily, as if borne down this way and that by the tremendous blasts.

"You've got to hurry up," shouted Mr. Rout, as soon as he saw Jukes appear in the stokehold doorway.

Jukes' glance was wandering and tipsy; his red face was puffy, as though he had overslept himself. He had had an arduous road, and had traveled over it with immense vivacity, the agitation of his mind corresponding to the exertions of his body. He had rushed up out of the bunker, stumbling in the dark alleyway amongst a lot of bewildered men who, trod upon, asked "What's up, sir?" in awed mutters all round him; down the stokehold ladder, missing many iron rungs in his hurry, down into a place deep as a well, black as Tophet,[1] tipping over back and forth like a seesaw. The water in the bilges thundered at each roll and lumps of coal skipped to and fro, from end to end, rattling like an avalanche of pebbles on a slope of iron.

Somebody in there moaned with pain, and somebody else could be seen crouching over what seemed the prone body of a dead man; a lusty voice blasphemed; and the glow under each fire door was like a pool of flaming blood radiating quietly in a velvety blackness.

A gust of wind struck upon the nape of Jukes' neck and next moment he felt it streaming about his wet ankles. The stokehold ventilators hummed: in front of the six fire doors two wild figures, stripped to the waist, staggered and stooped, wrestling with two shovels.

"Hallo! Plenty of draft now," yelled the second engineer at once, as though he had been all the time looking out for Jukes. The donkeyman, a dapper little chap with a dazzling fair skin and a tiny, gingery mustache, worked in a sort of mute transport. They were keeping a full head of steam, and a profound rumbling, as of an empty furniture van trotting over a bridge, made a sustained bass to all the other noises of the place.

"Blowing off all the time," went on yelling the second. With a sound as of a hundred scoured saucepans, the orifice of a ventilator spat upon his shoulder a sudden gush of salt water, and he volleyed a stream of curses upon all things on earth including his own soul, ripping and raving, and all the time attending to his business. With a sharp clash of metal the ardent pale glare of the fire opened upon his bullet head, showing his spluttering lips, his insolent face, and with another clang closed like the white-hot wink of an iron eye.

"Where's the blooming ship? Can you tell me? blast my eyes! Under

---

[1] *Tophet:* the Pit; Hell.

water—or what? It's coming down here in tons. Are the condemned cowls[1] gone to Hades? Hey? Don't you know anything—you jolly sailor-man you . . . ?"

Jukes, after a bewildered moment, had been helped by a roll to dart through; and as soon as his eyes took in the comparative vastness, peace and brilliance of the engine room, the ship, setting her stern heavily in the water, sent him charging head down upon Mr. Rout.

The chief's arm, long like a tentacle, and straightening as if worked by a spring, went out to meet him, and deflected his rush into a spin towards the speaking tubes. At the same time Mr. Rout repeated earnestly:

"You've got to hurry up, whatever it is."

Jukes yelled "Are you there, sir?" and listened. Nothing. Suddenly the roar of the wind fell straight into his ear, but presently a small voice shoved aside the shouting hurricane quietly.

"You, Jukes?—Well?"

Jukes was ready to talk: it was only time that seemed to be wanting. It was easy enough to account for everything. He could perfectly imagine the coolies battened down in the reeking 'tween deck, lying sick and scared between the rows of chests. Then one of these chests—or perhaps several at once—breaking loose in a roll, knocking out others, sides splitting, lids flying open, and all these clumsy Chinamen rising up in a body to save their property. Afterwards every fling of the ship would hurl that tramping, yelling mob here and there, from side to side, in a whirl of smashed wood, torn clothing, rolling dollars. A struggle once started, they would be unable to stop themselves. Nothing could stop them now except main force. It was a disaster. He had seen it, and that was all he could say. Some of them must be dead, he believed. The rest would go on fighting. . . .

He sent up his words, tripping over each other, crowding the narrow tube. They mounted as if into a silence of an enlightened comprehension dwelling alone up there with a storm. And Jukes wanted to be dismissed from the face of that odious trouble intruding on the great need of the ship.

CHAPTER FIVE

H E waited. Before his eyes the engines turned with slow labor, that in the moment of going off into a mad fling would stop dead at Mr. Rout's

---

[1] *cowls:* the horn-shaped openings of the ventilators on deck.

shout, "Look out, Beale!" They paused in an intelligent immobility, stilled in midstroke, a heavy crank arrested on the cant, as if conscious of danger and the passage of time. Then, with a "Now, then!" from the chief, and the sound of a breath expelled through clenched teeth, they would accomplish the interrupted revolution and begin another.

There was the prudent sagacity of wisdom and the deliberation of enormous strength in their movements. This was their work—this patient coaxing of a distracted ship over the fury of the waves and into the very eye of the wind. At times Mr. Rout's chin would sink on his breast, and he watched them with knitted eyebrows as if lost in thought.

The voice that kept the hurricane out of Jukes' ear began: "Take the hands with you . . . ," and left off unexpectedly.

"What could I do with them, sir?"

A harsh, abrupt, imperious clang exploded suddenly. The three pairs of eyes flew up to the telegraph dial to see the hand jump from FULL to STOP, as if snatched by a devil. And then these three men in the engine room had the intimate sensation of a check upon the ship, of a strange shrinking, as if she had gathered herself for a desperate leap.

"Stop her!" bellowed Mr. Rout.

Nobody—not even Captain MacWhirr, who alone on deck had caught sight of a white line of foam coming on at such a height that he couldn't believe his eyes—nobody was to know the steepness of that sea and the awful depth of the hollow the hurricane had scooped out behind the running wall of water.

It raced to meet the ship, and, with a pause, as of girding the loins, the *Nan-Shan* lifted her bows and leaped. The flames in all the lamps sank, darkening the engine room. One went out. With a tearing crash and a swirling, raving tumult, tons of water fell upon the deck, as though the ship had darted under the foot of a cataract.[1]

Down there they looked at each other, stunned.

"Swept from end to end, by God!" bawled Jukes.

She dipped into the hollow straight down, as if going over the edge of the world. The engine room toppled forward menacingly, like the inside of a tower nodding in an earthquake. An awful racket, of iron things falling, came from the stokehold. She hung on this appalling slant long enough for Beale to drop on his hands and knees and begin to crawl as if he meant to fly on all fours out of the engine room, and for Mr. Rout to turn his head slowly, rigid, cavernous, with the lower jaw dropping. Jukes

---

[1] *cataract:* waterfall.

had shut his eyes, and his face in a moment became hopelessly blank and gentle, like the face of a blind man.

At last she rose slowly, staggering, as if she had to lift a mountain with her bows.

Mr. Rout shut his mouth; Jukes blinked; and little Beale stood up hastily.

"Another one like this, and that's the last of her," cried the chief.

He and Jukes looked at each other, and the same thought came into their heads. The Captain! Everything must have been swept away. Steering gear gone—ship like a log. All over directly.

"Rush!" ejaculated Mr. Rout thickly, glaring with enlarged, doubtful eyes at Jukes, who answered him by an irresolute glance.

The clang of the telegraph gong soothed them instantly. The black hand dropped in a flash from STOP to FULL.

"Now then, Beale!" cried Mr. Rout.

The steam hissed low. The piston rods slid in and out. Jukes put his ear to the tube. The voice was ready for him. It said: "Pick up all the money. Bear a hand now. I'll want you up here." And that was all.

"Sir?" called up Jukes. There was no answer.

He staggered away like a defeated man from the field of battle. He had got, in some way or other, a cut above his left eyebrow—a cut to the bone. He was not aware of it in the least: quantities of the China Sea, large enough to break his neck for him, had gone over his head, had cleaned, washed, and salted that wound. It did not bleed, but only gaped red; and this gash over the eye, his disheveled hair, the disorder of his clothes, gave him the aspect of a man worsted in a fight with fists.

"Got to pick up the dollars." He appealed to Mr. Rout, smiling pitifully at random.

"What's that?" asked Mr. Rout, wildly. "Pick up . . . ? I don't care. . . ." Then, quivering in every muscle, but with an exaggeration of paternal tone, "Go away now, for God's sake. You deck people'll drive me silly. There's that second mate been going for the old man. Don't you know? You fellows are going wrong for want of something to do. . . ."

At these words Jukes discovered in himself the beginnings of anger. Want of something to do—indeed. . . . Full of hot scorn against the chief, he turned to go the way he had come. In the stokehold the plump donkeyman toiled with his shovel mutely, as if his tongue had been cut out; but the second was carrying on like a noisy, undaunted maniac, who had preserved his skill in the art of stoking under a marine boiler.

"Hallo, you wandering officer! Hey! Can't you get some of your slush-slingers to wind up a few of them ashes? I am getting choked with them here. Curse it! Hallo! Hey! Remember the articles:[1] *Sailors and firemen to assist each other*. Hey! D'ye hear?"

Jukes was climbing out frantically, and the other, lifting up his face after him, howled, "Can't you speak? What are you poking about here for? What's your game, anyhow?"

A frenzy possessed Jukes. By the time he was back amongst the men in the darkness of the alleyway, he felt ready to wring all their necks at the slightest sign of hanging back. The very thought of it exasperated him. *He* couldn't hang back. They shouldn't.

The impetuosity with which he came amongst them carried them along. They had already been excited and startled at all his comings and goings —by the fierceness and rapidity of his movements; and, more felt than seen in his rushes, he appeared formidable—busied with matters of life and death that brooked no delay. At his first word he heard them drop into the bunker one after another obediently, with heavy thumps.

They were not clear as to what would have to be done. "What is it? What is it?" they were asking each other. The boatswain tried to explain; the sounds of a great scuffle surprised them; and the mighty shocks, reverberating awfully in the black bunker, kept them in mind of their danger. When the boatswain threw open the door it seemed that an eddy of the hurricane, stealing through the iron sides of the ship, had set all these bodies whirling like dust: there came to them a confused uproar, a tempestuous tumult, a fierce mutter, gusts of screams dying away, and the tramping of feet mingling with the blows of the sea.

For a moment they glared amazed, blocking the doorway. Jukes pushed through them brutally. He said nothing, and simply darted in. Another lot of coolies on the ladder, struggling suicidally to break through the battened hatch to a swamped deck, fell off as before, and he disappeared under them like a man overtaken by a landslide.

The boatswain yelled excitedly: "Come along. Get the mate out. He'll be trampled to death. Come on."

They charged in, stamping on breasts, on fingers, on faces, catching their feet in heaps of clothing, kicking broken wood; but before they could get hold of him Jukes emerged waist deep in a multitude of claw-ing hands. In the instant he had been lost to view, all the buttons of his jacket had gone, its back had got split up to the collar, his waistcoat had

---

[1] *articles:* the ship's articles, setting forth the rights and obligations of the crew.

been torn open. The central struggling mass of Chinamen went over to the roll, dark, indistinct, helpless, with a wild gleam of many eyes in the dim light of the lamps.

"Leave me alone—damn you. I am all right," screeched Jukes. "Drive them forward. Watch your chance when she pitches. Forward with 'em. Drive them against the bulkhead. Jam 'em up."

The rush of the sailors into the seething 'tween deck was like a splash of cold water into a boiling caldron. The commotion sank for a moment.

The bulk of Chinamen were locked in such a compact scrimmage that, linking their arms and aided by an appalling dive of the ship, the seamen sent it forward in one great shove, like a solid block. Behind their backs small clusters and loose bodies tumbled from side to side.

The boatswain performed prodigious feats of strength. With his long arms open, and each great paw clutching at a stanchion, he stopped the rush of seven entwined Chinamen rolling like a boulder. His joints cracked; he said, "Ha!" and they flew apart. But the carpenter showed the greater intelligence. Without saying a word to anybody he went back into the alleyway to fetch several coils of cargo gear he had seen there —chain and rope. With these life lines were rigged.

There was really no resistance. The struggle, however it began, had turned into a scramble of blind panic. If the coolies had started up after their scattered dollars they were by that time fighting only for their footing. They took each other by the throat merely to save themselves from being hurled about. Whoever got a hold anywhere would kick at the others who caught at his legs and hung on, till a roll sent them flying together across the deck.

The coming of the white devils was a terror. Had they come to kill? The individuals torn out of the ruck[1] became very limp in the seamen's hands: some, dragged aside by the heels, were passive, like dead bodies, with open, fixed eyes. Here and there a coolie would fall on his knees as if begging for mercy; several, whom the excess of fear made unruly, were hit with hard fists between the eyes, and cowered; while those who were hurt submitted to rough handling, blinking rapidly without a plaint. Faces streamed with blood; there were raw places on the shaven heads, scratches, bruises, torn wounds, gashes. The broken porcelain out of the chests was mostly responsible for the latter. Here and there a Chinaman, wild-eyed, with his tail unplaited, nursed a bleeding sole.

They had been ranged closely, after having been shaken into submission, cuffed a little to allay excitement, addressed in gruff words of

[1] *ruck:* mob.

encouragement that sounded like promises of evil. They sat on the deck in ghastly, drooping rows, and at the end the carpenter, with two hands to help him, moved busily from place to place, setting taut and hitching the life lines. The boatswain, with one leg and one arm embracing a stanchion, struggled with a lamp pressed to his breast, trying to get a light, and growling all the time like an industrious gorilla. The figures of seamen stooped repeatedly, with the movements of gleaners,[1] and everything was being flung into the bunker: clothing, smashed wood, broken china, and the dollars, too, gathered up in men's jackets. Now and then a sailor would stagger towards the doorway with his arms full of rubbish; and dolorous, slanting eyes followed his movements.

With every roll of the ship the long rows of sitting Celestials would sway forward brokenly, and her headlong dives knocked together the line of shaven polls[2] from end to end. When the wash of water rolling on the deck died away for a moment, it seemed to Jukes, yet quivering from his exertions, that in his mad struggle down there he had overcome the wind somehow: that a silence had fallen upon the ship, a silence in which the sea struck thunderously at her sides.

Everything had been cleared out of the 'tween deck—all the wreckage, as the men said. They stood erect and tottering above the level of heads and drooping shoulders. Here and there a coolie sobbed for his breath. Where the high light fell, Jukes could see the salient[3] ribs of one, the yellow, wistful face of another; bowed necks; or would meet a dull stare directed at his face. He was amazed that there had been no corpses; but the lot of them seemed at their last gasp, and they appeared to him more pitiful than if they had been all dead.

Suddenly one of the coolies began to speak. The light came and went on his lean, straining face; he threw his head up like a baying hound. From the bunker came the sounds of knocking and the tinkle of some dollars rolling loose; he stretched out his arm, his mouth yawned black, and the incomprehensible guttural hooting sounds, that did not seem to belong to a human language, penetrated Jukes with a strange emotion as if a brute had tried to be eloquent.

Two more started mouthing what seemed to Jukes fierce denunciations; the others stirred with grunts and growls. Jukes ordered the hands out of the 'tween decks hurriedly. He left last himself, backing through the

---

[1] *gleaners:* literally, those who gather, from a field of grain, what has been left by the reapers.
[2] *polls:* heads.
[3] *salient:* prominent.

door, while the grunts rose to a loud murmur and hands were extended after him as after a malefactor. The boatswain shot the bolt, and remarked uneasily, "Seems as if the wind had dropped, sir."

The seamen were glad to get back into the alleyway. Secretly each of them thought that at the last moment he could rush out on deck—and that was a comfort. There is something horribly repugnant in the idea of being drowned under a deck. Now they had done with the Chinamen, they again became conscious of the ship's position.

Jukes on coming out of the alleyway found himself up to the neck in the noisy water. He gained the bridge, and discovered he could detect obscure shapes as if his sight had become preternaturally acute. He saw faint outlines. They recalled not the familiar aspect of the *Nan-Shan,* but something remembered—an old dismantled steamer he had seen years ago rotting on a mudbank. She recalled that wreck.

There was no wind, not a breath, except the faint currents created by the lurches of the ship. The smoke tossed out of the funnel was settling down upon her deck. He breathed it as he passed forward. He felt the deliberate throb of the engines, and heard small sounds that seemed to have survived the great uproar: the knocking of broken fittings, the rapid tumbling of some piece of wreckage on the bridge. He perceived dimly the squat shape of his captain holding on to a twisted bridge rail, motionless and swaying as if rooted to the planks. The unexpected stillness of the air oppressed Jukes.

"We have done it, sir," he gasped.

"Thought you would," said Captain MacWhirr.

"Did you?" murmured Jukes to himself.

"Wind fell all at once," went on the Captain.

Jukes burst out: "If you think it was an easy job——"

But his captain, clinging to the rail, paid no attention. "According to the books the worst is not over yet."

"If most of them hadn't been half dead with seasickness and fright, not one of us would have come out of that 'tween deck alive," said Jukes.

"Had to do what's fair by them," mumbled MacWhirr, stolidly. "You don't find everything in books."

"Why, I believe they would have risen on us if I hadn't ordered the hands out of that pretty quick," continued Jukes with warmth.

After the whisper of their shouts, their ordinary tones, so distinct, rang out very loud to their ears in the amazing stillness of the air. It seemed to them they were talking in a dark and echoing vault.

Through a jagged aperture in the dome of clouds the light of a few stars fell upon the black sea, rising and falling confusedly. Sometimes the head of a watery cone would topple on board and mingle with the rolling flurry of foam on the swamped deck; and the *Nan-Shan* wallowed heavily at the bottom of a circular cistern of clouds. This ring of dense vapors, gyrating madly round the calm of the center, encompassed the ship like a motionless and unbroken wall of an aspect inconceivably sinister. Within, the sea, as if agitated by an internal commotion, leaped in peaked mounds that jostled each other, slapping heavily against her sides; and a low moaning sound, the infinite plaint of the storm's fury, came from beyond the limits of the menacing calm. Captain MacWhirr remained silent, and Jukes' ready ear caught suddenly the faint, long-drawn roar of some immense wave rushing unseen under that thick blackness, which made the appalling boundary of his vision.

"Of course," he started resentfully, "they thought we had caught at the chance to plunder them. Of course! You said—pick up the money. Easier said than done. They couldn't tell what was in our heads. We came in, smash—right into the middle of them. Had to do it by a rush."

"As long as it's done . . . ," mumbled the Captain, without attempting to look at Jukes. "Had to do what's fair."

"We shall find yet there's the devil to pay when this is over," said Jukes, feeling very sore. "Let them only recover a bit, and you'll see. They will fly at our throats, sir. Don't forget, sir, she isn't a British ship now. These brutes know it well, too. The damned Siamese flag."

"We are on board, all the same," remarked Captain MacWhirr.

"The trouble's not over yet," insisted Jukes, prophetically, reeling and catching on. "She's a wreck," he added, faintly.

"The trouble's not over yet," assented Captain MacWhirr, half aloud. . . . "Look out for her a minute."

"Are you going off the deck, sir?" asked Jukes, hurriedly, as if the storm were sure to pounce upon him as soon as he had been left alone with the ship.

He watched her, battered and solitary, laboring heavily in a wild scene of mountainous black waters lit by the gleams of distant worlds. She moved slowly, breathing into the still core of the hurricane the excess of her strength in a white cloud of steam—and the deep-toned vibration of the escape was like the defiant trumpeting of a living creature of the sea impatient for the renewal of the contest. It ceased suddenly. The still air moaned. Above Jukes' head a few stars shone into a pit of black vapors. The inky edge of the cloud-disk frowned upon the ship under the patch of glittering sky. The stars, too, seemed to look at her intently, as if for the last time, and the cluster of their splendor sat like a diadem on a lowering brow.

Captain MacWhirr had gone into the chartroom. There was no light there; but he could feel the disorder of that place where he used to live tidily. His armchair was upset. The books had tumbled out on the floor: he scrunched a piece of glass under his boot. He groped for the matches, and found a box on a shelf with a deep ledge. He struck one and, puckering the corners of his eyes, held out the little flame towards the barometer whose glittering top of glass and metals nodded at him continuously.

It stood very low—incredibly low, so low that Captain MacWhirr grunted. The match went out, and hurriedly he extracted another, with thick, stiff fingers.

Again a little flame flared up before the nodding glass and metal of the top. His eyes looked at it, narrowed with attention, as if expecting an imperceptible sign. With his grave face he resembled a booted and misshapen pagan burning incense before the oracle of a Joss.[1] There was no mistake. It was the lowest reading he had ever seen in his life.

Captain MacWhirr emitted a low whistle. He forgot himself till the flame diminished to a blue spark, burnt his fingers and vanished. Perhaps something had gone wrong with the thing!

There was an aneroid glass[2] screwed above the couch. He turned that way, struck another match, and discovered the white face of the other instrument looking at him from the bulkhead, meaningly, not to be gainsaid,[3] as though the wisdom of men were made unerring by the indifference of matter. There was no room for doubt now. Captain MacWhirr pshawed at it, and threw the match down.

The worst was to come, then—and if the books were right this worst would be very bad. The experience of the last six hours had enlarged his conception of what heavy weather could be like. "It'll be terrific," he pronounced, mentally. He had not consciously looked at anything by the light of the matches except at the barometer; and yet somehow he had seen that his water bottle and the two tumblers had been flung out of their stand. It seemed to give him a more intimate knowledge of the tossing the ship had gone through. "I wouldn't have believed it," he thought. And his table had been cleared, too; his rulers, his pencils, the inkstand—all the things that had their safe appointed places—they were gone, as if a mischievous hand had plucked them out one by one and flung them on the

[1] *oracle of a Joss:* the grotto of a Chinese religious idol.
[2] *aneroid glass:* a barometric device.
[3] *gainsaid:* contradicted.

wet floor. The hurricane had broken in upon the orderly arrangements of his privacy. This had never happened before, and the feeling of dismay reached the very seat of his composure. And the worst was to come yet! He was glad the trouble in the 'tween deck had been discovered in time. If the ship had to go after all, then, at least, she wouldn't be going to the bottom with a lot of people in her fighting teeth and claw. That would have been odious. And in that feeling there was a humane intention and a vague sense of the fitness of things.

These instantaneous thoughts were yet in their essence heavy and slow, partaking of the nature of the man. He extended his hand to put back the matchbox in its corner of the shelf. There were always matches there—by his order. The steward had his instructions impressed upon him long before. "A box . . . just there, see? Not so very full . . . where I can put my hand on it, steward. Might want a light in a hurry. Can't tell on board ship *what* you might want in a hurry. Mind, now."

And of course on his side he would be careful to put it back in its place scrupulously. He did so now, but before he removed his hand it occurred to him that perhaps he would never have occasion to use that box any more. The vividness of the thought checked him and for an infinitesimal fraction of a second his fingers closed again on the small object as though it had been the symbol of all these little habits that chain us to the weary round of life. He released it at last, and, letting himself fall on the settee, listened for the first sounds of returning wind.

Not yet. He heard only the wash of water, the heavy splashes, the dull shocks of the confused seas boarding his ship from all sides. She would never have a chance to clear her decks.

But the quietude of the air was startlingly tense and unsafe, like a slender hair holding a sword suspended over his head. By this awful pause the storm penetrated the defenses of the man and unsealed his lips. He spoke out in the solitude and the pitch darkness of the cabin, as if addressing another being awakened within his breast.

"I shouldn't like to lose her," he said half aloud.

He sat unseen, apart from the sea, from his ship, isolated, as if withdrawn from the very current of his own existence, where such freaks as talking to himself surely had no place. His palms reposed on his knees, he bowed his short neck and puffed heavily, surrendering to a strange sensation of weariness he was not enlightened enough to recognize for the fatigue of mental stress.

From where he sat he could reach the door of a washstand locker. There should have been a towel there. There was. Good. . . . He took it out, wiped his face, and afterwards went on rubbing his wet head. He toweled himself with energy in the dark, and then remained motionless with the towel on his knees. A moment passed, of a stillness so profound that no one could have guessed there was a man sitting in that cabin. Then a murmur arose.

"She may come out of it yet."

When Captain MacWhirr came out on deck, which he did brusquely, as though he had suddenly become conscious of having stayed away too long, the calm had lasted already more than fifteen minutes—long enough to make itself intolerable even to his imagination. Jukes, motionless on the forepart of the bridge, began to speak at once. His voice, blank and forced as though he were talking through hard-set teeth, seemed to flow away on all sides into the darkness, deepening again upon the sea.

"I had the wheel relieved. Hackett began to sing out that he was done. He's lying in there alongside the steering gear with a face like death. At first I couldn't get anybody to crawl out and relieve the poor devil. That bos'un's worse than no good, I always said. Thought I would have had to go myself and haul out one of them by the neck."

"Ah, well," muttered the Captain. He stood watching by Jukes' side.

"The second mate's in there, too, holding his head. Is he hurt, sir?"

"No—crazy," said Captain MacWhirr, curtly.

"Looks as if he had a tumble, though."

"I had to give him a push," explained the Captain.

Jukes gave an impatient sigh.

"It will come very sudden," said Captain MacWhirr, "and from over there, I fancy. God only knows though. These books are only good to muddle your head and make you jumpy. It will be bad, and there's an end. If we only can steam her round in time to meet it. . . ."

A minute passed. Some of the stars winked rapidly and vanished.

"You left them pretty safe?" began the Captain abruptly, as though the silence were unbearable.

"Are you thinking of the coolies, sir? I rigged life lines all ways across that 'tween deck."

"Did you? Good idea, Mr. Jukes."

"I didn't . . . think you cared to . . . know," said Jukes—the lurching of the ship cut his speech as though somebody had been jerking him around while he talked—"how I got on with . . . that infernal job. We did it. And it may not matter in the end."

"Had to do what's fair, for all—they are only Chinamen. Give them the same chance with ourselves—hang it all. She isn't lost yet. Bad enough to be shut up below in a gale——"

"That's what I thought when you gave me the job, sir," interjected Jukes, moodily.

"——without being battered to pieces," pursued Captain MacWhirr with rising vehemence. "Couldn't let that go on in my ship, if I knew she hadn't five minutes to live. Couldn't bear it, Mr. Jukes."

A hollow echoing noise, like that of a shout rolling in a rocky chasm, approached the ship and went away again. The last star, blurred, enlarged, as if returning to the fiery mist of its beginning, struggled with the colossal depth of blackness hanging over the ship—and went out.

"Now for it!" muttered Captain MacWhirr. "Mr. Jukes."

"Here, sir."

The two men were growing indistinct to each other.

"We must trust her to go through it and come out on the other side. That's plain and straight. There's no room for Captain Wilson's storm strategy here."

"No, sir."

"She will be smothered and swept again for hours," mumbled the Captain. "There's not much left by this time above deck for the sea to take away—unless you or me."

"Both, sir," whispered Jukes, breathlessly.

"You are always meeting trouble half way, Jukes," Captain MacWhirr remonstrated quaintly. "Though it's a fact that the second mate is no good. D'ye hear, Mr. Jukes? You would be left alone if . . ."

Captain MacWhirr interrupted himself, and Jukes, glancing on all sides, remained silent.

"Don't you be put out by anything," the Captain continued, mumbling rather fast. "Keep her facing it. They may say what they like, but the heaviest seas run with the wind. Facing it—always facing it—that's the way to get through. You are a young sailor. Face it. That's enough for any man. Keep a cool head."

"Yes, sir," said Jukes, with a flutter of the heart.

In the next few seconds the Captain spoke to the engine room and got an answer.

For some reason Jukes experienced an access of confidence, a sensation that came from outside like a warm breath, and made him feel equal to every demand. The distant muttering of the darkness stole into his ears. He noted it unmoved, out of that sudden belief in himself, as a man safe in a shirt of mail would watch a point.

The ship labored without intermission amongst the black hills of water, paying with this hard tumbling the price of her life. She rumbled in her depths, shaking a white plummet of steam into the night, and Jukes' thought skimmed like a bird through the engine room, where Mr. Rout—good man—was ready. When the rumbling ceased it seemed to him that there was a pause of every sound, a dead pause in which Captain Mac-Whirr's voice rang out startlingly.

"What's that? A puff of wind?"—it spoke much louder than Jukes had ever heard it before—"On the bow. That's right. She may come out of it yet."

The mutter of the winds drew near apace. In the forefront could be distinguished a drowsy waking plaint passing on, and far off the growth of a multiple clamor, marching and expanding. There was the throb as of many drums in it, a vicious rushing note, and like the chant of a tramping multitude.

Jukes could no longer see his captain distinctly. The darkness was absolutely piling itself upon the ship. At most he made out movements, a hint of elbows spread out, of a head thrown up.

Captain MacWhirr was trying to do up the top button of his oilskin coat with unwonted haste. The hurricane, with its power to madden the seas, to sink ships, to uproot trees, to overturn strong walls and dash the very birds of the air to the ground, had found this taciturn man in its path, and, doing its utmost, had managed to wring out a few words. Before the renewed wrath of winds swooped on his ship, Captain MacWhirr was moved to declare, in a tone of vexation as it were: "I wouldn't like to lose her."

He was spared that annoyance.

CHAPTER SIX

On a bright sunshiny day, with the breeze chasing her smoke far ahead, the *Nan-Shan* came into Fu-chau. Her arrival was at once noticed on shore, and the seamen in harbor said: "Look! Look at that steamer. What's that? Siamese—isn't she? Just look at her!"

She seemed, indeed, to have been used as a running target for the secondary batteries of a cruiser. A hail of minor shells could not have given her upper works a more broken, torn, and devastated aspect: and she had about her the worn, weary air of ships coming from the far ends of the world—and indeed with truth, for in her short passage she had been very far; sighting, verily, even the coast of the Great Beyond, whence no ship ever returns to give up her crew to the dust of the earth. She was incrusted and gray with salt to the trucks of her masts and to the top of her funnel; as though (as some facetious seaman said) "the crowd on board had fished her out somewhere from the bottom of the sea and brought her in here for salvage." And further, excited by the felicity of his own wit, he offered to give five pounds for her—"as she stands."

Before she had been quite an hour at rest, a meager little man, with a red-tipped nose and a face cast in an angry mold, landed from a sampan on the quay of the Foreign Concession,[1] and incontinently turned to shake his fist at her.

A tall individual, with legs much too thin for a rotund stomach, and with watery eyes, strolled up and remarked, "Just left her—eh? Quick work."

He wore a soiled suit of blue flannel with a pair of dirty cricketing shoes; a dingy gray mustache drooped from his lip, and daylight could be seen in two places between the rim and the crown of his hat.

"Hallo! what are you doing here?" asked the ex-second mate of the *Nan-Shan,* shaking hands hurriedly.

"Standing by for a job—chance worth taking—got a quiet hint," explained the man with the broken hat, in jerky, apathetic wheezes.

The second shook his fist again at the *Nan-Shan.* "There's a fellow there that ain't fit to have the command of a scow," he declared, quivering with passion, while the other looked about listlessly.

"Is there?"

But he caught sight on the quay of a heavy seaman's chest, painted brown under a fringed sailcloth cover, and lashed with new manila line. He eyed it with awakened interest.

"I would talk and raise trouble if it wasn't for that Siamese flag. Nobody to go to—or I would make it hot for him. The fraud! Told his chief engineer—that's another fraud for you—I had lost my nerve. The greatest lot of ignorant fools that ever sailed the seas. No! You can't think . . ."

"Got your money all right?" inquired his seedy acquaintance suddenly.

"Yes. Paid me off on board," raged the second mate. " 'Get your breakfast on shore,' says he."

"Mean skunk!" commented the tall man, vaguely, and passed his tongue on his lips. "What about having a drink of some sort?"

---

[1] *the quay of the Foreign Concession:* the landing set apart for the use of European shipping interests.

"He struck me," hissed the second mate.

"No! Struck! You don't say?" The man in blue began to bustle about sympathetically. "Can't possibly talk here. I want to know all about it. Struck—eh? Let's get a fellow to carry your chest. I know a quiet place where they have some bottled beer. . . ."

Mr. Jukes, who had been scanning the shore through a pair of glasses, informed the chief engineer afterwards that "our late second mate hasn't been long in finding a friend. A chap looking uncommonly like a bummer. I saw them walk away together from the quay."

The hammering and banging of the needful repairs did not disturb Captain MacWhirr. The steward found in the letter he wrote, in a tidy chartroom, passages of such absorbing interest that twice he was nearly caught in the act. But Mrs. MacWhirr, in the drawing room of the forty-pound house, stifled a yawn—perhaps out of self-respect—for she was alone.

She reclined in a plush-bottomed and gilt hammock-chair near a tiled fireplace, with Japanese fans on the mantel and a glow of coals in the grate. Lifting her hands, she glanced wearily here and there into the many pages. It was not her fault they were so prosy, so completely uninteresting—from "My darling wife" at the beginning, to "Your loving husband" at the end. She couldn't be really expected to understand all of these ship affairs. She was glad, of course, to hear from him, but she had never asked herself why, precisely.

". . . They are called typhoons . . . The mate did not seem to like it. . . . Not in books . . . Couldn't think of letting it go on. . . ."

The paper rustled sharply. ". . . A calm that lasted more than twenty minutes," she read perfunctorily; and the next words her thoughtless eyes caught, on the top of another page, were: "see you and the children again. . . ." She had a movement of impatience. He was always thinking of coming home. He had never had such a good salary before. What was the matter now?

It did not occur to her to turn back overleaf to look. She would have found it recorded there that between 4 and 6 A.M. on December 25th, Captain MacWhirr did actually think that his ship could not possibly live another hour in such a sea, and that he would never see his wife and children again. Nobody was to know this (his letters got mislaid so quickly)—nobody whatever but the steward, who had been greatly impressed by that disclosure. So much so, that he tried to give the cook some idea of the "narrow squeak we all had" by saying solemnly, "The old man himself had a poor opinion of our chance."

"How do you know?" asked, contemptuously, the cook, an old soldier. "He hasn't told you, maybe?"

"Well, he did give me a hint to that effect," the steward brazened it out.

"Get along with you! He will be coming to tell *me* next," jeered the old cook, over his shoulder.

Mrs. MacWhirr glanced farther, on the alert. ". . . Do what's fair. . . . Miserable objects. . . . Only three, with a broken leg each, and one . . . Thought had better keep the matter quiet . . . hope to have done the fair thing. . . ."

She let fall her hands. No: there was nothing more about coming home. Must have been merely expressing a pious wish. Mrs. MacWhirr's mind was set at ease, and a black marble clock, priced by the local jeweler at £3 18s. 6d., had a discreet stealthy tick.

The door flew open and a girl in the long-legged, short-frocked period of existence, flung into the room. A lot of colorless, rather lanky hair was scattered over her shoulders. Seeing her mother, she stood still, and directed her pale prying eyes upon the letter.

"From father," murmured Mrs. MacWhirr. "What have you done with your ribbon?"

The girl put her hands up to her head and pouted.

"He's well," continued Mrs. MacWhirr, languidly. "At least I think so. He never says." She had a little laugh. The girl's face expressed a wandering indifference, and Mrs. MacWhirr surveyed her with fond pride.

"Go and get your hat," she said after a while. "I am going out to do some shopping. There is a sale at Linom's."

"Oh, how jolly!" uttered the child, impressively, in unexpectedly grave vibrating tones, and bounded out of the room.

It was a fine afternoon, with a gray sky and dry sidewalks. Outside the draper's Mrs. MacWhirr smiled upon a woman in a black mantle of generous proportions armored in jet and crowned with flowers blooming falsely above a bilious matronly countenance. They broke into a swift little babble of greetings and exclamations both together, very hurried, as if the street were ready to yawn open and swallow all that pleasure before it could be expressed.

Behind them the high glass doors were kept on the swing. People couldn't pass, men stood aside waiting patiently, and Lydia was absorbed in poking the end of her parasol between the stone flags. Mrs. MacWhirr talked rapidly.

"Thank you very much. He's not coming home yet. Of course it's very sad to have him away, but it's such a comfort to know he keeps so well."

Mrs. MacWhirr drew breath. "The climate there agrees with him," she added, beamingly, as if poor MacWhirr had been away touring in China for the sake of his health.

Neither was the chief engineer coming home yet. Mr. Rout knew too well the value of a good billet.

"Solomon says wonders will never cease," cried Mrs. Rout joyously at the old lady in her armchair by the fire. Mr. Rout's mother moved slightly, her withered hands lying in black half-mittens on her lap.

The eyes of the engineer's wife fairly danced on the paper. "That captain of the ship he is in—a rather simple man, you remember, Mother?—has done something rather clever, Solomon says."

"Yes, my dear," said the old woman meekly, sitting with bowed silvery head, and that air of inward stillness characteristic of very old people who seem lost in watching the last flickers of life. "I think I remember."

Solomon Rout, Old Sol, Father Sol, the Chief, "Rout, good man"—Mr. Rout, the condescending and paternal friend of youth, had been the baby of her many children—all dead by this time. And she remembered him best as a boy of ten—long before he went away to serve his apprenticeship in some great engineering works in the North. She had seen so little of him since, she had gone through so many years, that she had now to retrace her steps very far back to recognize him plainly in the mist of time. Sometimes it seemed that her daughter-in-law was talking of some strange man.

Mrs. Rout junior was disappointed. "H'm. H'm." She turned the page. "How provoking! He doesn't say what it is. Says I couldn't understand how much there was in it. Fancy! What could it be so very clever? What a wretched man not to tell us!"

She read on without further remark soberly, and at last sat looking into the fire. The chief wrote just a word or two of the typhoon; but something had moved him to express an increased longing for the companionship of the jolly woman. "If it hadn't been that Mother must be looked after, I would send you your passage money today. You could set up a small house out here. I would have a chance to see you sometimes then. We are not growing younger. . . ."

"He's well, Mother," sighed Mrs. Rout, rousing herself.

"He always was a strong healthy boy," said the old woman, placidly.

But Mr. Jukes' account was really animated and very full. His friend in the Western Ocean trade imparted it freely to the other officers of his liner. "A chap I know writes to me about an extraordinary affair that happened on board his ship in that typhoon—you know—that we read of in the papers two months ago. It's the funniest thing! Just see for yourself what he says. I'll show you his letter."

There were phrases in it calculated to give the impression of light-hearted, indomitable resolution. Jukes had written them in good faith, for he felt thus when he wrote. He described with lurid effect the scenes in the 'tween deck. ". . . It struck me in a flash that those confounded Chinamen couldn't tell we weren't a desperate kind of robbers. 'Tisn't good to part the Chinaman from his money if he is the stronger party. We need have been desperate indeed to go thieving in such weather, but what could these beggars know of us? So, without thinking of it twice, I got the hands away in a jiffy. Our work was done—that the old man had set his heart on. We cleared out without staying to inquire how they felt. I am convinced that if they had not been so unmercifully shaken, and afraid—each individual one of them—to stand up, we would have been torn to pieces. Oh! It was pretty complete, I can tell you; and you may run to and fro across the Pond to the end of time before you find yourself with such a job on your hands."

After this he alluded professionally to the damage done to the ship, and went on thus:

"It was when the weather quieted down that the situation became confoundedly delicate. It wasn't made any better by us having been lately transferred to the Siamese flag; though the skipper can't see that it makes any difference—'as long as we are on board'—he says. There are feelings that this man simply hasn't got—and there's an end of it. You might just as well try to make a bedpost understand. But apart from this it is an infernally lonely state for a ship to be going about the China seas with no proper consuls, not even a gunboat of her own anywhere, nor a body to go to in case of some trouble.

"My notion was to keep these Johnnies under hatches for another fifteen hours or so; as we weren't much farther than that from Fu-chau. We would find there, most likely, some sort of a man-of-war, and once under her guns we were safe enough; for surely any skipper of a man-of-war—English, French, or Dutch—would see white men through as far as row on board goes. We could get rid of them and their money afterwards by delivering them to their Mandarin or Taotai, or whatever they call these chaps in goggles you see being carried about in sedan chairs through their stinking streets.

"The old man wouldn't see it somehow. He wanted to keep the matter quiet. He got that notion into his head, and a steam windlass couldn't drag it out of him. He wanted as little fuss made as possible, for the sake of the ship's name and for the sake of the owners—'for the sake of all concerned,' says he, looking at me very hard. It made me angry hot. Of course you couldn't keep a thing like that quiet; but the chests had been secured in the usual manner and were safe enough for any earthly gale, while this had been an altogether fiendish business I couldn't give you even an idea of.

"Meantime, I could hardly keep on my feet. None of us had a spell of any sort for nearly thirty hours, and there the old man sat rubbing his chin, rubbing the top of his head, and so bothered he didn't even think of pulling his long boots off.

" 'I hope, sir,' says I, 'you won't be letting them out on deck before we make ready for them in some shape or other.' Not, mind you, that I felt very sanguine[1] about controlling these beggars if they meant to take charge. A trouble with a cargo of Chinamen is no child's play. I was tired, too. 'I wish,' said I, 'you would let us throw the whole lot of these dollars down to them and leave them to fight it out amongst themselves, while we get a rest.'

" 'Now you talk wild, Jukes,' says he, looking up in his slow way that makes you ache all over, somehow. 'We must plan out something that would be fair to all parties.'

"I had no end of work on hand, as you may imagine, so I set the hands going, and then I thought I would turn in a bit. I hadn't been asleep in my bunk ten minutes when in rushes the steward and begins to pull at my leg.

" 'For God's sake, Mr. Jukes, come out! Come on deck quick, sir. Oh, do come out!'

"The fellow scared all the sense out of me. I didn't know what had happened: another hurricane—or what. Could hear no wind.

" 'The Captain's letting them out. Oh, he is letting them out! Jump on deck, sir, and save us. The chief engineer has just run below for his revolver.'

"That's what I understood the fool to say. However, Father Rout swears he went in there only to get a clean pocket handkerchief. Anyhow, I made one jump into my trousers and flew on deck aft. There was certainly a good deal of noise going on forward of the bridge. Four of the hands with the bos'un were at work abaft.[2] I passed up to them some of the rifles all the ships on the China coast carry in the cabin, and led them on the bridge. On the way I ran against Old Sol, looking startled and

---

[1] *sanguine:* cheerful; hopeful.
[2] *abaft:* toward the stern.

sucking at an unlighted cigar.

" 'Come along,' I shouted to him.

"We charged, the seven of us, up to the chartroom. All was over. There stood the old man with his sea boots still drawn up to the hips and in shirt sleeves—got warm thinking it out, I suppose. Bun Hin's dandy clerk at his elbow, as dirty as a sweep, was still green in the face. I could see directly I was in for something.

" 'What the devil are these monkey tricks, Mr. Jukes?' asks the old man, as angry as ever he could be. I tell you frankly it made me lose my tongue. 'For God's sake, Mr. Jukes,' says he, 'do take away these rifles from the men. Somebody's sure to get hurt before long if you don't. If this ship isn't worse than bedlam! [1] Look sharp now. I want you up here to help me and Bun Hin's Chinaman to count that money. You wouldn't mind lending a hand, too, Mr. Rout, now you are here. The more of us the better.'

"He had settled it all in his mind while I was having a snooze. Had we been an English ship, or only going to land our cargo of coolies in an English port, like Hong Kong, for instance, there would have been no end of inquiries and bother, claims for damages and so on. But these Chinamen know their officials better than we do.

"The hatches had been taken off already, and they were all on deck after a night and a day down below. It made you feel queer to see so many gaunt, wild faces together. The beggars stared about at the sky, at the sea, at the ship, as though they had expected the whole thing to have been blown to pieces. And no wonder! They had had a doing that would have shaken the soul out of a white man. But then they say a Chinaman has no soul. He has, though, something about him that is deuced tough. There was a fellow (amongst others of the badly hurt) who had had his eye all but knocked out. It stood out of his head the size of half a hen's egg. This would have laid out a white man on his back for a month: and yet there was that chap elbowing here and there in the crowd and talking to the others as if nothing had been the matter. They made a great hub-bub amongst themselves, and whenever the old man showed his bald head on the foreside of the bridge, they would all leave off jawing and look at him from below.

"It seems that after he had done his thinking he made that Bun Hin's fellow go down and explain to them the only way they could get their

---

[1] *bedlam:* the mad-house; a corruption of *Bethlehem*, the name of the old hospital for the insane in London.

money back. He told me afterwards that, all the coolies having worked in the same place and for the same length of time, he reckoned he would be doing the fair thing by them as near as possible if he shared all the cash we had picked up equally among the lot. You couldn't tell one man's dollars from another's, he said, and if you asked each man how much money he brought on board he was afraid they would lie, and he would find himself a long way short. I think he was right there. As to giving up the money to any Chinese official he could scare up in Fu-chau, he said he might just as well put the lot in his own pocket at once for all the good it would be to them. I suppose they thought so, too.

"We finished the distribution before dark. It was rather a sight: the sea running high, the ship a wreck to look at, these Chinamen staggering up on the bridge one by one for their share, and the old man, still booted and in his shirt sleeves, busy paying out at the chartroom door, perspiring like anything, and now and then coming down sharp on myself or Father Rout about one thing or another not quite to his mind. He took the share of those who were disabled himself to them on the No. 2 hatch. There were three dollars left over, and these went to the three most damaged coolies, one to each. We turned-to afterwards, and shoveled out on deck heaps of wet rags, all sorts of fragments of things without shape, and that you couldn't give a name to, and let them settle the ownership themselves.

"This certainly is coming as near as can be to keeping the thing quiet for the benefit of all concerned. What's your opinion, you pampered mail-boat swell? The old chief says that this was plainly the only thing that could be done. The skipper remarked to me the other day, 'There are things you find nothing about in books.' I think that he got out of it very well for such a stupid man."

MAN AND THE SEA

1. What are the details of Captain MacWhirr's appearance? What do his "shore" clothes suggest about his personality and habits? What do you make of his apparent inability to furl an umbrella?

2. Consider Captain MacWhirr's home life. How does Conrad make sure that the reader will have a distinct reaction to it? What seems to be Captain MacWhirr's attitude toward his family?

3. What dominant impressions do Captain MacWhirr, Mr. Jukes, and Solomon Rout have of the *Nan-Shan*? Can you explain the differences in their attitudes toward the ship?

4. In what sense is Captain MacWhirr an unimaginative man? How does his conversation with Jukes about the Siamese flag demonstrate his deficiency? What is his attitude toward idle conversation? What is his response to the mate's use of figurative language (page 326)?

5. It would seem that Jukes has the sort of imagination that his captain lacks. How do the mate's letters to his Atlantic Ocean friend demonstrate his imaginative powers? In the matter of confronting the typhoon, what advantages and disadvantages are provided by the imagination of Mr. Jukes?

6. How does Conrad let us see that, whatever his limitations, Jukes has a certain measure of professional competence?

7. On what does Captain MacWhirr base his decision to head his ship right through the storm? Why does Conrad call MacWhirr's explanation to Jukes "a confession of faith"?

8. "We are on board, all the same," says Captain MacWhirr when Jukes complains that the *Nan-Shan* is no longer a British ship. What is the Captain's brand of patriotism? Or, to put it another way, to what specifically does Mac-Whirr feel he owes allegiance? Compare him in this respect to Jukes.

9. Jukes' letter to his friend in the Atlantic about the typhoon has "phrases in it calculated to give the impression of light-hearted, indomitable resolution." How close is such an impression to the actual state of Jukes' feelings during the storm? What does Conrad mean when he notes that Jukes wrote such phrases "in good faith"?

10. The Captain thinks of the boatswain as an excellent petty officer. Mr. Jukes considers the boatswain worthless. How can you explain the difference in the two men's attitudes?

11. What is Jukes' reaction to Captain MacWhirr's order to pick up the scattered Chinese dollars at the height of the storm? How do the engineering officers affect his actions at this point?

12. The second mate is a character who appears as a type so regularly in Conrad's work that he deserves some close attention, if only to establish some broad outlines of the author's moral point of view. What is characteristic of the second mate's behavior during more or less normal times aboard the *Nan-Shan*? What are his actions during the typhoon? What does he say to his friend on shore after he has been paid off? How do these things join to make up the picture of a contemptible character?

13. After Mr. Jukes has reported his successful handling of the Chinese, Captain MacWhirr goes into the chartroom where he checks and rechecks the fantastically low barometer readings. "The experience of the last six hours had enlarged his conception of what heavy weather can be like." What, at this point, does he expect from the storm? What specific details of the experience in the chartroom cause his feeling of dismay to reach "the very seat of his composure"? What does he then reflect about the trouble 'tween deck? How does the rest of this scene affect the reader's attitude toward MacWhirr?

14. Explain the disagreement between Captain MacWhirr and Mr. Jukes about what should be done with the Chinese and their dollars when the *Nan-Shan* reaches port. What do Jukes, Rout, and MacWhirr do and say in the last action of the novel? Is there any indication that they have changed since we first met them?

15. What happens to the letter which Captain MacWhirr writes to his wife after the typhoon? How does his account of the storm affect the readers of the letter? What does Solomon Rout write his wife about the typhoon?

16. In the last sentence of the story, Jukes refers to MacWhirr as "such a stupid man." He has, of course, indicated his low regard for the Captain's intellect on other private occasions. But do these words provide an adequate statement of the chief mate's feelings about Captain MacWhirr throughout the tale? Consider, among other specific incidents, Jukes' feelings during the conversation on the speaking tube in the final paragraphs of Chapter IV.

TYPHOON: *An Afterword*

Typhoon was first published in 1903. It is a fine example of the use Conrad made of a form unusual, especially at that time, in English fiction. Unfortunately we have no exact name—like the French *nouvelle* or the Italian *novella*—for fiction of this length, which can be seen as a long short story or as a short novel. Conrad wrote a number of tales of this intermediate length—*The Secret Sharer* and *Heart of Darkness* are other excellent examples—and in such stories he often made use of incidents he had heard about, in talk with other sea captains, years before in remote places.

Typhoon is based upon such an account—an account of a ship, crowded with Chinese coolies, that runs into appalling weather in the North China seas, an area that has always had a sinister reputation. However, in an "Author's Note," Conrad tells us that he needed more than this incident: "I felt that to bring out its deeper significance which was quite apparent to me, something other, something more was required; a leading motive that would harmonize all these violent noises, and a point of view that would put all that elemental fury into its proper place."

He needed, in fact, a central figure, not only a particular kind of man, capable of facing the terrible fury of wind and sea, but a man who would serve as a symbol of what seemed to Conrad to be essential manhood. He would have to display those qualities that Conrad especially admired. He would have to be—as we say now—both an anti-hero, comically different from any accepted figure of romance, and yet in essence a hero, symbolic of man's defiance of the dark and treacherous elements. Conrad found him, as he tells us, in Captain MacWhirr, an imaginary character, but, he adds, "the product of twenty years of life. My own life."

MacWhirr seems at first a comic character, satirically drawn: almost a faceless little man wearing a skipper's peaked cap. Hardly anybody notices him. His own wife and children, far away in London, do not trouble to read the long letters he writes to them. He is almost entirely without imagination; after the droll episode of the Siamese flag, his lively young first mate, Jukes, thinks him a wooden-headed old plodder. But it is MacWhirr who takes his ship through that typhoon without losing his sense of responsibility, his nerve, his power of command. And that is not all—the key to the story is here—for there is something else he never loses, namely, his deeply rooted acceptance of a common human obligation. At the very height of the menace, he cannot ignore the thought of those battened-down coolies, maddened by the loss of their savings and by sheer terror, fighting down there in the dark. Jukes and the crew must restore order, must pick up the money and keep it safe; obligations must be honored, typhoon or no typhoon. Do we all, we wonder, carry at certain times like this a cargo of maddened coolies, screaming and fighting in the dark, and must there be somewhere in our personalities a MacWhirr clinging to the bridge, still giving orders that may bring us through to decency and untarnished honor?

Certainly there are some moments in this tale when MacWhirr turns into an heroic Everyman, defying the total menace of this dangerous planet. This one, to a reader who has really given himself to it, experienced it, is unforgettable:

> And again he heard that voice, forced and ringing feebly, but with a penetrating effect of quietness in the enormous discord of noises, as if sent out from some remote spot of peace beyond the black wastes of the gale; again he heard a man's voice—the frail and indomitable sound that can be made to carry an infinity of thought, resolution, and purpose, that shall be pronouncing confident words on the last day, when heavens fall, and justice is done—again he heard it, and it was crying to him, as if from very, very far—"All right."

Possibly this is too rich a mixture, too rhetorical and grandiloquent, for some more austere contemporary tastes—and Conrad, later, could do better—but it remains a memorable and deeply significant moment.

As an example of the art of narrative, no doubt a minor art but one too many of our novelists neglect, *Typhoon* in its opening passages cannot be praised. It is uncertain in its progress, wobbles both in time and place, and it is not until the *Nan-Shan* sets out, with the barometer falling and falling, that the narrative moves forward steadily, holding us in its grip. In a preface to an earlier story, Conrad had written, "My task which I am trying to achieve is, by the power of the written word, to make you hear, to make you feel—it is, before all, to make you *see*." Here, once the ship and the story are really moving, he does make us hear, he does make us feel, he does make us *see*. Consider this, one of twenty passages that might be quoted:

At its setting the sun had a diminished diameter and an expiring, brown, rayless glow, as if millions of centuries elapsing since the morning had brought it near its end. A dense bank of cloud became visible to the northward; it had a sinister dark olive tint and lay low and motionless upon the sea, resembling a solid obstacle in the path of the ship. She went floundering towards it like an exhausted creature driven to its death. The coppery twilight retired slowly, and the darkness brought out overhead a swarm of unsteady, big stars, that, as if blown upon, flickered exceedingly and seemed to hang very near the earth . . .

It is like a sinister and mysterious passage for the orchestra, horns sounding above the low throbbing and quivering of strings, a wonderful little prelude to the great storm passages that follow, drums and cymbals clashing, brass blaring, woodwind shrieking. It is *writing,* and if you think it easy, sit down and try to match it.

The end of the story, with the typhoon left behind, offers us a fine scattered shower of ironies, some grim, some comic. And just as the reader should yield himself to the storm, *experience* it and not simply read about it, he should return to this ending, this battered arrival in port and all that follows, and mark and taste and relish all its ironies. Remember then this writer who came from far inland to sail all the seas, who compelled himself to create sensitive and musical prose in a language not his own, who did not allow himself to be defeated by failure nor deluded and spoiled by success: a captain among men, a writer for writers.

J. B. P.

THE GROWTH OF
THE ENGLISH LANGUAGE

The Twentieth Century

You who have spent your entire lives in the twentieth century have probably accepted our language as you hear and see it, without much thought as to how it grew and became what it is now. The chapters running through this book have, we hope, given you a new outlook on language—an understanding that it is not a static thing, but a living, changing organism just as a human body is. Just what English will be one or two hundred years from now we cannot say, but we are quite sure that our present-day language will still be understandable, even if it is dubbed quaint or archaic. Not only the sound of the language but its terminology will differ. Every new advance in technology, science, and even in international relations will add new terms to the vocabulary, probably at the rate of about one thousand words per year. Meanwhile, older terms may well fade out of the language.

The first half of the twentieth century has brought some interesting developments. During the decade of peace before there was such a thing as a world war, there was a miniature war over Simplified Spelling. The movement was started toward the end of the nineteenth century by a group of people who deplored the unphonetic spelling of English and thought that the time had come for drastic action. In 1906, President Theodore Roosevelt directed the Government Printing Office to use three hundred simplified forms. This edict brought on a minor crisis. Protesting letters flooded the White House and storms of disapproval shook the editorial columns of newspapers and magazines. The President retracted his order. Though the Simplified Spelling Board continued to issue new lists from time to time, it never regained the prestige it had lost. Such an experience shows the impossibility of performing a major operation on language. It must change slowly by natural forces which neither man nor reason can completely control.

George Bernard Shaw continued to make caustic thrusts at our illogical language. In the Preface to *Pygmalion* he says: "The English have no respect for their language, and will not teach their children to speak it. They spell it so abominably that no man can teach himself what it sounds like. It is impossible for an Englishman to open his mouth without making some other Englishman hate or despise him. German and Spanish are accessible to foreigners; English is not accessible even to the Englishman. The reformer England needs today is an energetic phonetic enthusiast. That is why I have made such a one the hero of a popular play."

Yet Shaw, who left a good deal of his personal fortune to the cause of simplified spelling, was actually misguided. English is undoubtedly one of the two or three worst spelled languages on earth. But so rapid are the changes occurring at present in English pronunciation that even if we spent the billions of dollars needed to change over to simplified spelling, we would be obliged to make major changes in another seventy-five years or so.

Many Americans think that the British tend to pronounce words even less according to the spelling than we do. The fact is that Americans prefer accentual patterns different from those of British English. We give value to every syllable of *dictionary* and *millinery,* while the British slur the unaccented syllables until the words sound like *diction'ry* and *millin'ry.* This disparity between spelling and pronunciation is especially true of place names. Some of the most striking examples are Harwich (Hăr'idge), Greenwich (Grĕn'ich), Leicester (Lĕs'ter), Cirencester (Sis'eter), and Featherstonehaugh (Feest"nhay). We also have to watch out for family names, for Beauchamp is pronounced Bee'cham, and Cholmondeley is Chŭm'ly. Sometimes the difference between British and American pronunciation is merely a matter of accent, as when the Englishman says *munici'pal* and *labor'atory.*

English spelling deviates from American spelling in such words as: *storey* (of a house), *pyjama, kerb, tyre* (of a wheel), *gaol* (jail).

Americans abroad encounter different names for many ordinary objects. The Englishman's car wears a bonnet instead of a hood. He takes a tram instead of a streetcar; drives a lorry instead of a truck. He goes to the cinema instead of the movies. He enjoys a spot of tea in the afternoon. At dinner he uses a serviette instead of a napkin. When his wife wants a spool of thread, she asks for a reel of cotton. But misunderstandings because of terminology are decreasing as the interchange between the two countries increases.

World events have given us hundreds of new words. What first appeared as servicemen's slang has often proved useful enough to be accepted in good standing. The new world of the air has produced an entire vocabulary unknown a hundred years ago. Interest in medicine and psychiatry has introduced many new scientific terms. The inventions of the last fifty years have required new terms to describe them. Who can measure the possible effect of broadcasting on unifying speech? Already the British Broadcasting Corporation has appointed a board of six men to endeavor to arrive at a set standard of speech. (The background of these six men is rather surprising—there is one Scot, two Welshmen, one Irishman, and one American by birth, leaving only one who is thoroughly English.) It is possible that movies, radio, and television may have an effect on speech similar to that of printing on spelling.

On the whole, the style of expression of the twentieth century has been much less formal and ornate than that of the nineteenth century. Simplified spelling may have failed, but simplified style has succeeded. Credit for this may be given to the influence of journalism, certain authors like Hemingway who have a large following, and the increased tempo of life which can no longer tolerate verbosity and complicated structure. There has been great reaction against the teaching of formal grammar; some schools do not teach it at all. Those who do have eliminated many of the terms and constructions that were derived from Latin and have made English grammar follow more closely the natural form of the language.

What about English as a world language? It is now the mother tongue of two continents, North America and Australia, besides other widely scattered parts of the British Commonwealth. It is the chief secondary language of most of Western Europe, India, Japan, the Pacific Islands, and some parts of China. Its lack of complicated inflections and involved grammar make it a fairly easy language to learn, even though the discrepancies between spelling and pronunciation are a stumbling block to foreigners.

Thus we see that the English language, which started as a mere rivulet, has grown into a mighty river. What its social and cultural future may be we can only guess, but we can ourselves participate in its linguistic future as sensitive users of English words.

GLOSSARY

The definitions supplied in this glossary apply to each word as it is used in the textbook. With very few exceptions, words that are footnoted in the text are not included in the glossary.

A

absolve (ăb·sŏlv′). To set free (from an obligation or from the consequences of guilt.)

abyss (à·bĭs′). Something deep, vast, bottomless. *Adj.*, **abysmal.**

accession (ăk·sĕsh′ŭn). 1. Coming to the throne. 2. Addition.

accost (ă·kŏst′). To speak to first with aggressiveness.

affability (ăf′à·bĭl′ĭ·tĭ). Graciousness.

aggrieve (ă·grēv′). Distress; offend.

alchemy (ăl′kĕ·mĭ). Medieval chemistry; the power to change something ordinary into something valuable.

allude (ă·lūd′). To refer indirectly.

amiable (ā′mĭ·à·b′l). Goodnatured; friendly. *Noun*, **amiability** (ā′mĭ·à·bĭl′ĭ·tĭ).

analogy (à·năl′ŏ·jĭ). A degree of similarity between different things.

analytical (ăn′à·lĭt′ĭ·kăl). Able to separate a subject into its parts and to describe each part critically.

animosity (ăn′ĭ·mŏs′ĭ·tĭ). Hostility; ill will.

annihilation (ă·nī′ĭ·lā′shŭn). Total destruction.

annuity (à·nū′ĭ·tĭ). A yearly allowance.

antagonist (ăn·tăg′ŏ·nĭst). Opponent; adversary.

anthropomorphic (ăn′thrŏ·pŏ·môr′fĭc). Representing God in human form.

apathy (ăp′à·thĭ). Indifference; lack of emotion or excitement.

apropos (ăp′rŏ·pō′). As suggested by; with respect to.

arbitrary (är′bĭ·trĕr′ĭ). Unreasonably ruled by one's own wishes.

aridity (à·rĭd′ĭ·tĭ). Dryness; lack of variety.

arrogant (ăr′ŏ·gănt). Haughty.

ascendency (ă·sĕn′dăn·sĭ). Control; domination.

aspect (ăs′pĕkt). Look; air; appearance.

assail (ă·sāl′). To attack, often with harsh words. *Adj.*, **assailable.**

assimilate (ă·sĭm′ĭ·lāt). To incorporate or absorb.

attribute (ă·trĭb′ût). *Verb*, to consider that something belongs to someone else. *Noun*, **attribute** (ăt′rĭ·būt). A quality or characteristic.

audacity (ô·dăs′ĭ·tĭ). Boldness. *Adj.*, **audacious** (ô·dā′shŭs).

augment (ôg·mĕnt′). To increase.

austere (ôs·tēr′). 1. Stern; severe. 2. Unadorned; simple.

B

bannister (băn′ĭs·tēr). A row of upright supports topped by a railing, along a staircase.

barrow (băr′ō). 1. A hill or mound, often an ancient burial ground. 2. A wheelbarrow.

belligerent (bĕ·lĭg′ēr·ĕnt). Warlike; quarrelsome.

benign (bē·nīn′). Kind; gentle. *Noun*, **benignity** (bē·nĭg′nĭ·tĭ).

bestial (bĕst′yăl). Beastly; brutish.

betel (bē′t′l). The nut of a climbing pepper vine, often chewed by natives of the Far East.

bilious (bĭl′yŭs). Suffering from a disorder of the liver; generally ill-tempered, sickly in appearance.

bizarre (bĭ·zär′). Odd; eccentric; fantastic.

āpe, chăotic, bâre, ăt, ăttend, ärt, flåsk, átop; ēke, mĕrely, ĕlect, ĕcho, prudĕnt, doēr; ītem, ĭnn, rarĭty; ōde, ŏpaque, fôr, dŏt, lôft, cŏnfide; sōōn, tŏŏk; sour, toil; cūbe, ûnique, tûrn, sŭp, ŭntil. bar; church; dog; ardûous; fat; go; hear; jail; key; lame; meat; not; ring; pay; ran; see; shell; ten; there, thick; pastûre; vast; wind; **yes; zoo, zh = z in azure.**

blatant (blā'tănt). 1. Offensively obtrusive. 2. Noisy; clamorous.

bode (bōd). To prophesy. *Noun*, **bodement** (bōd'mĕnt).

brogue (brōg). A pronunciation in a dialect.

burlesque (bûr·lĕsk'). An imitation which makes fun of a literary or dramatic work.

buttress (bŭt'rĕs). *Noun*, a projecting structure to support a wall. *Verb*, 1. To support; to prop. 2. To protect.

C

canny (kăn'ĭ). Shrewd; clever.

capitulate (kȧ·pĭt'ů·lāt). To make terms of surrender.

caricature (kăr'ĭ·kȧ·tûr). *Noun*, a picture, or description, exaggerating a person's peculiarities or defects. *Verb*, to make a caricature of.

cataclysm (kăt'ȧ·klĭz'm). Violent upheaval.

caustic (kôs'tĭk). Sharp; satirical.

cede (sēd). To give up; to yield.

circumvent (sûr'kŭm·vĕnt'). 1. To go round. 2. To gain an advantage by strategy.

colloquy (kŏl'ȯ·kwĭ). A formal conversation.

comingle (kȯ·mĭng'g'l). To mix or mingle.

complacent (kŏm·plā'sĕnt). 1. Satisfied. 2. Self-satisfied. *Noun*, **complacence.**

compunction (kȯm·pŭngk'shŭn). Regret; a sense of guilt.

condescend (kŏn'dē·sĕnd'). To show courtesy with an air of superiority. *Noun*, **condescension.**

conjure (kŭn'jẽr). 1. To summon or to bring to mind as if by magic. 2. To plot together; to plan in secret. 3. (kŏn·jŏōr'). To plead with; to implore. *Noun*, **conjurer** (kŭn'jẽr·ẽr). A magician.

connive (kȯ·nīv'). 1. To pretend ignorance. 2. To cooperate secretly.

connoisseur (kŏn'ĭ·sûr'). One competent to pass critical judgment.

consecration (kŏn'sē·krā'shŭn). 1. Setting apart for a holy use. 2. Dedication; devotion.

consequential (kŏn'sē·kwĕn'shăl). Self-important.

consummate (kŏn·sŭm'ĭt). Perfect; in the highest degree.

contumely (kŏn'tů·mē'lĭ). Contemptuous treatment; scorn.

conventionalize (kŏn·vĕn'shŭn·ăl·īz). To represent in a typical manner.

conviviality (kŏn·vĭv'ĭ·ăl'ĭ·tĭ). Gaiety; festivity.

copious (kō'pĭ·ŭs). Rich; full.

covert (kŭv'ẽrt). A shelter; a protection.

cow (kou). To frighten.

culminate (kŭl'mĭ·nāt). To reach a climax.

D

dauntless (dônt'lĕs). Bold; fearless.

decorum (dē·kō'rŭm). Dignity; formal behavior. *Adj.*, **decorous.**

deference (dĕf'ẽr·ĕns). Honor; respect. *Adj.*, **deferential** (def'ẽr·ĕn'shăl).

deft (dĕft). Skillful; nimble.

deprecate (dĕp'rē·kāt). To disapprove of. *Noun*, **deprecation** (dĕp'rē·kā'shŭn). *Adj.*, **deprecatory** (dĕp'rē·kȧ·tō'rĭ).

despondency (dē·spŏn'dĕn·sĭ). Depression; dejection.

despot (dĕs'pŏt). A tyrant. *Adj.*, **despotic** (dĕs·pŏt'ĭk).

diabolical (dī'ȧ·bŏl'ĭ·kăl). Devilish; fiendish.

diadem (dī'ȧ·dĕm). A crown.

diffidence (dĭf'ĭ·dĕns). Shyness; lack of self-confidence. *Adj.*, **diffident.**

disarm (dĭs·ärm'). To make friendly; to make harmless.

discomfiture (dĭs·kŭm'fĭ·tûr). Frustration; overthrow.

disconcerting (dĭs'kŏn·sûrt'ĭng). Embarrassing; upsetting.

disconsolate (dĭs·kŏn'sō·lĭt). Deeply dejected; sad.

disreputability (dĭs·rĕp'ů·tȧ·bĭl'ĭ·tĭ). A low or dishonorable act or state.

āpe, chăotic, bâre, ăt, ȧttend, ärt, flåsk, ȧtop; ēke, mẽrely, ĕlect, ĕcho, prudĕnt, doẽr; ītem, ĭnn, rarĭty; ōde, ȯpaque, fôr, dŏt, lŏft, cŏnfide; sōon, tŏŏk; sour, toil; cūbe, ûnique, tûrn, sŭp, ŭntil. bar; church; dog; ardůous; fat; go; hear; jail; key;

divert (dĭ·vûrt'). *Verb*, 1. To amuse; to entertain. 2. To turn to a different purpose. *Noun* (dĭ'vûrt). *Slang*. An odd or different person.

dogmatist (dŏg'mȧ·tĭst). One who states his beliefs positively, as if they were facts. **dogmatic** (dŏg·măt'ĭk). Dictatorial.

dolorous (dŏl'ēr·ŭs). Painful; sorrowful.

draught (drȧft). A drink.

E

ecclesiastical (ĕ·klē'zĭ·ăs'tĭ·kȧl). Pertaining to the church.

edifying (ĕd'ĭ·fī·ĭng). Morally instructive or beneficial.

effigy (ĕf'ĭ·jĭ). A pictured likeness.

egoistical (ē'gō·ĭs'tĭ·kȧl). Excessively self-centered.

ejaculate (ė·jăk'ū·lāt). To exclaim; to utter suddenly.

emanate (ĕm'ȧ·nāt). To flow out or spring from.

embolden (ĕm·bōl'děn). To make bold or brave; to encourage.

emporium (ĕm·pō'rĭ·ŭm). A department store.

enigma (ė·nĭg'mȧ). A riddle. *Adv*., **enigmatically** (ē'nĭg·măt'ĭ·kȧl·ĭ).

estheticism (ĕs·thĕt'ĭ·sĭz'm). Devotion to principles of beauty and good taste.

ethics (ĕth'ĭks). Moral principles. *Adj*., **ethical** (ĕth'ĭ·kȧl).

evanescent (ĕv'ȧ·nĕs'ĕnt). Fleeting; short-lived.

eventuality (ė·vĕn'tū·ăl'ĭ·tĭ). An outcome.

exaltation (ĕg'zôl·tā'shŭn). The feeling of extreme personal well-being; elation.

execration (ĕk'sė·krā'shŭn). A curse.

exemplary (ĕg·zĕm'plȧ·rĭ). Worthy of imitation.

exotic (ĕks·ŏt'ĭk). Something foreign; belonging to another part of the world.

expostulate (ĕks·pŏs'tū·lāt). To reason earnestly with someone (usually on a fault of his conduct); to remonstrate.

extortionate (ĕks·tôr'shŭn·ȧt). Oppressive; exorbitant.

exult (ĕg·zŭlt'). To rejoice triumphantly. *Noun*, **exultation** (ĕk'sŭl·tā'shŭn).

F

felicity (fė·lĭs'ĭ·tĭ). 1. Happiness; success. 2. A pleasing expression or language.

filial (fĭl'ĭ·ȧl). Befitting a son or daughter in relation to a parent.

fillip (fĭl'ĭp). Something that stimulates.

flag (flăg). To lag.

forte (fōrt). One's special talent; that in which one excels.

furtive (fûr'tĭv). Secret; stealthy.

G

garish (gâr'ĭsh). Gaudy; glaring.

genuflect (jĕn'û·flĕkt). To bend the knee, as in worship.

guile (gīl). Treachery; craftiness.

gumption (gŭmp'shŭn). Common sense.

gyrate (jī'rāt). To whirl or rotate; to move in a spiral. *Noun*, **gyration** (jī'rā'shŭn).

H

herculean (hûr·kū'lē·ăn). 1. Very difficult or dangerous. 2. Of extraordinary strength or size.

I

ignominy (ĭg'nō·mĭn·ĭ). Disgrace. *Adj*., **ignominious** (ĭg'nō·mĭn'ĭ·ŭs). Disgraceful.

imminent (ĭm'ĭ·nĕnt). Threatening to occur at any moment. *Noun*, **imminence**.

impalpable (ĭm·păl'pȧ·b'l). Too delicate to be easily seen or felt.

impeccable (ĭm·pĕk'ȧ·b'l). Faultless.

impecunious (ĭm'pė·kū'nĭ·ŭs). Habitually without money.

impenetrable (ĭm·pĕn'ė·trȧ·b'l). Unable to be penetrated; unfathomable.

imperceptible (ĭm'pēr·sĕp'tĭ·b'l). Not evident to the senses or mind; very slight.

imperious (ĭm·pēr'ĭ·ŭs). 1. Lordly; domineering. 2. Urgent; compelling.

---

lame; meat; not; ring; pay; ran; see; shell; ten; there, thick; pasture; vast; wind; yes; zoo, zh = z in azure.

imperturbable (ĭm′pēr·tûr′bȧ·b′l). Serene; not capable of being disturbed.

impotence (ĭm′pȯ·tĕns). Inability to bring about a result.

impresario (ĭm′prä·sä′rĭ·ō). One who sponsors, produces, or manages a concert, theatrical show, opera, or the like.

inclement (ĭn·klĕm′ĕnt). Harsh; severe.

incontinent (ĭn·kŏn′tĭ·nĕnt). Not restraining the passions or appetites.

incorrigible (ĭn·kŏr′ĭ·jĭ·b′l). Uncontrollable; bad beyond correction; unchangeable.

incredulity (ĭn′krē·dū′lĭ·ti). State of being skeptical; a withholding of belief.

indiscretion (ĭn′dĭs·krĕsh′ŭn). An unwise or incautious act.

indite (ĭn·dīt′). To write.

indomitable (ĭn·dŏm′ĭ·tȧ·b′l). Unconquerable.

inexorable (ĭn·ĕk′sȯ·rȧ·b′l). Unyielding; not to be persuaded.

inextricable (ĭn·ĕks′trĭ·kȧ·b′l). 1. Forming a maze from which it is impossible to get free. 2. Incapable of being untangled; unsolvable.

infinitesimal (ĭn′fĭn·ĭ·tĕs′ĭ·măl). Immeasurably small; very minute.

ingenuous (ĭn·jĕn′ū·ŭs). Naive; innocent.

ingratiating (ĭn·grā′shĭ·āt′ĭng). Bringing or working oneself into another's good graces or favor.

interloper (ĭn′tēr·lōp′ēr). Intruder.

interpose (ĭn′tēr·pōz′). 1. To place between. 2. To inject a remark into a conversation between or among others.

irrelevance (ĭr·rĕl′ē·vȧns). Inappropriateness to the subject. *Adj.*, **irrelevant.**

J

jocular (jŏk′ū·lēr). Given to jesting; merry; witty.

judicial (jṓ·dĭsh′ăl). 1. Impartial. 2. critical.

L

labyrinth (lăb′ĭ·rĭnth). A maze of complicated paths.

lagoon (lȧ·gōōn′). A shallow pool; usually connected with the sea.

lavish (lăv′ĭsh). To give generously.

libretto (lĭ·brĕt′ō). The text or words of an opera or other long musical composition.

librettist (lĭ·brĕt′ĭst). The writer of a libretto.

limbo (lĭm′bō). A place of confinement, neglect, or oblivion.

loquacious (lȯ·kwā′shŭs). Talkative.

lorry (lŏr′ĭ). A large, low truck.

luminous (lū′mĭ·nŭs). Shining.

lurid (lū′rĭd). 1. Ghastly pale; dismal. 2. Harshly vivid; marked by violent passion.

M

magisterial (măj′ĭs·tēr′ĭ·ăl). Commanding; pompous; having the manner of a magistrate, an important public official.

magnanimous (măg·năn′ĭ·mŭs). Generous; noble; honorable.

malefactor (măl′ē·făk′tēr). One guilty of an evil deed; a criminal.

malignity (mȧ·lĭg′nĭ·tĭ). Bad influence; evil.

malicious (mȧ·lĭsh′ŭs). Filled with hatred or ill will.

manifest (măn′ĭ·fĕst). *Verb*, to display; to make evident. *Adj.*, apparent; evident. *Noun*, **manifestation** (man′ĭ·fĕs·tā′shŭn). A display; a disclosure.

memoir (mĕm′wär). An account of one's own life or experiences.

mendacity (mĕn·dăs′ĭ·tĭ). Lying.

mettle (mĕt″l). Temperament involving vigorous spirit, fortitude, and courage. *Adj.*, **mettled, mettlesome.**

mezzotint (mĕd′zȯ·tĭnt). An engraving on copper or steel.

millennium (mĭ·lĕn′ĭ·ŭm). The period of greatest happiness and prosperity.

mobile (mō′bĭl). Easily moved; expressive.

modulation (mŏd′ʊ·lā′shŭn). Variation or inflection of tone.

molest (mō·lĕst′). To annoy; to inter-

āpe, chăotic, bâre, ăt, ȧttend, ärt, flȧsk, ȧtop; ēke, mērely, ĕlect, ĕcho, prudĕnt, doēr; ītem, ĭnn, rarĭty; ōde, ȯpaque, fôr, dŏt, lŏft, cŏnfide; sōōn, tōōk; sour, toil; cūbe, ûnique, tûrn, sŭp, ŭntil. bar; church; dog; arḓůous; fat; go; hear; jail; key;

fere with. *Noun*, **molestation** (mō'-lĕs·tā'shŭn).

multiplicity (mŭl'tĭ·plĭs'ĭ·tĭ). A great number.

N

nonchalance (nŏn'shȧ·lȧns; –läns). The condition of being nonchalant; casual; unconcerned.

novice (nŏv'ĭs). 1. One who has just entered a religious order. 2. A beginner in any field.

O

obsequious (ŏb·sē'kwĭ·ŭs). Fawning; servile.

oratorio (ŏr'ȧ·tō'rĭ·ō). A dramatic text, usually on a Biblical theme, set to music with instrumental accompaniment and performed without scenery, costumes, or action.

orgy (ôr'jĭ). Excessive indulgenée in some activity.

orifice (ŏr'ĭ·fĭs). A mouthlike opening.

ostentation (ŏs'tĕn·tā'shŭn). Proud show.

ottoman (ŏt'ȯ·mȧn). A stuffed footstool or couch.

P

palatable (păl'ĭt·ȧ·b'l). Pleasing to the taste.

palpable (păl'pȧ·b'l). 1. Capable of being touched or felt. 2. Easily perceived; obvious.

panoply (păn'ȯ·plĭ). 1. A suit of armor. 2. Anything that protects completely or forms a magnificent covering.

paradox (păr'ȧ·dŏks). A statement that seems absurd or contradictory but is really true.

paroxysm (păr'ŏk·sĭz'm). A sharp attack of pain; a spasm.

pathos (pā'thŏs). The quality or power that awakens feelings of pity and sympathetic sadness.

pedant (pĕd'ănt). One who shows off his knowledge. *Adj.*, **pedantic** (pĕ·dăn'tĭk). Overly precise.

peremptory (pĕr·ĕmp'tȯ·rĭ). Masterful; positive.

perennial (pĕr·ĕn'ĭ·ăl). Enduring; living through the years.

perfidy (pûr'fĭ·dĭ). Faithlessness; treachery.

perfunctory (pĕr·fŭngk'tȯ·rĭ). Indifferent; mechanical.

pertinacious (pûr'tĭ·nā'shŭs). Stubborn; persistent.

petulance (pĕt'ū·lȧns). Peevishness; fretfulness.

phonetics (fȯ·nĕt'ĭks). The science of speech sounds as elements of language.

piquancy (pē'kȧn·sĭ). A delightful, charming quality.

pirouette (pĭr'ōō·ĕt'). To whirl rapidly on the toes or on one foot.

plaintive (plān'tĭv). Sorrowful; mournful.

plausible (plô'zĭ·b'l). 1. Seemingly worthy of approval. 2. Apparently true.

poach (pōch). To hunt or fish illegally on another's property. *Noun*, **poacher**.

portent (pōr'tĕnt). 1. A forewarning; an ominous meaning. 2. A marvel. *Adj.*, **portentous**. 1. Ominous. 2. Monstrous.

precipitation (prē·sĭp'ĭ·tā'shŭn). 1. Act of falling or rushing headlong. 2. Haste; acceleration.

predestined (prē·dĕs'tĭnd). Fated; destined or determined beforehand.

premonition (prē'mȯ·nĭsh'ŭn). A foreboding; a warning in advance.

prodigious (prȯ·dĭj'ŭs). Extraordinary; marvelous.

prolific (prȯ·lĭf'ĭk). Producing abundant results; fertile.

propitiate (prȯ·pĭsh'ĭ·āt). To win over; to make favorable.

prosaic (prȯ·zā'ĭk). Dull; unimaginative.

protract (prȯ·trăkt'). To prolong; to lengthen.

proximity (prŏks·ĭm'ĭ·tĭ). Being very near to; closeness.

purblind (pûr'blīnd'). Lacking in vision or understanding.

---

lame; meat; not; ring; pay; ran; see; shell; ten; there, thick; pastûre; vast; wind; yes; zoo, zh = z in azure.

Q

quarto (kwôr′tō). A book size, about 9½ x 12 inches, smaller than a folio.

quench (kwĕnch). 1. To suppress; to calm. 2. To put out; to extinguish. 3. To relieve, as thirst.

querulous (kwĕr′ů·lŭs). Fretful; peevish.

R

recluse (rē·klōōs′). A person who lives alone and secluded from the world.

refectory (rē·fĕk′tō·rĭ). A dining hall in a monastery. **refectory table.** A long, narrow, wooden dining table.

rejoinder (rē·join′dēr). Answer; reply.

relegate (rĕl′ē·gāt). To remove to a less desirable situation; to put out of sight or mind.

remonstrate (rē·mŏn′strāt). To protest. *Noun,* **remonstrance** (rē·mŏn′străns).

replica (rĕp′lĭ·kȧ). A reproduction; a close copy.

repudiate (rē·pū′dĭ·āt). 1. To disown; to refuse to listen to or recognize. 2. To reject.

resolute (rĕz′ȯ·lūt). Determined; steadfast.

ribaldry (rĭb′ȧld·rĭ). Coarse, vulgar joking.

roseate (rō′zē·ăt). Rose-colored; hence happy, optimistic.

rudiment (rōō′dĭ·mĕnt). A basic principle; a first step.

ruminate (rōō′mĭ·nāt). To muse; to ponder.

S

sagacious (sȧ·gā′shŭs). Shrewd; watchful. *Noun,* **sagacity** (sȧ·găs′ĭ·tĭ).

sallow (săl′ō). A pale yellow-red color suggesting sickliness (in describing the skin or complexion).

scrutinize (skrōō′tĭ·nīz). To examine critically; to look at closely.

sedentary (sĕd′ĕn·tĕr′ĭ). Accustomed to sitting for long periods of time and taking little exercise.

senility (sē·nĭl′ĭ·tĭ). The physical and mental weakness of old age.

sensuous (sĕn′shōō·ŭs). Appealing pleasurably to the senses.

sinister (sĭn′ĭs·tēr). Threatening; indicative of lurking evil.

sordid (sôr′dĭd). Filthy; base.

staid (stād). Sober; sedate.

stentorian (stĕn·tō′rĭ·ȧn). Extremely loud (from *Stentor,* a herald in Homer's *Iliad*).

stratagem (străt′ȧ·jĕm). A trick designed to deceive; deception.

supine (sū·pīn′). 1. Lying face upward. 2. Inactive; passive.

surplice (sûr′plĭs). An outer garment of white linen with wide sleeves, worn by clergymen.

T

tendril (tĕn′drĭl). A slender, leafless climbing part of a plant that attaches itself to something and supports the plant.

tenterhooks (tĕn′tēr·hōōks′). (Used with *on*). In suspense; under a strain.

tippet (tĭp′ĕt). A scarf or scarflike garment of cloth or fur.

toady (tōd′ĭ). To fawn upon or flatter; to cater to.

transfigure (trăns·fĭg′ûr). To transform; to change in appearance; to cause to shine.

truculent (trŭk′û·lĕnt). Fierce.

tumult (tū′mŭlt). Agitation; violence. *Adj.,* **tumultuous** (tū·mŭl′tū·ŭs). Stormy.

U

unabashed (ŭn′ȧ·băsht′). Not embarrassed.

unassailable (ŭn′ȧ·sāl′ȧ·b′l). Not capable of being attacked.

undeviating (ŭn·dē′vĭ·āt′ĭng). Not changing or turning aside from a set course.

undulate (ŭn′dů·lāt). To rise and fall in waves; to surge.

unduly (ŭn·dū′lĭ). Excessively.

unimpeachable (ŭn′ĭm·pēch′ȧ·b′l). Blameless; unquestionable.

āpe, chăotic, bâre, ăt, ȧttend, ärt, flăsk, ȧtop; ēke, mẽrely, ĕlect, ĕcho, prudĕnt, doēr; ītem, ĭnn, rarĭty; ōde, ȯpaque, fôr, dŏt, lŏft, cŏnfide; sōōn, tŏŏk; sour, toil; cūbe, ūnique, tûrn, sŭp, ŭntil. bar; church; dog; ardŭous; fat; go; hear; jail; key;

unostentatious (ŭn′ŏs·tĕn·tā′shŭs). Without show; quiet.

untenable (ŭn·tĕn′á·b'l). Incapable of being held or defended.

unwonted (ŭn·wŭn′tĕd). Unaccustomed; unusual.

V

vacuity (vă·kū′ĭ·tĭ). 1. A vacancy; a void. 2. Emptiness; hollowness. 3. Vacancy of mind; mental emptiness.

vehement (vē′ĕ·mĕnt). Furious.

vehicular (vē·hĭk′ů·lēr). Pertaining to or serving a vehicle.

velocity (vĕ·lŏs′ĭ·tĭ). Speed; rapidity; swiftness of motion.

venerable (vĕn′ēr·á·b'l). Commanding respect, usually because of age or dignified position.

vernacular (vēr·năk′ů·lēr). Native or commonly spoken language.

vestige (vĕs′tĭj). A trace.

vestry (vĕs′trĭ). A room in a church in which the vestments or robes of the clergy are kept along with the sacred vessels used in services.

vindicate (vĭn′dĭ·kāt To justify; to clear of suspicion.

volatile (vŏl′á·tĭl). Lively; lightheaded.

voluble (vŏl′ů·b'l). 1. Turning; rotating. 2. Speaking fluently. **volubility** (vŏl′ů·bĭl′ĭ·tĭ). Talkativeness.

W

wattles (wŏt′lz). Twigs and easily bent rods woven together and used for walls, fences, etc., or to support straw thatch in a roof.

whist (hwĭst). An old card game for four players, the forerunner of bridge.

writhe (rīth). To twist violently.

---

lame; meat; not; ring; pay; ran; see; shell; ten; there, thick; pastûre; vast; wind; yes; zoo, zh = z in azure.

Special Indexes

READING SKILL STUDY AIDS appear, as listed here according to subject, on the following pages. The names in parentheses indicate the authors of the selections after which each Study Aid appears.

Character, Following Development (Maugham), 60; Comparison of Works by the Same Author (O'Connor), 150; Conflict, Analyzing (Coppard), 33; Fantasy, Appreciating (De la Mare), 91; Figurative Language, Understanding (Spender), 110; Ideas, Analyzing (Chesterton), 97; Mood, Analyzing (Mansfield), 68; Poetic Language, Appreciating (Thomas), 114: Purpose, Recognizing an Author's (Orwell), 169; Satire, Understanding Shaw's, 272; Style, Analyzing an Author's (Tomlinson), 156; Appreciating an Author's (Churchill), 187; Suspense, Reacting to (Sansom), 53; SEE ALSO: *Reading the Short Story* (Conrad), 23

"THE POWER OF WORDS" FEATURES: Creating Effect (De la Mare), 91; Word Discrimination (Pearson), 138

SUGGESTIONS FOR WRITING appear on the pages listed, following selections by the authors specified: 107 (Betjeman), 104 (Brooke); 161 (Huxley, Aldous), 69 (Mansfield), 61 (Maugham), 192 (Priestley), 131 (Strachey), 157 (Tomlinson), 176 (Woolf)

GENERAL INDEX

ADVENTURES IN LITERATURE SERIES

LAUREATE PAPERBACK EDITION

ADVENTURES IN READING
VOLUME 1 Short Stories
2 Nonfiction
3 Poetry, the Epic, and Drama
4 Dickens' *Great Expectations* (abridged)
5 Scott's *Ivanhoe* (abridged)

ADVENTURES IN APPRECIATION
VOLUME 1 Short Stories
2 Nonfiction and the King Arthur Legend
3 Poetry and Drama
4 Eliot's *Silas Marner* (abridged)
5 Dickens' *A Tale of Two Cities* (abridged)

ADVENTURES IN AMERICAN LITERATURE
VOLUME 1 Modern Fiction, including Crane's *The Red Badge of Courage*
2 Modern Nonfiction, Modern Poetry, and Modern Drama
3 "The Colonial Time" through "New England's Golden Years" (1600–1860)
4 "Growth and Conflict" through "Time of Change" (1840–1910)

ADVENTURES IN ENGLISH LITERATURE
VOLUME 1 The Anglo-Saxon Period through The Seventeenth Century
2 Shakespeare: Songs, Sonnets, *Macbeth,* and *Hamlet*
3 The Eighteenth Century through The Victorian Age
4 The Modern Age, including Conrad's *Typhoon*

Accompanying the anthologies: test booklets for each grade; booklets of programed instruction in reading and literature; teacher's manuals; long play records

L
M
N
O
P
O
R